Cornell University Library
MT 220.M43

The act of touch in all its diversity :a

PIANOFORTE
TONE-PRODUCTION

BY TOBIAS MATTHAY

THE ACT OF TOUCH IN ALL ITS DIVERSITY. An analysis and synthesis of Pianoforte Tone-Production.

THE FIRST PRINCIPLES OF PIANOFORTE PLAYING. Being an extract from the author's "THE ACT OF TOUCH." Designed for school use, and including two new chapters, DIRECTIONS FOR LEARNERS AND ADVICE TO TEACHERS.

SOME COMMENTARIES ON THE TEACHING OF PIANOFORTE TECHNIQUE. A Supplement to "THE ACT OF TOUCH" and "FIRST PRINCIPLES."

LONGMANS, GREEN AND CO.
LONDON, NEW YORK, TORONTO, BOMBAY, CALCUTTA AND MADRAS

THE ACT OF
TOUCH
IN ALL ITS DIVERSITY

AN ANALYSIS AND SYNTHESIS OF
PIANOFORTE TONE-PRODUCTION

BY

TOBIAS MATTHAY

FELLOW AND PROFESSOR OF THE ROYAL ACADEMY
OF MUSIC, LONDON, ETC.

NEW IMPRESSION

LONGMANS, GREEN AND CO.
39 PATERNOSTER ROW, LONDON E.C. 4
NEW YORK, TORONTO
BOMBAY, CALCUTTA AND MADRAS

1924

COPYRIGHT, 1903, BY
LONGMANS, GREEN, AND CO.

First Edition December 1903. Reprinted May 1905

Reprinted September 1911
,, February 1914
,, June 1916
,, July 1919
,, April 1921
,, July 1924

Made in Great Britain

To

MY FELLOW WORKERS AT THE

PIANOFORTE

STUDENTS, ARTISTS, AND TEACHERS

"There can be no effect without a cause."

PREFACE.

ABILITY to understand and feel Music, and ability to communicate such perceptions to others by means of an instrument, are two totally distinct accomplishments. They have often been confused, owing to the fact, that it is impossible to achieve a really satisfactory musical performance without their happy combination.

To become pianoforte players, we must learn Music, and must acquire Taste, but we can only succeed in expressing what we feel, musically, by means of *the physical act of key-depression.* In short, the purely physical act of playing consists solely of an ACT of Touch,—an act of Tone-production. All the gradations of Agility (fleetness of finger), Duration (staccato and legato), as well as all the contrasts of Tone-inflection depend solely and directly on the nature of this act; and it is therefore upon our expertness in the ART of Touch that the whole superstructure of Pianoforte-playing rests. The Art of Touch may indeed be concisely defined as: *command over the Means of Expression.*

This Art thus forms the very Foundation (the Elements or Rudiments) of Pianoforte-playing; and it can no more be a "gift" (as so often supposed) than is the art of articulate Speech itself; for it can be acquired by every person of average intelligence. Its precise place in the scheme of Pianoforte Education need not here be further dilated upon, since

Part I. is devoted to that purpose; and the reader is referred to the Summary of this Part, on page 40.

A performer can indeed prove himself to be *musical* only to the extent of his command over touch variety. It is the constant flow of note to note touch-inflections that forces one to realize that a performer is a sentient being. And it is just this Art of Touch, that will for ever defy mechanical imitation; and will for ever render the simplest performance, coloured by human fingers, immeasurably superior to the most complex one obtained by mechanical agency, however perfect the machine.

Although it is only thus, by perfecting himself in the Art of Touch, that the player can obtain the means of expressing his musical sensibilities, yet until within quite recent years the paramount necessity of studying this problem had not begun to dawn upon teachers, artists, and students.

As the true fundamentals of this Art remained practically unrecognized, no serious attempt could be made to give *direct* instruction in it. True, it was recognised that the musically endowed evinced a "finer touch" than did others less endowed; but this, it was assumed, was owing solely to some occult influence over the keyboard, the possession of which enabled the favoured ones to produce tone of a better quality and of finer gradations;—and there is some half-truth in this, for it is certain that the possession of a musical ear, and a strong wish for musical expression, will undoubtedly compel the player to experiment at the keyboard, until he does sooner or later discover for himself at least *some* of the mechanical Means that will conduce to success. True, also, that the more serious teachers have insisted upon the necessity of good quality and variety of Touch. But even the greatest, so far, have relied almost exclusively upon empirical methods or upon the force of Example. Or they have insisted upon what is after all a mere *accompaniment* of good touch, i. e.: Position and Movement—thus placing "the cart before the horse." True it is, moreover, that the necessity of rationally studying this problem has lately made itself keenly felt, especially in America. How pressing this need is, becomes only too painfully evident, when one has to teach those who have already formed wrong muscular-habits, and when one is compelled to witness the ineffectual struggles of many even of the musically endowed in the Examination-room, and Concert-room, who, were they not thus handicapped by faulty habits (acquired through ignorance of these Rudiments) could give free vent to the powers of perception and imagination evidently latent in them!

Obviously the only way to succeed in the attempt rationally to learn and teach the Act of Touch in all its immense variety, is, first to discover through ANALYSIS how the successful players obtain their effects, and then to test such Analysis, by observing whether the *act* of touch, built up in accordance with such analysis, does give the anticipated tonal-results. Having thus determined the structure of all varieties of touch, and the *permits* to Agility, we ought then to be in a position directly to help ourselves and others towards their acquisition.

The Means of Touch-variety or Key-treatment having thus been analysed, it follows that all who will take the trouble to master the subject—all who will take the trouble to understand the requirements of Key and Muscle, and will take the trouble to form these into physical and mental habits—will be able to acquire the language of Expression. Everyone may thus be enabled to gain power of Agility and Colouring; and even the musically endowed, may, by *directly* acquiring a tone-palette (or Touch-palette) thus save years of time, which would otherwise be wasted in futile experiments, and in forming bad habits.

As I have now for a great number of years applied such Analysis and Synthesis of Touch in my daily work of teaching, doing so always with increasing directness, and mainly ascribe such success as I have had as a teacher (and my pupils, also, as teachers) to the resulting ability to point out *the immediate causes of the observed faults*, and the *direct means of their correction*—to the ability to show explicity HOW to command the physical fulfilment of each interpretative and technical detail, I have long been urged to render this knowledge more widely accessible, and the present little work is the result.

In endeavouring to place the many unfamiliar facts and new ideas before the reader, there was however this dilemma to face: that innumerable prejudices and fallacies would have to be combated, and that to do this would render the treatise too elaborate for the Schoolroom; whereas, to limit it to direct information in its concisest form (as required for the Schoolroom) might render its teachings liable to misconception, and unacceptable to the prejudiced.

To overcome this difficulty, the work has been laid out in four Parts, as follows:—Part I, is purely introductory, and purposes to show the relation the study of Touch bears to the general problems of Pianoforte-education. This is followed by the practical Parts, II to IV.   Part II, " The instrumental aspect of Key-treatment," demonstrates the nature of the mechanical difficulties to be overcome,—what are the requirements of the key, and how the key must be treated for each kind of effect. Part III, " The muscular-aspect of Key-treatment," exhibits the muscular difficulties of the problem, and their solution—the muscular means we must adopt, to fulfil the key's requirements. Finally, Part IV deals with the positional aspect of the subject—the postures and movements which must, or may, accompany correct key-treatment. Each of these practical Parts consists first of a Preamble, giving a general idea of the matter to be dealt with, followed by a number of chapters, providing explanatory details; each of these chapters being followed by a RECAPITULATION, and each of the Parts again by a SUMMARY; the concluding chapter of the work, moreover, giving a Glossary of the whole. A system of Notes accompanies the text, and *Appendices*, which follow each Part, give further opportunity for detailed instruction.

In this way, the close enquirer may obtain full information in the chapters, while the less advanced student can be referred to these Recapitulatories and Summaries. These, in fact, form a work *complete in itself*,—a digest or extract, designed for school use. This Digest or Extract, is intended for publication in a separate form later on, to render it more easily available for such purpose.

The work, it will be seen, is entirely explanatory. It has nothing to do with any particular system of exercises or studies, etc. The *Student* can apply its teachings at any stage of his progress, since it applies in all cases, whatever the system of teaching or exercises adopted in other respects.

The *Artist* can learn from it the reason of his greater or lesser success technically, and how further to improve his powers of Expression. The *Teacher* will find it useful at every step; and finally the *Critic* can find in it a basis for his technical opinions.

This work may presently be followed by an extra Part— Part V, giving certain exercises for acquiring Muscular-discrimination, which have been found useful in direct teaching.

Coming now to the end of the years of labour expended on this little volume, the late Professor TYNDALL'S words recur to me: "The ease with which an essay is read, is often a measure of the laboriousness with which it has been written;"—and in concluding, I can only express the hope that my readers may find some measure of correspondence between my labour in this instance, and its result!

I must also here take the opportunity of thanking the many kind friends who have encouraged me in my self-imposed task, and to acknowledge the valuable help given me in the revision of the proofs, etc., by Mrs. Kennedy-Fraser, of Edinburgh, and others.

Tobias Matthay.

Hampstead, London,
    July, 1903

RECOMMENDATION.

In studying this work, each of the four Parts should be taken in the following order:

I. The Preamble to each Part.
II. The Contents of each chapter.
III. The Summary of each chapter.
IV. The Text of each chapter, with re-study of the Recapitulatories.
V. The Recapitulatory or Summary of each *Part*, to concentrate the knowledge acquired.
VI. The student should afterwards constantly refer to the Recapitulatories, whenever he perceives technical difficulties between himself and his interpretative intentions.

The reader may here be warned against a mistake often made, viz.: the assumption, that an author must needs be in the wrong, because a reader fails to understand the facts dealt with!

Granted, that it is wrong to accept any teachings unless one's reason is convinced of their truth, nevertheless it is still more deeply wrong, to be convinced that such teachings are untrue, because they happen, perhaps, to be in complete opposition to doctrines faithfully clung to for years! Only by a rigid analysis of facts can we hope to eliminate untruth, and the author begs for such test, convinced as he is that the facts here stated become only the clearer, the more they are subjected to examination.

CONTENTS.

PART I.—INTRODUCTORY.

CHAPTER I.

PREAMBLE.

PAGE

The absurdity of attempting to teach Pianoforte Playing, without teaching the Elements of "Touch".—Comparison of Empiric with Rational, or Direct, methods of teaching.—Practice unprofitable, unless it tends towards the *acquisition of Variety in Touch, through the* formation of correct habits.—Only by a preliminary practical understanding of the *Laws* of Tone-production can this be ensured.—Such understanding insufficient by itself, the rules of procedure must be fixed into Mental-Muscular Habit.—The form of Attention a fully-trained Artist gives during the act of performance, must hence widely differ from that required from a Learner.—Comparison of the Accidental with the Rational methods of attaining Touch.—The Highly-talented may happen to discover correct forms of tone-production, the Less-talented will probably fail.—Tone-production discovered by accident is easily forgotten; whereas, this is not likely, once the facts are understood.—The rational method of acquiring Tone-production premises knowledge of the laws that govern it.—The formation of correct habits of Touch is ensured, when we understand what Treatment the Key requires for each different kind of sound, and the nature of the Muscular-Conditions by means of which such Key-treatment can be fulfilled.—Three stages of acquaintanceship are possible with regard to Tone-production, viz.: (a) Ability to obtain the effects from the instrument, while ignorant of the processes adopted; (b) Understanding the nature of these processes, how key and limb have to be treated for each effect; (c) Perception of the reason for such treatment 1

CONTENTS.

CHAPTER II.

THE PROBLEM OF PIANOFORTE TRAINING.

PAGE

Successful Performance consists in the combination of two distinct processes: the mental act of Musical Perception, and the physical act leading to its Execution.—The first process implies Musicianship; the second, Executantship.—Neither avails, unless Attention is forthcoming from both sides during the act of performance.—Musicianship has a dual aspect: the Emotional, and the Intellectual; both sides must be trained.—Emotional training permits us to *feel* Music; Intellectual training permits us to *see* the Musical Shapes through which Feeling is expressed.—Executantship similarly has a dual aspect: one, implying Artistic Judgment, and the other, implying Command over the Art of Tone-Production.—Artistic-judgment comprises: (a) Familiarity with the possible Instrumental effects; (b) Judgment, as to their appropriate Application; and (c) Keenness of Pulsational-Sense, of perception of Time-lapse.—Command over Tone-Production involves special training for the particular instrument; it implies Ability to draw from it every effect dictated by our Musicianship, and our Artistic-sense 9

CHAPTER III.

THE PROBLEM OF EDUCATION IN THE ART OF TONE-PRODUCTION.

The Art of Tone-production comprises the production of all possible Sound-effects from the instrument: those of Tone-Quantity; those of Tone-Quality; those of Continuance; it includes also the attainment of *Agility*.—The laws of Tone-Production apply equally to everyone, gifted and non-gifted.—Certain endowments render easier the acquisition of Agility; these are distinct from those which constitute a large Pianoforte-*Voice*.—Even the smallest natural Piano-voice, when properly produced, is capable of far larger volume of tone, and its modifications, than is generally supposed possible.—"Stiff" fingers and wrists also indicate faulty habits, rather than natural incapacity.—Facility in Tone-production rests on knowledge and physical attainments, in two distinct directions: Instrumental education and Muscular Education.—The Key-treatment required for each kind of sound must be understood; and the muscular Conditions consummating each shade of treatment must be forthcoming 21

CHAPTER IV.

THE PROBLEM OF MUSCULAR EDUCATION.

Consists of two steps.—We must learn to discriminate the right muscular-conditions from the wrong ones; we must then learn to apply these correctly-discriminated Conditions to the Keyboard, both as regards amount and duration.—The *First* step in Muscular-education can be carried out apart from the Pianoforte keyboard.—It is a process of *Elimination* of not-required activities.—The result is Freedom of action.—The needful muscular activities and inactivities produce two distinct classes of effects; Visible effects, in the shape of movements, and Invisible effects in the shape of stresses and tensions.—The mode of imparting the Visible actions; also, the Invisible actions.—Warning not to overlook ultimate Object, Sound excitation, during such process of Muscular-education.—The *Second* step in muscular-education demands a keyboard, and that of a good instrument.—We must here learn to *time* the muscular-act both to *commence* and to *cease* at the right moment.—We must learn to gauge the intensity of the Muscular-act in obedience to the needs of the Key, before, during, and after its descent 25

CHAPTER V.

THE FINAL PROBLEM: THE UNION OF EXECUTION WITH CONCEPTION.

The completion of the act of Tone-production arises at a definite point in Key-descent, and at a definite moment of Time; herein lies the means of Union.—This Union is accomplished, by *timing* a muscular-act, of requisite intensity, to culminate the mechanical operation upon the key in absolute correspondence with the degree and time which our conception of the Music demands for each note.—Execution fulfils Conception, when Key-arrival "at Sound" corresponds with the musically-*intended* moment of tone-excitation.—Only through the Ear can we be promptly enough notified of the moment when the act of "Touch" is consummated: the moment of transition from Silence to Sound.—Alertness of Ear, hence, the final and most important problem of Executive-education.—Final definition of the Four Elements which together constitute the Act of Attention required in performance.—Warning not to forget the ultimate Object in endeavouring to fulfil the Means.—Even Attention itself must not be given for its own sake.—In performance, our consciousness must always be a supreme desire to perceive Music, for the sake of communicating it . 30

CHAPTER VI.

CONCLUSION, AND SUMMARY.

Realization of the components of Pianoforte Education will enable us to locate each fault.—This will enable us to correct each fault separately, the quickest and surest way.—It will enable us the better to Practise, Criticise, Play, and Teach 37

Summary, a Table, giving the relationship of the various components of Pianoforte Education 40

APPENDIX TO PART I.

NOTE   I. *On Listening* 40
NOTE II. *On Rhythm* 41
NOTE III. *As to Gymnastics* 42
NOTE IV. *Piano-talent* 42
NOTE   V. *As to Self-consciousness and Nervousness* . . . 43
NOTE VI. *Musical Feeling* 43

PART II.—KEY-TREATMENT FROM ITS INSTRUMENTAL ASPECT.

CHAPTER VII.

PREAMBLE: THE MAIN INSTRUMENTAL FACTS.

The Pianoforte consists of two distinct portions, the instrument proper, and the set of machines provided to excite it into sound.—The Sounding-board with its strings forms the instrument proper.—The Key with all its appurtenances forms the exciting Tool.—This only serves to transmit Speed to the string.—Sound can only be excited by giving Motion to the Key, nothing else forms Tone-production.—The application of Energy must be so Timed during key-descent, as to culminate coincidently with the moment that tone begins to appear.—Hitting or Striking the key is as fallacious as Pressing it upon its bed.—We must realise the key's weight and resistance through the fingertip, and must overcome this resistance so as to *aim* the hammer-end of the key against the string.—Thus used, the key forms but a mechanical elongation of the finger.—The act of aiming involved in creating String-speed by means of the hammer-end, includes three points: (a) the full key-speed intended must be reached as the sound arises; (b) the Energy applied must cease at that moment; (c) the manner of its application must be determined—*suddenly* applied energy creates "brilliant" tone, harsh and non-carrying; *gradually* applied energy creates "sympathetic" tone, singing and carrying.—The *first* lesson of key-treatment is, that every note must be musically intended as to Time and Tone; the *second* lesson is, that the culmination of each key-descent must be made to coincide with such intention 47

CHAPTER VIII.

THE INSTRUMENT.

The outer Case contains the sounding-board, the strings and frame and the Mechanism, or "action."—Description of the Sounding-board.—The Strings and Frame.—Description of the components of the Mechanism—*Firstly*: A compound Lever, to facilitate the transmission of speed to the string—its resemblance to a see-saw, since all speed transmission-power vanishes with the key's full depression—*Secondly*: The Escapement, to allow the hammer to fall away from the string the moment that tone-production is completed.—The Repetition contrivance—*Thirdly*: The Check, to prevent rebound of the hammer—*Fourthly*: The Damper, to stop the sound when the key is released—*Fifthly*: The Damper-Pedal, which raises all the dampers simultaneously—Correct Pedalling—The Sostenente pedal—*Sixthly*: The Una Corda pedal and its substitutes.—Recapitulation 52

CHAPTER IX.

ON SOUND.

The physical nature of Sound.—Concussions travel through the air as areas of alternate compression and rarefaction.—We are unable to identify air-concussions individually when repeated more frequently than about sixteen per second.—Beyond that speed they blur into a continuous ear-impression.—The sensation of Noise arises when the ear-impression is derived from an irregular sequence of impacts.—We hear a Musical-note when the continuous ear-impression arises from a regular sequence of impacts.—The Pitch of a note depends on the component number of impacts that form such ear-impression; the ear counts these component impacts and delivers the result as a musical-sensation; the higher the number, the higher the note.—Loudness depends on the intensity of the individual air-disturbances, the more violent the vibrations the louder is the sound.—A sound wave reaching us may be simple in its structure, or compound.—Thence arises the sensation of difference in the Quality of the sound, a powerful means of expression. 64

CHAPTER X.

THE STRING, ITS BEHAVIOUR DURING THE VARIOUS FORMS OF TONE-PRODUCTION.

PAGE

We create sound from the Pianoforte by causing a String or set of strings to move.—The string, in moving, beats the air, and is said to vibrate.—The length, tension and thickness of the string determines how often per second it will be compelled to complete its vibration.—The actual Speed with which the string moves must not be confused with this rate of vibration.—The sounding-board, owing to its large surface, magnifies the effect of the string-movements for our ear.—The string is set in motion by the hammer reaching it, and slightly driving it out of its place of rest.—The hammer shares its speed and momentum with the string during this moment of contact.—The string is then left free to continue in gradually decreasing movement, unless checked by the damper's descent.—The *act* of tone-production ceases with the first outward swing of the string.—Each act of tone-production is therefore of exceedingly short duration, never taking longer than it does in the shortest Staccato.—It is quite distinct from the act of retaining the Key depressed, whence arises Tenuto and Legato.—Loudness depends upon the extent of ground covered by the string during each vibration.—The string's vibrations are necessarily completed during the same period of time, whether these vibrations are ample or small in extent; the string must hence be made to move *faster* for a loud note than for a soft note.—The Quality of the sound depends upon the manner in which the string is reached.—Sudden application of energy causes the harsher harmonics of the string to appear, whereas gradual application of energy causes the string movements to be simpler in character, and therefore more beautiful, pleasant, and carrying in tone-result. 69

CHAPTER XI.

THE KEY—THE STRING-MOVING IMPLEMENT—ITS BEHAVIOUR AND REQUIREMENTS DURING THE ACT OF TONE-PRODUCTION.

The key enables us to propel the String into great speed.—It is a machine complete for each note.—The term Key here includes the whole leverage-system, with all its attached contrivances.—Weight and muscular-energy have to be brought to bear upon our end of this lever; they are translated by it into Speed at the hammer-end.—The key considered as a mechanical continuation of our finger.—All application of energy must be fulfilled before the key-descent culminates in sound, *since the hammer then slips off the end of the hopper.*— The laws of key-movement.—We can rest upon the key up to certain point of heaviness without its giving way; slightly more weight than that causes the key to give way at its softest; still greater weight and energy are needed to induce tone louder than *pp.*—The fallacies of Key-striking and Key-bed squeezing.—Key-speed can be induced Suddenly or Gradually; illustration of the difference.—The more gradually key-speed is induced, the more beautiful is the tone-character.—*Tenuto* arises when the weight that just suffices to bear the key down, is permitted to *continue* on it beyond the moment that tone-emission begins. —*Legato* arises when such Tenuto-causing weight is *transferred* from key to key.—Super-Legato.—*Staccato* arises when all weight and energy bearing upon the key is accurately and completely *ceased* the moment that tone begins; the key is thus left free to rebound, even with the finger lying thereon.—No force greater than is needed to prevent such rebound (in Tenuto and Legato) should ever be permitted to reach the key-bed, except momentarily in an extreme form of Staccato.— Summary.— Recapitulatory, and Conclusions drawn from Part II 78

APPENDIX TO PART II.

Note (I.)   VII. *On Choice of Instrument* 91
Note (II.) VIII. *Tone-exciters* 93
Note (III.) IX. *On Quality of Sound* 93
Note (IV.) X. *On the Fallacy of Key hitting or Striking* . . . 96

PART III.—KEY-TREATMENT FROM ITS MUSCULAR ASPECT.

CHAPTER XII.

PREAMBLE: SYNOPSIS OF THE MAIN MUSCULAR FACTS.

Muscular Condition is by far the most important problem to be dealt with in considering the act of Touch.—The eye here often proves misleading, as the visible movements accompanying Touch give but little clue to the actual muscular processes of activity and inactivity, through which, alone, we can influence the key.—The muscular-*components* are

CONTENTS.

three in number : (1) Finger down-exertion, (2) Hand down-exertion, and (3), Arm-weight, occasionally supplemented by shoulder-weight.—It is owing to the great number of combinations these offer us, that Variety in touch (and Expression) becomes possible.—Two apparently antagonistic forces arise from the combination of these three components (or ingredients) of Touch, which meet at the Wrist-joint; where a down-stress is produced by the force derived from LAPSE of arm-support, and where an *upward* stress is produced by the exertions of the Hand and Fingers reacting from the keys.—Since the latter exertions are the main ones employed to induce the act of key-descent, it follows, that the sensation of work done during key-descent must be felt to be *upwards;* upwards by reaction (or recoil) from the key against the Knuckle, and again upwards against the Wrist, and even in extreme cases against the Shoulder.—Touch can therefore be defined as an act of *Levering* Weight upon the key during the latter's descent.—All exertions employed at the Pianoforte must exhibit absolute freedom, so far as possible; however vigorously we may wish to urge one set of muscles into activity, we must not permit this to influence the *opposite* set into activity.—Movement must appear in some portion of the superimposed limb when a key gives way; this may take the form of either Arm-movement, Hand-movement or Finger-movement.—Which of these three movements ensues, depends on the relative balance existing between the three muscular-components during key-depression.—Arm-touch arises, when the arm-weight released exactly *balances* the exertion of the other two components during key-descent; Hand-touch (Wrist-touch) arises when hand-exertion is slightly in excess of the other two components; while Finger-touch arises when that component is slightly in excess.—Moreover, we have the option of not applying all three components against the key, simultaneously.—Owing to this option, we are able to provide forms of Technique suitable for ponderous passages and agile passages, respectively.—Agility depends muscularly on the careful elimination of all arm-*exertion* (and even Weight) for the time.—We must in such case rely almost exclusively on finger and hand exertions; and must in extreme cases of Agility, even restrict ourselves to the unaided exertion of the finger.—In both the latter cases, the arm "floats" over the key-board, supported by its own muscles.—Three principles of muscular-*combination* are thence deduced, which are so important as to deserve the title, *Species.*—The *first* Species of Touch-construction depends on finger-exertion alone, with passive hand and self-supported arm; permits fullest degrees of Agility, but restricts Tone-variety to the narrowest limits.—The *second* Species gives hand-exertion behind that of the finger, while the arm remains self-supported; permits greater variety of tone-quantity, while slightly reducing Agility-power.—The *third* Species gives arm-weight (individually released for each sound) in addition to the other two components; while considerably hampering Agility, this species offers the fullest variety not only of tone-amount, but of *quality*.—Beauty of quality in any tone above a *piano* is only attainable under this last Species.—Contrasts in *quality* depend on the option we have in this third species, of *initiating* (or "willing") the muscular-act into operation either (a) by Weight-release, or (b) by Muscular-exertion (of the finger and hand); the remaining components participating in both cases, but doing so in automatic response, either (a) to such willed Release, or (b) to such willed Exertion.—The tendency is towards the "singing" (or "sympathetic") tone-character, when this initiatory-prompting is by Release of arm-weight; and the tendency is towards brilliancy and even harshness, when this Initiative dates from finger and hand Exertion.—The two forms of key-attack thus obtained (i. e., (a) Weight-touch, and (b) Muscular-touch) are so important in their distinctions, as to deserve the name of Sub-genera.—These distinctive tendencies (toward singing and brilliant qualities, respectively) are materially enhanced by the *two opposite modes of finger-use* available, with their correlated opposite conditions of the Upper-arm.—The "Flat-finger-attitude" reduces the whole limb to its most elastic condition; its *clinging* action upon the key demands a corresponding release of the Upper-arm or Elbow, and it thus furthers *gradual* key-attack, and has been recognized as "pressure-touch" or "melody-touch."—The "Bent-finger-attitude," on the contrary, reduces the elasticity of the finger, hand and arm; and while the *thrusting* action of the finger here demands a forward tendency of the Upper-arm and Elbow, it thus furthers *sudden* key-attack, and has been recognized as "hammer-touch" or "passage-touch."—To obtain Tone-beauty in its fullest measure, we must combine the "Flat-finger" attitude with Weight-touch, unalloyed.—To enable us accurately to obtain the musically-desired tone from the muscular-operation intended to produce it, we must learn to "AIM" this operation during key-descent; we must learn to direct it so that it may culminate and *cease* at the very moment that Production ceases, the moment when Sound-emission commences.—All force applied to induce key-descent must cease at that moment, whether derived from Weight-release, or from Muscular-exertion.—We can only be apprised with sufficient directness of the moment when this culmination and cessation is demanded, by *listening* for the moment of sound-beginning.—The result thus obtained is STACCATO, since the key is here left free to rebound.—To obtain TENUTO, we must rest continuously upon the key-board with sufficient weight, to compel the finger and hand *slightly* to continue their work upon the key *beyond* the moment of sound-emission.—Such "Resting" is a process quite distinct and independent from the one that induces key-descent.—Such Tenuto-inducing Resting should, moreover, be no heavier than will just suffice to overbalance the key into descent.—LEGATO is obtained by the intervention of successive fingers during the continuance of such tenuto-inducing Resting.—The Resting is in this case transferred from key to key by the successive *lapse* in each successive finger's weight-supporting exertion.—The conception of *all* Touch moreover implies some form of Resting, and all Touch is therefore *dual*.—It implies (1) an act (the "Added-impetus") individually directed against each key to induce its depression, and (2), an act of Resting, continuous during each phrase, and sufficiently cumbrous in Tenuto and Legato to retain the keys depressed, and light enough in Staccato *not* to influence the key into descent.—All touch is thus *compound* in its nature; the only exception is the absolute *pianissimo*, when this is Tenuto or Legato.—This is the only form of Simple-touch; since the Resting itself here suffices to produce the required tone, as well as the effect of tenuto or legato.—Rotary Adjustments of the Fore-arm *conditions* are important; they greatly influence the extreme fingers at the two opposite sides of the Hand; these fingers are thus rendered equally available for strong or light action against the key; this furthers not only evenness of touch, but also the individualization of Melody notes from accompaniment.—Horizontal (lateral) movements of the Hand and Wrist are required to enable us to connect succeeding fingering-positions in unbroken sequence.—We also require side-to-side movements of the fingers themselves, to bring these over the required notes; and for the same purpose, horizontal movements of the Fore-arm alone, or in combination with the Upper-arm; also slight vertical-movements of the Wrist-joint, to enable us alternately to reach black and white keys in octave passages, without disturbing the Elbow 101

CHAPTER XIII.

THE LINK BETWEEN KEY AND MUSCLE—OUR SENSE OF KEY-RESISTANCE.

Each difference in sound-kind, exacts a difference in our application of energy to the key; we therefore need to be constantly reminded how much energy is required *by the key*, to insure certainty of execution and accuracy, artistically.—The key itself warns us of its requirements, if we constantly *watch* the resistance it offers, before and during depression, since such resistance varies with each key, and the use it is put to.—Our "Resistance-sense" (the muscular-sense and its coöperatives) can alone transmit this information to us.—Such Resistance-sense hence forms the LINK between the inanimate keyboard and our living muscles.—So intimate may this union become by this means, that the key will seem to be a physical-continuation of our finger itself.—The condition of our muscles must arise in *strict response* to the key's felt resistance.—Muscular-sensation arises purely from resistance opposed to muscular-exertion.—Even the slight muscular-exertion of the finger that supports the loose-lying hand upon the un-depressed key, is ample to excite the sensation.—A slight wedging of the fingers between hand and key renders the sensation more pronounced.—We must not mistake the mere sensation of Touch (or Contact) for the required sensation of Resistance.—The fact of our thus watching Key-resistance, also induces us to attend *musically;* for we cannot attend to the key, and choose what to do with it, and when to do it, without constantly referring to our musical Feeling and Judgment.—*Recapitulatory* 119

CHAPTER XIV.

ON KEY-CONTACT :—THE NATURE OF THE IMPACT OF THE FINGER AGAINST THE KEY.

Hitting the key has been found equally pernicious, whether regarded from the instrumental or the muscular aspect, since it precludes our employing the "Resistance-sense."—The finger-tip must therefore reach the key with no greater force than the key will bear without being thereby deflected, if Beauty and Accuracy of tone are required.—This will enable us to "take hold of and weigh the key, before *using* it.—The preliminary gentle fall of the limb upon the key, should be as far removed from a muscular exertion as possible.—The process of *pressing the key into movement* (Tone-production) only commences *after* we have reached the key-surface.—This latter process need not be separate from the preliminary one; for the comparatively slow preparatory descent upon the key may be immediately followed by the act of key-depression itself.—In this case there will be an unbroken descent of the limb (even from a well-raised position) down to the place in key-descent where sound arises; the latter part of the descent being however far speedier than the first part.—Or, contact with the key may instead be made some time *before* the key's depression is musically due; several fingers may thus be "ready" in certain swift passages.—An instructive lesson in non-hitting.—The finger, although reaching the key without actual blow, can nevertheless act against it either *suddenly* or *gradually*.—This difference depends on the muscular-*condition* of the arm, hand, and finger, discusssed later.—Approximation towards key-attack by blow, permissible for the harsher sound-kinds.—The mistake of employing harsh sounds, under the impression that they are effective; such harsh sounds, although noisy close by, do not carry in the Concert-room.— Key-contact and the subsequent key-descent constantly require adjustment to the particular needs of each instrument.—A heavily felted hammer requires far more "driving" in brilliant passages than does a harder one.—The harder hammer permits far greater range of tone-*quality*; but the *elasticity* required for the more sympathetic effects must in this instance be provided by the player's muscles, operating under the requisite conditions.—Movements preceding key-depression should be as ample as convenience allows.—Exaggerated importance must not be attached to such preliminary lifting, otherwise stiffness and worse will ensue.—The true object in well-lifting a limb, is not to enable one to hit harder, but that we may reach and move the key with more ease and *freedom;* and so that the individual fingers may be better discriminated in finger-passages.—Rather than allow oneself to think of the actual lifting-process, one should think of "playing from a (moderate) distance."—Ample movements, when possible, more healthy for the muscles concerned.—More appropriate for slow passages than for quick ones.—Two contradictory fallacies have arisen from (a) the desirability of giving ample preliminary movements, and (b), the necessity of determining the "giving-way-point" of the key; hasty generalizations having produced the doctrine of exaggerated limb-raising, in one case, and the fetish of never quitting the keyboard, in the other case.—Reconciliation of these two "Schools" found in the basis of (perverted) truth underlying both fallacies.— Accuracy in expressing ourselves musically is found to depend, in the first place, upon proper Key-contact.—*Recapitulatory* . . . 125

CHAPTER XV.

THE TWO CONCEPTS AND ACTS, OF "RESTING" AND "ADDED-IMPETUS."

It is necessary to possess clear and definite general concepts of Touch.— Touch consists of two main concepts and acts; (a) that of Resting upon the keys, and (b) that of Key-deflection, or the Added-impetus. —Touch is therefore *dual* in its nature.—Grounds upon which this conception of Touch is based.—The muscular consideration of Touch re-enforces the teachings of Part II., *Firstly:* that all passages (both Legato and Staccato) consist of a string of *dis-connected* muscular-

CONTENTS. xxvii

operations against the key-board, excepting in absolute *pp*, the "weighed" form of *pp*-tenuto or legato; and *Secondly*: that these separate muscular-acts are accompanied by a *continuous* act of light Resting, continuous for each phrase, but not heavy enough in Staccato to cause down-retention of the keys.—All touches (except the *ppp*) consist therefore of a series of *discontinuous* operations against the key-board to form the tone, in combination with a *continuous* one, a sub-stratum of Resting; the former determining the Tone-kind, and the latter determining its Duration.—The reason why so many fail to discover that the act of tone-production is dis-continuous and quite a short-lived operation, is, that quick passages and legato passages present a *continuous* effect to the ear, which is here misleading.—Since all touches are compound (excepting that solitary exception the *ppp*-ten. or leg.), it follows, that Purpose in performance must be so directed, as to insure the resting being *real* and of the required kind, and also to insure the Added-impetus being of the required kind, and that the latter is moreover accurately *timed* to culminate and *cease* with its consummation in Sound.—This consummation forms the Deed, itself, of tone-production.—" Aiming" at the Pianoforte hence means, that we must *finish* each key-descent at the moment that the sound is musically due; thus compelling the actual production of the sound to coincide with the pre-imagined Time-place and Tone-kind. —It follows, that the muscular act of tone-production must be commenced *before* its completion is musically due.—*Recapitulatory* . . 135

CHAPTER XVI.

THE NATURE OF THE LIMBS EMPLOYED, AND THEIR MUSCULAR EQUIPMENT.

The Upper-arm, Fore-arm, Hand and Finger form four separate levers.—Each lever is individually provided with muscles, and can therefore be placed in a state of action or inaction independently or conjointly with the others.—The muscles that provide the energy, are not necessarily found on the same part of the limb they serve to energize.—The muscular-provisions: the fingers can be exerted upwards or downwards, or from side to side; the hand has similar facilities; the fore-arm and upper-arm likewise.—The fore-arm can also be *rotated*, either by exertion or lapse of exertion; its condition in this respect has far-reaching influences.—Rotation of the upper-arm assists the taking of "skips."—The fingers can be applied in two opposite Attitudes; the Thrusting (or Bent) attitude, and the Clinging (or flat) attitude.—The *visible* difference between the Thrusting and Clinging attitude is best exhibited, when the finger is well raised; in which

xxviii   CONTENTS.

                                                                    PAGE
case the Thrusting-finger starts from a well-curved position, whereas the Clinging-finger starts from an almost straight position.—Besides having the power to *move* each part of the whole limb, individually, we are also able to exert these same muscles, *without* any corresponding movement of the limb.—Amongst the hidden stresses thus produced, are found the most important actions and in-actions required in playing.—There are several causes that may prevent visible movement from arising from muscular-exertion, beneficial and otherwise.— If the *opposite* exertion is permitted to come into operation with the required one, restraint or even rigidity supervenes.—All Stiffness of Finger and Wrist can under normal conditions be directly traced to such faulty Muscular-condition.—Ease in Technique and Expression hence demands as a first law, that we must as completely as possible relax all muscles opposite to the ones required to do the work of tone-production.—Passivity of the opposing muscles can be directly learnt. —The means of doing so.—*Recapitulatory* 147

CHAPTER XVII.

THE MUSCULAR ACTIONS AND INACTIONS CONCERNED IN THE ACT OF TOUCH.

All good touch implies Weight levered upon and against the key during its descent, by means of the Finger and Hand.—The weight is that of the Arm, sometimes supplemented by Shoulder-weight, and even Body-weight.—All exertion is *upwards* by recoil, upwards against the Knuckle, against the Wrist, and the Shoulder when necessary; the Basis for this Exertion is the weight of the Arm, and even that of the Body.—Although Body-weight is thus ultimately available, Body-*down*-force must never be substituted; the body must be purely passive.—The sensation accompanying key-depression is invariably *upwards*, a sensation of stepping-up on to the keys.—The reasons for this.—The three main muscular *components* of Touch: Finger-exertion, Hand-exertion, and Arm-weight with its coöperatives.—The three main *principles of combination* available of these, forming the three Species of Touch-construction; to be dealt with in Chap. XIX. —Arm-weight available in two distinct forms: either passive or active. —In the first case the arm is fully self-supported; in the second case it is more or less released during the act of Touch.—Two distinct sources of Energy must be recognized: (a) the Element of Exertion, that of the finger and hand, and (b), the Element of Weight, that of the Arm, etc.—These two Elements meet at the Wrist-joint; Exertion there bearing *upwards* (by reaction from the key), and Weight there bearing downwards (by release).—*Quantity* of tone depends on the total amount of energy derived from these two sources, and applied during key-depression.—*Quality* of tone mainly depends on *which* of these two sources *starts* the operation of both against the keys, thus forming the distinction between Weight-touch and Muscular-touch.—The tendency is towards *beauty* of tone when the tone-producing muscular-combination is *initiated* by Weight; while brilliancy or aggressiveness supervenes when the Initiative is by Exertion.—The rationale of this difference.—The two opposite Attitudes of the Finger available, the *clinging* and the *thrusting*, with their correlated Upper-arm tendencies.—These modify the contrasts in Tone-quality derivable from difference in the locality of the Initiative.—The clinging (or *flat*) finger enhances the sympathetic effects, while the thrusting (or *bent*) finger assists brilliance.—The two opposite kinds of Technique thus derived.—The flat finger, and its more or less loose-hanging arm; and the bent-finger, with its more or less forward-supported upper-arm.—Illustration of the opposite character of the resulting stresses.—The bent-finger unbends towards, and with the key; whereas the flat-finger remains straight, or tends to bend.—The differences in result are owing to contrasts in the *elasticity* of the limb under the two opposite conditions.—Whichever finger-attitude is employed, the KNUCKLE-PHALANX should invariably be relied upon for most of the work.—The *common* fault of relying too much upon the front two joints, and its results.—The device of inverting the hand, for the purpose of acquiring a true notion of the two opposite finger attitudes.—The two rules regarding Touch-quality deduced from the foregoing.—The distinctions of movement, respectively termed Finger-touch, Hand-touch, and Arm-touch; by no means the radical distinctions of kind, generally supposed.—Most of the sets of Condition (that form a given tone-character) can be accompanied optionally either by Finger, Hand or Arm movements.—The cause is found in *one* of the touch-components slightly out-balancing the other two.—Arm-touch.—Hand-touch (so-called "Wrist-touch"). —Finger-touch.—The relative sensations of Finger, Hand, and Arm-touches.—Arm, Hand and Finger movements, when appropriate.— The speed of the passage is the main cause that determines choice; thus: Arm-movement for slow successions of chords or notes, and for the initial notes of phrases; Hand-movement, when the passage is too quick to admit of arm-movement; and Finger-movement, for passages still faster.—Finger-movement, also employed in the slower, and slowest passages, since Legato can only be obtained by finger-intervention.—Exceptions to these rules, and combination-movements. —Choice of Muscular-*combination* more important than choice of Movement.—How Arm-weight is obtained by release of the support-

Missing Page

Missing Page

Hand or Arm touches); Agility is limited, owing to the rapid re-iterations required of alternate release and self-support of the arm.—Note, showing *Glissando* to be closely related to *ppp*-transfer-touch.—*The Second Species of Touch-formation :* (Finger and Hand exerted, with arm self-supported) permits greater Agility than Species III.; Tone quality limited to the muscularly-initiated variety, with its less sympathetic effects, only modifiable by the contrasts between Thrusting and Clinging-attitudes; Tone-quantity also more limited than in Species III.; while Finger and Hand movements are alone available.—*First Species of Touch-formation:* (Finger exertion alone, with loose-lying hand and self-supported arm) offers unlimited scope as to Agility (or Velocity); has the drawbacks, that Tone-amount available is very small, and that variations in Tone-quality are impossible, except for the slight modifications between Thrusting and Clinging.—The determining-reasons between choice of " flat " and " bent " finger attitudes.—The immediate cause of the difference between the two finger-actions, found in the condition of the arm; since upper-arm weight cannot be individually lapsed beyond a certain speed, *forte* passages beyond that speed *must* be played with supported upper-arm (2nd Species) and with "bent" finger.—The true nature of the muscular difficulties that *prevent* agility; to overcome them we must be able to provide either 2nd or 1st Species (when necessary in Thrusting-attitude); i.e., we must be able to provide conjoint exertion of the finger and hand, without this leading to arm down-exertion; and finger-exertion, even, without this leading to hand-exertion.—The imperative necessity of timing and ceasing all tone-productions either as single notes or as groups of notes, not only for the sake of Agility but also for the sake of accuracy in Expression.—Systematic teaching of Muscular-discrimination again proved to be urgent.—General directions as to the appropriate application of the three Touch-formations.—The Cantando and Cantabile.—The ever-present question of Staccato *v.* Legato.—The question of order of Study.—Warning reiterated, that caution is necessary while studying muscular-conditions; we must never forget that our Purpose must ever be : *Music, through Key-movement.*—Recapitulatory.—TABLE, showing relationship between Touch-construction, Movement, and the Resting . . . 214

CHAPTER XX.

ENUMERATION AND CLASSIFICATION OF TOUCHES.

Necessary brief review of the main muscular-facts and touch-formations.— The main facts: The Resting; the Added-impetus; the three distinct Species of Touch-construction; the two radical touch-distinctions, Weight-initiated *v.* Muscularly-initiated: and the distinctions between Clinging and Thrusting attitudes.—The three Species of Touch-construction form the chief basis both for Enumeration and for Classification.—Review of these species and their potentialities.— Classification points:—(A) the difference of Resting, exhibited as between Legato and Staccato; (B) the different aspects of Movement, exhibited as Finger-touch, Hand-touch, and Arm-touch; (C) the different forms of Touch-construction, exhibited under each of these headings:—*Division I*, STACCATO: (a) *Finger-staccato*, eight distinct kinds; (b) *Hand-staccato* ("*Wrist*"-*staccato*), six distinct kinds: (c) *Arm-staccato*, four distinct kinds.—*Division II*, TENUTO or LEGATO (the act of Resting, unassisted, serves as a tone-producing agent for *ppp*-Tenuto and Legato): (a) *Finger-Legato and Tenuto;* ten distinct varieties; (b) *Hand* ("*Wrist*") *Tenuto*, eight distinct varieties; (c) *Arm Tenuto*, six distinct varieties.—42 distinct kinds of touch can thus be formulated; we must, however, NOT thus think of them in Practice; we must, instead, first learn them in the guise of the *comparatively few* fundamental principles of muscular-action and application quoted; must subsequently learn to apply these more and more unconsciously, until Musical-sense at last prompts their application. —The distinctions requiring constant supervision are: (a) Weight *v.* Muscular touch, (b) Flat *v.* Bent attitude, (c) Resting at surface or bottom of key—*Recapitulatory* and Summary.—TABLE I: Enumeration-summary; TABLE II: Classification under Legato *v.* Staccato, and under Movement.—TABLE III: Final Classification, from the Colourist's point of view, viz.: Weight-touch *v.* Muscular-touch, etc 238

CHAPTER XXI.

RECAPITULATORY OF THE MAIN CONCLUSIONS OF PART III.

APPENDIX TO PART III.

Note XI.	"*The foundation touch and mono-method fallacies* .	.	264
Note XII.	"*Exaggerated finger-lifting,*" etc. .	. . .	265
Note XIII.	"*The province of automaticity*" .	. . .	266
Note XIV.	"*On arm-weight*" .	. . .	267
Note XV.	"*Bent*" v. "*Flat*" *finger-attitude* .	. . .	268
Note XVI.	"*Incorrect v. correct finger-technique* .	. . .	269
Note XVII.	"*Certain exceptional forms of Legato and Staccato*	.	271

PART IV—"ON POSITION."

CHAPTER XXII.

SYNOPSIS OF THE MAIN ASPECTS OF POSITION.

Correct posture, during rest and movement, follows almost as a necessary consequence when the correct muscular Actions and Inactions are being fulfilled.—The importance of Position has been greatly exaggerated.—Forms no guarantee whatever of correct Key-treatment, although ease of posture is helpful in its attainment.—Position not the Cause of good technique, although it may arise as a Result of such.—The fallacy of seeking to obtain good technique by insisting on the imitation of posture.—The ground covered by Position.—Variation of Position necessary with each individual.—It has nevertheless some important aspects, where variation from the normal would prove impedimental.—The three points of greatest importance—(a) Position of Shoulder: sufficient distance between it and the keys to enable the arm to be sufficiently unbent, thus rendering the whole of its weight available.—(b) Posture of finger: sufficient preliminary curve when used in thrusting touch, and flatter when used for clinging touch.—(c) Posture of Wrist or Hand laterally: fingers and hand pointing in same direction as keys, for Five-finger position; turned inwards for single-note Scale, with slight additional lateral movements for Arpeggio; and turned outwards, when Double-notes-passages travel outwards.—Subsidiary details: (a) Wrist-level, not too exaggeratedly high or low; (b) Knuckle well away from keys, and not held "in" relatively to the fingers and wrist; (c) the seat, sufficiently distant from instrument, while central and not too high.—Fallacy to consider the reaching of the correct keys purely as one of the problems of Position, since it should mainly depend on the proper fulfillment of the Act of Resting.—The latter, properly executed, causes us to find each key from each preceding one.—A sequence of notes hence realized as a succession of distances accurately judged from each preceding key.—Position is finally found of importance, although not so important as has been imagined 273

CHAPTER XXIII.

THE DETAILS OF POSITION.

Vertical aspect of Finger-position.—The two distinct positions of the finger, corresponding to the Thrusting and Clinging attitudes of the finger and arm.—More noticeable when the finger is raised, than when it is depressed.—The nail-phalanx shows the difference most; this must be *vertical,* when the finger is raised previously to the action of thrusting-touch; whereas it may remain flat in clinging touch.— The movement of the finger towards the key can in some measure show us whether the touch-action is good or otherwise; the fault of hitting can thus be detected by the eye.—The tip of the finger reaches the key in " bent-finger " touch, while the fleshy part reaches the key in "clinging-touch."—In bent-finger touch, the fingers should be all nearly equally bent, but if the fifth is abnormally short, it may be slightly straighter.—Ample preliminary movement of the finger is healthy, provided there is time for it, and provided it does not lead to stiffness and hitting.—Position of the thumb—corresponds in its differences to those of the fingers in a measure.—The thumb should not be held contracted against the hand, an often-found fault.— Thumb movement arises near the wrist-end of the hand.—Finger-position in Hand-touch.—The fingers should assume their deflected position relatively to the hand, while the hand is rising from the preceding chord or note.—Down-movement of the finger simultaneously with that of the hand, is a combination only rarely required.— Finger-staccato; there are two kinds, corresponding to the two attitudes of the finger and arm, the " thrusting " and the " clinging."— The return-movement differs in correspondence with these attitudes. —In *bent*-finger staccato-touch the finger re-ascends into the initial position, whereas in *flat*-finger staccato-touch the two front phalanges continue their movement *beyond* the moment that tone-emission commences, while the knuckle-phalanx rebounds with the key.—*Horizontal* aspect of finger-position.—Varies with each different kind of passage.—Five-finger fingering positions allow the middle-finger and hand to point in the direction of the length of the key.—The places on the key that should be reached by the fingers in such fingering position.—It is a fallacy to suppose that the fingers must reach the keys all in a straight line.—With the thumb on the black keys, the edge of the black keys must be considered to form the limit of the key-board.—Single-note Scales and Arpeggi require the hand and fingers to point inward as the normal position, so as to give freedom of movement to the thumb.—In the arpeggio, lateral movements of the hand and wrist are required in addition, to facilitate the extensions of the fingers and thumb.—In double-thirds scales, the hand and fingers are turned in the direction in which the scale is travelling at the time.—In other double-notes passages, lateral movements of the wrist and hand are required in addition.—The curve of the thumb.—Looking down upon the thumb, its nail phalanx should always be in the same line as its key, unless we wish to sound two adjacent notes with

CONTENTS.

it, when it should be at an angle with the keys.—The thumb should therefore assume a convex curve, when it is extended from the hand, as it always should be, unless required under the hand.—The position of each key, should, whenever practicable, be derived from the position of the preceding key, or keys; and each finger, moreover, should be in position on its key, *before* the act of key-depression is begun—two rules that automatically fulfil themselves, provided we insist on due observance of the Act of Resting, in one of its two aspects.—Position *inside* the key, is however of even greater importance than this *feeling* of each key before key-depression; accuracy of Expression immediately depends on due observance of these rules.—To prevent risk of note-"splitting," we should be careful to try to reach each key in its centre.—Position of the hand and knuckles.—The hand should not slope towards the little-finger, but should be level, excepting when it apparently tilts in the act of Rotation-touch. —The Knuckles.—Should not be allowed to sink in; they should be kept sufficiently well off the keys, owing to the natural reaction of the fingers against the keys during key-descent.—Relatively to the Wrist, the Knuckle may be either level or somewhat higher.—The actual height varies with the kind of touch used, and it differs with different conformations of hand, and the height of seat adopted.—The "knuckle-in" fallacy.—Beginners should at once be taught to recognise, how the knuckle can easily be kept up, if a proper action of the fingers is adopted, and provided down-arm force is eliminated. —Vertical movement of the hand; exhibited as Hand-touch (so-called "Wrist-touch").—In hand-touch the knuckles rise and fall bodily.—The extent of the movement of the hand need not exceed the depth of the key; and the movement should not be of greater extent than this, in very rapid passages.—In slower passages the hand may rise off the key, and in this instance it is muscularly an advantage to do so.—Excessive raising of the hand in hand-touch is as strongly to be deprecated, as an excessive raising of the fingers in finger-touch; and whatever the amount of raising, it should only be undertaken for the sake of *freedom* of motion.—The fallacy of considering "Wrist-touch" to consist of a throwing-up of the hand.—The position of the wrist vertically.—Its elevation above the key-board should arise as the natural consequence of a proper balance between the exertion elements of the finger and hand, and the element of arm-weight.—On the whole, the most natural position of the wrist relatively to the knuckle is about on a level with the latter; but a higher or lower variation of this is admissible, provided there is no exaggeration either way.—In Hand-touch (Wrist-touch) this normal (about level) position is the most natural; but a slightly raised position is found more comfortable for rapid octaves, etc., by many players.—The fallacious doctrines of exaggeratedly high wrist and low wrist.—The wrist-height should vary slightly in the case of passages requiring the use of the thumb on alternate white and black keys; a slight raising for the white key, and lowering for the black key enables the thumb to reach both, and thus obviates what would otherwise have to be a clumsy movement of the elbow, fore and aft.—Lateral movements of the wrist, reviewed; also the lateral movements of the fore-arm and upper-arm, which bring the fingers over their keys.—Definition of these requirements in passages of short extension and large extension, respectively.—Instruction as to these movements and the lateral movements of the Thumb, respectively in the Scale and the Arpeggio; the greatest care here necessary in primary instruction.—The rotary movements of the Wrist and Hand (really of the Fore-arm), which constitute Rotation-touch.—Position of the Fore-arm.—Position of the Upper-arm and Elbow.—It is the most important law of Position that *the Shoulder must be sufficiently removed from the key-board* to enable the arm to be opened out almost into an obtuse angle; freedom and the use of Arm-weight are otherwise greatly impeded.— Sideways, the Elbow should not be pressed against the body, but its position varies, with the part of the key-board the hands are employed upon.—Arm-touch movements, of two kinds: (a) of the whole arm, and (b) of the forearm only.—The importance of the loose-lying hand in this connection.—Position of the Body.—Two alternative positions available, either (a) almost erect, or (b), leaning forward from the hips (but without stooping).—Choice depends on the relative measurements of the body and the arm, and on the inexorable requirements of the opened-out arm.—Position of chair.—In the centre of the instrument; sufficiently removed from it to admit of the opened-out arm, and of a height that will allow the fore-arm to be about level with the key-surfaces.—Unnecessary movements.—Should be avoided when possible.—In the learning stage many secondary movements are unavoidable so that we may be able to test ourselves for freedom, accuracy of aim, etc.; such movements should, however, be gradually reduced to the smallest limit compatible with due fulfilment of their purpose, once that Freedom, etc., has been conquered.—Summary of the main points requiring attention 278

Recapitulatory of this Chapter and of Part IV. 308

Main Points of Position.—Summary. 315

CHAPTER XXIV.

CONCLUSION:

GLOSSARY AND SUMMARY OF THE MAIN TEACHINGS OF THIS WORK.

PART I. Introductory :—The act of playing; musical perception; technique; key-treatment.—PART II. Key-treatment, instrumental aspect; —Definition of the act of Tone-production; loudness; beauty; cessation of the act of touch; key-resistance; energy required.—PART III. Key-treatment, muscular aspect :—Key-resistance gauged through the muscular-sense.—The dual aspect of Attention in playing.—Key-contact not really a blow.—The duplex nature of the act of touch; the two acts of Resting and Added-impetus.—The act of Resting, its duration, and its two forms: either at surface or at bottom-level of keyboard, forming respectively Staccato and Legato.—The Added-impetus, its duration and its forms of construction, muscularly.—The three muscular Components of Touch.—The three Species of Touch-construction.—The sensation of work done, always upward.—The determining cause of Movement during the act of touch; i. e., the difference between Finger, Hand, and Arm touches.—The distinctions between Muscular-touch and Weight-touch arising from the two alternative modes of starting the Third Species into operation, with its tendencies toward brilliance and roundness of tone, respectively.—Playing too far down insures bad tone-quality.—Quality also influenced by alternative Attitudes of Upper-arm in conjunction with the Finger: the Thrusting and Clinging finger respectively helping brilliant and sympathetic effects.—The importance of the knuckle-phalanx's action in both finger-attitudes.—The automatic inducement of Arm-weight cessation in the Added-impetus.—The automatic Transference of the Resting-weight.—The necessity for eliminating all contrary exertions from those required in playing.—The importance of constant rotary adjustments of the fore-arm, and freedom therein, in conjunction with vertical and horizontal freedom of the Wrist-joint.—PART IV. On Position: The imperative necessity for room between the shoulder and the key-board.—The difference positionally between bent and flat finger.—The lateral adjustments of the hand and wrist for each particular kind of passage.—The supreme importance of properly preparing every finger over every note, and of tonal-aiming: each key's position found from its predecessor, and acted upon only down to sound-consummation.—Warning in conclusion, not to forget the musical purpose of Technique, whilst studying the details of muscular and instrumental action which render its attainment alone possible; i. e., the muscular-act must always be supplied only in answer to the felt needs of the key, key-needs, determined by the ever-present attention of our Musical-consciousness and Imagination.—Final summary of main points to be insisted upon in teaching ourselves and others 317

APPENDIX TO PART IV.

Note XVIII. "*The Fallacy of Position-Worship*" 324
Note XIX. "*The straight fifth finger*" 326
Note XX. "*The high wrist and the low wrist dogmas*" . . 327

INDEX TO THE PREAMBLES, RECAPITULATORIES, AND TABLES

Part I. INTRODUCTORY.

	PAGE
Preamble	1
Conclusion and Summary (Chapter VI.)	37
Table; the Act of Playing	40

Part II. INSTRUMENTAL ASPECT OF KEY-TREATMENT.

Preamble. " Synopsis of main instrumental facts "—Chapter VII.	47
Recapitulatory of Chapter VIII. "The instrument"	60
" " Chapter IX. " On Sound "	68
" " Chapter X. " The String "	76
" " Chapter XI. " The Key " ; (§ 18)	87
Recapitulatory and Summary of Part II.	89

Part III. MUSCULAR ASPECT OF KEY-TREATMENT.

Preamble. Synopsis of the main muscular facts—Chapter XII.	101
Recapitulatory of Chapter XIII. " The Link between Key and Muscle"	124
" " Chapter XIV. " On Key-contact "	134
" " Chapter XV. " The Concepts of *Resting and Added-impetus.*"	143
Table of the two Concepts, etc.	146
Recapitulatory of Chapter XVI. " The limbs employed "	156
" " Chapter XVII. " The muscular *Actions and Inactions*".	197
Table of the main muscular discriminations required	195
Recapitulatory of Chapter XVIII. " The Three Muscular Tests"	212
" " Chapter XIX. " The Three Species of Touch-formation "	232
Table, showing relationship between Touch-construction, Movement, and the Resting	237
Recapitulatory of Chapter XX. " Enumeration and Classification of Touches "	248
Tables of Enumeration and Classification	251–4
Recapitulatory of Part III. (Chapter XXI.)	255

INDEX TO PREAMBLES AND RECAPITULATORIES

Part IV. ON POSITION.

	PAGE
Preamble. "Synopsis of main aspects of Position;" Chapter XXII	273
Recapitulatory of Chapter XXIII. : " *Positional Details,*" and of Part IV. Close Summary of Position	315
RECAPITULATORY, CONCLUSION and SUMMARY of whole work—Chapter XXIV	317
Final Summary	323
The " *Contents* "	xv

PIANOFORTE TONE-PRODUCTION.

PART I.

INTRODUCTORY.

GENERAL ASPECT OF THE PROBLEMS OF PIANOFORTE PLAYING.

CHAPTER I.

PREAMBLE.

§ 1. THE attempt to teach, or to learn the readings of pieces of Music, before the *Means* of rendering them has been mastered by the aspirant, is quite as great an absurdity, as endeavouring to insist on the subtle details of the elocution of a poem, while one is as yet unable to pronounce the words of the language in which it is written. Still more absurd is the practice of the teacher-beginner, old or young, who gives *Chopin* Ballades, and *Beethoven's* Moonlight Sonata to school-girls, as yet incapable of giving a good account of *Schumann's* "Merry Peasant"!

Surely it is pure folly to attempt to teach pieces, or studies, or even Technical exercises, until at least the actual *Elements* of the question of *Tone-production* itself are understood by the pupil,—and master! Such folly shows crass ignorance of the whole problem of Pianoforte Education. Indeed, it does not deserve the name of "teaching," for it is mere dabbling!

INTRODUCTORY.

§ 2. However, the signs of the times clearly point to the fact, that it is beginning to be generally felt, that the same educational methods should be applied to the Pianoforte, as have long ago been adopted in other branches of Education.

§ 3. Let us consider, then, the difference between the empiric and the rational or "*direct*" systems of teaching:

The empiric method of Pianoforte Education consisted in choosing pieces, studies, and technical-exercises, more or less suitable for the learner, and then leaving him to make tentative efforts to perform these; the comparative failure that resulted from his helpless undirected flounderings, being corrected—as it was supposed, by scolding, bullying, or encouraging him into trying again, according to the temper of the instructor!

A rational scheme of Education, on the contrary, would consist: in analysing the subject to be taught; analysing also the successful doings of successful artists; thence deducing the laws and rules that govern successful performance; and then *directly* communicating such laws of procedure to the pupil, instead of leaving him to discover them for himself.

This has been done in the study of Language, and to a certain extent in that of Music; for in the one case, the rules of Grammar and of Syntax, in the other case, the rules of Harmony and Composition form (or should form) rules of procedure at the moment acceptable to the Majority. Such formulating of Knowledge has been methodically done in the case of Mathematics, Physics, and the Sciences generally; it there means, formulation of the knowledge *so far* gained of the *immediate Causes that underlie each Effect.*

Evidently, teaching, as applied to Science, Harmony, or Language, does not here signify, that the discovery of the implicated Laws shall be left to each individual learner. On the contrary, the student is in each case informed of the already perceived laws and rules of procedure. Hence, he can in this case, at once "start fair," and can make practical use of such information; and may even go further, and discover fresh truths;—instead of having to experiment for years, or maybe

PREAMBLE.

a lifetime, in his endeavours to rediscover for himself facts, already understood by others.

§ 4. Clearly therefore, we cannot even *commence* really profitable practice at the instrument, until we have attained conscious (or unconscious) sense of the inexorable laws that govern its effects.

Until we have such sense, we shall risk forming wrong habits, which must then be first crushed, before we can hope to make a step forward.[1]

It is the formulation of these Laws of Tone-production, which is attempted in this present work.

§ 5. It is true, the rules of Grammar, of Harmony, or of Composition, are found to be of little practical value, *until subconsciously employed; i.e.:* until we are not only able to act in accordance with such rules, but are able to do so without self-conscious attention to them. This hence involves, that such rules must be made into habits of mind; but this applies equally to Thought and Invention in other forms of human activity.

This subconscious mastery of already-discovered rules and facts, which must precede original thought and invention in the case of the other sciences, certainly applies with equal force to the inexorable *laws* (not mere rules) of the art of Tone-production by means of the Pianoforte.

Habits of thought, and of action, must be formed in accordance with such laws, before the knowledge thus gained, can become available for free playing; just as no treatise on Harmony, Grammar, or Science, can lead to results of any real value, until similar habit has been accomplished.

Whereas, the forming of *Correct Habits* can at once be enforced, when the laws, or at least the rules of procedure, are known.

---

[1] If correct habits are not at once formed, at least *thrice* the time will have to be spent. There is the time wasted in fixing the wrong habit; then the time required to weaken that wrong habit to the point of effacement; then, at last, the time needed to form the correct mental-muscular connections.

How requisite, therefore, that these laws — the Elements of Pianoforte playing, should be thoroughly understood!

INTRODUCTORY.

§ 6. It follows, both with regard to the question of playing generally, and to that of Tone-production in particular, that the *Form of Attention* required from a fully-trained Artist, must necessarily widely differ from that required of a Student, who is as yet still undergoing the process of *learning to attend* and to *act*,—provided he is undergoing that process successfully.

This fact cannot be too strongly insisted upon.

Our calligraphy, for instance, receives no detailed attention, when we *have* conquered the process of writing; we then merely "wish" a word to appear on the paper, and, lo! our muscles provide the whole of the complex behaviour required, in response to the mere *general direction,* wish, or thought, given for that word—with all its component letters;—we no longer have to consider whether it is a hook, an up-stroke, or a down-stroke, that is wanted; habits formed long ago, unconsciously guided by the eye, provide all the complicated movements, in answer to what is hardly even a conscious wish!

But what a different matter, *before* we had attained such facility! Do we not remember the time, when, as little ones, our pen refused even to make up or down strokes respectably? Did we not then consciously, with all our will and might—with tongue protruding, from the unwonted mental struggle—have to direct that floundering pen according to that so well-remembered " copy,"—which from its very perfection of line and curve, seemed hopelessly beyond imitation?

Do we not find a similar impediment in our Pen-speech—and in our Tongue-speech, when we attempt to be fluent in a Language, only somewhat unfamiliar?

Yes, the act of playing, is a widely different experience from the act of *learning* to play! Practically everything we learn, has first to be done consciously; and also very often self-consciously too! Only by habit can we ultimately succeed in "naturally" accomplishing the required actions. The greater the talent, the greater the speed and the less the *apparent* effort with which we learn, that is all. Playing forms no exception to this universal law.

§ 7. The art of Tone-production itself can be acquired in two quite distinct ways:—The empiric, *i.e.*, hap-hazard way, and the *direct* way.

In the hap-hazard way, we experiment at the key-board until we happen to hit on those particular conditions of key and muscle, which alone will serve to give us each of the chameleon-like varieties of tone-colour it is possible to obtain from the instrument, and without which, expression remains impossible.

It is possible to succeed in learning in this way; but to do so, we must possess a quite exceptionally good ear for tone-*Colour*,[1] an ear that will instantly warn us, when we converge towards, or diverge from, the tone-quality desired. . . . We must also be provided with a *Musical Instinct* sufficiently keen to detect the necessity for tone-subtleties in playing. In addition, we must have a keen musical *Memory*, to keep these effects before us, otherwise the sound of the wrong tones will assuredly blunt our sense of beauty and variety of tone-colour, and will tend to lessen our desire for improvement in this direction. We must besides have good healthy *Muscles*, that will almost without instruction act "freely," *i.e.*, in definite sets; so that, having accidentally obtained a right sound, we shall be able, at will, to repeat the desired effect. For this repetition can only be assured, if we have succeeded in mentally noting both the aural effect, and the *Muscular-Sensations* accompanying the mechanical consummation of the sound; for it is only by having the power to recall these muscular-sensations, that we shall be able to ensure the recurrence of the musical effect.

It is obvious then, that to learn tone-production in this way, needs a superlative equipment musically, and physically. Even assuming however that we do possess such exceptional talent, musically, aurally, and muscularly; so far from their correct production being discovered, it may after all take us years before the existence of the complete gamut of tone-possi-

---

[1] *i.e.*: Perception of the distinction between Tone-qualities; or "Clang-tints," as the late PROFESSOR TYNDALL proposed terming them.

INTRODUCTORY.

bilities is even suspected, and we may altogether fail ever to stumble upon some of the most important or even simplest varieties![1]

And even then,—how often is the "doing" after all forgotten! No, to learn in this way, is by no means the best way, even for the gifted! For the ordinary mortal, it is quite an impossible way. Hence arises the fact, that so far, it has been the specially gifted that alone have shown good colour-technique at the Pianoforte.

The other way of learning, being direct and immediate, is far simpler :—

In this rational form of learning, after Tone-production of every kind has been analysed, we must first learn to understand the laws that govern Key-Treatment; and we must then learn to understand the nature of the Muscular-acts required from us, to fulfil those key-requirements.[2]

Knowing what to do to the key, and knowing also how muscularly to consummate such *use* of the key, we shall then be in a position *directly* to start forming these acts into habits of muscle and mind. In this way we shall gain a true Technique, in the widest sense of that word. Although this will not allow

---

[1] Much of that conflict of opinion, and apparent contradiction, we find between the upholders of rival "methods" and "systems" of pianoforte playing (and of singing !) arises from non-perception of the fact, that a really great Master-artist, be he Pianist, Violinist, or Vocalist, never restricts himself to *one* single form of "touch" or tone-production. On the contrary, we find, that he constantly changes from one tone-kind to another. It is mostly by such means, indeed, that he is able to express those subtly-varying moods he perceives in the music he undertakes to interpret.

The "method"-maker, on the contrary, having discovered one or other way of effectively using the Pianoforte-key, or human-voice, allows himself to be misled into fancying, that that particular way is the only "right method." Consequently he then decries everything that does not happen to fit in with his narrow views; and forces his pupils to perform whole works with but one tone-colour throughout, varied merely in its intensity.

[2] This involves the understanding of some of the elementary facts of physiology, anatomy, and even of psychology; also a clear understanding of the obvious mechanical laws of action and inter-action involved. Such understanding, however, does not trench on these subjects beyond their most elementary stages. We have to deal, indeed, with such elementary, every-day, facts, that unless these are already fully understood—apart from the Pianoforte, true "Education" on the part of the individual, can hardly be said to have begun.

us to translate into sound, that, which we do *not* in the first instance musically *see;* yet it will enable us at least fully to express such modicum of musical-sense, as we are able to perceive.

In fact, we shall find, that a great deal of bad playing does not arise so much from want of musical taste, or musical judgment, as from wrong mental-muscular habits; and that it is these that prevent the expression of sense. Hardly any player, excepting the very greatest, is quite free from such faulty habits.

When such faulty mental-muscular habits are numerous, and are strongly fixed, we have what is practically a "ruined" Piano-voice. Such a case differs however, from the parallel in Singing; for in the latter case the instrument itself may be permanently injured; whilst a cure is always attainable at the Pianoforte; although it is idle to expect it, unless dead-in-earnest purpose is forthcoming from both learner and teacher.

§ 8. *Three* stages of acquaintanceship with Tone-production are possible : viz.—

a) : We may be able to produce any sound we wish from the instrument—sound of any kind, within the limitations of the instrument, and at any speed of succession.

b) : Beyond that : we may understand, what are the actions (of key, and muscle) that will effectually lead to such attainment.

c) : Still further : we may KNOW WHY those actions must be so.

= *i.e.* :—

a) : Acquaintanceship, *in the first sense*, is strictly speaking, no knowledge at all. All it implies, is, the ability to provide at will every possible contrast; as derived from remembrance of the personally-experienced sensations accompanying each kind of effect.

This may serve the Artist well enough; although, even *his* failures would be less frequent, could he trace effect back to its cause.

b): Acquaintanceship, *in the second sense*, forms *practical* knowledge of the subject.—It signifies, knowledge of the Key-treatment, and of the muscular actions and inactions that will lead to each desired tone-result. It is the Teacher's domain, as it will enable him to show and describe the means to be adopted to ensure the appearance of each possibility of Contrast. Without such knowledge, he cannot teach at all, in the rational acceptation of that word.

c): Acquaintanceship, *in the third sense*, forms practical *Explanation* of the facts; knowledge of the *immediate* causes to which each effect must be traced [1]; knowledge of the Laws on which are based the Rules derived from analysis of successful playing.

Knowledge of the subject, to this intimate extent, almost trenches, it is true, on the domain of the Theorist and Scientist. Nevertheless, it is well for both Teacher and Artist to possess it; for it will serve to give him assurance, that his teachings and doings rest upon ascertained laws; and that he is not perchance following the merely arbitrary fancies of his own brain. He is then also safe-guarded from falling a victim to such fancies, and to the many fallacies by which he is liable to be carried away, without such definite knowledge.

§ 9. The *Object* of the following work, is, in the first place, to urge a more serious, rational, and direct study of the art of tone-production, and therefore of PLAYING generally. In the second place, it is an attempt to provide the *Material* for such practical study of the problem and its direct teaching. It also proposes to provide some measure of Explanation of the Laws immediately involved, put in as summary a form as is consistent with clearness. It is therefore divided into Parts. The first Part forms a short analysis of the process of Pianoforte Education and Playing; and at the same time attempts to convince the yet unconvinced, of the necessity of the *rational* study of the art. This part is followed by others, in

---

[1] *Ultimate* "explanation" is of course no more possible in these matters than it is of any of the other every-day facts of existence. The very narrow limitations of the human mind surround us with the Unknowable at every turn.

which it will be attempted to give the necessary information, in successive and logical steps.

Short and practical directions, as to the various touch-elements follow; also, the exposition of a series of mental-muscular exercises, independent of the key-board,—"Relaxation studies"—by means of which the necessary muscular conditions (visible and invisible) can be most quickly acquired, and subsequently retained.

I hope to follow this work, with others, dealing more minutely with the processes of Practice, Performance, and Teaching.

§ 10. Much tautology and repetition, will be found in the following pages,—and no doubt many other literary sins! As my endeavour is, to form a *useful*, rather than an ornamental work, I do not hesitate to sacrifice all literary exigencies, whenever my pedagogical experience prompts me to do so, for the sake of the student.

Experiment at the key-board, and away from it, should accompany the reading of the letter-press. This will assist in the understanding of the matter put forward.

CHAPTER II.

THE PROBLEM OF PIANOFORTE TRAINING.

§ 1. SUCCESSFUL PERFORMANCE, when analysed, is found to resolve itself into the nice combination of *two quite distinct processes:*

I. *The purely mental*[1] *process of apprehension and conception of the Music to be performed;* and

II. *The mental-muscular process, of communicating such conception to others;* this being done through the physical act of

---

[1] The term "mental" is here used as signifying "emanating from the *Brain*." It therefore includes musical emotion and feeling, as well as intellectual perception.

producing the requisite sounds[1] from the instrument; a physical act consummated through the agency of certain of our limbs against the Pianoforte-key.

Both of these processes must be successful, if consummate performance is to result. The first process implies MUSICAL INSIGHT on the part of the performer,—musicality, musicianship.

The second process implies special *Instrumental-Insight* and *Attainments* on his part; the art of performance proper. EXECUTANTSHIP.

To have something to express, implies imagination, invention. To be able to communicate it, no matter whether in English or in Hindustani, or by means of the Pianoforte ivories, implies conquest of "Technique" in the real sense of that much-misunderstood and much-abused word. Mere knack in scampering over the key-board at a great rate, or playing very loudly or softly at will, is but a very small part of Technique. To have good Technique, means, not only being able to do all that, but to be able to do a great deal more besides. For it means, being able to provide all possible tone effects of which the instrument is capable; and the capacity to apply these in the best of Taste. Technique itself hence implies: knowledge, judgment and imagination; as well as the physical habits that will enable us to obtain from the instrument the tones required to build up the imagined musical edifice.[2]

---

[1] By "requisite sounds" is not meant merely "the right notes," but also the right *Tone-kinds* to form those requisite tone-contrasts by means of which alone, musical sense can be made evident to the listener.

[2] A performance can only appeal to us, through the medium of *Contrast*;—through contrasts of Pitch; of note-combination (harmony); of Time-pulse and its divisions; speed of movement (tempo); of *Tone* quantity, quality, and duration. It is owing to his having the power to choose different degrees and combinations of these, that the real Artist is able to affect us.

Like everything else, a performance is necessarily built up of *ultimate units*. These ultimate units, in the case of a musical performance, consist of separate individual sounds, or "notes." Every one of these necessarily has its distinct influence on the effect of the *Whole*. Hence, in performance, there is no such thing as a note of no consequence; for the least-accented note demands quite as much care in performance as the most accented one; both will equally ruin the resulting Music-picture, if not kept in their place. Each note must therefore enter at the precise Time-place, and must be of the

THE PROBLEM OF PIANOFORTE TRAINING. 11

§ 2. Moreover, it is not enough to *be* Musicians and Executants. It is not enough to have the ability to see musical-sense, and to have ability to execute it, but we must not forget actually to *use* both those faculties at the moment of performance. For there is a vast difference between merely *hearing*, and really *listening*. It is the distinction between merely sounding notes automatically, and sounding them with musical *Purpose*. As performers, it is just as futile to imagine the musical *end* in view without purposing its fulfilment, as it is to purpose the fulfilment of mere sounds, while losing sight of the fact that they should fulfil a Musical Aim.

In a word, both musical and executive *Attention* is required. (*Vide Note I., Appendix.*)

§ 3. We ourselves cannot be conscious of giving such attention at the time, if it be really successfully provided. Obviously, successful attention implies that our whole consciousness—our "whole Body and Soul"—is taken up with musical perception and its translation into actual sound. We therefore cannot also use our consciousness at that moment to analyse that very act.

If, however, we possess the power of mental *post*-analysis, then we shall be able clearly enough to realise the nature of the attention required from us.

Having realised its nature, we shall then, vice versa, also be able to instruct, stimulate, and compel ourselves and others to give it.[1]

exact duration, tone-quantity and quality, that will best fit it to fulfil its mission.

Judgment is hence required for each and every note. We shall see later on that such judgment can only be derived from *perception* of the music ;—*Emotional* perception, and *Intellectual* perception. From such perception must date the conscious or un-conscious judgment that *every* note demands in performance, if it shall properly fit into the picture.

[1] To many Artists, self-analysis seems totally denied. Hence, such fail to recognize the *processes* of their own acts, both mental or physical. Indeed, once having learnt to act properly, knowledge of the process appears useless to such, and may be so, in some measure. This is the reason why artists, as a rule, actually resent the mere idea of "attention" or "execution"; since the very fact of their giving such good attention prevents their personally becoming aware of the act. This is also the reason why most artists prove themselves such indifferent teachers, although they often do stimulate (as Liszt did)

INTRODUCTORY.

§ 4. This dual aspect of all Performance applies equally to all the Arts; simple or complex. An act of conception, and an act of execution are always implied: Ability to provide those acts, and Will to apply them at the moment.

Definitely to express even the simplest shape, our mind must will the doing; must first successfully grasp it—imagine it, and must then by means of successful mental and physical technical attainments, express it.

It applies to every word we write, even to every letter forming each word; and it applies to every note we play.[1] For instance, if we would delineate on paper, even so simple a shape of definite proportions as a triangle, it is evident that our imagination must first vividly picture the extent of the lines constituting it, and where these lines shall meet, before our executive faculty can begin to draw it. The necessary executive attainments here consist in responsiveness on the part of our muscles to the mandates of our inner sight,—a perception gained through training and experience.[2]

True, we may "let our pencil wander over the paper." But if we really do this without previous mental picturings, then the result will be mere scribbling. Exactly analogous are the Sound-results arising from indefinitely, inefficiently guided fingers at the Pianoforte; they form mere musical scribbling.

§ 5. Here it will be as well at once to endeavour to show what it is that constitutes *Definiteness* in performance—what it is that constitutes "*Grip.*" (*Vide Chap. IV.*, §§ *10 and 11.*)

The same laws apply to musical perception as apply to

---

by their exhibition of unbounded enthusiasm. Obviously, as we cannot show that which we have not perceived, it follows, that without conscious or unconscious analysis we cannot hope to become cognisant of what there is to teach.

And as the self-analysis required must be that of an actual artist, we here see why really "great teachers" are even rarer than great artists.

[1] A great deal of technique is ultimately provided by automatic, or semi-automatic actions. These have nevertheless to be definitely stimulated. We cannot *learn* to make even the strokes and hooks, etc., forming *one* letter, without copious conscious attention directed upon the problem.

[2] In fact it comes to this, that we have practically to project an imagined shape upon the paper, and to insist upon our muscles fulfilling the lines thus imagined.

every other kind. All perception, and all knowledge itself, being purely *relative*, it follows that it is only by *Contrast* that we can perceive; that it is only through its contrast with something else, that we can become aware of anything.

For instance, we can only realise a solid object, like the surface of a table, by its contrast to the surrounding air. Moreover, both our sense of touch and our sight will only inform us of the *Point of Demarcation* between solid and air,—it is only the *surface* we can thus become aware of.

Now, if we wish *definitely* to perceive even one note, it is obvious that there must also be some such line of demarcation —or surface!—which can be appreciated by our *Ear*.

This we find to be the case. For to the musical ear there is a perfectly definite point, a mentally solid fact realisable; and that is, the point of demarcation between *Silence* and *Sound*, when each sound actually commences to issue from the Pianoforte. It is just this line of demarcation, this point, this tone-*surface*, that alone can give us the opportunity definitely to pre-judge, purpose, and in consequence, definitely to perform any note. (*Vide Note II., Appendix*.)

Notes, thus definitely *meant* as to time, can then be grouped together, first to form minute *Shapes* in the way of ideas and motives, then whole phrases; then the smaller and larger sections or contours of a movement; and finally, into a complete and living organism,—a *Whole* musical-work.

"Shape," in performance, therefore eventually resolves itself into RHYTHM, both in its narrowest, and in its widest sense. The constituent *atoms* (the single sounds) must, each one, have its definite place in the scheme of the Whole, if that is to be satisfactory. To enable us to succeed in this, the work as a Whole must constantly be kept in mind,—while yet, for the sake of it, carefully placing each and every note at the precise *time-spot* thus dictated; and not only that, but at the exact tone-amount—and more important still—at the exact tone-*quality* thus demanded. Unless this be accomplished, the resulting music-picture can neither be homogeneous, nor perfectly harmonious, nor *just* in its outlines; while the expression of the *emotional*-import underlying these mere shapes (popularly mal-termed " soul ") obviously remains quite impossible.

§ 6. The measure of our success then depends absolutely on the degree of strength and perfection of the necessary emotional and intellectual conceptions formed. It also depends upon the accuracy with which our executive ability is able to translate these mental pictures into physical fact.

At first sight, it seems pure supererogation to have to insist on such self-evident facts. It is however most necessary to do so, for the grossest misconceptions of the whole problem of pianoforte practice and teaching arise directly from failure to grasp this premise : that the two processes of artistic-perception and of artistic-execution are quite distinct accomplishments; and that therefore, good Execution is by no means a necessary consequence of good musical Perception.

To sum-up : it is clear, that Pianoforte-Education must needs consist of two perfectly distinct branches: a), that we must learn accurately and vividly to use our powers of Perception ; and b), that we must learn as accurately to *translate* such perceptions into actual sound, *i.e.* :

I.) : We need emotional and intellectual training, sufficient to make us MUSICIANS ;— and thus enable us to " attend " musically.

II.) : We need artistic and physical training, sufficiently to make us EXECUTANTS—and thus enable us to "attend" executively.

MUSICIANSHIP:—

§ 7. Both the Musical Imagination and the Judgment must be trained : such musical imaginative-power as we happen to possess, must be trained, to enable us to be vividly impressed by the Beautiful in Music, and to enable us to realise the human emotions that the composer endeavours to convey to us through the medium of music-language. Without such emotional appreciation, all modern music remains a sealed book.—And BACH and MOZART are as intensely "modern" in this respect, as is WAGNER!

In addition to training in emotional-appreciation of music, training is also demanded in the *intellectual* appreciation of music-*Matter* itself. It is only by this means that we shall be enabled to perceive the *shapes* the composer has employed through which to express his feeling.

This involves training that shall enable us to perceive FORM. Form in its true sense, not merely in the restricted, narrow and conventional sense,[1] but *Form* or *Shape*, from its largest manifestations, down to its minutest details; *Rhythm* primarily, manifested as this is, in the larger contours of movement as *Climax*, and through its smaller sections, down to its component phrases and constituent ideas.

It involves, also, training to enable us to understand the material from which these shapes are built up:—the contrasts of Pitch, of Duration, of vertical note-combination (Harmony) and their juxtapositions (harmonic progressions) and the recognition of the ornamentation of these by passing notes and suspensions, etc.

Appreciation of musical Form, Shape, or Rhythm, in this sense, is a purely intellectual act. Education in it, is therefore comparatively easy.

Appreciation of emotion in Music, on the other hand, is a more difficult matter, for it depends not only on appreciation of the Beautiful as Music—on inner "ear," but it depends also on Feeling—in the sense of human sympathy. Education in this direction, though possible, is far more difficult, for the requisite "understanding" can only be obtained by a training of the faculty of human insight; through contact with and interest in our fellow-creatures; through the multifarious experiences of a rich life.[2]

---

[1] A musical building (or Form) if well proportioned both in its largest as in its smallest details, will be perfectly good, even if the particular "form" it takes is quite unconventional, and has never before been employed. We must have shapeliness, but it need not be mere copy of the tested and accepted!

[2] Refer to *Note VI., Appendix.*

EXECUTANTSHIP :—

§ 8. We must remember that *Technical-Ability* merely signifies: ability fully to communicate to others, that which we do musically *see*. "Technique" signifies just that; all that, nothing beyond that, but also nothing *less* than that.

Hence, however great our capacity as musicians,—however keen and intimate our perception of musical sense; the power of communicating such perceptions is absolutely limited by our capacity as Executants.

§ 9. The *Intellectual* interest of Music is made evident in performance, by clearly *showing* the musical "shapes"—the musical architecture.

The *Emotional* effect of Music, on the other hand, mostly depends upon the use of Tone-*Colouring*.

Performance cannot be clear unless the musical shapes are clearly seen and shown; whereas *"Feeling"* can only be expressed when Tone-colouring is employed to vivify those shapes. This can be intensified by Time-colouring—the *Rubato*.

By "colouring" is here meant not only contrasts of tone-*Amount*, but contrasts in that far more important department, that of *Quality*.[1]

Evidently it is range of "colouring"—range of contrast in tone-*kind*, that constitutes the most important item in one's technical equipment.

The proof of this is: that this very item is the point that most distinguishes the *Technique* (N.B.: the "technique") of a really great performer-artist from that of the less great; for his range of tone-shadings is far greater; his distinction between shadings far more subtle.

. This also holds good in all the other arts: in their particular way.[2]

---

[1] There are some who even deny the very existence of the fact, that variety in Tone-QUALITY can be produced from the Pianoforte! The explanation is obvious enough. Either, they suffer from a physical disability which prevents their discerning such contrasts; or they have never happened to discover the *Doing*. Possibly, they may never have experimented on an instrument sufficiently good!

[2] For instance, while *Shakespeare* is generally acknowledged to be the greatest literary giant, he also displays the largest vocabulary—the largest as-

§ 10. Executantship or Technical-ability, when analysed, resolves again into two very distinct accomplishments :—
I.): *Artistic-Judgment* pianistically, including also pulsational-judgment.
II.): Mastery over THE ART OF TONE-PRODUCTION.

§ 11. *The term "*ARTISTIC JUDGMENT*" as here used implies :—*
a): Knowledge of the whole range of instrumental effects and possibilities;
b): Judgment to enable us to select precisely those instrumental-effects that will most fully convey to the hearer the musical emotions and shapes which our Musical-faculty enables us to see;
c): Ability accurately to gauge TIME-LAPSE, in the minute apportionments requisite in the passing-by of the tone-picture. This last involves training the *Pulsational-sense* to a degree of efficiency.

§ 12. Pulsational-training does not form special training for any particular instrument; manifestly it is needed for every kind of musical performance.

It is a training that will enable us vividly to recognise *Time-Place* in a regular succession of small Time-distances, such as are covered by bars and their divisions; that will enable us accurately to judge the "Time-place" for every note filling up such comparatively gross time-lapses; and will enable us also to realise those larger pulsations of Rhythm built up from the combinations of bars, and even phrases.[1]

Pulsational-training, it is, that will enable us to watch time-pulse as a living fact, when we have once started some particular swing in our mind; thus enabling us to keep such train of Pulse vividly before us, while we proceed to fit our performance into its inexorable LAW.

Moreover, it will ultimately enable us to recognise and re-

sortment of word-shadings. In the same way we find that the greater the musical composer, the more complete is his use of the full gamut of harmonic possibilities, the greater the range of his rhythmical contrasts.

[1] *Vide* again *Note II., Appendix.*

assert such recurrences of Time-division, even when we choose to deviate from their *straight path*, as in that higher exhibition of Pulse and Rhythm, implied in the RUBATO.

For true *Rubato* implies that we dare not lose sight of the inexorable Pulse, even when we do choose to omit direct reference to it for a while.

That is: although we may, in obedience to our emotional-sight of the music, elect to make our performance either lag behind or press in advance of the relentless succession of Time-beats, yet we must continue to feel the persistence of this same Pulse, so that we can resume its sequence as if it had been unbroken. Unless we can succeed in this, we shall break instead of "bend" the Time; when the infallible result will be, that all *Continuity* in the composition under interpretation will be hopelessly broken-up.

Rubato is then, an accomplishment of the pulsational-sense, that enables us to *bend* the lines of our performance shapefully, while not impairing their continuity;—a bending, without which truly *musical* (as the converse to merely mechanical) performance remains unattainable; and without which, all real emotional effect must remain impossible of full realisation.

§ 13. The other two items constituting "*Artistic Judgment*," do however require much special training. Training as distinct from general pulsational training, as it is distinct from that of general musicianship. For we must have special knowledge of all the effects — MEANS OF EXPRESSION, of which the particular instrument is capable;[1] and we must possess the judgment and taste that will enable us to select precisely those means that will best convey our musical sense.

Such training is to be obtained:

a), by listening to the doings of good players, when one has learnt how to "listen";

---

[1] Including its capacity of contrast in every way:—of forte with piano; legato with staccato; "sympathetic" tone-quality with the "hard" variety; Accentuation, both by means of Tone, and by means of Time;—in a word, the whole realm of phrasing and "colouring."

b), by oneself experimenting at the instrument, and profiting from such experiences;

c), by the surest, and most direct method, viz., by taking advantage of the guidance of a teacher; always provided, such teacher himself fully possesses not only the necessary knowledge and experience, but is also able to communicate it.

§ 14. *The Art of Tone-Production.*—Manifestly, our power of communicating the verdicts given by our musical feeling and knowledge, and by our artistic-judgment, is *strictly limited* by the extent of our power to make the instrument respond to our wish with exactitude, and in the end unconsciously.

In other words: any artistic-judgment, musicianship, or feeling that we may possess, must perforce remain mute, unless we also possess ability to *draw* the sound-effects, thus dictated, *from the instrument;* and are able to do so with accuracy and with certainty.

Here we are face to face with a training, special to the particular instrument chosen. It is this special training—this latter section of the Executive side of Playing—the Art of Tone-production at the Pianoforte—the very BASIS OF EXPRESSION—with which the present work proposes to deal.

In the next chapter, we will a little more closely consider what is meant by this "Art of Tone-production," and how this art is to be acquired.[1]

---

[1] The uncultivated ear often fails to distinguish between good and bad tone-production. There are plenty of minds, otherwise "musical," who yet seem quite content to acquiesce in the rawest of tone qualities, and paucity in variety. No doubt this arises from ignorance that *there is something better* to be obtained from the instrument than what they are accustomed to. Also, there is no doubt that those few, who are really very highly gifted executively, are *not content* with such raw tones; but that they do strive might and main to discover the ways of good tone, in consequence of discomfort caused to their sensitive ear. Hence, also, the popular fallacy (popular even amongst musicians) that beautiful tone-production necessarily denotes "musicality" on the performer's part. True, up to now, owing to the prevailing ignorance of the whole subject, it has been only the few gifted ones, who have arrived at beauty and variety of tone.

Good tone-production is not to be measured by mere quantity of sound. Mere noise, and Tone of good volume and beauty—and consequent *carrying* power, are two quite distinct things.

Many a street-singer makes plenty of sound—of a villainous description! We sometimes even hear performers in the Concert-room, who sing as execra-

CHAPTER III.

THE PROBLEM OF EDUCATION IN THE ART OF TONE-PRODUCTION.

§ 1. No effect can possibly arise from the instrument without a physical cause. Being caused, there must be laws that determine each effect. Every possibility of sound-quantity and quality; and of continuation—of legato and staccato; and every possibility of speed in note succession—Agility; all must rest on physical facts.

Moreover, that these physical facts with regard to the KEY may be fulfilled, again absolutely depends on our employment of the requisite muscular *Conditions ;* conditions of activity and of relaxation.

i.e.: When the exact Treatment needed *by the key* is fulfilled for each possible sound-effect, then only can each effect result; but these possible different treatments of the key can only be fulfilled by the employment of Muscular-Conditions, each correspondingly different for each sound-kind ; muscular-conditions, many of which give no evidence of their existence to the eye. The needs of the key must be fulfilled, but these must be fulfilled by our muscles in the easiest possible way.

Tone-production, in a word, is the art of drawing any kind of sound from the instrument at will, in chameleon-like variety;—any quantity, any quality, momentary or sustained; and it also includes the problem of Agility.

Tone-production is hence a question of Mechanics, Physics, Physiology, and of Psychology too. It is an art that does not rest on mere "rules," mostly at the mercy of taste—like

bly, but are nevertheless accepted by a section of the public, owing to the presence of sensationally enormous voices !
Likewise at the Pianoforte, it is not difficult for one gifted with a good "Piano-voice" to stir up the air (and our ears) with masses of sound of a kind, and also to gain considerable facility in *agility,* and to do this in spite of a radically wrong "production"; but such lamentable cases of misapplied energy, and misapplication of a good "voice," must not be allowed to confuse the real question at issue : that good tone-production will enable even naturally good "voices" to succeed incomparably better than they could do without it.

those of language, or of harmonic-etiquette; for it rests on physical LAWS, inexorable as those of mathematics.

The art of tone-production implies implicit obedience to the *laws* that govern sound-excitation through movement of the Pianoforte-Key; an Art, not perfect, nor even possible in some directions, unless we are able muscularly to fulfil these key-*needs* in the *easiest* possible way.

§ 2. The laws of tone-production apply equally to all sorts and conditions of players.

For as tone-production absolutely depends on accurate obedience given to the mechanical, physical, and psychological laws involved, it therefore follows that such laws, being inexorable, apply to all players, no matter how much they may differ in muscular or in musical conformation.

These very laws, indeed, also entail slight modifications of activity and of *Position*, with different sizes of hand and finger; and differences of size and weight of arm.[1]

§ 3. The idea that there are "stiff" hands and fingers which have to be ground down to suppleness by interminable exercises, is also mostly based on fallacy; except in those rare cases of incapacity through rheumatism, etc.

"Stiff" wrists, "stiff" fingers, are as a rule, merely the outcome of incorrect muscular action—*impeded* action. *i.e.*: Action impeded by the unnecessary, and harmful associated action of the *opposite* muscles.[2]

Some people naturally possess muscular *Insulation*, as it were. Others will make ten times the necessary effort, even in such familiar actions as raising their hands to their hats!

It is such so-called "stiffness," *i.e.*, *restrained*-movement and action, that directly prevents many a Student and Artist from attaining good Pianoforte *Speech*.

[1] Correct "position" of the limbs employed is almost a necessary consequence, when the correct conditions of muscle are fulfilled. The converse is however by no means true. For it by no means follows that "correct position" necessarily also entails correct muscular activity and inactivity; although this forms one of the current superstitions (or displacements of cause and effect) with regard to Pianoforte-technique!
[2] Sometimes, however, they result from sheer ignorance of the nature of the Key's mechanism,—and its laws of treatment.

Not only does weak and bad tone result from such bad *Production*—tone, bad both as to quantity and as to quality; but agility, accuracy in legato and staccato, and accuracy even in Time and Rhythm itself, all seem almost impossible of attainment under such conditions. (*Vide* §§ *3 and 5, Chap. IV.*)

Whereas, all becomes easy and certain, as soon as the muscular and physical laws involved are strictly obeyed.

§ 4. Those who are naturally gifted with such muscular "insulation," easily acquire facility in that department of Tone-production that gives AGILITY,—"technique" in the popular but false and narrow acceptation of that word.

Such, also easily acquire facility in those other, but far more important departments of "technique," in its proper and fuller sense—facility in providing Tone-Varieties of every kind.

Such endowment indeed forms both Talent in tone-production, and "Finger-talent;"—an endowment quite distinct however from the one that enables us to attain a *really* large tone at the Pianoforte, and which latter therefore forms what may be termed a good Pianoforte-VOICE.

We must not forget, that such endowments are moreover perfectly distinct from a Musical-talent, however often they may be mistaken for such.

It is evident then, that physical endowment for the Pianoforte is as divergent as that for vocal performance, and that at the Pianoforte we may evince a naturally large "voice." This depends on the actual size of the Arm-muscles, etc.,—that is, provided these are thoroughly "healthy"—*i.e.*, easily "insulatable" and easily *fully relaxable*.[1] For it is the *amount* of Arm-weight we can set free, that forms the possible extent of our real voice, *in "singing" tone-quality*, at the Pianoforte.

---

[1] Really complete relaxation may possibly be physically unattainable, perhaps even undesirable, pathologically considered; but the term thoroughly conveys, what has *practically* to be striven for. For it is the completest possible *Relaxation* of all muscles that should be passive, that forms the real "secret" of all good tone-production (including Agility) at the Pianoforte;— just as it is the secret of beauty of tone at any other musical instrument—or indeed of good muscular technique applied to anything else.

We have an instance even, in the DELSARTE system of gesture, which evidently rests on the same truth as a basis.

Now a properly produced Voice "carries" well, and sounds *fuller*, than a badly produced one. Precisely analogous is the case at the Pianoforte; and it is astonishing to most people, how large is the compass of contrast of which even the *smallest* Pianoforte-voice is capable, once the problems of correct tone-production have been mastered.

"Good" tone-production hence signifies: that we do make the best possible use of such "voice" as we may be endowed with; that we succeed in fully employing, and accurately directing it against the key-board.

§ 5. *We learn* from all this, that facility and education in the art of tone-production, rest on two distinct kinds of *Knowledge* and *Attainments* :—

a), We must understand *how to treat the instrument;* and b), we must be able to provide *the requisite muscular conditions* to enable us to fulfil such treatment.

Education in Tone-production hence divides into the two departments :—

I.) : *Instrumental education*, and

II.) : *Muscular education*.

§ 6. We will now consider these two departments in slightly further detail:

INSTRUMENTAL EDUCATION: This implies, that we must learn thoroughly to understand the nature of the instrument, and the conditions under which alone it will respond to our wish.

i.e.: We must learn thoroughly to understand what is the nature of the particular *treatment* the *key* demands for each and every sound-kind, and shading; since it is alone through such difference in treatment that each difference in Tone can be induced.

§ 7. *MUSCULAR EDUCATION :* This implies, that we must acquire, and must subsequently form into habit, all those different sets of muscular-*conditions* (of activity and relaxation) which alone will best enable us to fulfil these differences in key-treatment, essential for the production of each difference in sound-shading. For we see, that as contrast in sound can only be induced by contrast in key-treatment, therefore, to secure such contrast, the muscular conditions must also in each instance be modified.

Such habits of muscular-combination, must then subsequently be associated mentally with their results in SOUND.

Ultimately this will enable us to provide these muscular-conditions automatically—in *direct Response* to each stimulus from our musical imagination and judgment.

In fact, we cannot be said perfectly to possess "The Art of Tone-production," until such muscular-response is absolutely in accord with every musical wish that we may feel; that is, until Muscle unerringly responds to the promptings of Musical Feeling.[1]

---

[1] *i.e.:* We must first realise (consciously, or unconsciously) *how we must muscularly act* in order to obtain each possible effect from the instrument, through its keys. Having successfully learnt to provide the muscular conditions that will give the correct key-treatment, it still remains necessary to form these muscular-conditions into HABIT.

Habit of this kind, must be so strong, and of such nature, that it will be prompted into action simply by association of ideas; so that the mere imagining of a sound-shading, will automatically prompt its muscular realisation—its physical realisation through the key-board.

For we must always remember, that until the requisite muscular-habits are thus formed for each sound-shading, it remains just as impossible to allow the *musically*-artistic mind full sway, as it remains impossible to converse freely in a language, the words of which have still to be summoned up by a conscious act of volition.

In fact, that we must not rest, until Feeling is able to prompt action, applies with equal force here, as in other forms of Conduct. For it is Feeling eventually that acts as the great motive force in conduct. A few words of quotation from that greatest of English philosophers, HERBERT SPENCER, will prove of service in this connection. Regarding the relationship of Feeling and Conduct, he says: "It is never the knowledge which is the moving agent in conduct; but it is always the feeling which goes along with that knowledge, or is excited by it. The truth that recklessness brings *distress*, fully acknowledged though it may be, remains inoperative." . . . "The mere cognition does not affect conduct—conduct is affected only when the cognition passes out of that intellectual form in which the idea of distress is little more than verbal, into a form in which this term of the proposition is developed into a vivid imagination of distress—a mass of painful feeling." . . . "It is thus with conduct of every kind."

"Already we have seen that the connexion is between action and feeling; and hence the corollary that only by frequent passing of feeling into action, is the tendency to such action strengthened. Just as two ideas often repeated in a certain order, become coherent in that order; and *just as muscular motions, at first difficult to combine properly with one another and the guiding percep-*

CHAPTER IV.

THE PROBLEM OF MUSCULAR EDUCATION.

§ 1. Training in this latter branch of instrumental education—in the acquisition and application of the requisite Muscular-Conditions, is again a twofold problem: consisting as it does, of two distinct STEPS:—

Step I.: We must gain the requisite MENTAL-MUSCULAR DISCRIMINATION.

i.e.: We must learn mentally to distinguish the muscular-conditions that *are necessary*, from those that *impede* the desired result in Tone. In a word, we must learn to provide the activities wished for, and no others.[1]

Step II.: We must learn to APPLY *these correctly-discriminated Muscular-conditions, to the* KEY-BOARD.

i.e.: We must learn ACCURATELY to TIME the *Commencement*, and also the *Cessation* of the correct muscular-operations; and we must accurately gauge their degree, according to the "needs of the key."[2]

---

tions, become by practice facile, and at length automatic; so the recurring production of any conduct by its prompting emotion, makes that conduct relatively easy. Not by precept, though heard daily; not by example, unless it is followed; but only by action, often caused by the related feeling, can a moral habit be formed." . . . "And yet this truth, which Mental Science clearly teaches, and which is in harmony with familiar sayings, is truth wholly ignored in current educational fanaticisms."—"The Study of Sociology," pp. 359, 367.

[1] Practically, even the simplest movement or activity of a limb, needs a complex set of co-ordinated muscular actions and cessations for its fulfilment. What we have to do, is to learn to obtain just the needful and complete muscular-processes. This is the interpretation desired for the term, "mental-muscular discrimination."

[2] To be more explicit:—As regards Step I.): We must *learn to distinguish* the particular set of muscular-conditions (active and passive) which will best serve to induce each one of those different modifications of key-treatment (both during and after descent) from which arise: a), all the possible varieties of tone-*Quality* and *Quantity;* and of *Duration;* b), those modifications of muscular-condition that will best serve towards the attainment of AGILITY; and c), those that will best provide the requisite side-to-side movements of Finger, Hand, and Arm, which enable us to bring the Finger-tips over the required notes.

As regards Step II.): We must learn to *gauge* and *time* these muscular-ex-

§ 2. We will now consider a little more closely the process of education implied in these two steps.

The *first* of these two steps, the acquisition of the requisite mental-muscular discriminatory power, dealing as it does with the power of distinguishing between the desirable and undesirable Muscular-conditions, is not really special to the instrument.

Most of such requisite *discriminatory* power can therefore primarily be acquired, away from the Pianoforte keyboard.[1]

In fact, in many cases, it is a distinct advantage thus to set about its acquisition, since, away from the instrument, there is not the same overwhelming association of ideas which recall any WRONG HABITS acquired there; and therefore the impediments to progress are not so great.

§ 3. The process of acquiring such requisite muscular-discrimination, whether at the key-board or away from it, is one of ELIMINATION. That is, a process of elimination of the non-required activities; a process similar to that by which we acquire the muscular-habits of our daily lives.[2]

ertions and lapses so that they shall be accurately applied to the purpose in view:—to the requirements of key-treatment. *i.e.*:—a): We must learn to time them to COMMENCE upon contact with the key, and not before; so that there shall be no *Waste* and *In-Accuracy* caused by concussion against that surface; b): We must learn to *time* them to CEASE the very instant they have completed their duties against the key—so that the Energy set free by the muscles shall fulfil its purpose in making *Sound* only, and shall not instead be wasted (and worse than wasted) against the pads under the key; c): We must learn similarly to *gauge* and *time* the before-mentioned horizontal movements of Finger, Hand, and Arm, so that we may with *certainty* always find the required notes,—having already learnt to make the requisite movements themselves with perfect ease.

[1] For the purpose of acquiring these elementary "muscular-discriminations" a set of "Relaxation"-exercises will be given in Part V.; these will cover the whole ground of the special muscular activities and in-activities required at the Key-board. They can be practised at any odd moments during each day, as they require no key-board; familiarity with the needed muscular conditions can thus be both gained and retained, and the muscles kept "in form." (*Vide Note III., Appendix.**)

[2] When we start life, we have hardly any power of muscular-discrimination. We begin by kicking-out legs and arms, in our efforts to attain some-

* These "Relaxation Studies" have since been published as a separate work by Messrs. Bosworth.

THE PROBLEM OF MUSCULAR EDUCATION. 27

§ 4. It is by such process of mental-muscular elimination, that we have to learn:—

a), to distinguish the required exertions of each separate portion of the limbs;

b), to provide these with *perfect freedom*,—*i.e.*, with elimination of the opposite muscular-activities;[1]

c), to learn *promptly* to cease the required exertions; so that we shall, when at the key-board, be able accurately to *aim* the force set free upon the key, only towards the production of Sound.[1]

§ 5. The muscular activities and in-activities required, moreover produce two distinct classes of effects:

a): Those that provide actual *Movements*, and which therefore become *Visible;* and

b): Those that produce *Stresses* and *Tensions*, without immediately causing any movement, and which therefore remain quite *Invisible.*

Of these two classes of effects, by far the most numerous are those *undiscernible* by the eye.

---

thing. It is only by degrees that we learn to *eliminate* leg-movement when we wish to move an arm; only after much experimental failure, that we learn sufficiently to eliminate wrong muscular activity, to obtain a single definite movement of one limb; we require still longer experience before we can definitely *aim* such movement. For instance, it is only gradually that we learn to guide a spoon into our mouths, and not into our own, or our nurse's eye! Having then learnt to distinguish such already complex muscular problems, we learn in course of time, even to locate the activity of one finger from another.

But how far are we even then from using each Finger, Hand, or Arm, at its *Easiest!* For the delicate shadings of muscular-condition required at the Pianoforte remain impossible of attainment, unless each muscular condition can be thus provided absolutely without restraint.

The particular talent that makes for their quick acquisition, has already been alluded to. (§ 7, *Chap. I., also Vide Note IV., Appendix.*)

[1] Many people experience great difficulty in thus providing one set of muscular-exertions, while keeping the *opposite* set passive. As already alluded to, it is just to such *impeded* muscular-action, that has to be attributed the common experience of "stiffness," clumsiness and general difficulty of movements so fatal to all playing.

It is indeed to imperfection in this particular kind of muscular-*Segregation* to which we must often trace that want of Agility,—so often falsely attributed to "insufficient practice"; and to which we must also often trace that *lack of Tone,* lack of *Delicacy,* and lack of subtlety in Tone-*Shading*—in a word, lack of EXPRESSION so lamentably prevalent.

§ 6. The problem of *directly* teaching the particular muscular conditions that do provide visible result in the shape of movement, is comparatively simple; description, example, and imitation suffice, provided absolute "freedom" during movement be insisted upon.

§ 7. The problem of *directly* dealing with the *Invisible* ones, and their omission, is however more difficult; indeed at first sight it would seem almost as difficult as that of directly teaching those required in vocal tone-production.

This, however, is not so. For these invisible activities and relaxations can be described and shown, in the first instance, by permitting *movements* to result from them; having thus been learnt or taught, they can afterwards be applied under the slightly altered circumstances that prevent their becoming evident to the eye.

§ 8. Once the desired muscular-combinations have been successfully attained, we can proceed to fix them in the memory. This can only be done by taking mental note of the *Muscular-Sensations* accompanying their application. It is by subsequently recalling such sensations, that we shall be able to re-enact the muscular conditions at will; and by doing this with sufficient frequency, we shall be able to form them into Habits. Such habits have subsequently to be applied not only to the instrument, but to Music itself; so that we can ultimately form that further habit,—that of associating the requisite muscular-habit with each sound-effect.

For, as has been previously insisted upon, it is only in this way that we shall eventually be able to provide the required tones, in strict response to our musical-judgment—and thus at last enable Feeling, the great prompter, to have full sway.

§ 9. Here is the place, urgently to warn both Learner, and Teacher, of the great danger there is, of *too exclusively* thinking of the required muscular-attitude, when endeavouring to alter a muscular-habit *at the* KEY-BOARD. There is danger, at such times, of dwelling upon such desired muscular-attitude, limb-movement, or mere position, and of coming to look upon these *as the Object* to be attained; meanwhile forgetting the ultimate object of such muscular-correctness! (*Vide also* § 7, next Chapter.)

Therefore, whenever we conduct muscular experiments at the Key-board, we must be careful to keep such muscular-conditions in view solely *as the Means* to an end. That end is: to MAKE SOUND by means of inducing movement in the Key;— a Sound-excitation, moreover, that must always be definitely TIMED; and definitely gauged as to kind. (*Vide also* § 7, next Chapter, page 34.)

§ 10. This now brings us to a closer consideration of that *Second Step* in muscular-education—the correct Gauging and Timing of the correctly chosen muscular-conditions. We shall moreover realise, that it is in such Timing that immediately lies the LINK that unites the purely mental act of musical-determination with the physical act of Tone-production.

For we shall see that it is on the ground of RHYTHM that they coalesce.

§ 11. As regards Education in this Second Step—the application of the results of muscular-condition to Key-necessities, manifestly, a Key-board is here absolutely essential.

It is true, a *dumb* key-board may quite well serve to teach us, and to enable us to retain, those particular muscular-gaugings that enable us to find the right notes; this being a matter that depends merely on our muscularly gauging with accuracy the distances to be traversed on the key-board—through side-to-side movements of Finger, Hand, and Arm.[1]

But beyond that point, a *speaking* key-board becomes imperatively necessary, by which to teach ourselves the HABIT

---

[1] Our EYE can only guide us, in the case of large skips; with plenty of time provided by the composer for taking them.

Everything else consists of movement far too swift for the guidance of the eye to be of any direct use.

The eye can only help us indirectly; it can only remind us of the actual *size* of the distances to be traversed; it cannot really guide our fingers or hands during their movements. This is plain from the fact, surprising to so many people, that we can equally well "find" our notes, whether we look at the portion of the key-board in actual use, or instead remind ourselves of the *distances* involved, by keeping our eyes riveted on similar distances *at the opposite end of the key-board!*—or even situated on another key-board!

of accurately Timing and accurately Gauging the *degree* of those other muscular acts, those that directly make tone.

The reason why this can best be accomplished at the Pianoforte key-board itself is clear enough:—

Since both Time and Degree of the muscular-conditions are determined by, and must hence be gauged by the particular resistance offered by each individual key; and as this resistance differs not only in different instruments, but differs indeed with different keys of the same instrument; and, moreover, as such resistance differs with the SPEED at which we endeavour to impel each particular key's descent during a musical performance; it follows: *That unless we firmly ingraft this habit* of Attention (and of eventual unconscious *Obedience*) to the varying necessities of key-resistance, we shall remain but "mechanical" performers; mechanical executants moreover, without even the element of Certainty to commend us.[1]

CHAPTER V.

THE FINAL PROBLEM: THE UNION OF EXECUTION WITH CONCEPTION.

§ 1. It has been pointed out (§ *5, Chap. II., page 12*) that there is but one way by which to attain *definiteness* in our playing; and that is, by pre-determining the Time-Place of each note by means of our musical consciousness.

[1] Some of the more rough-and-ready Gauging and Timing may if necessary be acquired at a semi-dumb key-board, provided it be not allowed to breed carelessness of attention to the Quality in Key-descent. Much good practice can undoubtedly be obtained there by those who have really mastered Tone-production, and who possess firmly fixed habits in this respect.

Without the use of a good Pianoforte, it is however impossible either to acquire, or to retain, those finer and subtler manipulations of the Key-Descent which are the means of all real beauty and expression in performance.

And the more perfect the instrument employed for this purpose, the more profitable will the Practice-hour prove. For the larger and the more subtle the compass of tone-varieties the instrument offers, the more are we likely to be urged to their employment, and the more are we likely to hear when we do wrong.

Recognition of this fact has been aptly expressed by EUGEN D'ALBERT,

THE UNION OF EXECUTION WITH CONCEPTION.

Accurately to realise this musical wish, it follows: that we must *time* the tone-production of each desired note, so that it may reach *Completion* at such pre-determined moment. In other words, it is in this *Accurately Timed* application, culmination, and consequent cessation of the correct muscular-*act* against each individual key, that lies THE POINT OF UNION between Conception and Execution. This last fact must be thoroughly grasped.

On its conscious (or unconscious) realisation, directly depends "Grip" in performance, Mastery of the subject—Mastery in Practice, Playing, and in Teaching. This point must be insisted upon, even at the risk of tautology.

§ 2. We have seen, that the accurate timing of our muscular operations against the key, signifies: (*Chap. IV., § 1, Step II.*) that we must not time these either too early, or too long; but that they must culminate at a certain point in key-descent, and must then promptly cease; they being after that moment useless, and worse, as regards the act of sound-making.

In the culmination and instantaneous cessation of the muscular impetus that provides Key-movement, we have here available an absolutely *definite* point in the process of tone-production, definite physically and mentally.

Definite, because it represents a definite place in key-descent; again, because at that point, the completion of the tone-production is clearly realisable by our outer ear as the beginning of sound;—and once more, because the point of transition between Silence and Sound is a clearly definite one in the element of Time, and can therefore be purposed in this respect.

For the particular moment when tone *begins* to be emitted from the instrument, also forms the *conclusion of the act of tone-production;* and it is this moment, this definite physical

when, in presenting his portrait to that great master Piano-maker, he wrote: "Meinen besten Clavier-lehrern und liebsten Freunden, den Bechstein-schen Flügeln"—" To my *best* Piano-*Teachers* and dearest friends, the Bechstein Grands."

fact, that we can seize hold of by the mind, through the ear, if we are careful to be on the alert for it.

Consequently, if we succeed in making this definite physical fact arise in absolute *coincidence* with the Time-place (and Tone-kind) pre-determined by our musical-consciousness, it follows, that we have then succeeded in physically realising our musical emotion—that we have that moment forced execution to obey conception—for they have coalesced, have united, in thus coinciding.

§ 3. We shall now be able to realise the necessity of the final, and probably most important item, in a Performer's Aural-Education, viz.:

ALERTNESS OF EAR:—

Alertness as to the moment of Time, when sound begins.[1]

For it is only by LISTENING outwardly, that we can *guide* or *aim* that accurate culmination and cessation of the muscular-act, which forms the Union of Tone-production with Conception.[2]

§ 4. In short, and this forms an excellent working definition of the act of Execution: *We must learn to be* AURALLY *on the alert, so that the right muscular-act shall consummate key-movement at the very moment dictated by our musical-consciousness.*

FURTHER DEFINITION OF ACT OF PLAYING:—

§ 5. We shall now be in a position to realise, further, that the act of *Attention* needed in playing, although it seems but a

---

[1] Alertness in this respect, must not be confused with that other form of ear-alertness, subtlety of discriminatory-power as to tone-kind — kind, as regards quantity, quality, and duration. The importance of this latter form of alertness is obvious enough without further comment.

A strong bias towards giving aural-attention in both these respects, constitutes one of the most necessary sides of the talent that enables a performer-artist to become a possibility.

"Ear" of this kind, is evidently also quite another thing from "ear" in that other sense, that of musical imaginativeness. It is the latter that makes for invention, for composition; but not necessarily also for performance.— In the performer's case it is the outer-ear that must imperatively be keen; although its effective employment is nevertheless limited by the extent of his "inner-ear,"—or Imaginativeness. (*Vide Appendix, Note IV.*)

[2] *i.e.* : It is only by listening *Physically*, along with that other *Inner*-listening or alertness of the imagination, that we can aim the muscular act.

single flash of consciousness, is really a compound act, and that it must embrace *two* distinct purposes :—
{ *I*: *The act of judging* WHAT *each sound effect should be,*
{ *II*: *The act of judging the means for its physical fulfilment.*

The first implies, that we must purpose to obey the *Music*; and the second implies, that we must purpose to obey the *Piano-key*.

We have already seen, that to succeed in this dual act of judgment, we must appeal both Inwards and Outwards; *i.e.*, we must appeal Inwards—to our inner-consciousness of Musical-Necessity; and we must appeal Outwards—to Instrumental-Necessities. Now we shall discover that these two acts themselves once again segregate, each into two distinct subdivisions of Intelligence; thus proving the Act of Attention in Playing ultimately to consist of four components. For we find : a): that we must mentally try to *see Where* each note must begin as to Time; and b): what its degree of *Importance* is in the scheme of the piece—thus determining its tone-shade; c): we must, through our *Muscular-Sense*, try to judge what energy the key needs, to move it at the required speed; and d): we must through our *Outer-Ear* watch for the moment in key-descent when cessation of that energy becomes due.

This single thought-flash (volition, or act of consciousness) must hence embrace *four* points in reality :—*Where*, and *How*, each sound must be ; *Where* the key begins (to resist), and *Where* its movement-possibility ends—in sound.[1]

If but one of the four components of this act of attention is absent, then we have failed to attend properly, and our play-

[1] This may appear very complex at first blush ; but in reality it is no more complex than many acts of our daily lives. Nothing, indeed, that can be dignified with the name of thought, consists of a mere simple sensation. Consider, for example, the act of taking a stroke at Tennis. When analysed, it displays an almost identical complexity with the mental-muscular act, of playing a note *with Intelligence* at the Piano !—There is : a) our consciousness of the ball coming across the net towards us ; b) our resolve, to place it in the corner of the opposite court, furthest removed from our opponent ; c) our judgment of the *Weight* of our own racket, unconsciously derived from our constantly balancing and swinging it ; and d) our calculation of the degree of energy required to be *added* to that racket's swing, which shall place the ball in the pre-conceived SPOT,—not of Time, but of Tennis-court !

D

ing will consequently prove unsatisfactory to that extent. (*Vide Note IV., Appendix.*)

The solution of this problem of *Attention* also forms the means of willing the *Union* between Execution and Conception; for it means, a determination to be *definite;* a determination definitely to *aim* the completion of each note's tone-production to a pre-determined spot in Time.

Thus making Co-incident the: { *Time,* when sound of a particular shade [is judged to be *due*, *Time,* when it is physically *consummated*.

§ 6. The following little plan sums up this question of "attention," both for Artist and Student, both for Teacher and Critic:

The Act of INTELLIGENCE *In Playing,* implies :

Attention Inwards— to enable us to obey Music :	*Attention Outwards*— to enable us to obey the Key :
This implies use of our Musical-Imagination so that by perceiving Musical-Emotion and Musical-Shape, we shall be able to judge the TIME-SPOT *and* TONE-KIND *due for each note.*	This implies Attention *Muscularly and Aurally,* to enable us to *Feel* key-resistance before and during [descent, and to *Hear* the completion of key-descent.

Or finally, to put the case as a positive direction :

I : *We must try to SEE the Emotion, and the Musical-material ;*—
—the latter being the material-shapes of Time (rhythm) and Tone, through which the former is exhibited ;
and II : *We must try to OBTAIN this mentally-pictured Music from the Keys;*
—by employing our knowledge of the requirements of Key-treatment, and our muscular-adaptations to these.

The latter moreover involves, that we must give :
a) *Muscular-Attention* to the key-Resistances, and [key-descent.
b) *Aural-Attention* to the beginning of each sound—the consummation of

§ 7. A warning is here once again urgently necessary, similar to the one on page 29, § 9, Chap. IV. If, in our endeavours to fulfil all the elements that together form successful performance, we permit these *Means*, even for a moment, to become our paramount object and aim, then we shall after all fail to achieve success.

Even the very act of endeavouring to give *Attention* may cause us to fail! For we may try to "attend" simply for the sake of attending successfully; we may try to give our consciousness to one, or to all of the four points of Attention enumerated, and yet fail to play successfully! Fail we assuredly shall, unless we bear in mind that even Attention itself must not be given for its own sake, but must instead be given as a consequence of our intense wish and purpose to *see* Music, so that it shall become living sound.

Here, again, we are face to face with that well known law, that applies with equal force to Playing, as it does to all other Arts, namely: that the moment we attend to the Means—for the sake of fulfilling these means, that very moment witnesses the collapse of our Art.

That is, all the means enumerated must indeed be fulfilled; but we cannot ultimately succeed, unless we attend to Music itself as the supreme object to be attained by them.[1] We must be *busy* emotionally and intellectually. We must try to see what phase of emotion each phrase presents, and we must use our intelligence so that we may perceive the musical shapes employed, and so that we may perceive the executive requirements needed for their interpretation. We shall thus be able to secure for each note-atom its proper place in the musical-scheme as a Whole,—and we shall thus be giving expression to Music itself.

The sequence of Cause and Effect, will moreover be synthetically in the reverse order to this summary analysis, when we sit down to play a piece of music:—

For we must not try to play a note until we are ready to

---

[1] It is of no use remembering: that the keys must be rightly used; nor that "we must muscularly fulfil key-treatment at its easiest"; nor that "we must attend to the Key as to the resistance it offers, and to the point in its descent where cessation of our muscular application is demanded"; nor that "we must fulfil these two physical acts because of the moment in Time, and because of the kind of Tone required for each note," *so long as we do these things for their own sake*. No, we must attend to these things only for the sake of the Feeling that we perceive, and to which we wish to give expression.

"listen," as the Artist says; listening here signifying, that we must try to perceive, or see *Music*. This signifies that we must at that very moment, try to realise what the Music means; what it is; how it feels; how it *should* sound. "Seeing" music in this sense, is a supremely vital experience; it is something absolutely vivid.[1]

In short, whenever we sit down at the piano, to play or to practise Music, our motive must never deteriorate into playing for the sake of personally doing well. Our supreme wish must be, to strive to perceive Music; *i.e.:* we must *try* to *see*, rather than try to *do*.[2]

§ 8. In a word, the act of Volition in performance, must ultimately centre in a supreme endeavour to *feel* music-sense, so that others may be moved by it. Attention and Execution must be provided only in response to this all-powerful motive, the wish to see and exhibit Music itself.

We shall then find ourselves in harmony with Herbert Spencer's teaching, that "Feeling[3] is the great motive power of Action," and we shall then prove ourselves not mere Artisans, but true Artists.

---

[1] Although we may have played a passage a thousand times, yet, the moment we do succeed in actually re-seeing it, that moment the music becomes a thing absolutely fresh and new. Although the particular experience may be similar in character to previous ones, yet this experience will be quite apart from those, because of its freshness. The passage will seem alive at that very moment, because our brains—our feelings, are vividly awake to the impression.

This is the supreme experience to aim for, each time we endeavour to play Music. Its attainment—the perception of music, being in the shape of Feeling, will then serve as an omnipotent motive-power for those necessary mental and physical processes of Tone-production that ultimately enable us to communicate the musically *Seen*, to others.

[2] We must give ourselves up to the emotions that live behind the dead signs of music-notation: since it is only to the extent that we allow such human and artistic Emotion to take possession of us, that we can succeed in portraying it;—that is, always provided we do possess the requisite power of Execution.

The moment we permit the "Doing"—our well-Doing, to become the object striven for, that moment we become self-conscious; instead of musically-conscious; with equally disastrous results here as in our daily lives, when, instead of looking outside of ourselves, we allow our own self-advancement to become the prime consideration. (*Vide Note V., Appendix.*)

[3] *Vide Note VI., Appendix.*

CHAPTER VI.

CONCLUSION AND SUMMARY.

§ 1. We have now indicated what are the elements of Pianoforte playing and education; and also what are the elements of Education in Tone-production. To enable these indications to be of any practical value, it is necessary thoroughly to realise, that each *perfection*, and each *want of Perfection*, should in each individual case, be traced to its immediate cause. Unless this be done, we shall after all have mere empiric floundering, instead of that *direct* teaching of oneself and others, which we find to be possible.

§ 2. It follows, if we would properly practise, play or teach, that we must *localise* each want of perfection, must trace it to its cause amongst those various elements that together form Pianoforte Education and playing.

i.e.: On realising that the performance of a piece, passage, or even a single note, has proved inadequate, we must analyse the fault; reflection will then enable us to discover its true nature. For instance, we must investigate whether it is lack of musical insight that has caused the lapse, or whether it is simply owing to inefficient attention in this respect; or to lack of understanding of how the key should be treated, or to inattention in this respect; or whether faulty muscular habit is the cause; or that inadequate "aiming" of the muscular conditions, resulting from aural or muscular inattention.

The fault having thus been "hunted home" and thoroughly located, we shall then be in a position clearly to point it out, and also *directly* to proceed to its correction.

§ 3. Now, since we can only *learn*, or *think*, one thing at a time, it follows, as a matter of course, that we can only correct one fault at a time.

This fact is indeed one of the most important deductions

forced upon us, by the preceding contemplation of the real constituents of Pianoforte Education.[1]

§ 4. The ends of Pianoforte Education are hence best attained, not by the interminable and senseless repetition of Pieces, Studies, Scales and Technical exercises, all given with quite hap-hazard tone-production, and misnamed "Practice;" but, on the contrary, by the teacher (or self-teacher) first realising what is the nature of the habits to be acquired.[2]

Possessing the requisite knowledge of what to strive for, we shall then begin by essaying to produce correctly one sound at a time, thus obtaining the opportunity to form that habit of mind, that perceives in Key-treatment during descent, the only possible means of obtaining any desired sound; and the opportunity to form the co-related muscular habits that serve to fulfil such Key-treatment. We shall then proceed to apply tone-production, thus acquired, to the various passage-forms from which Music is built up, and here the practice of Tech-

---

[1] Wrong muscular habits, and wrong ways of looking at Piano-playing, so often formed during the child-stage, and so difficult to eradicate afterwards, are very generally to be traced directly to this want of localising-power, on the part of the teacher. Instead of being expected to learn one thing at a time, the child is expected to learn musically to speak, read, and even write, all at the same time!

Instead of being first shown how to produce sounds from the instrument, and to recognise these, and to recognise the element of Time in their production; the music-page is placed before the child's dazed eyes, and it is asked to translate those written signs into sounds, when instead, it is the sound-making itself and recognition of the sounds made, that should receive the fullest possible attention. The result of this struggle to learn to do several things at the same time, is, that the mental struggle engenders a *muscular struggle*. No thought can be given to what really are the necessities of the key, or what are the real muscular-means required for this key-treatment. Undirected efforts, amounting to spasms, result as a consequence,—and are calmly permitted by the "teacher!"—while, so far from learning to *read* Music, the child instead contracts that vicious habit, that of *spelling* notes.

A child, before it touches the instrument, should be made to understand that a definite musical-sound is the thing required, not a mere putting down of keys anyhow. Sequences of sounds should then be learnt from the teacher's dictation, portions of the material of music—scales, etc., and actual simple tunes.—In this way, the child begins by understanding that musical sense is required, and that this sense must be drawn from the keys. Time enough, then, as a separate phase of education, to teach the written signs representing musical letters, words and phrases!

[2] Habits, we must remember, that include not only the necessary habits of muscular co-ordination, but habits of mind as well as of body; habits of musical attention, and habits of muscular and aural attention.

nics, of scales and arpeggi, etc., becomes necessary, within reasonable bounds. In addition, we then require the practice of Studies, to give us *endurance* of Mind and Muscle.

The practice (study and playing) of much real music should moreover be contemporaneous with such study of the Means of Expression, so that that supreme necessity may *infallibly* be fulfilled:—the mental association of Touch-method with musical sense and emotion.

§ 5. We now realise how expedient it is, first thoroughly to understand the nature of the very elements or Constituents of Pianoforte-education, before going further, and proceeding to form habits.

Earnest study of the preceding pages is therefore invited, before attempting to master the matter dealing with the details of tone-production itself; which will be presented in the following Parts.

These Constituents of Pianoforte Education are summarised in the accompanying Plan. . . . Understanding the facts there presented will assuredly help us the better to practise, criticise, play, and teach!

SUMMAR[Y]

THE AC[T]

—is accomplished by the

I:

CONCEPTION,

—the Perception of Musical Sense.

The power of perceiving musical sense depends on the degree of our

MUSICIANSHIP.

Musicianship, the power of understanding Music, has two sides :—

(a):
The EMOTIONAL SIDE; and

(b):
The INTELLECTUAL SIDE;

AR[

Emotional Musical-ability, or *Musical-Feeling*, permits us to perceive : the *Emotional Import* of Music.
It permits us to perceive, and enjoy, the sensuously Beautiful in Music ; and its parallelism to Human emotion.

Intellectual Musical-ability, or *Musical-Reasoning*, permits us to perceive : the *Musical-Shapes* employed to convey such emotion.
It permits us to perceive, and enjoy, the perfections shown in the musical structure ; workmanship —in its largest and smallest manifestations.
It enables us to perceive Rhythmical structure ;— the facts of Climax, or Crisis, in its large swings of form, and in its smaller ones of the Phrase and its subdivisions—down to its component ideas.

Artistic edge of, a the instru[ment] it is alo[ne] sense as [It also [ity ; a se[enough t[even whe[rily suspe[

Training is hence required in both the departments, *Conception* and *Executio*[n]
Moreover, such Training can only bear fruit, provided ATTENTION is conse[
This Act of *ATTENTION* or *VOLITION* in performance, although apparen[

FOU[

MUSICAL attention.—*Inwards* :—

(I):
As to TIME;

(II):
As to TONE;

—WHERE each note should begin;

—HOW each note should sound.

—An Attention, Judgment, and consequent Volition originating from our Musical Feeling and Intelligen[ce] provided we insist on these faculties determining the proper mission of each Note,—as *Part of a* WHOLE.

The Result to be obtained by such perfect act of Attention and Volition is : that the **PLACING** (bo[th]
The result moreover is : that the Muscular-Conditions, necessary to consummate this " *Placing,*" wil[l]
Firstly, by our Muscular-sensation—of the key's resistance before and during descent :
Secondly, by our Aural-Sensation—of the commencement of tone, arising from the compl[

The supreme necessity for an unbroken continuity of Attention and Judgment in both these particulars, bec[

PART I.

'LAYING

wo quite distinct acts :—

II:

EXECUTION;

—the Communication of such perception to others.

The power of communicating musical sense, depends on the extent of our

EXECUTIVE-ATTAINMENTS.

Executantship, the power of expressing that which one perceives, has two sides :—

(b):

UDGMENT; and THE ART OF TONE-PRODUCTION:

t, embraces : Knowl- | This implies, *Ability* to obtain from the instrument, every possible kind of tone
in the application of | of any Quantity, Quality, Duration ; and at any Speed of succession. It embraces
fects, through which | Agility, and Colouring.
e to translate such | Adeptness in the Art of Tone-making has two separate aspects :—
:rceive musically.
pulsational sensibil-
hat should be keen
ontinuance of Pulse,
rations are tempora-
in "*Rubato.*"

(aa) : (bb) :
INSTRUMENTAL-KNOWLEDGE; and MUSCULAR-HABIT.
—*Consciousness of what are the require-* —*Muscular-ability, to fulfil these re-*
ments of the Key. *quirements, correctly formed and viv-*
idly retained.

Muscular-Habit, implies two distinct things :—

(aaa) : (bbb) :
Muscular-Discrimination ; *Muscular-Application.*
The power to provide the requisite The power to apply these to the Re-
Muscular *Activities,* and *Inactivities.* quirements of the Key, as to *Time* and
Degree.

all the subsidiary aspects of these.
unconsciously given during the Act of Playing.
\s flash of consciousness, must nevertheless comprise
O*NENTS :—*

PHYSICAL attention,—*Outwards :—*

(III) : (IV) :
As to RESISTANCE, *As to PLACE, in KEY-DESCENT,*
Experienced from each KEY; *WHERE each Sound BEGINS;* *
ttention and Judgment by means of : the —Attention and Judgment, by means of : the
MUSCULAR-SENSE. AURAL-SENSE.

ne and as to Tone) of each and every note, will be *directly prompted* by our Musical Feeling and Intelligence.
d, and "Aimed"—*i.e.,* ceased :—

ch Key-movement.

evident, when the real problems of Tone-production itself are considered, as they will be, in Parts II. and III,

APPENDIX TO PART I.

"*ON LISTENING*"

NOTE I.—For § 2, Chapter II., page 11. It is so very easy not to "listen" properly; but instead, merely to *hear*. In the latter case, the only result can be, that we simply hear that which our automatic centres happen to play; whereas, by listening—outwardly and *inwardly*, we shall perhaps succeed in "doing" that which our inner ear directs.

Our eyes can give us a similar difference of experience; for we may look at a page, a picture, or a scene, and fancy we "see"; and yet all the while, we are not even trying to perceive. A fact we shall immediately discover, if we try to reproduce that page, picture, or scene!

It is the same, if we wish to communicate an idea. Unless we ourselves definitely try to *see* that thought, we shall certainly be unable to communicate it.

We can neither paint, draw, nor write successfully, unless we have an inner picture we wish to fulfil through the implement in our hands.

In fact, a keen—but unconscious—*analysis* of the thing that is to appear, has all the while to precede the "doing." To the extent that such analysis is efficient, to that extent only can the Artist "see" or "feel," as he puts it,—he himself being naturally unaware of his own mental processes. To communicate the thing seen, he must have the power of execution; he must have the knowledge and experience that will *unconsciously* guide him to choose the exact combinations of colours and shapes, that will render his *Conceptions*—facts of the *Imagination*—into physical *Actuality*.

It is customary to quiz a novice, experimenting with a gun, and to assert, that having aimed most carefully, he after all closes his eyes before pulling the trigger!

It is however no exaggeration to assert that ninety-nine out of every hundred Piano students act analogously at their instrument! Even if they do go so far as to think of the actual key they mean to deal with, yet, when it comes to the act of depressing it—the very process itself of *using* it to excite sound, then they end, after all, by making an un-*Aimed* muscular effort,—*with their Ears perfectly shut*, so far as attention is concerned! In playing, *it is the propulsion of the key during its short descent, that has to be "aimed"*; merely to reach the right key, and to get it down "somehow," does not constitute a musically-directed sound.

The mistake arises, from not perceiving that each musical sound must be as much the outcome of the musical Will, as must be the lines constituting a drawing, or piece of penmanship. Non-perception of the fact that a *Sound* is a mere unit, meaningless by itself, arises from the fact, that a musical sound is a so much rarer experience for the majority of individuals, than is the experience of impressions caused by light;—shapeliness being conveyed to us through our eyes all day long.

It is owing to such comparative rarity in the experience of musical-sounds, that something seems actually accomplished when a Piano-key has been made to deliver some sort of sound—no matter how bad, nor how inappropriate!

A mere sound nevertheless no more constitutes musical-sense, than does a mere line constitute a picture when presented to the eye.

The moral hence is: that Sound-making only rises above mere tone-*scribbling* when we insist on guiding the requisite Units into a vivid musical-Drawing.

"ON RHYTHM"

NOTE II.—For § 5, Chapter II., page 13. There are three distinct ways in which we can pre-determine a single sound. Three distinct forms of Practice result from this fact:

I: At a sufficiently slow rate of movement, we can give *conscious* attention to each note beforehand; consciously determining not only its Moment and Tone, but also consciously determining *how* it shall individually be obtained from the instrument. Such careful manipulation, demanding as it does a distinct thought *before* each note, requires considerable time. It is the only way to learn new habits of tone-production. Hence arises the conviction forced upon most players, sooner or later: the need for really SLOW PRACTICE.

II: We can, at a quicker *tempo*, still consciously will the Time and Tone for each individual sound; although we shall be unable at that speed to pre-realise the means of tone-production involved for each individual sound. Tone-production must obviously in this case be forthcoming as a previously-formed habit; Habit in this case stimulated into activity by the mere wish or direction for a particular sound-kind.

III: The speed may however be so great as to preclude our directing even the Time of each individual note by a conscious act of volition. The necessary "willing" has then to be relegated to a faculty we possess, that of *semi-automatically* Timing the inside components of note-groups.

It is a faculty of the ear and muscles, analogous to the one we use through the eye, which enables us at a glance to discern the exact number contained in a small group of objects, without our actually "counting them up."[1] We thus discriminate between the various sets of leger lines; the lines that constitute the difference between semi-quavers and demi-semi-quavers; and the sets of lines that form the staves.

We can in fact at great speed, only " will" whole sets of notes. The notes and figures that belong to the Beats being known, the latter are kept in view, and the passage is thus steered along by their means. The inner notes of each beat are in this case merely felt as subdivisions of time *leading up* to each imminent Time-pulse. For instance, at great speed, groups of four semi-quavers, must be felt as three segmental points of *Crotchet-Division, leading up to* the beginning of the next Crotchet, or Pulse.

This learning to *direct* the minute subdivisions of Time by means of this semi-automatic or unconscious faculty, forms a very important detail in a Performer's Education.

Camille Stamaty, one of the teachers of Liszt, constructed a whole school of Technics—much superior to "Plaidy"—keeping this necessity in view; the suggestive title of the work being: "Le Rhythme des doigts."

[1] It is said there have been show-men who have trained this faculty to the extent of being able to distinguish at a glance the exact number of balls thrown down, up to about thirty!

"AS TO GYMNASTICS"

NOTE III.—For § 3, Chapter IV., page 26. While on the subject of muscular-training, it may be well to point out, that ease in acquiring the requisite discriminatory-power and its application to the instrument, is much facilitated by the possession of *healthy* muscles. Most forms of gymnastics and calisthenics further such healthy condition of the muscles; but the best exercises for this purpose are those that alternately give Full Contraction and Full Extension of the muscles involved. An urgent warning is here however necessary, since harm instead of good may result from the practice of all gymnastics, unless the requirements of correct tone-production are constantly borne in mind. Hence the reason, why there is such divergence of opinion amongst musicians respecting the use of gymnastics away from the keyboard; though the same rule holds good even more forcibly at the keyboard itself;—for even more harm in habit-forming can be done at the key-board, than away from it!

Whenever gymnastics of any kind are practised, this must imperatively be done not with "force," but with the most perfect *freedom* possible. There must not be the slightest suspicion of *restraint* or friction, or "force," in the movements themselves, however great the energy that may be exerted against some *outside* object. It is (and it cannot too often be repeated) from the unintentional employment of the "opposing" muscles, that arises the tendency toward "stiff" or restrained action, which proves so baneful to Technique in every sense.

To allow oneself the slightest tendency toward stiffness, whilst practising gymnastics of any kind, is a fatal obstacle against the attainment of either *Agility* or *Accuracy* in Tone-Response.

"PIANO-TALENT"

NOTE IV.—For §§ 3 and 5, Chapter V., pages 32 and 34. Here once again, is a point where natural endowment differs widely. Those who, without effort, unconsciously give Attention with full purpose, possess indeed "talent" in the most important respect of all :—

For talent itself, in its most general sense—that exhibition of a *strong bias* toward some particular pursuit, may be defined, from its results, as simply : *ability to learn with ease.*

Now our ability to learn anything, directly depends on the power of our *Memory*—its impressionability, and its retentiveness; and memorizing again directly depends on the degree of Attention we can provide. Hence, it is, that Power of Attention, or ability to acquire this, is synonymous with : good memory, ease in learning, and in a word "Talent."

A few words of Summary, may prevent misapprehension with regard to the question of Pianoforte "talent :"—

Special phases of endowment are needed in addition to general Musicality.

These are : a good "piano-voice"—the possession of a sufficiently ample muscular endowment, combined with Ease in mental-muscular discrimination; a good "Ear," not only for Time, but also particularly for the discernment of subtle distinctions in tone-quantity, and above all, in tone-*Quality ;* "Brains" to enable Attention to be given, combined with a personal bias toward giving the particular form of Attention demanded in playing.

These particular endowments are nevertheless not very far-reaching, unless there be besides, a general endowment musically. Musical imaginativeness is required, both emotionally and intellectually. Without that, nothing vivid can be done, however excellent the other, the special, phases of Talent.

Moreover, even such endowments do not constitute a player. To succeed as an Artist, we need besides all that, PERSISTENCE. That depends on character, on our real love for the Art, and whether we possess Health sound enough to stand the necessary close application.

For eventually, as RUBINSTEIN once said to us Royal Academy Students: "real *Hard Work* is the only road to success."

"*AS TO SELF-CONSCIOUSNESS AND NERVOUSNESS*"

NOTE V.—For § 7, Chapter V., page 36. This dread horror kills many a possible player. Perhaps the following advice may help to eradicate the nervousness resulting from self-consciousness. Try to realise, that when your audience is really listening, that at that moment they cannot really be conscious of you at all; for their attention is then given to Music alone, just as yours should be.

Even if a thousand people are looking at the same spot that you are looking at, that fact will not render you self-conscious, nor "nervous." No, even if they are shouting at the same object that you are shouting at, nor will that do so. Hence, in performing, try to realise, that the audience is not listening to you, but is listening to the same Music that you are listening *for*; *i.e.*: that Observation is being directed to the same spot, by yourself and your audience.

It is your duty to "look," with your ears, *at* a certain spot in Music at a definite time; realise that your listener is looking at that same musical-spot, and that moment you cease being aware that he is listening to *You*, personally.

Moreover, once you feel that that listener's attention is directed to the same musical *Point* that yours is, it will intensify your attention to it, and you will see the music more vividly than in the practise-room!

It is impossible for the listener to concern himself with *you* personally, if he is listening to the sounds provided by your fingers in obedience to your musical wish; and vice versa: if the listener is aware of you, then he cannot at that moment be aware of the music provided, and the performance cannot then be under criticism. Hence, in either case, there is nothing to be self-conscious about!

In a word, force yourself to realise that the listener is watching for that which you also are trying to hear, and all self-consciousness with its consequent nervousness inevitably vanishes at that moment.

Incapacitating nervousness during performance is therefore usually only the result of sheer inattention.

The causes of such inadequate attention are various.

They may prove at once remediable by a better understanding, and a consequent better practice, of that which constitutes Performer's Attention.

Inadequacy and Uncertainty of Technique (*i.e.*, of *Tone-production* itself) does however form perhaps the most potent factor in causing our attention to be distracted from where it should be.

"*MUSICAL FEELING*"

NOTE VI.—For § 8, Chapter V., page 36. The following speculations may prove helpful to some; and may serve to make clearer some points otherwise generally obscure.

The full explanation or interpretation of what it is that constitutes "Musical Feeling" yet remains to be achieved. Meanwhile, there is this to be

APPENDIX TO PART I. 45

noted: that musical emotion is not IDENTICAL with the emotions of ordinary life, but is instead merely *parallel* to such.

Emotion, experienced apart from music, may stimulate a composer or player to the endeavour to record such feeling through the medium of musical sounds. . . . It is however impossible for him directly to communicate a DEFINITE emotional message through that indefinite medium, Music;—a consummation only faintly possible even through the medium of Words; although we here have definite symbols to remind us of already approximately experienced sensations. All a composer can do, in using Music for the expression (or vent) of his emotion, is to write the *musically beautiful*, so that the effect of such Beauty shall arouse a parallel emotional state in the listener, to the state of mental-excitement under which the composer was labouring, when he penned the music.

In a word, it is the sensation of the Beautiful that successions and combinations of notes can convey to us, that has to be used as a vehicle to arouse emotion. Ultimately it is a manifestation of the Beautiful in Sound that the composer—and player—has to rely upon to create emotion in us, and thus to suggest pain or pleasure, etc., through its parallelism in mental result.

That Ugliness is employed in music, does not weaken this contention; on the contrary, it strengthens it; since it is only by Contrast that we can perceive anything; either by our senses or by our reason. We are compelled to employ what can aptly be termed the Unbeautiful in music, so that that intensely emotional result, the sensation of the Beautiful, shall by contrast be rendered possible.

Thus we have recourse to extreme dissonances and ultra-chromatic passages, the moment we wish to portray extreme emotion,—since extreme emotion borders on pain. The continued TENSION caused by dissonance resolved on dissonance here provides an effect upon our nervous system analogous to that caused by extreme emotion apart from music. . . . It is because of this parallelism of the EFFECTS of musical-feeling to ordinary Feeling, that we find Music such a more powerful, subtle and direct means of arousing Emotion (always however really indefinite) than words can ever be, however powerfully penned.

These considerations will also render clearer, why the experiences of Life—with its extremities of emotion—are essential, before we can hope to realise the presence of such parallelisms in the music of the great Tone-poets.

The significance of the phrase " to Listen Inwardly " will now also be better understood; for it means, that we must try to perceive, must lie in wait for the Beautiful in Music;—as exhibited through its Rhythmical-shapes, enforced by Melody and Harmony. All this indicates what should be our mental attitude toward Music during performance.

For it is manifest, that it is useless, or nearly so, to strive to see Emotion APART from the musically-Beautiful in the work under interpretation. If we make this mistake, and give our whole mind up to the endeavour to guess how the composer " felt," or how we ought to " feel," then we shall assuredly fail to perceive the real *emotion* the music was intended to engender through its beauty, and we shall instead lapse into mere sickening Sentimentality.

PART II.

KEY-TREATMENT FROM ITS INSTRUMENTAL ASPECT.

CHAPTER VII.

PREAMBLE :

SYNOPSIS OF THE MAIN INSTRUMENTAL FACTS.

IN PART I., Pianoforte Playing and Education was analysed into its constituents. It was found to consist of two distinct branches, since it demands both Musical and Executive attainments. Executive attainments were found to embrace, a), those relating to Artistic-taste in the application of the possible instrumental-effects ; and b), those relating to the ACT by means of which such effects become physically realised.

This Act of Tone-production, or Key-Treatment, was again found to possess two distinct aspects,—the Instrumental and the Muscular. We will first deal with the former.

Education in the Instrumental-aspect of Tone-production implies learning to understand the requirements, *in the shape of Key-movement*, that must be fulfilled for the production of each possible kind of tone.

A GENERAL GLANCE at this part of the subject is desirable, before proceeding to a more detailed analysis of the instrument and its mechanism, and its principles of action :

§ 1. Much misconception of Key-treatment directly arises from failure to grasp the sufficiently obvious fact, that the Pianoforte consists of *two distinct portions*, each as distinct from the other as the Violin is from its Bow.   This mental difficulty occurs, because the Pianoforte encloses within its outer CASE both the musical instrument itself, and the machine for exciting it into sound.

The instrument proper should be considered to consist of the Sounding-board with its bridges supporting the strings, and the strong frame that enables the latter to be kept at tension; whilst the TOOL for exciting it into sound, and controlling its cessation, is formed by the Key-board with all its appurtenances.   The first portion is analogous to the Violin itself; whilst the second portion, the key-board, is analogous to the Bow.   At the Pianoforte, however, instead of the instrument being provided with but *one* Tool for exciting sound, we are here provided with some eighty separate tools, or machines, for transmitting *movement* to the String.

§ 2. For it is only by giving *motion* to the key, that we can, through its hammer-end, communicate motion to the string,— a transfer of energy that can only be effected during the hammer's brief contact and movement *with* the string, before the rebound of both occurs.[1]

Let us then at once thoroughly realise this important fact, that it is only through KEY-MOVEMENT that we can produce sound[2]; and that all energy that shall produce sound, must

---

[1] It is the string, which in turn communicates its motion to the connected sounding-board; the two together thus causing vibrations in the surrounding atmosphere. These vibrations, on reaching the Ear, are by that organ transformed into nerve vibrations; and it is these that finally reach our Brain, there arousing the SENSATION OF SOUND.

[2] Much misconception as to Key-treatment at once vanishes, the moment we realise, that the Key forms but a machine, lever, handle, or Tool to enable us conveniently to create SPEED in the String.

Herein lies the *radical* difference in treatment required by the Organ and the Pianoforte Key,—a difference that has been at times overlooked owing to the mere visual similarity of the two key-boards.

The energy that makes the organ-pipes speak, is derived from the Organ blower, or engine. It follows that the depression of a key here requires—one might say—but a *passive* act, like opening a valve or tap, since such *opening* of the key merely serves to permit the mechanically stored-up energy to reach and operate upon the pipes. In the case of the organ-key it therefore makes practically no difference *how* the key is treated *during* its descent; provided that a certain promptness of attack is forthcoming.

The case is widely different at the Pianoforte, where, on the contrary, the sound is the direct outcome of the performer's own physical energy, delivered to the key during descent. It follows that key-depression must here be in the nature of a *positive*, active operation, carefully chosen, and graded in its application; since it is such application of energy to the key that constitutes

therefore be delivered to the key *before*[1] and *during* the latter's descent; and that this energy must be so timed, as to produce the greatest key-speed at the very moment that sound-emission is *heard to commence*—a moment that corresponds to the place in key-descent where the hammer rebounds from the string.

§ 3. Realising that our object must be to create Key-movement, we shall then neither attempt to hit or strike the key—as if it were a ball or nail, nor shall we attempt to jam it down upon its "bed"—as if it were a nut-cracker! We shall, on the contrary, project our minds as it were to the *hammer-end* of the key; and our purpose will be, to move the string by means of that hammer-end. In a word, we shall not try to *play the key-board*—or at it; but shall instead try to play the *strings* by means of the key.[2]

Now we never dream of *hitting* or *striking* the Tennis-racket, the Violin-bow, or the Billiard-cue; instead, we take them up—take hold of them, and USE them. And that is precisely how we should treat the Pianoforte-key:—When we wish to play a note, we must first equip or "arm" our finger-end with the implement we wish to employ—and that is the key. We must take hold of that key, by placing a finger-tip against its surface; and thus enable ourselves to *realise* its weight and resistance, through the *muscular-sense*. Thus realising the weight of the Tool we mean to employ, we must then proceed positively to AIM with its opposite end,—the hammer-end.

It is of no use "aiming" *at* the Key, we must aim *with* it;

---

the material act of Sound-making,—for all differences in tone-result here absolutely depend on the *speed* attained during the short transit of the key from its surface level to its full depression, and on the *manner* in which the ultimate degree of speed is attained.

[1] *Some* energy must indeed be delivered to the key, before it will even *begin* to move.

[2] To enforce this upon our minds, we should remember, that although we play the Harp with our fingers,—since it is these that pluck the strings; yet we do not play the violin, "with our Arm," but with the Bow; for it is by means of the latter, in contact with the string, that we try to draw sound from that instrument. It is in this sense, that we do not at all play the Pianoforte " by our Fingers, Hands, and Arms," but instead play it by means of the Key.

E

for the key is not to be regarded as a ball, but rather in the light of a racket, cue, or other Speed-tool.[1] With the finger thus equipped, the key will be felt to be but a mechanically-provided *continuation* of the finger itself,—an intimate connection and elongation of our body, ending only with the hammer-tip; and we shall feel that it is with that end of this tool (thus under our immediate control) that we have to aim, and create speed in the string.

§ 4. This Aiming or directing of the Key, comprises three points:

a): We must aim the key, so that its *full speed* is reached at the moment that the hammer-end is in communication with the String — the moment that the escapement permits the hammer to rebound with the string—the moment that we can *hear* the beginning of the sound, if we listen for it.

b): We must *cease* to apply energy against the key at that same moment; excepting that slight residuum of weight that is required in Tenuto and Legato, to prevent the key from rebounding.[2]

c): We must determine *in which manner* the required speed shall be reached,—for if the total energy is applied *suddenly*, then the result is a "brilliant" but "short" tone; whereas, if it is instead applied *gradually*, then we shall obtain a true "singing," or "sympathetic" tone, of good carrying power.

§ 5. To sum up:

The *first* lesson in Key-Treatment we have to learn, is, that the Time-place and Tone-value of every note must be musically realised and intended.

The *second* lesson, is, that the Key must be *aimed* to culminate its speed in sound, at that very moment.

These two things must *coincide*.

We must therefore aim, or direct, the key into Speed, and di-

[1] For the same reason we must not press that tool upon its bed; since the key-beds are not like ripe fruit, out of which sound-juice can be squeezed.
[2] Else, instead of causing musical sound we shall cause the various portions of the mechanism to be jarred and forced against each other, to their manifest detriment; and to the great detriment also of all correct Execution.

PREAMBLE. 51

rect its increase in Speed during its short journey, so that we shall compel the String to *begin* its sound at the very instant that that sound is musically imperatively DUE. We shall then have correctly obeyed our Time-sense, and our Tone-sense; and having thus definitely compelled Tone-production to fulfil our musical conception, a clear and definite impression will consequently be conveyed to the listener; for we shall have succeeded in transmitting to him the same musical impression with which we ourselves were impressed.[1]

[1] The main difference between other forms of "aiming" and that required by the Pianoforte-key, is, that we must employ our EAR to guide the muscles that fulfil Key-movements; whereas we employ the EYE to guide our muscles in the case of the tennis-racket, billiard-cue, pen, pencil or brush.

There are, however, many analogies in the use of the Piano-key to that of the racket, cue, bat, golf-club, cycle-pedal, or other speed-tools.

For instance, we must in all cases, *weigh*, balance, or judge the weight or resistance of the tool itself, before we can successfully supply the requisite energy, and can aim this to its purpose. Again : we do not aim such a tool *as a whole*,—as we should a ball or stone, when throwing it ; no, on the contrary, we aim with the *end* of the tool—the end furthest away from us. For it is manifestly the doings of that end that concern us, when we wish definitely to project or impel a Ball—or a String—by means of such a speed-tool. Therefore it is with that end of the tool that our mind must be busy.

Moreover, it is not enough merely to aim Racket or Piano-key so that Ball or String shall be reached and moved "somehow." No, if we mean to have effective "play," we must see that the energy we supply to the ball or string is carefully directed to a definite *purpose*, when using the racket or the key ; —an object-less and clumsy result will otherwise accrue. If we merely dab our keys down somehow, we may obtain a tone of some kind ; but it cannot then be in accurate response to musical-feeling, for none is in question ! The law applies to all tools that require any accuracy in their use ;—we must be careful, in applying the "business-end" of such a tool to the object it is desired to take effect upon, that it is there directed by a definite wish of ours ; a wish of which we may or may not be conscious at the time.

Thus, we must feel a Time and Tone as imperatively *due*, owing to our musical-sensibilities being directed upon the work under interpretation ; and must place the needful key (or keys) into intimate connection with our brain through the muscular sense. We must then *use* that key in accordance with the laws of its application ;—*i.e.* : we must remember to *move* it while it is movable, and obtain from it during the short space it is movable, either the *suddenly* or the *gradually* consummated degree of speed, that our inner-ear demands in Tone-value.

Once again, in a word : the key-descent must be aimed or directed to that spot in descent, where its culminating motion initiates Tone :—that spot in key-descent being made to correspond with the Spot in Time and Tone dictated by our musical conscience.

CHAPTER VIII.

THE INSTRUMENT.

The strong outer CASE of the Pianoforte serves but as a support and protection for the instrument-proper. This consists of: a), the SOUNDING-BOARD; b), the *Strings*, with a *Frame* to keep them at tension; hereto is added, c), the MECHANISM, consisting of a series of little *machines*, complete for each note, by means of which our finger-tip is enabled to communicate motion to the strings.

We will glance at these points for a moment in further detail:—

A: *The Sounding-Board, or Sound-Board.*

§ 1. This forms the most vital portion of the instrument. It is analogous to the whole body of the instrument, in the Violin family. It is a carefully constructed, large, thin, resonant sheet of wood, somewhat bulging in the centre, and of almost the same dimensions as the case itself in a horizontal Grand, with the exception of a portion that has to be omitted, to allow the hammers to reach the strings.

B: *The Strings.*

§ 2. These are of steel wire, and are strung across the face of the sounding-board, the strain being for the most part taken by pins at each end. A small portion of the strain is, however, borne by wooden *bridges* fixed to the sounding-board; these latter serve to secure an intimate contact between strings and

---

[1] The surface of the string is too small to affect a large volume of air, hence the device of a sound-board. The vibrations of the string are communicated to it, and as this large surface disturbs much more air at each vibration, we are better enabled to hear the sound initiated by the string. (*Vide* § 3, *Chap.* X.)

sounding-board. The pins at each end of the string are kept apart by a strong *frame*. In the old instruments this frame was formed of large timber-baulks, but in modern instruments, it almost universally takes the far better form of an iron or steel casting. Such metal frame is better calculated to resist the enormous strain created by the tension of so large a number of strings. The pin at one end of the string is fixed in the steel frame itself; the other pin is set in a wooden plank (supported by the frame) so that it can be rotated by means of a tuning-key; the string is in this way wound or unwound, and the tuning is effected by the consequent alteration of the string's tension.

The higher octaves of the instrument have *three* strings tuned in unison for each note, these three strings being simultaneously reached by the same hammer; these strings are short and comparatively thin. The strings are longer and somewhat thicker in gauge the lower the pitch of the notes. As the lower part of the instrument would require strings of impracticable length, these are instead made slower in vibrational-number by being weighted; copper or other wire being coiled upon them for this purpose. Such more ponderous strings give more sound than the thinner and shorter ones belonging to the higher octaves; the number of strings for each note is therefore correspondingly reduced in the lower octaves,—first to *two* only, and then, for the lowest octave, or so, to a single string for each note.

It may be noticed in passing, that much of the success of an instrument depends on the proper choice of length and thickness of string for each note,—or "scaling" as it is termed.

C: *The Mechanism, or "Action."*

§ 3. FIRSTLY: This consists essentially of a *compound lever*; the end which is presented to us of this lever is faced with ivory or ebony, while the other end carries a wooden hammer, covered with layers of felt.[1] The mission of this leverage-

---

[1] The diagram Fig. 1, found at end of this chapter, will help to render the following explanations clearer.

system is to render great speed at the hammer-end easy of attainment, so that this can there be transmitted to the string. As the fulcrum of this leverage-system is far closer to our end of the key than to the hammer end of it; it follows, that the hammer moves through some *two inches* of space,—with correspondingly increased speed, for the mere ⅜ inch or so that the ivory-end of the lever can be depressed.

The depression of our end of the key beyond that depth is arrested by a felt pad—the "key-bed" as it may conveniently be termed.

The mechanism is so adjusted, that the hammer gives its energy up to the string JUST BEFORE THE KEY REACHES THIS PAD.

Here we realise, that all *misdirected* effort, on the part of the performer (*i.e.*: effort ill-timed or ill-directed in its application to the key during descent) is spent merely on these key-beds. The energy intended to create sound is thus more or less lost, and the mechanism of the instrument is over-driven—to its manifest injury, and to the detriment of the quality of the tone. Hence it may be useful to regard the key as a See-Saw; for the key is so weighted, that although it seems level or nearly so when at rest, yet it is in reality *tilted-up* toward us,—ready to have its *other* end, the hammer-end, tilted up during the act of sound-excitation.[1]

§ 4. SECONDLY: The most important of the several devices with which this leverage-system is provided, is the ESCAPEMENT.

This enables the hammer to fall away from the string the moment its mission is completed; and this, although the player may retain the key in its depressed condition.[2]

We should however be unable to *repeat* the note, without

---

[1] The simile of the See-Saw is a peculiarly suggestive one ; for if we stand on the ground, and desire the opposite end of a see-saw to fly up swiftly, we know that we must apply all the energy at our disposal *before* our end of the lever reaches the ground, since all speed-making is impossible after that moment. (*Vide* §§ *5 and 6, Chapter X.; also Note to* § *11, Chapter XI.*)

[2] The tone would be killed in its very birth, were the hammer to remain against the string ; just as would happen, if we, in sounding a bell, continued pressing the striker against it, instead of allowing the latter to rebound with the return-wave of the metal of the bell.

first allowing the key to rise back fully to its surface level, if this "escapement" allowed the hammer to fall completely back to its place of rest. To obviate this inconvenience (and consequent risk of non-repetition of the note) all good modern Grands and some Uprights are provided with a supplementary device. This device, while it allows the hammer to rebound with (and from) the string, and thus leaves the latter free to continue in vibration, yet keeps the hammer fairly close to the string's surface so long as the key is kept fully depressed; the slightest rising of the key from its depressed condition, here suffices to enable one to repeat the note; for the hammer does not in this case fully fall back, unless the key is also allowed to rise beyond a certain point.

An "action" (or mechanism) thus provided, is termed a REPETITION-ACTION;—a term that must not be confounded with "check-repetition," or "check"-action, which is quite another thing.[1]

§ 5. THIRDLY: In the older instruments, the hammer was left free, after its rebound from the string. This rendered it liable to bound back against the string on its own account, re-striking the string once or twice before finally coming to rest. The tone was thus ruined, since such re-striking would not be likely to occur in re-enforcement of the string's move-

[1] The Escapement takes the form of a little crank termed the "hopper." The hammer is supplied with a little button (termed a "roller") on its underside, close to its hinge-end; by this means the hammer lies loosely upon the hopper, and is thereby lifted when the key is depressed. The mechanism is so arranged, that this hopper or crank is tilted at the right moment during key-descent; the hopper in consequence slips or "hops" from under the hammer's button, and the hammer is thus left free to rebound from the string; and is thus prevented from jamming, or "blocking" against the string, and stopping its vibrations.

In the Repetition-action, a subsidiary lever is employed to catch the hammer when it thus rebounds; this prevents the latter from falling completely back, and holds it in readiness to have the hopper re-slipped under its button, without much raising of the key.

Reference should here be made to Fig. 1,—diagram of Action, to be found at end of this chapter.

The extent of the effectiveness of this repetition-device can be tested in the following manner:— Continue repeating a note with one finger, meanwhile gradually lower the key with a finger of the other hand—thus by degrees limiting this key's ascent. The repetition is proved to be the more perfect, the smaller the ascent required by the key, to enable it to speak again.

ment; intentional rapid repetition was also but a precarious matter under this arrangement.

A "check-repetition" was consequently devised. A "check" —a little wooden jack covered with leather or felt is here provided, this rises as the key descends, and is so adjusted that it catches a projection on the end of the hammer, when this falls back, thus precluding any further motion, until released by a sufficient ascent of the key.

§ 6. We see, therefore, that a "repetition-action" renders easier quick repetitions of the same note; whereas, a "check-repetition-action" prevents the hammer from rebounding on its own account, and thus marring the sound.

§ 7. FOURTHLY: A DAMPER is provided to stop the vibrations of the string when the key is allowed to ascend to its normal position. The damper consists of a little wooden block, faced with soft material, and pressed upon the string by its own weight and a soft spring. When the key is depressed, the damper is lifted off the string just before the hammer reaches the latter, and the string is thus left free to continue in vibration until the key is released. When the key is released, the damper again falls into its place upon the string, reaching it just before the key reaches its uppermost limit; the damper thus "damps" (*i.e.*, stops) the string's vibrations in the same manner that one stops the sounding of a bell by gently touching it.[1]

§ 8. FIFTHLY: We have the Damper-Pedal; the right-foot Pedal.[2] This, on being depressed, raises the whole of the dampers off the strings, thus leaving all the latter free to

---

[1] The highest octave-and-a half, or so, is left damperless. This is for two reasons; 1), these strings possess comparatively little power to continue sounding, and 2), being left free to vibrate, they do so in sympathy with lower notes when these are sounded, thus increasing the brilliancy of the instrument.

[2] The damper-pedal is often misnamed the "loud" pedal; whereas it is in truth but a *sustaining*-pedal. Its depression causes but little increase in actual loudness, although it does cause a more resonant effect. This increase in resonance arises from the fact, that every *higher* string that happens to be in tune with a harmonic (or upper partial) *of the one sounding*, is bound to sound in sympathy with it. Moreover, *lower* strings than the one sounded are also bound to be set into sympathetic vibration with it, provided the note actually sounded occurs in the harmonic series of these lower strings. These latter, however, will not in this case sound their own fundamental note, but will in-

sound. On letting the pedal rise, any strings that happen to be sounding are then promptly stopped.

We see therefore, that to obtain a *legato* effect by means of the Pedal, we must let the pedal *rise* as we depress the keys forming the next chord; both the depression of the key and the ascent of the pedal being completed at the same moment. Since the dampers cannot reach their strings until the Pedal is nearly quite up, and as the dampers also act in the same way in connection with the rising key, it also follows that it becomes an inexorable rule in *legato* playing, *not to depress the pedal at the same moment as a key* the sound of which we wish to sustain, but instead to do so immediately *after* the completion of the descent of such key. Correct Pedalling during Legato—the putting *down* of the Pedal, thus forms a close *syncopation* following the sounding of the notes.[1]

stead vibrate at the particular harmonical division that corresponds to the note of the higher-sounding string.

This very interesting fact should be realised by experiment. Depress, without sounding, the notes forming the harmonics of a low note; then ask someone to sound that "fundamental" strongly, and to let go its key at once. All the harmonically related strings (as under, *vide* A) will then be distinctly heard. The B flat will however be rather unclear, owing to the harmonic 7th

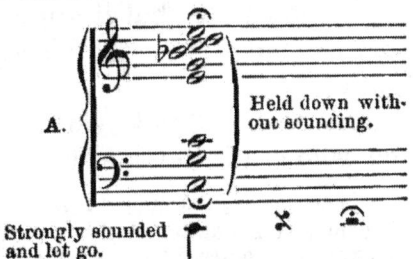

A. Held down without sounding.

Strongly sounded and let go.

being flatter than the "equal temperament" 7th; the higher harmonics are also fainter.

Again, instead of this, hold down without sounding, the lowest of these notes—the C. On then sounding any of the *upper-partials* strongly, and at once letting go their keys, we shall find that this low string is then sounding —not as its own proper note, but as one, *or more*, of these upper-partials. This can be proved by letting its key rise, when they at once cease. The whole chord formed by these harmonics can thus be heard issuing from the *single* string. Each string, therefore, which can give the note sounded as a harmonic, and all the strings which are themselves harmonics of that note, sound in sympathy with it and thus re-enforce it when the pedal is down. (*Vide Note* to § 3, *Chapter X.*)

[1] To render this clear, we should remember that the fingers must in Legato keep the damper of each note *away from* its *strings*, until the moment

To sum up Pedal-action in Legato:—The Pedal must ascend as the next key or group of keys is descending, and this ascent must be so timed that the dampers reach the strings at the very moment that the next sound commences; or they must do so slightly later, if *Legatissimo* is required.

§ 9. A "*Sostenente*" Pedal is added to a few instruments, and forms a *supplementary* Damper-Pedal. This is so contrived, that its depression, immediately *after* the depression of any key or keys (as in the act of ordinary correct pedalling), will prevent these implicated dampers *alone* from falling upon their strings until this pedal is again released. It thus enables us to sustain individual sounds by means of the foot.[1]

§ 10. SIXTHLY: There is the pedal operated by the left foot— the "soft pedal." Several distinct devices have been adopted by different makers in connection with this pedal. None but the true *Una Corda* pedal should however be encouraged, since that is the effect intended in the works of BEETHOVEN, CHOPIN, SCHUMANN, and others of the great Pianoforte Masters —an amply sufficient reason.[2]

The danger of the *una corda* being ousted from the Horizontal Grand is happily now past; but it appears to have become quite customary to omit it from the Upright, and this is greatly to be deplored.

This una-corda device—the "mit Verschiebung" of the Germans—shifts the whole of the instrument's "action" a

---

when the succeeding sound commences—or even beyond that moment. The consequence of depressing the pedal simultaneously *with* the keys would be, that the dampers of the *preceding* notes would not reach their strings at all, thus causing an ugly cacophonous effect—"smudging," in fact.

[1] The contrivance consists either of a string placed across the whole length of the damper-wires, or of a complete set of little levers, which, when pushed forward by that pedal, form a stop and engage with any damper-wires that happen to be raised past this device, thus preventing their return when the attached keys are allowed to rise.

[2] To deprive the instrument of this beautiful effect for the sake of convenience and cheapness in manufacture, or from faddist ideas as to its being "injurious to the instrument," is in fact a piece of sheer commercialism and vandalism. Granted that the relentless use of the *u. c.*—its continuous use, and under a rough imperfectly trained touch, will tend to throw out the unisons, and may under severe treatment even tend to twist the hammer-shanks; nevertheless this forms no indictment against the *u. c.*, for an appliance can only be designed for *use*, not for mis-use!

little to one side. Consequently, in the older instruments (which possessed but two strings to each note) *one* string only was reached by each hammer, whence the term. In modern instruments the hammers are only shifted to the extent of missing *one* of their *three* strings.

The adjustment should be so arranged that the less-used, softer, and un-cut surface of the hammer reaches the remaining strings. Thence partially arises that peculiar, softer tinge of tone-quality obtainable from this device. The main cause of the difference however is: that with the shifted action, we have *one* string excited *sympathetically*—entirely without percussion, the hammer reaching only the other two strings; this gives a mellowness to the sound that is quite unattainable by any other means; not even by the most perfectly "sympathetic" key-treatment or "touch."

§ 11. The substitutes for the true *una corda* are of two kinds:—

The first consists of a *strip of felt*, which is made to intervene between the hammer and the strings when the pedal is depressed. It is an execrable contrivance, the effect of which reminds one of a dog with his head in a sack.[1]

The other device is a less objectionable one, inasmuch as it is at all events not evil-sounding. Here the depression of the pedal brings the whole of the hammer-heads *closer to the strings*. As this lessens the distance the hammer-heads can travel, this reduces the leverage the mechanism offers under ordinary circumstances; whence it follows that the same degree of energy delivered to our end of the key will nevertheless create less speed at the hammer-end, and hence less tone. Such power-cheating device is a quite unnecessary appendage to the instrument, since the very softest sound is quite easily attainable, once the true principles of muscularly producing it are understood; for absolute *pp* is then found to be at once the simplest, easiest, and most secure of all touch-kinds.

[1] The term "celeste" pedal has been applied to this contrivance by some of its makers, possibly on the ground of its singular inappropriateness; or is it that its effect of "distance" is supposed to be suggestive of Heaven?

§ 12. The acquisition of good Tone-production is materially facilitated by the possession of a good instrument; for the better the instrument, the stronger is the prompting towards variety in tone, and the more perceptible are the aural differences that result from good or bad production. Some hints on the choice of an instrument are therefore given in the Appendix to this Part, Note VII.

§ 13. Reference should now be made to Fig. 1, forming a Diagram of the "action"; as the various points can here be studied. Opportunity offering, the student should however not fail to investigate an actual "key"—preferably that of a Grand. This opportunity offers itself in the detached "action" exhibited by most of the makers in their showrooms.

RECAPITULATORY

1): The outer case of the instrument contains *two* distinct portions; the Instrument-proper, and the Implement by which to excite it into sound.

2): The instrument-proper consists of : a), the Sounding-board, and b), the Strings, with the wooden or iron Frame to take their tension.

3): The exciting-implement consists of the "Action" or Mechanism.

4): This Action, or Mechanism, comprises the Key and all its appurtenances; these include:—

a): A Leverage-system, see-saw like, designed to facilitate the attainment of a high degree of velocity at the Hammer-end, and thus to communicate Energy to the String in the Form of Motion.

b): The Escapement, a device to enable the hammer to rebound with and from the string, while the key remains depressed.

c): A supplementary device, to enable Repetition to be easily effected.

d): A "check," to catch the hammer on its rebound from the

THE INSTRUMENT.

string, so as to prevent its re-striking the string by a further rebound.

5) : The "action" has the following accessories:—

aa): The Damper, to stop the string's vibrations when the key is allowed to rise.

bb): The damper Pedal, to raise the whole of the dampers off the strings, and thus leave them free to vibrate.

cc) : The soft pedal, the UNA CORDA pedal.

KEY-TREATMENT; INSTRUMENTAL ASPECT.

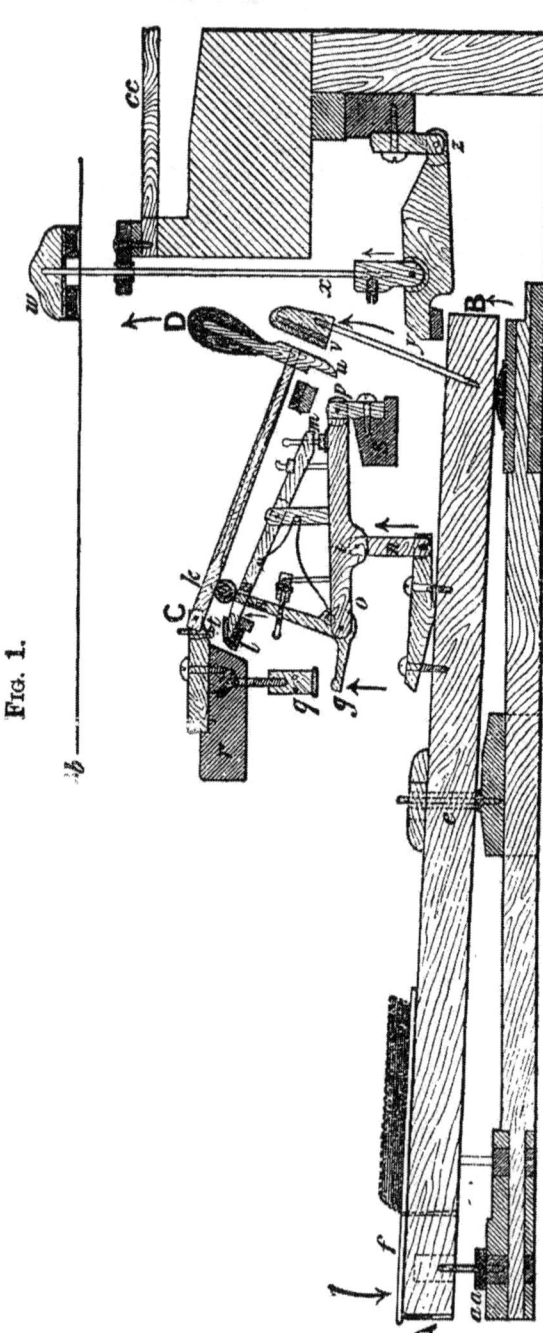

Fig. 1.

DESCRIPTION OF FIG. 1.—The above Diagram forms an illustration of the best type of present-day "Grand-action"; it is a type now adopted as to its principles by all the great makers, although each has slight modifications as to details. It is from a tracing for which I am indebted to the great kindness of Messrs. C. BECHSTEIN.

We, as Pianists, should regard the whole of the mechanism from A to D, inclusive, as "KEY." The Piano-mechanic however often technically applies this term merely to the wooden rocker $A—B$. This rocker is pivoted at e and carries a finger-*plate* of ivory or ebony at f.

$C—D$ is the "hammer" pivoted at C; it has a leather-covered "roller" attached to its underside at k. r and s are *immovable* planks reaching across the full width of the key-board.

The compound ESCAPEMENT is formed by the two straight levers $p—o$, and $l—m$, and by the bent

THE INSTRUMENT.

lever or L-crank g—h (termed the "hopper") in conjunction with the before-mentioned "roller" attached to the hammer, and the adjustable set-off screws q and t.

The operation of the escapement is as follows:—

So long as the key remains unmoved, the Hammer rests, supported through its Roller k, upon the end h of the hopper; this latter being for this purpose passed *through* an aperture in the lever l—m, the "escapement-lever."

When the key is depressed, the whole of the levers concerned in the escapement are raised through the Upright n, and through them, the hopper-supported hammer.

Both the end C of the hammer, and the point p of the lever o—p however remain stationary, owing to their being pivoted to the planks r and s.

To prevent the hammer, on reaching the string, from "blocking" against it, the set-off nut q is so adjusted as to cause the hopper to tilt its g-end against this nut at the right moment. As the levers continue to rise while g is arrested by q, it follows that h slides from under the Hammer-roller, and as the rise of l has also been meanwhile arrested by the screw t, the hammer is thus left free to fall back. It cannot however, fall far away from the string, so long as the key is kept fully depressed, owing to its now resting on the lever l—m.

It is the latter lever that will enable us now to repeat the note without a full ascent of the finger-end of the key being previously required. For if the key is allowed to rise even slightly, then h will at once slightly descend, as will also the m end of the escapement-lever l—m; but as l is under a slight pressure from the spring underneath, it continues for awhile pressing *upward* against its screw t and thus holds the hammer still raised, though not in actual contact with the string. Meanwhile, a moment will however soon be reached, when the Hopper (actuated by the same spring that also gives life to the escapement-lever) will again be able to slip into position under the hammer-roller. We shall thus be able to repeat the note at will. The neat way in which the escapement-lever (l—m) thus as it were *lifts* and replaces the hammer upon the top of the hopper is a real marvel of mechanical ingenuity.

v is the Check; the u end of the hammer is caught by this on its recoil from the string.
w is the damper, lying on its string; and y—z is a little crank by which this is lifted through its wire x by the end of the rocker $A\,B$ when the key is depressed.

At aa we also see the felt pads that prevent the key being taken down too far—the "key-beds" as they are here termed.
bb represents the position of the string.
cc, the edge of the sounding-board.
The arrows indicate the direction of the movements resulting from key-depression.

CHAPTER IX.

ON SOUND

§ 1. If we would possess the power of obtaining at will every possible kind of sound from the instrument, we must first realise what the instrument itself requires from us for each tone-shading.

To form any clear ideas on this subject, it is essential that we should acquire at least a slight—elementary—understanding of:

a): The nature of the phenomena of *Sound* itself.

b): The nature of the *String's* activity during sound-excitation.

c): The nature of the various kinds of treatment the *Key* demands, by means of which we are able to induce the desired kinds of string-movement.

d): The nature of the mechanical laws governing the application of energy to our end of the key.

We will now glance at these points in due succession, since this will help us to understand Key-treatment "from its instrumental aspect."[1]

On Sound.

§ 2. Oscillations, in the sense of areas of alternate compression and rarefaction, travelling through the atmosphere, are, when they reach the *Ear*, transformed into Nerve-vibrations by that organ of sense. Such nerve-vibrations, are once

---

[1] We shall then further have to learn to understand Key-treatment *from its "Muscular Aspect"*; to learn what is required of our muscles, and to learn to provide these requisite muscular actions and inactions.

more transformed on reaching the living Brain, there giving rise to the sensation or consciousness of Sound.[1]

§ 3. The repetition of such concussions of the air, perceptible through the ear, remain distinguishable as separate shocks—or ear-impressions, provided they do not recur oftener than about sixteen times per second. Beyond that limit— 16 per second,[2] these separate impressions merge into each other; and we can then perceive but a *continuous* sensation through the ear, analogous to that produced upon the eye, when a point of light is moved in front of it with sufficient rapidity. For in this case also, the image ceases to remain recognisable as a point—of light, and becomes instead a continuous eye-impression—a streak of light; of which the pyrotechnic device, the "catherine-wheel," is a familiar illustration.

§ 4. Such continuous ear-impressions may either be built up of a *regular*, or of an *irregular* sequence of concussions:

Sound caused by an irregular sequence, is apprehended as *noise;* whereas Sound caused by a regular sequence, is apprehended as a *musical note, i.e.:* A continuous ear-impression, caused by an irregular set of repetitions forms but a *noise;* whereas, we shall experience a musical-sound—or *note*, when the component concussions of such continuous ear-impression are regular in character; and this, however short such impressions may be as regards actual duration.

§ 5. Sounds even that appear to us as *instantaneous* aural-impressions, are nevertheless most probably built up of many air-oscillations, regular or irregular.

Any apparently instantaneous ear-impression—such as a

---

[1] Such recurrences or phases of alternate compression and rarefaction travelling through the air or other suitable medium, are termed "vibrations." It is found that these must however be well marked and definite, if they are to affect our ear; since there is after all a limit to the latter's sensitiveness.

[2] A good deal of confusion arises from there being a difference in the nomenclature of vibration-numbers in different countries. In our country, each "vibration" is understood to include a complete cycle of compression and rarefaction, the two together forming but one single attack on our ear; but in France for instance, the two alternate states are both counted, so that a note here said to be of 16 vibrations is there said to consist of 32.

F

66 INSTRUMENTAL ASPECT OF TONE-PRODUCTION.

rap on the table with a pencil, or the click of a ratchet against the teeth of a ratchet-wheel, or a single puff of air [1]—will moreover, when regularly repeated, fail to remain recognisable as a *separate* impression beyond a speed of 16 repetitions per second, as already previously pointed out.

§ 6. We have learnt, that the stream of ear-impressions caused by regularly-repeated impacts becomes *blurred* into a continuous musical-sound, when these impacts reach about the number of 16 per second.[2] This sound is the note C, an octave lower than the lowest Pianoforte C, and termed " 32-foot " C in the terminology of the Organist. Any excess in the number of impacts received by the ear beyond 16 per second causes a corresponding *rise in Pitch* beyond 32-foot C; for the greater the number of the component ear-attacks per second, the higher is the translated note; such rise in acuteness continuing until the number of repetitions is so high, that a point is reached where our ear will no longer serve to render us conscious of their existence.[3]

It is in fact the function of the ear to *count* the number of impacts received, and discriminating thus the differences in vibration-number, to deliver the result to our consciousness, translated into a mental impression,—that of contrast in Pitch.

§ 7. Understanding that it is the number of vibrations com-

---

[1] The Syren is an example of this class of tone-exciter. Or we can imitate the effect with our lips,—as we in fact do in the case of the Brass instruments, where the lips are helped by the mouthpiece to become vibrating reeds. (*Vide Note VIII., Appendix to Part II.*—"*On Tone-exciters.*")

[2] To be more accurate: when the regularly-repeated impressions on our *consciousness* reach that number.

[3] Sound altogether vanishes from our ken when the impacts reach a speed of about 4,500 per second. This is because our organ of hearing is not adapted to receive nerve-excitations at a quicker rate than that. We do nevertheless possess nerve-ends differently *armed* or *equipped*, by means of which we are able to distinguish vibration-rates far quicker than those of Sound, even at their speediest. There are those different and far quicker vibrations, for instance, that form the physical *reality* of Light and Heat. Furthermore, there are forms of vibration, such as Electricity, for the perception of which we are entirely unprovided with any organs, and have therefore to rely on the artificial *organs* of the laboratory. Those inclined to be interested in this subject should refer to a delightfully vivid lecture on "The Senses" by Professor Croome Robertson, to be found amongst the popular "Manchester Science Lectures"—Fifth Series (John Haywood).

pleted per second that determines the Pitch of a note, we have further to realise :—that it is upon the *Intensity* of these vibrations, that depends its *Loudness, i.e.:* The zones of alternate compression and rarefaction reaching a given spot in a given time, may be of small or of great intensity—may be small or great disturbances, and the impacts received by our ear from these may therefore be of little or of great violence; it is this distinction that causes the difference in sensation between loudness and softness,—that causes the difference in Tone-amount.

§ 8. But there is yet one other difference to be accounted for, and that is the difference in the *character* of the sound,—the difference in *quality*, "timbre," or "clang-tint."

To realise the nature of this difference, we must understand that the waves of alternate compression and rarefaction that reach our ears, are nearly all *compound;* excepting such almost "pure" sounds as those of the Tuning-fork, and the "Open-Diapason" of the Organ, which are almost characterless in consequence of such freedom from Harmonics.

That is:

The series of evenly-timed impacts upon our ear-drum, that forms a musical-note, may be accompanied by other series of *fainter and quicker-timed* impacts; these latter (technically termed harmonics or upper-partials) form mathematical time-divisions of the principal set of impacts. It is the presence of such *harmonics*—various in their combination and relative strength—that gives the particular character, or Quality, to each sound.[1]   This fact it is that enables us to distinguish between one instrument and another, between Flute and

---

[1] The aspect of the waves we perceive on the surface of the sea, can give us some insight into the nature of Compound Sound-Waves. We find, that the long sweeping waves are ornamented with countless small wavelets. Both pursue their course, while the main wave nevertheless remains the fundamental fact.

In this sense the analogy is a good one, but we must remember, that we do not have to deal with a surface-wave, in the case of sound vibrations, but have to deal with a transmission of energy in all directions from a centre—in a series of ever-widening spheres of compression-points with intervening spheres of rarefaction.

Clarionet, Trumpet and Oboe, Violoncello and the Human-voice; and allows us even to distinguish one voice from another; indeed enables us to recognise even one Pianist from another, owing to divergences in habits of Key-attack.

The production of different *qualities* of sound from the same instrument, also forms one of the most powerful means of expression at our disposal.

RECAPITULATORY

a): A musical-sound (or note) consists of a series of concussions, equally timed and of equal strength, recurring at a sufficiently great speed to render it impossible for us to recognise the separate impacts delivered upon our ear, which consequently blurs them into a continuous sense-effect.

b): Pitch, is the term used to designate the difference between a high and a low speed in the repetitions of the ear-impacts,— forming the difference between a high and low sound.

c): The pitch of a note depends solely upon the *frequency* with which the air is disturbed or beaten in a given time.

d): The Amount of Tone depends on the Intensity of such disturbance.

e): Most notes are built up of a fundamental strong series of ear-impacts, accompanied by divers quicker and weaker impacts, termed Harmonics.

f): Divergence in the Character, Timbre, or Quality of the tone, arises from the difference in the combination and strength of the harmonics heard with the fundamental sound.

CHAPTER X.

THE STRING: ITS BEHAVIOUR DURING THE VARIOUS FORMS OF TONE-PRODUCTION.

§ 1. In the sound emitted by the Pianoforte, the requisite air-concussions are induced, by setting a *String in Motion.*

The two ends of the string are fixed points; the string can however be driven aside from its position of repose (in a direction at right angles to its length) owing to its elasticity. If it is thus driven aside, this same property of elasticity will then cause the string to rebound, provided it is left free to do so, and it will then continue in *vibration* (*i.e.*, to-and-fro oscillation) until the energy communicated to it during its first deflection is exhausted; unless such gradual dissipation of the original impetus is prematurely arrested by the mechanical means provided by the descent upon it of the Damper.[1]

§ 2. The Length, Tension, and Thickness of the String determines how quickly it shall complete its vibration—to-and-fro. It is upon the frequency of the completion of such vibrations that depends the aural effect of Pitch; for the greater the number of complete vibrations per second, the

---

[1] The string, in thus beating or whipping the air, does not exactly strike it. The attack delivered upon the air by the string is rather in the nature of a *compression* in one direction, while it leaves a *rarefaction* in the other. The particles of air in immediate contact with the string, cannot cease to exist in front of the latter's swift advance, hence they are, as it were, heaped or crushed upon each other,—thus causing a momentary area of compression. Owing to the extreme elasticity of the medium, this wave of compression is passed on from particle to particle, and is followed by its natural consequence —a rebound. We must not imagine that a current is produced in the air; it is simply the vibration that is transmitted, much in the same way that ever-widening circles arise on the surface of a sheet of water, disturbed by the falling of a stone into it. The air waves are however transmitted not in circlets, but in ever widening spheres—of alternate compression and rarefaction. (*Vide Note to* § 8 *of last chapter.)*

more acute the sound; and the fewer the vibrations the lower is it.[1]

It is here imperative not to confuse speed in the reiteration of these completed side-to-side movements, with *the actual speed at which the substance of the string is travelling through the atmosphere.* The two are quite distinct phenomena. (*Vide* § *8.*)

§ 3. As the slender String presents so small a surface for contact with the air, and is therefore unable to create a sufficiently considerable atmospheric disturbance to be conveniently appreciated by the ear, it is found desirable to bring the SOUNDING-BOARD into requisition.

The large sensitive surface of the sounding-board is in secure contact with the strings of the Pianoforte through the intervening bridges; and the sounding-board is thus compelled to vibrate in sympathy with the strings; and as a large area of vibrating material is here presented to the air, a far larger volume of air is in this way set in motion than could be

---

[1] As the vibrations of a String are mostly too minute and rapid to be discernible by the eye—excepting those of the lowest Bass strings, we may better learn to understand the phenomena of Vibration, by studying other forms of it. The oscillation of a Pendulum offers us such opportunity; so does a person sitting in a swing. A bunch of keys, suspended at the end of its chain, also forms an admirable illustration; and one moreover that is always conveniently available.

Now we shall find, on experimenting with one of these, that the to-and-fro swings of such pendulum remain the same as regards the number completed in a given time, so long as we leave the length of the pendulum unaltered; that the oscillations will complete themselves more rapidly if we shorten it; and that they will take longer to do so if we lengthen it; and this, while the actual speed of the mass through the air *remains unaltered;* always excepting, that the originally given impetus will by degrees exhaust itself. We shall moreover find, that we shall obtain *twice* the number of complete vibrations if we shorten the pendulum to one third of its length; and that it will take the pendulum twice as long to complete its recurring journeys, if we give thrice the length of pendulum.

Somewhat the same thing applies to the Pianoforte string. For we shall find that if we touch it *gently,* midway between its two ends, whilst it is sounding, that its division into two *halves* in this way will cause the two segments to continue in vibration, each on its own account; and as the two halves will now complete their vibrations in exactly half the time of that of the whole string, we shall now hear the sound an octave higher. This experiment will at once give us a practical insight into the nature of "harmonics." We can continue the experiment; and by successively touching the vibrating string at a third of its total length, or at a quarter, eighth, or sixteenth, etc., of its length, we shall obtain its higher harmonics—the twelfth, the double-octave, the third above that, etc. (*Vide Note to* § *8, Chapter VIII.*)

accomplished by the unaided string. The larger volume of air thus disturbed gives us a correspondingly magnified sensation of sound.

§ 4. In the Pianoforte, the String is set in motion by the hammer. This is effected in the following manner:

The hammer, moving swiftly and with great momentum, on reaching the string, carries this with it—a short distance out of its plane when at rest.[1] The extent of the deflection, thus caused, depends upon the degree of speed and momentum with which the hammer is moving. Such deflection of the string by the hammer seems infinitesimal to the eye; yet the short distance thus covered by the two in conjunction, amply suffices to enable the hammer to SHARE ITS SPEED AND MOMENTUM WITH THE STRING. The string, having thus been driven out of repose, rebounds, owing to the elasticity of its substance, takes the hammer back with it, and thus helps the latter to rebound and to catch against the "check" ready to receive it.

The string meanwhile continues its journey to-and-fro, owing to the momentum it has acquired from the hammer during their shortlived connection; and this momentum is gradually exhausted, unless arrested by the damper's descent.

§ 5. The fact particularly to be noticed in this connection, is, that the *act of tone-excitation* at the Pianoforte must necessarily be fully completed within the course of but one single "vibration" of the string. Indeed the time available is even more limited than that, since it is only while the string is being driven *outwards* from its position of rest, that the hammer can communicate its speed and momentum to the string; and it is therefore only during *one quarter* of one complete to-and-fro oscillation of the string, that we have the opportunity of conveying Energy in the form of Motion to it.

[1] This forms but a very rough-and-ready description of the known facts; but it suffices to enforce the point which it is imperative we should realise, viz.: *that tone production can only be attained by communicating Motion to the string.* (*Vide* §§ 7 and 8.)

This being the vital point that concerns us as Pianists, it is deemed inadvisable to give here a more minute description of the manner in which the string starts on its journey. Further detail would lead rather to confusion than to clearness, until this main fact is grasped.

72   KEY-TREATMENT; INSTRUMENTAL ASPECT.

This is the fact that in the first instance determines the treatment we have to mete out to the string through the Pianoforte mechanism. We must therefore vividly and constantly bear in mind, that since *we cannot influence the string beyond the moment of its first swing outwards*, it follows, that we cannot influence it beyond the moment *when sound breaks silence*,—unless we repeat the act of tone-production.

§ 6. We are here brought face to face with the truth so often lost sight of in playing and teaching; viz., that the act of tone-production at the Pianoforte is not only a DISCONTINUOUS act, separate for each note, but that it is one of exceedingly short duration; of no greater duration in fact than it is perceived to be in the sharpest *Staccatissimo*.[1]

Indeed, we shall presently find *(Chapter XV., etc., Part III.)* that here the Ear itself is apt to mislead one thoroughly at the Pianoforte, since the *continuous* aural effect of *Tenuto* or *Legato* may easily prompt us to a continuous muscular act in the place of the proper one,—one that is individually directed for each key-descent and carefully *ceased* on reaching sound,—excepting always that slight residue of weight, which we shall find is necessary when we wish to retain the keys depressed in *tenuto* and *legato*.[2]

§ 7. Coming now to the problem of Tone-Amount, we find that the degree of comparative *Loudness* of a note directly

---

[1] We shall presently realise that there is a single exception to this rule, for we shall find that when the key is *weighed* into sound at its softest, that this act of weighing may in this case be *continued beyond* the moment of tone-emission; the result forming the true *pp*-Tenuto. (*Vide next chapter, also Part III.*)

[2] It may here prove useful to compare this form of String-excitation to that employed in the Violin family:—The Pianoforte hammer can give but one single impulse to its string; whereas, the Violin-bow imparts a continuous series of impulses to its string. The action here is, that the Bow carries the string along with it, some little distance out of the latter's position in repose. The greater the weight brought to bear upon the string through the bow, the greater will be the frictional contact between the two, and the more will the string consequently be carried out of its place, before the frictional union between the two is overcome by the tension thus caused in the string. The string flies back, owing to its elasticity, the moment this tension becomes too great; the impetus thus gained, then carries it beyond its natural point of rest, when it again falls an easy prey to the continuously moving bow, which then again automatically grips hold of it, and once more wrenches it along.

depends upon the "*amplitude*" of each vibration of the string.

That is: the louder the sound required, the *further apart must be the extreme points to which the string swings*, when beating the air in conjunction with the Sounding-board.[1] For we have learnt, in the preceding chapter, that it is upon the degree of the air-disturbance (of alternate compression and rarefaction) that depends the loudness of the note.

§ 8. Now, as each particular string is compelled always to *complete* each of its vibrations in the *same period of time*, no matter how great or small the amplitude of such vibration

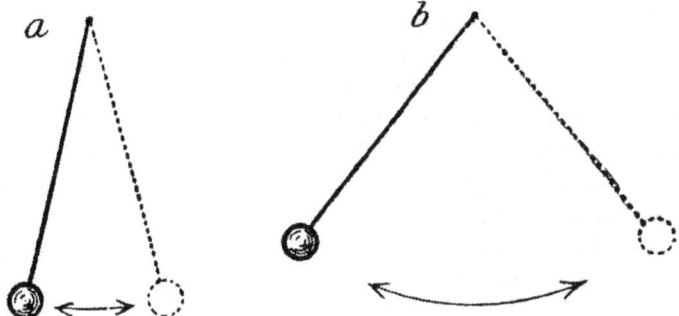

FIG. 2.—Comparison of large with small oscillations of a pendulum; both taking same space of Time for their completion.

may be; it follows, that to enable the substance of the string to cover the *greater space* traversed for a louder note, it must here be made to *move at a greater Speed*. Fig. 2 will make this clearer; for it will be seen, that the greater the space traversed by the same pendulum in the same time, the more swiftly must it move to complete its journeys.

§ 9. We learn herefrom a fact of the utmost importance, and that is, that Tone-*quantity* is strictly determined by the String's Speed:—that the amount of Tone therefore depends

---

[1] This increase in the amplitude of the string's vibration for each increase in tone-amount, can even be observed by the eye, in the case of the low Bass-strings.

solely upon the *degree of speed* which we can manage to communicate to the string.[1]

§ 10. Coming now to the question, what it is in the nature of the String's behaviour that gives rise to the aural effect of difference in the *Quality* of the sound,—difference in *timbre* or Clang-tint, we find that the facts so far understood on this point, indicate, that the difference is of the *same* nature as that difference which we Pianists find it necessary to make in our treatment of the Key, to induce those tone effects.[2]

§ 11. It is found that the difference in the string's behaviour that gives us differences of tone-quality depends *on the manner* in which the string is started upon its journey; and it is evident, that the difference between the production of the harsher, "Brilliant" tone-qualities, and the more pleasant "Sympathetic" qualities, lies in a greater or lesser percussiveness; for the string is in the first case set a-going with abruptness, suddenness and absolute Percussion, whereas in the second case, speed is imparted to it, with a far more *gradual* application of the total Energy employed.

It is found that a too sudden application of energy tends to cause the string to move off rather into segmental vibration,

---

[1] To enforce this point, we should always recur to the simile of the Swing, or Key-chain. (*Vide Note to* § *3 of this chapter, page 70.*) For we shall find on repeating this experiment, that the number of completed oscillations in any given time remains practically the same, *whether we complete the swings in great sweeps, or in small ones.* Whence we deduce the fact, that far more ground must be covered in the same space of time when the swings are "ample" than when they are small in extent. It is also manifest that the person, String, or bunch of keys thus swinging, must *travel at greatly increased speed* to enable this greater distance to be covered in the same space of time during each swing; and finally it is evident, that in this case a more effective "shove-off" must have been delivered;—unless the requisite speed is added during *successive* swings by muscular exertion, as can be done in the case of the Violin-string, or in that of a person on a swing,—but which remains impossible in the case of Pianoforte Tone-production.

[2] We shall find in the next chapter, that the more *suddenly* the key-depression is effected, the more harsh ("*brilliant*") and "short" will be the resulting sound-quality; and that the more *gradually* the key-depression is effected, the more "*sympathetic*," singing, and carrying will the sound be;—Part III. will further show us how these differences in Key-treatment result from the selection of the particular *muscular conditions* proper for each difference.

than into those complete vibrations—of its whole length—that enforce the fundamental sound.[1]

The more these segmental vibrations (or harmonics) preponderate, especially the higher and harsher ones, the worse is the sound in every respect;[2] it is less beautiful, and less full, and it is less able to travel or "carry."[3]

[1] Helmholtz has pointed out that a soft hammer coming into contact with the string "lies longer" on it than a harder hammer; *i.e.*, the soft hammer does not instantly bound off, but the momentum with which it is moving drives its soft armature accumulatively against the string before the rebound arises. The Piano-makers sometimes make evil use of this knowledge—which they have acquired through practical experience. They supply hammers so soft that a harsh tone almost becomes impossible of attainment on instruments thus provided. Such heavy felting of the hammers, or "toning" of them, although it does in a measure prevent the instrument from sounding unpleasant, even under the hands of the worst player, and although this may enhance its commercial value with some patrons, nevertheless renders it comparatively inefficient as an instrument for the production of *Variety* of tone. It cannot therefore so well reflect the moods of the player through the "colouring" agency, and such instrument should therefore be shunned equally by Artist and Student.

[2] *Vide* § 8, *Chapter IX., page 67.*

[3] *Helmholtz*, in his "*The sensations of tone, as a physiological basis for the theory of music,*" maintains, that the difference in quality is caused by the difference between a mere KNOCK and a "SHOVE-OFF" of the string by the Hammer;—circumstances that certainly do apply at our end of the Key. He says: "In "Pianoforte playing the effect of the tone-excitation by means of the hammer "depends on the length of time the latter *remains lying* on the string. For if "the soft elastic surface of the hammer is brought against the string without "audible blow, then the movement has time to propagate itself before the "hammer springs back, and *increases* gradually and constantly during the "time of contact;"—*i.e.:* during one *quarter* of one complete string-vibration.

This indeed seems to form the true explanation of the Phenomenon. SUDDEN attack of the string no doubt tends to produce but a concussion at the string's surface, causing it as it were, to "wriggle off" into movement; hence a poor sound, harsh with harmonics, which although *noisy* in close proximity, exhibits but small *carrying* power. GRADUAL attack of the string tends, on the contrary, to give it a really far greater momentum, the resulting vibrations partaking rather of the simple (fundamental) type than of the compound (harmonic) type; we consequently here obtain a large volume of pure, rich sound, that carries well, even at its softest.

The example of the Swing, or bunch of keys on their chain, may here again help us to a better appreciation of the facts: If we desire to give a person seated in a swing a good "shove-off," it is useless to endeavour to do so by means of a sudden jerk or knock; we should on the contrary thus risk upsetting his balance on the seat! The only (and familiar) way to secure an effective result, is, to apply force *gradually:* by allowing our hand gently to come into contact with the person—without concussion therefore, and *realising the degree of the resistance to be overcome*, we increase the energy of the push given, as the speed is felt to increase by virtue of it.

We shall also find, when the treatment of the key comes to be considered,

RECAPITULATORY

a): At the Pianoforte, the requisite concussions that form sound are communicated to the atmosphere by means of to-and-fro motions (vibrations) of the String, enhanced by the Sounding-board.

b): The greater the *number* of such vibrations completed by the String per second, the *higher* (more acute in Pitch) is the resulting note.

c): The greater the *extent* of these String vibrations, the *louder* is the note.

d): The string must therefore traverse space more *quickly* the louder the note; since the time available (in which to traverse the larger distance embraced by the more ample vibration) remains the same as for a softer note.

e): To produce much tone, we must therefore induce *much movement* in the string. For the more quickly the string is made to move, the greater will be the distance it can traverse during the course of each complete vibration.

that we here have a very suggestive analogy, as to how we should *use the key* for Sympathetic tone.

Another experiment forms a good demonstration in this connection :—One end of a long rope being fixed, take hold of the other end, and give it a violent jerk. The rope will here be seen to "wriggle" into little curves. Instead of this jerk, now give a carefully "aimed," gradual swing to the rope, and one may succeed in causing it by such means to swing in but one single curve, with hardly any subsidiary ones.

A point that however still requires elucidation, is, the exact manner in which the hammer-end is able to *transmit* to the string the KNOWN differences in key-treatment that do cause the known differences in the string's vibrations—whence arise those differences in Quality, perceptible by the ear.

As this subsidiary part of the problem still awaits final solution, we can here only rely on hypothesis and surmise, instead of upon fully ascertained facts.

This point, although extremely interesting, is however of but small moment here, where we are not concerned in completing the acoustical explanation of the effects we hear, but are concerned with the way in which these effects are to be obtained from our end of the Key. On this latter point there is happily no question of "hypothesis," since the facts are all proven,—as are also the muscular-ones by means of which we are able to fulfil such laws of key-treatment.

Those interested in this detail will find some remarks bearing on it on referring to the Appendix of this Part, Note No. IX., "On Quality."

f): The string is set into motion by the felt-covered end of the Pianoforte mechanism—the hammer.

g): The hammer, upon being brought into contact with the string, *shares* its speed with the latter whilst deflecting it. Both thereupon rebound; and the hammer, falling away from the string, leaves the latter free to continue in vibration, gradually expending the energy communicated to it, unless stopped by the Damper.

h): The hammer can therefore only communicate movement to the string during the latter's *first* vibration; and can only do so, during the first *quarter* of such first to-and-fro movement of the string.

i): As the hammer *ceases to influence* the string the very moment that *Sound begins,* it follows, that this moment *forms the conclusion and cessation* of the Act of Tone-production; for the string cannot move quicker than it does at that moment, since it has ceased to be under the influence either of Key or Finger.

j): Tone-production at the Pianoforte is therefore a *discontinuous* Act; an act separate for each note; and one that *ceases* with the moment when Silence changes into Sound.

k): Beauty in the Quality of a sound, depends on the string's vibrations tending rather toward the *simple* types of movement than toward the *compound* forms;—the resulting tone is thus less embarrassed with the harsher harmonics.

l): This simplicity in the string's vibration that furthers beauty of tone (vibration of the string rather as a whole than in sections) depends on the *manner* in which movement is communicated to it.

m): The *harsher* effects arise, when the string is *suddenly* set in motion; whereas the more *sympathetic* effects arise only when the string is set in motion as *gradually* as possible.

CHAPTER XI.

THE KEY—THE STRING-MOVING IMPLEMENT, ITS BEHAVIOUR AND REQUIREMENTS DURING THE ACT OF TONE-PRODUCTION.

§ 1. The manner of attacking and using the Pianoforte-key is necessarily determined by the requirements of the String.

The Key's requirements have therefore been foreshadowed, and have in fact already been clearly indicated in the last chapter.

§ 2. Our unaided finger would find it impossible to propel the string into adequate speed;—a convenient implement, tool or *machine* is therefore offered us for this purpose in the shape of the Pianoforte Key.

This Key, with its attached Mechanism or Action, is individually complete and separate for each note.

§ 3. It is important that the term "key" should here convey more to the mind than is suggested by the mere sight of its Ivory or Ebony-clad ends. By "Key" we must understand: the *whole* lever with its attached contrivances,—from the ivory or ebony end, to the opposite Hammer end.[1]

§ 4. Since the main object of this *machine* is, to enable the finger to communicate more Speed to the string than the finger could without being thus equipped, it follows, that we

---

[1] Manifestly, a significance far beyond the usual one is here attached to the term "key:"

As ordinarily employed, it is applied to the visible plates that receive the Finger's contact. We find, on the other hand, that a Piano-regulator speaks of "removing a key" from the instrument; he applying the term to the long wooden rocker or lever (vide A—B, in both Figs. 1 and 3) to one end of which the finger-plates are attached; and which is quite separate from the rest of the "action" in most instruments.

As Pianists, it is however essential that we should regard the whole of the compound-leverage system (from A to D inclusive, Figs. 1 and 3) as "Key" or Implement. In this sense therefore is it, that the Key is applied to the String to move it,—just as another kind of key is applied to a lock to unlock it.

must look upon the Key as *a contrivance to help us to translate Energy into Speed.*

The energy requisite for this purpose is derived from Weight, and from direct Muscular-exertion brought to bear upon the key.[1]

§ 5. This work of translation is accomplished by the key through the agency of the compound leverage-system it offers us. As we have already learnt (§ *3, Chapter VIII.*), the depression of our end of the key-lever to its fullest extent of about ⅜ inch, causes the opposite end (with its felt-covered hammer) to rise some two inches. Now it is obvious that the hammer-end must travel at far greater speed than does our finger-tip in contact with the key, since the hammer traverses so much greater a distance than does *our* end of the key. (*Vide Fig. 3.*[2])

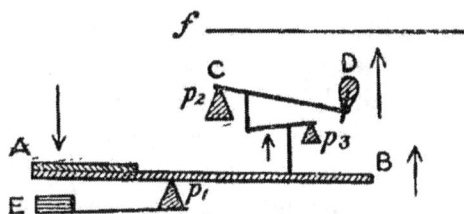

Fig. 3.—Diagrammatic representation of the *principle* of the compound-leverage involved, with omission of all details of the mechanism.

A—B wooden rocker, with finger plate at A. C—D hammer. f string. E keypad. $p1, p2, p3$, are immovable centres or pivots.

It is well therefore to regard the key as a mechanical CONTINUATION OF OUR FINGER, to enable us more easily to induce String-speed.

§ 6. To induce movement in the key-end presented to us, we must bring greater Weight or Power into opposition with it, than it itself represents, when in a state of rest.[3]

[1] This part of the problem is dealt with in Part III.
[2] We must however understand, that what we gain in speed in this way, has to be supplied as extra Energy at our end of the key. The key being a kind of See-Saw, upon the opposite end of which is the object that has to be speeded—into sound.
[3] By " weight " of key, we must here understand not only its actual weight, but also the *friction* of the attached mechanism,—in fact the inertia of the whole mass.

Such weight-opposition can only become translated into Key-*speed*—and string-speed—and Tone, provided its full application is consummated before the key's descent culminates in Tone.

§ 7. The key therefore *ceases* to induce string-speed the moment the beginning of Sound is heard; for the key-lever as it were *falls in twain* at that moment; *i.e.:* the hammer at that moment slips off the hopper, rendering it impossible for us further to influence the string through its agency, unless we first allow the key slightly to rise, and thus regain control over the hammer. (*Vide Chapter VIII.,* §§ *3 and 4, and Fig. 1, page 62.*)

This very potent fact in tone-production must always be kept in view.

§ 8. The action and reaction of Weight, Force, or Energy, in this connection, is, roughly speaking, as follows:

a): We shall obtain *no* key movement, so long as the weight or energy we apply to the key does not *more* than equal the resistance which the key itself offers us when in a state of rest.

b): We shall obtain the *softest* sound possible from the instrument, if we bring weight or energy upon the key-surface up to the point that the latter's opposition to Movement is just overcome. For the key will then be exactly outbalanced, and it will then (and thus only) give way at the most gentle speed compatible with its sounding at all,—giving the effect of absolute *pp*.

c): To obtain *more sound* than this real *pp*, we shall have to apply far greater Weight (or Energy) than this to the key; and the *louder* the sound required, the *greater* will have to be the *sum* of such application of Power. For increased Power will be as it were *swallowed up*, before we can obtain the desired increase in Key-speed—and String-speed—and Tone.

d): Whence we also find, *vice versa*, that the Key *resists us* with increased effectiveness, with every increase in the speed we endeavour to induce in it; and this in spite of the fact, that the key's actual weight remains the same.

§ 9. A pair of scales may render these points clearer:

a): If we place, say, a pound-weight in *each* of the pans,

we shall find that they merely balance each other, producing a state of equilibrium ;—*no* movement will thence ensue.

b) : Whereas, if we gently add weight to one of the pans, as for instance, by pouring sand into it rather sharply, then a moment will arrive when that pan's inertia will be just overcome; it will be overbalanced, and in giving way to this slightly greater weight, it will sink down and cause the pan at the opposite end of the lever to rise—also quite gently.

c) : Again, if instead of thus carefully adding weight only up to the point that the pan will just give way, we bring a whole extra pound or more to bear upon it, then we shall find that the opposite pan no longer rises gently as in the last experiment, but that it now does so with extremely increased swiftness. Here we see indicated, the nature of the divergence in Treatment demanded by the key, respectively during the production of *pianissimo* and *fortissimo*.

§ 10. In other words:

a) : So long as we do not bring Weight or Energy to bear upon the key, *beyond* the latter's resistance to movement, *we may rest on its surface* without causing any movement whatsoever.

b) : If however we wish to induce sound, and that of the softest possible amount, then we must *add* weight or energy to that already resting upon the key at surface-level, until the key is just *overbalanced* into descent. This we can do with perfect accuracy, provided we *watch* the resistance the key offers to movement, by means of our *muscular sense*. It is the muscular-sense (with its co-operatives) that alone can accurately apprise us of the particular moment when the key *begins* to give way, and which can therefore also warn us when to discontinue the addition of weight or Power, if we mean *pp*.[1]

---

[1] Such estimate of key-resistance can be formed in two ways, for it is formed differently in a slow passage than it is in a quick one : We can derive it in a slow passage from the resistance *each individual key* can then be felt to offer ; in more rapid passages we must depend on the *general impression* of resistance the whole key-board offers, as our fingers pass across it.

Allusion to the duties of the muscular-sense and its co-operatives is here unavoidable, although premature. This matter receives further consideration in the next Part. *(Vide Chapter XIII.)*

G

c) : If moreover, we wish to produce a sound *louder* than this real *pp*, then manifestly we must add weight or energy upon the key in excess of the amount that we find suffices merely to overcome its inertia—as in *pp*. In fact, the louder the required sound, the greater must be the Energy we bring to bear upon our end of the key, for the hammer will then move more swiftly, the string-speed will be greater, and the sound correspondingly louder.

§ 11. All this plainly teaches us to recognise the Key in its true aspect; viz.: to recognise it as a *long lever* or machine, intended to enable us to obtain a high velocity by means of its hammer-end.

Once recognising this fact, we are inevitably forced to the conclusion, the true one: that any *percussion* caused at the key-surface forms absolute MIS-USE of the Pianoforte tone-producing mechanism.

The supposition, that Tone-production at the Pianoforte should be attained by any *real* unmitigated hitting or "striking" at the keys, being thus proved to be a complete fallacy—except in mere appearance, it follows that we are compelled to discard all doctrines of tone-production based on this fallacy; unless beauty of tone, ease and certainty are not worthy of consideration.   To harbour such conception of the act of Pianoforte tone-production is almost equally far from the truth, as it would be to suppose a "stroke" at Tennis or Billiards to consist of an act of "striking" the racket or cue itself.[1]

---

[1] This fallacy has probably arisen, like so many other indefensible dogmas relating to Pianoforte-technique, owing to the initial mistake, that of studying the VISIBLE effects—of the *limb-movements*, etc., that accompany correct production—instead of studying the laws involved in the use of the Pianoforte key itself, and the muscular CONDITION of the implicated limbs. The comparatively swift (AND CORRECT) movements of Finger, Hand and Arm towards the key-surface may indeed easily be mistaken for hitting; but the fact remains, that the true artist rarely permits himself really to hit at the keys; on the contrary, he always "follows-up" his keys, however much it may seem to others, and even to himself, like "punching the key-board."

It should be noted, that the main fact against "key-hitting" is, that CONCUSSION is thus caused at the key-surface,—between that and the finger-tip. This forms so much waste of Energy; the molecular vibrations of the key and finger-tip, thus caused, replacing to that extent the *intended* motion of the whole body of the key itself. The further disadvantage is, that *accuracy*

THE KEY.

Meanwhile, we must never lose sight of the all-important fact, that we must apply *all* the energy intended to produce Tone, *before* the moment when it becomes too late to do so; else we shall squeeze the key-beds, instead of making tone. That is: we must always remember, that it is too late to make sound when the key has reached its bed, and that the act of tone-production itself is always as short-lived as it is obviously enough proved to be in *Staccatissimo*, and that we must therefore be constantly on the alert with our Ears, so that the very beginning of Sound-emission may instantly warn us that the opportunity for inducing String-speed by means of the Key is past.[1]

§ 12. Coming now to the divergences in key-treatment that determine the differences in TONE-QUALITY, we will first return once more to our pair of scales, which will enable us to realise another instructive fact:

We shall find that we can make the addition to the load on

of expression must needs remain unattainable; since we have in this instance no means of accurately feeling the degree of resistance each key offers, and cannot therefore accurately *guide* it to its musically-intended consummation in tone-shading.

There are other facts besides: The one pointed out above, that the key is a lever by which to move the string, should prove ample to prevent our looking upon the key in the light of a ball, etc. Experiment has moreover proved that the hammer instantly *flies off* the "action" when the key is really hit—in which case all the elaborate leverage-system provided, by which *gradually* to induce movement, becomes useless. Again, if the key is driven down over-suddenly by a really forcible blow, it is exceedingly probable, that the "hopper" then instantly slips from under the hammer, thus similarly rendering futile the carefully planned leverage-system of the key.

Vide Note X., Appendix, "On key-hitting," which gives further details, and a summary on these points.

[1] Ignorance of this simple law—one would think it to be self-evident enough to occur to a child—often leads to the monstrous fallacy, and to the consequent complaints uttered by Pianists, that it is their supposed "*want of Strength*" that prevents their obtaining the full measure of intended tone! Those huge exertions we so lamentably often witness, even on the platform, are generally the immediate result of the performer not having so far recognised this very first and obvious fact connected with his instrument, viz., that Tone-production absolutely *ceases* when the key-bed has been reached—or even before that; and that all the labour expended on the key-beds is but sheer waste, and is but impedimental to accurate expression.

We may rest perfectly assured, when we see a performer labouring at his instrument as if he were lifting oxen, that he has certainly *not* conquered the mere "Elements" of using the key-board correctly,—has not learned his technical A B C, however admirable his artistic instincts may be in other ways.

one pan (*vide* § *8 and 9*) by letting go the intended weight either *suddenly*, or by letting it slip through our fingers more *gradually*. We thus have the option of adding a given weight in either of these two ways, before the pan in question reaches its full depression.

We can moreover, in either case, employ a weight sufficient to cause even a very swift ascent on the part of the opposite pan.

The distinction thus illustrated, is, that we can either *suddenly* or *gradually* induce a great speed in that opposite pan.

It is just such a distinction between suddenly or gradually applied force, that will, in the case of the Pianoforte-key (by inducing the contrast between suddenly or gradually-reached Key-speed) enable us to cause the aural contrast between "Brilliant" and "Sympathetic" tone-qualities.[1]

§ 13. The nature of this divergence between the production of "brilliant" and "sympathetic" tone-qualities—the difference between Sudden or Gradual key-attack, or the French "avec attaque" and "sans attaque"—may become plainer through the following considerations and diagrams (*vide Fig. 4*), illustrative of the two opposite extremes of this nature in key-treatment:

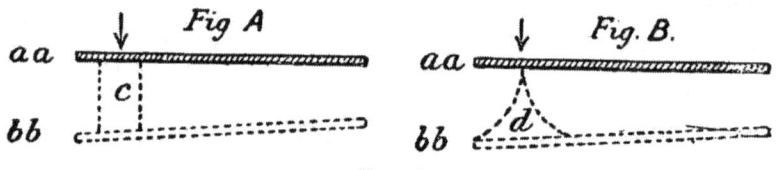

Fig. 4.

Of the two horizontally converging thick lines in both the above diagrams, the *upper* one (*aa*) illustrates the position of our end of the key when at rest—at "surface-level"; the lower

---

[1] In other words: The more *suddenly* we attack the key, the harder, shorter, and less carrying will be the resulting tone; and the more *gradually* we propel the key into full speed, the more "sympathetic"—resonant, rich, full and carrying—will be the tone, and the more controlled will it be.

A really *hit* key cannot for this reason give a beautiful sound; although it may seem to cause much commotion and noise close to the instrument. Refer again to *Note X., Appendix*, "On key-hitting."

of these lines represents the position of the key's surface when fully depressed.

The vertical (dotted) lines in both diagrams are meant to exhibit the *degree* in the key's motion *during descent*, respectively in brilliant and in sympathetic tone-production.

In diagram *A*, we have Energy applied *suddenly*—"avec attaque." Here the dotted lines *c* (supposed to represent the degree of speed) are seen to start at once *some distance* apart, but they remain *only thus far apart* to the end of the key's descent; for the key-descent is so *sudden* that it is practically impossible to attain any *increase* in speed during it.

In diagram *B*, the key has on the contrary been reached practically without percussion, without suddenness,—"sans attaque." The dotted lines *d* therefore here commence together, and they *widen out* to represent the Speed-*crescendo* that can now be induced during descent; for the key is in this case started on its journey almost imperceptibly, but has energy applied to it in *increasing ratio* during its short-lived descent, thus giving that almost unpercussive attack *of the string* whence arises Beauty of tone and control of gradation.[1]

§ 14. We now come to the distinctions between *Tenuto, Legato, and Staccato*.

To induce TENUTO, we must *continue* applying the Weight

---

[1] It seems well-nigh incredible that we should thus be able to GRADE the motion of a key (as demanded for sympathetic tone) during the minute interval of time expended during key-descent. Many of the muscular-acts of our every-day existence are however found to be equally minutely graded, when we analyse them.

It is even possible (although extremely difficult) directly to grade key descent in this requisite manner by an exertion of the Will. This is however happily unnecessary, otherwise our Technique would for ever remain cumbrous and uncertain; for we can, by supplying the requisite MUSCULAR CONDITIONS, encompass this end in quite a simple and reliable way, and it is thus that the effect of sympathetic-tone is wrought in actuality.   By in fact placing the various muscles belonging to the Finger, Hand and Arm in the requisite relationship to each portion of the limb and the key, we are able to apply energy through so elastic a medium, that the desired gradation during key-descent accomplishes itself almost automatically, and with corresponding certainty.

To enable us to provide these requisite muscular-conditions, we must study key-treatment from its *Muscular Aspect*. This aspect of the study of Touch is dealt with in Part III. and the Parts that follow it.

that just proves sufficient to overbalance the key into descent —into its *softest* sound,[1] BEYOND THE MOMENT THAT THAT SOUND BEGINS; for it is obvious, that the amount of weight that proves ample to cause the key's deflection, *must also suffice to retain it depressed* and prevent its rebound, and thus keep its damper raised.

Tenuto thus involves: that a light weight, sufficient to depress the keys, must *continue* resting on them *after* the completion of the act of Tone-production.

§ 15. LEGATO is induced in the same manner; the weight that suffices to depress the key, and which, if continued, therefore suffices to keep it depressed will, *if passed-on (or transferred) from key to key*, create that merging of one sound into the next, termed *Legato*.

This *Transfer* of light weight should be effected at the very moment that the next key's descent is desired to *commence*. The descent of the new key is in this way so timed, as to meet the ascent of the previous key about half-way, or thereabouts; the damper of the ascending key will consequently reach its strings at the very moment that the next sound *begins;* and one sound will thus be caused neatly to merge into the next, without smudge, and without break in continuity.[2]

This light weight, thus resting on the key-beds in Legato, and thus transferred from note to note, is contemporaneously *continuous* with the duration of each musical phrase; it in fact here forms the *Act of Phrasing*.

SUPER-legato, *legatissimo*, is induced by slightly *deferring the transfer* of the light weight thus continuously resting on the key-board during each musical phrase, *beyond the moment* that the next sound commences. The sounds consequently slightly overlap; causing an effect somewhat akin to the *glissando* of Violin playing, and to the *portamento* of Singing.

§ 16. To obtain STACCATO, we must *cease* all weight and

---

[1] *Vide* §§ *8, 9* and *10.*
[2] *Vide* remarks on legato pedalling, etc., *Chapter VIII.*, § *8, page 57.*

force at the very moment that sound-excitation is completed, excepting that slight amount of weight that the key can bear at its *surface*-level—the amount the key can bear *without* deflection.

If we succeed in doing this, the key will be free to rebound, and will do so instantaneously—even carrying up with it, the super-imposed finger.[1]

The following experiment should here be made. *(Vide Fig. 5.)*

Take a large lead pencil, the larger the better, and preferably armed with a rubber-end. Hold this vertically between the thumb and index finger, letting its end rest on a key in the centre of the key-board.

Now sharply depress the key by means of the pencil; *but cease* the grip on the pencil *accurately* at the moment that sound begins.

If the down-impetus is ceased accurately enough—instantaneously that sound arises, then the key, in recoiling, will drive the pencil up, the latter slipping through the fingers;—the result being an absolute staccato.

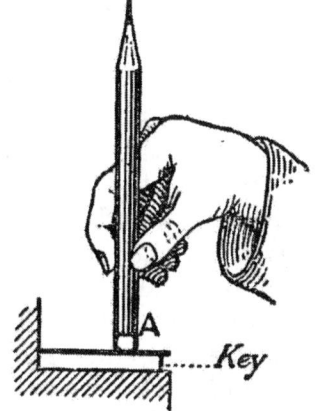

FIG. 5.—A, a pencil, or other smooth object.

§ 17. No greater Weight or Force than just suffices to prevent such rebound of the key in Tenuto and Legato, should therefore ever be allowed to rest on the key-*bed*. In fact it is unnecessary that more force than this, should ever even *reach* the key-bed; except in a comparatively rare effect, a forced variety of Staccato, in which the rebound of the key and finger is assisted by delivering a blow to the key-bed, analogous to a jump or "kick-off."[2]

§ 18. *To sum up this Chapter:*

We find that the Key is a Speed-tool; and that the laws

---

[1] The act of Resting on the keys, in its two forms—the one so light as to have no effect upon the keys, as in Staccato, and the other slightly heavier, so as to compel their continued depression, as in Tenuto or Legato—will be found more fully considered in Part III., for such Resting forms one of the chief concepts of correct Touch.

[2] There is also a certain form of cumbrous *cantabile*, in which slightly more weight may reach the key-beds than is necessary to ensure legato or legatissimo.

that govern the use of other speed-tools must therefore equally apply in the case of the Pianoforte key.

We should always bear in mind, as previously suggested, that this Tool is akin to the *See-Saw* in principle.[1]

This will prevent our being tempted either to *squeeze* it upon the pads beneath, or to *punch* its surface viciously, in our efforts to make Tone by its means.

We shall then, on the contrary, take hold of it—*upon* it, and realising its resistance, feel it to be so intimately in connection with our finger-tip, as to seem literally a *continuation* of it.

Projecting our minds meanwhile to the opposite end of this tool—the hammer-end, we shall bring Force in the shape of Weight and Muscular-exertion to bear upon its *handle*—its ivory or ebony end.

We shall so TIME the application of this force, both as regards Amount and Gradation, that we shall ensure that the desired speed of the Key—and String—is reached before our end of the tool is brought into contact with its underlying pad, and we shall thus have succeeded in obtaining the exact tone-shading which our musical conscience prompted us to desire.

---

[1] It is well to keep this simile in mind, since it is so manifestly futile to continue pressing down one end of a See-Saw, after this has reached the ground, if our purpose be to induce movement at its other end. (*Vide also* § *3, Chapter VIII., page 54.*)

RECAPITULATORY AND SUMMARY

OF THE MAIN CONCLUSIONS OF

PART II

a): The Pianoforte Key is a machine to facilitate the production of Speed in the String. It is a compound-lever, akin in principle to the See-saw.

b): It follows, that Tone-production can only be effected by giving Motion to the Key; since this forms our only means of conveying motion to the String.

c): Energy brought to bear upon the Key *ceases* to create Tone, the moment that the place in key-descent is reached, where the hammer's motion culminates, and causes Sound to *begin*.

d): The act itself of Tone-production can hence never take longer than it does in the most extreme *Staccatissimo*.

e): The Ear apprises us of this moment more quickly than can any other of our senses; hence we must *listen* for the beginning of sound, if we would have Accuracy in tone-production.

f): The greater the total speed we induce during each individual key-descent, the greater is the Tone-*quantity*.

g): The more *gradually* this key-speed is attained, the more beautiful is the Tone-*character*,—the fuller, more "sympathetic," singing and carrying is its *quality*, and the finer the control.

h): The more *sudden* the key-depression, the harsher is the resulting Tone-quality; it may be more "brilliant," but it will be less effective in carrying power.

i): The *softest* possible sound is obtained, when *Weight* is brought upon the key until a point is reached where the key's opposition (or resistance) to movement is just overcome—and it consequently slips down with the most gentle movement compatible with its hammer reaching the string.

j): Such amount of Weight, allowed to remain resting upon

the key, *beyond* the moment that the latter's full depression is reached, forms the effect of TENUTO. The duration of such Tenuto is determined by the duration of such Resting.

k): The effect of LEGATO is induced by *transferring* such continuously resting light Weight from key to key; such Transference being unbroken for each Musical Phrase.

l): Weight of less amount than this, *insufficient* therefore to cause key-depression, may be left resting on the keys without causing either Tenuto or Legato.

It is such *lightness* in resting, that forms the Basis of all STACCATO effects, provided it is combined with an accurately-aimed Promptness in the *cessation* of the Energy that causes key-*descent*; for the keys are in this case left free to *rebound* the moment that Tone-production is completed.

m): Such combination (of light Resting and accurate Ceasing of the act of key-depression) also forms the secret of all great Agility in playing.

n): It is futile to *squeeze* the key upon its bed with the object of inducing Tone; since sound, if produced at all, is given off *before* the key reaches its full depression.

o): It is almost as futile to attempt to obtain good tone by *knocking* the key; since the concussion here caused at the key-surface forms *waste* of the Energy intended to create tone, and thus engenders *inaccuracy* in the tonal-result,—the actual tone obtained not corresponding to the tone intended.

p): We find (also vide Part III) that instead of squeezing the key-bed, or hitting the key-top, that correct Tone-production demands:—that the finger be brought comparatively gently into contact with the key-board surface, so that the Energy requisite to move the key may be there estimated by our *sense of key-resistance*. As the key-resistance varies with each change in Tone-shading, this will lead to the requisite *muscular-conditions* being almost automatically prompted into existence,—in accurate response therefore to the dictates of our musical-consciousness as to Time, Tone-amount, Tone-quality, and Duration.

APPENDIX TO PART II.

"ON CHOICE OF INSTRUMENT"

NOTE VII.—For § 12, Chapter VIII., page 60. The main points that should be tested by the student, and artist, when choosing an instrument, are as follows:

1: Extent of the Tone-compass. This should form the most important element determining choice; for the larger the possible range and *variety* of tone, the more will "colouring" be stimulated.

2: Delicacy of the action. Responsiveness of the instrument's "touch." The key should slip down "clean"—with the least possible amount of friction. This does not imply that the key may not be considerably weighted. Friction is impedimental, but *weight* is not. A certain amount of weight is indeed desirable, as this permits the "Resting" at surface-level of the key to be more robust; thus not only enhancing one's sense of security, but also tempting one toward correct key-treatment, since key-tapping is more easily discerned to be futile in the case of the more heavily-weighted key.

Heaviness of this kind must, moreover, not be confused with "stickiness" during descent—stickiness is a sure sign of a badly constructed mechanism, or of one in bad condition.

A sufficiently weighted key is also quite a distinct thing from a heavily-felted, or deeply "toned" hammer—a hammer softened by pricking. Difficulty of enunciation is caused in the latter case, and the term "heaviness of touch" is here often misapplied. *Vide* § 5.

3: Sustaining-power, or as it would be better termed, *continuation*-power of the sounds, especially at and just above the centre of the instrument.

There are moreover two different points to be noticed in conjunction with this: (a) Sustaining-power in respect to the degree of sound continuing during a long note, and (b), sustaining-power in the very percussion itself of the sound—*i.e.*, a certain "thickness" as against "shortness" in that initiatory percussion of each sound, a percussion inseparable from our instrument—excepting when it is almost eradicated under the finger of an expert "sympathetic" player.

4: Accuracy in the Damping. In this respect there must be absolute promptness and completeness. The sound must cease instantly the dampers reach the strings. Any continued "buzzing" makes for bad training, both in Staccato and in Legato, and also in Pedalling.

5: Hardness of hammer. For the platform, and for the student's practice-room, a considerably "hard" hammer is found helpful; the hammer should at all events not be over-felted or over-"toned." In the Concert-room, it undoubtedly helps the artist, for he can hear what he is doing; in the Study, the harder hammer is more likely to lead to the acquisition of true *pp* (and all other forms of correct and sympathetic touch) than is the soft hammer.

The soft hammer is apt to hide faults in key-attack to a considerable extent, wherefore it is exceedingly beloved by amateurs of the insincere type. The harder hammer, on the other hand, gives far more pointed warning to the ear, of the commencement of each sound; and how important this is, we shall understand better presently. Enough, that those who have acquired correct forms of key-treatment, need no blanket of felt to hide their wrong-doing.[1]

It is of course possible to have hammers too hard, for it is true that an instrument with a really large tone, requires a considerable thickness of hammer-felting to allow its tone to be displayed to best advantage.

6 : **The pads under the keys** should preferably be of the harder type. The harder key-bed, through its sharper resistance, gives better warning than does the softer key-bed, of the moment when the tone-producing stresses have completed their duties; the harder pad thus helps to warn us not to carry these stresses beyond their proper place in key-descent. An ideally perfect executant would indeed be he, who could be so accurately led by his Ear, as to be able entirely to avoid playing against the key-bed in almost all forms of tone-production; he would be so perfect, that he could play without damage on an instrument altogether unprovided with pads under the keys! An ideal perfection of technique neither reached within measurable distance so far, nor ever likely to be reached!

7 : **Depth of touch.** A deep touch is preferable to a shallow one. It renders command over the finer tone-shadings more easy. An instrument that gives its tone out sharply, is for this reason usually provided with more depth in key-descent (to render *pp* easier) than is an instrument that has a more gradual sound-*projection ;* both in the case where this slowness in sound-emission is caused by mere relative softness or " toning " of the hammers, and in the case where it is caused by the peculiarity of the sounding-board, as it is in some good Pianos :

8 : **Some instruments are far more slow of speech than others.** It takes longer for each note sounded to develop its full tone.

It should be noted that this difference is quite distinct from that comparative difficulty or ease of enunciation arising from the relative hardness or softness of hammer-covering. *Vide* § 5. It is a difference to be attributed to divergence in the construction of the sounding-board itself. It seems, that the sounding-board that gives out its full sound more gradually for each note, although far more trying to play upon than the one that sharply defines the beginning of each note, is nevertheless found to "carry" far better and to sound fuller in a large concert-room. On this point we must individually suit ourselves, bearing in mind, that the happy medium is the best in such cases.

9 : **The " repetition " power** should be tested, as suggested in *Note* to § 4, Chapter VIII., page 55.

A bad " repetition " does on the whole no harm in the study, since it merely forces one to allow the keys to rise well for each note in passages of repeated notes. A good repetition is however essential for the concert-room. The closer down the repetition is available the better. It not only renders the repetition of notes more certain of attainment, but also allows of certain extremely rapid *pp* shakes, etc., that are quite impossible on an instrument that demands a nearly fully raised key for each repetition of a note.

---

[1] There is an authentic case of one artist of considerable renown, who plays on an instrument usually provided with rather over-felted hammers, and who, careful and " knowing " man that he is, insists on having the hammers of his Concert-grand *pared down* under his own direction before appearing at important engagements !—a practice of proved advantage both to himself and to the particular instrument he uses.

"TONE-EXCITERS"

NOTE VIII.—For § 5, Chapter IX., page 66. There are innumerable means of producing the required concussions or disturbances in the atmosphere, that allow our ear to perceive a musical-note.

A ratchet-wheel, or even the edge of a coin will suffice, when rubbed against a metal or paper card; for the card will "beat" the air, in successively slipping off the teeth of the wheel or coin. The "reed" of a Clarionet, Organ-pipe, etc., is a closely-related form of exciter. Such "reed" consists of a slight tongue of metal or wood. It is fixed at one end, and free at the other; and it is accurately fitted into a little doorway, or aperture, opening from a wind-chamber. The reed is thus free to vibrate while nearly closing the wind-chamber behind it. The consequence is, that the free end of the reed is displaced when sufficient air-pressure is brought to bear behind it. The air, in escaping, momentarily reduces this wind-pressure, and the reed then falls back owing to its elasticity and recloses the door-way; the rapid reaction of these forces thus gives us the requisite air-concussions. In the Whistle, Flute, or "Flue" organ-pipe, such "reed" takes the form of a *sheet of air*. This thin sheet of air is driven against a sharp metal or wooden edge, and as this air-sheet cannot as it were *stand* against this edge, it fluctuates from side to side, thus beating the air exactly in the same manner as its wooden or metal relative.

The String beats the air much in the same way as a "reed" does; but its action is adequately considered in Chapter X.—"The String."

"ON QUALITY OF SOUND"

NOTE IX.—For § 11, *Note* 3, Chapter IX., page 76. THE EXPLANATION of the process by which the Hammer is able to *transmit* those known differences in Key-treatment to the String, that cause the latter to emit either a purer or an impurer sound, has not yet been finally determined.

We do know *what is the nature of the difference in Key-treatment* that gives us the contrasts in Tone-quality. We also know what is the result upon the String,—for we know that it vibrates more as a whole, when emitting the purer (or more sympathetic) qualities of sound; while it vibrates more in individual segments of its whole length, when emitting the more impure (or harsher) qualities of sound. We know, moreover, that it is started off more abruptly by the hammer when producing the harsher sounds, than it is when producing the more sympathetic sounds; and we know that in the latter case the hammer "lies longer" on the string. Again, we know, what is the physical difference in the resulting sound-waves,—for analysis proves that the harsher the sound-quality the more is the fundamental found to be prominently accompanied by a greater number of the higher and harsher upper-partials. But we do not know HOW these differences in key-treatment during descent are actually *transmitted* to the string by the felt-covered end of the hammer; at this point experimental science at present still fails us,—although it is quite certain that such transmission does take place, since each difference in key-treatment infallibly induces its particular concomitant difference in sound-shading.

Several hypotheses are here available:

1: The most plausible one, is, that the hammer does remain in communication with our end of the key—and our finger-tip—up to the moment that the string is fully deflected. If this is the true solution, then it is easy to conceive how the *gradually increased speed in key-descent* (derived from elastic conditions of the arm and finger) that gives a singing, sympathetic or pure tone, causes the hammer to "lie longer" on the string, than it does under the impulse of a *suddenly depressed* key. The gradually increasing speed of the player's finger-tip would here obviously "shove" instead of jerk the string into movement. This hypothesis, however, meets with the following objections :

The escapement (*vide* Fig. 1, Chap. VIII., page 62) is so adjusted, that the hopper is tilted from underneath the hammer when the latter is still about one-sixteenth of an inch distant from the string. The hammer would thus appear to lose connection with the finger-tip before the string is even reached ! This certainly does happen *when the key is so slowly depressed as to cause no sound;* for the hammer can then be seen to fall back, without reaching the string at all.

It has, however, not been finally decided by experiment, how the escapement really does act *during the process of successful tone-production;* and the surmise is therefore permissible, that the hopper does *not* thus act—does not act so soon—when the key is depressed with sufficient momentum to cause even the faintest sound,—a considerable degree of momentum being required to overcome the friction of the action, and thus to allow the hammer to reach its string, even for the softest sound,—a degree of energy ascertained by the resistance the key (and action) offers to a "clean" weighed-down descent.[1]

Is it not possible, that the gradual application of energy to the key during correct touch may here cause the escapement to fail in its action until a later moment ?—until in fact it is helped by the extra impetus derived from the string itself, when the latter returns after its first outward swing ?—a later action of the hopper that may arise possibly owing to a greater frictional-contact being set up between hammer and hopper during *correct*-touch, than is set up during a slow, non-sounding key-depression ? That the hammer does *not* fly off the hopper during the last part of its journey to the string in *sympathetic* touch, but instead appears to remain in connection with the rest of the key, up to the last moment of the act of tone-production—up to the moment that the string itself is able by its recoil to *assist* the hopper—is a conclusion that seems forcibly pointed to, when we experiment with a note that "blocks ;" *i.e.*, when we experiment with a key that has its escapement so mal-adjusted as entirely to prevent the hammer from slipping off the hopper. That is : if we adjust the hopper-nut (q., Diagram Fig. 1) in such a way that the hopper is *not* tilted early enough, then the hammer will be unable to slip off the hopper, and the hammer will in consequence remain a rigid part-and-parcel of the key, even when it reaches the string. The hammer will consequently be forcibly jammed against the string and will remain against it, if the finger-tip fully depresses the key, thus quite killing the sound in its very birth.

Now, it is most noteworthy, that we can nevertheless produce quite a beautiful tone, even with the escapement thus mal-adjusted, provided we are now *more careful in "aiming"* the Key-descent—provided we are careful enough not to drive the key *too far down*. That is : we shall find, if we are careful to apply the desired degree of energy so that this shall culminate and cease at a point *not quite so far down in key-descent as usual*, that the string then seems able to drive the hammer back with it ; and that a perfectly sym-

---

[1] The *unclean* sensation of the escapement giving way with great friction results from a *false* touch,—where the key is "put down" instead of weighed down. In this latter case one is never *sure* of one's *pianissimo*. This "sticky" sensation vanishes, the moment we employ correct touch ; and *pianissimo* is then indeed at once the simplest and surest touch of all.

pathetic tone is then in consequence easily attainable, even under these adverse conditions of the instrument!

Moreover, we find, on making the opposite mal-adjustment,—so that the hopper is tilted from underneath the hammer-button much too soon, long before the key has reached its full depression,—that the production of resonant "sympathetic" tone, then becomes a practical impossibility.

In fact, if only the adjustment is bad enough, or if the hopper-spring has become displaced, then it become impossible to obtain any tone whatever!

It is certainly conceivable, that the greater the momentum of the hammer, when it finally reaches the string, the *longer* will it then "*remain lying*" upon the latter,—the more will the string-surface be driven into it,—the flatter will the hammer in consequence become,—and the "less acute" will then be the angle subtended by the string in its initial push-off;—thus bringing the process into accord with HELMHOLTZ's teaching, as to the difference in attack that causes the string to move off in comparatively *pure* (fundamental) sound rather than in harmonics of the harsher kind.

The consideration of this point may be helped, by reflecting on the different result that arises from the impact of two bodies on the same surface, one of which is a heavy ball, and the other a light one. The difference in *momentum* will be great, although both balls may reach the surface with identical speed. If we then imagine such surface to be represented by a tense string, we can easily conceive how Helmholtz's "elastic" and therefore "longer-lying" hammer will result when there is much weight behind it—*i.e.*, the weight of the player's arm; whereas a hammer with less weight behind it would fly back too early,—before having had time to impart that full swing to the string that makes for beauty of tone.

Another suggestive fact in this connection, is, that an elastic substance *flattens* upon impact. GANOT[1] says, that if a billiard ball were to strike an inked ground, it would be found to exhibit a greater circle of ink at the place of impact, the more forcible the impact;—*i.e.*: that the more forcible the impact, the more would the ball be momentarily flattened,—a fact that vividly suggests what it is that may happen to the properly-used Piano-hammer,—a flattening that may be absent when the hammer reaches the string with but little momentum or added weight.

2: The opposite theory may also be tenable: viz., that a too sudden propulsion of the key may cause the escapement to act instantly;—too soon therefore to allow of sufficient momentum being attained by the hammer. For it is possible that the little spring that keeps the hopper under the hammer-roller (*vide* Fig. 1) may prove insufficiently strong to do its duty (to retain the hammer on the hopper) in the case of a too sudden key-attack, and that the hammer will therefore here instantly slip off the hopper; with the consequence, that we shall fail to influence the hammer sufficiently, and that our energy will be greatly wasted.

3: One of the reasons why a too sudden attack of the key, in the shape of a *real hitting* or striking of it, causes a thin quality of tone, is, because the hammer then evidently *instantly flies off the hopper*.

This here again deprives us of all opportunity of "following-up" the hammer, or of inducing much momentum in it; for the hammer here quits the action (bounds off from its support) before the key can well be got under way.

That the hammer does thus bound off the hopper, making a bad tone, the reader should prove for himself, by the following experiment:—

Place some incompressible object, such as a piece of wood, under the

---

[1] "Physics" translated by E. Atkinson.

edge of one of the damper-less keys.[1] This wooden stop should be so arranged as to prevent the key being depressed beyond a very small extent,—a 16th or 32nd of an inch is ample. We now have a key in which the action *cannot carry the hammer far upwards toward the string.* On now *hitting* the key, it will be found that the hammer nevertheless reaches the string. The concussion at the key-surface is thus proved to cause the hammer instantly to fly off the hopper; while the resulting tone-quality is distinctly of that well-known, thin, nasal, hard and unsympathetic type, apparently so gratifying to key-"striking" fanatics.

4: Another alternative hypothesis, once suggested to me by an amateur, a mining engineer, is, that the hammer-shank itself may momentarily *bend* under the strain, when too suddenly called upon to move the comparatively heavy hammer-head, and that the hammer may then reach the string at a wrong angle. This suggestion does not however appear to have much to recommend it.

5: The exceedingly harsh effect produced by forcibly "over-driving" the keys, most probably arises owing to the whole action itself bodily rising by recoil from the wrest-plank,—*e.*, Fig. 1. There seems nothing to prevent its doing so, and all the delicate adjustments of the key would in that case be momentarily rendered of no avail; the direct and inelastic transmission of such "brute force" may even lead to the breakage of hammer-shanks and strings.

MANY FACTS may in the end be found to contribute to the ultimate explanation here still needed. Perhaps some of the above speculations—they are put forward merely as such—may contribute to this desideratum.

Meanwhile, whatever may prove to be the ultimate explanation, nothing can alter the proven facts as to *what we have to do at our end* of the key.

These latter are the facts we are more immediately concerned with in this work, and these latter facts we must thoroughly realise, if we would expeditiously learn to play and teach in the easiest and surest manner.

"THE FALLACY OF KEY-HITTING OR STRIKING"

NOTE X.—For notes to §§ 10 and 11, Chapter XI., pages 81-82. As this iniquitous doctrine is still rampant all over the Globe, it behoves us well to consider the many facts and arguments that prove its utter falsity.

No doubt it was the influence of a certain German CONSERVATORIUM that gave it such wide currency. It was there adopted now some decades ago, and soon became disseminated in all directions—with the rapidity of a disease-microbe; teachers and institutions all over the Globe accepting it apparently without reflection, as if it were "Gospel-Truth!"

A vast number of persons no doubt imagine that they attack the key by means of a blow, when they really do nothing of the kind.[2] Again, there are many, who, being conscientious devotees at this false shrine, try hard to obey its doctrines, and who, while really somewhat percussing the key-surface, do nevertheless produce some good tone—occasionally; a success due to the fact, that their ear has led them unconsciously to "follow-up" such blow (although

---

[1] It is necessary to use one of the keys without dampers, as the experiment would otherwise be vitiated, owing to the damper failing to rise in time.

[2] There are also many who use the misleading expression "to strike the key," merely from want of a better term, never intending to convey the idea of a real stroke at all.

faulty in itself) by a *proper use* of the key during its subsequent descent. The latter class more particularly—being wrong-doers more in theory than in actual practice—will find it difficult to realise how thoroughly useless and impedimental real key-percussion must be. Having once formed a conception of a muscular-act, it is always difficult to rearrange such conception, and to see the thing in a new light. It is peculiarly difficult in the present case, since well-raised fingers, hands and arms, do really prove helpful—when the Tempo is slow enough to admit of such preliminary movements without impeding the speed,[1]—and since such commendable preliminary ample raising of the limb, and subsequent comparatively quick descent to the key-surface, is also so easily mistaken by the eye for a real hitting.

The deplorably evil effects of deliberately teaching key-hitting have proved incredibly far-reaching and disastrous to the progress of our art. The mechanically-wrong principle it involves, not only leads with absolute certainty toward paucity of tone, and evil-sounding tone ; but it also renders all subtlety, accuracy and certainty of EXPRESSION a physical impossibility. Worse than this even, for it leads as a corollary to a stiffening of the limbs employed,—a restrained use of the muscles, the dangers of which will be better understood after consideration of Part III. This "held" condition of the arm, etc., gives rise to all kinds of physiological trouble—such as Piano-cramp, inflammation of the tendons—so often wrongly ascribed to "weak hands." Moreover, it is not alone from this involved stiff-held condition of the limbs that such trouble arises : for it arises also directly from the severe *concussions* against the key-surface that are inseparable from the attempt to hit the key into sound. Such concussions indeed tend to form practically so many incipient *sprains* of the finger, hand ("wrist") and arm-muscles !

But the power of fetish-worship is such—even in this twentieth century—that all powers of reasoning, perception and common-sense seem to desert the sufferer, once he comes under a spell such as this ! Cases have come under my own observation, where teachers (otherwise apparently quite intelligent) were thus afflicted to such a state of imperviousness to outside impressions, as to completely close their ears, eyes, and musical-feeling to the experience of their every-day teaching-lives ;—although these latter experiences formed heaven-shrieking testimony to the fallacy of the premises upon which their "method" had been built ![2] For instance, there have been cases, when such teachers have received as new pupils, such who already possessed considerable fluency in the production of beautiful tone in great variety, and Agility also. Yet these pupils, incredible as it may seem, were deliberately made to *unlearn* their really correct and facile forms of production, so that their doings might be made forsooth to LOOK LIKE Piano-playing in conformity with this orthodox fetish-worship ! The natural result being, that these pupils played worse at each lesson ! Such result might, one would think, have caused a suspicion to enter the teachers' minds that the "system" might after all be at fault ?—Not so, the want of subsequent success, and eventual supervention of inflamed tendons, was here instead complacently attributed to "want of soul," "want of muscle," and "weak wrists," on the part of the unfortunate pupils !

Let us then sum up the main facts against key-striking, and the disadvantages that directly arise therefrom.

---

[1] Owing to the fact, that ample movement before key-contact, does tend to ensure greater *freedom* of movement when the key is actually reached and is being depressed.

[2] In a word, instead of employing the aural faculty in the Class-room and Concert-room,—instead of employing the most natural, direct and important channel for information,—such teachers appear carefully to shun all ear-impressions ; and endeavour to teach rather by eye than by ear. To such it would appear to signify more, how the thing looks, than how it sounds !

H

APPENDIX TO PART II.

To attempt to make sound by really hitting at the key-surface causes:—

I: LOSS OF ENERGY, with its consequences, paucity of tone, and limitation of contrast-power in this direction.

II: IMPOSSIBILITY OF PRODUCING A MUSICAL OR SUBTLE QUALITY OF TONE; and again, loss of contrast-power in this direction.

III: REDUCTION OF ACTUAL TONE-RESULT TO MERE CHANCE, with its corollary: loss of Expression-power—from the resulting tones not being those intended.

IV: Liability to PHYSICAL-DISABLEMENT, in the shape of inflamed tendons, and worse.

The following are the chief reasons why these disadvantages accrue from key-hitting:

a): *It is mechanically thoroughly wrong and ineffective;* since the key is but a tool, intervening between finger-tip and string, for the purpose of setting the *latter* into motion. To knock the key-lever, forms as absurdly great a misapplication in the use of this tool, and forms as wasteful and disadvantageous an application of muscular-energy, as would be the case, were we to hit the handle of a tennis-racket, hammer, oar, or cue, or to stamp upon a cycle-pedal, instead of using those tools properly.

b): *We cannot estimate* the weight of the tool itself, nor the amount of energy required to move it at any particular grade of speed, or increase of speed during its movement, if we hit the end of the lever we are using,—whether this be that of the Piano-key, or any other of the just-mentioned tools; and it follows that we cannot direct such tool with any accuracy, and that we cannot therefore obtain any intended subtle result.

c): *Loss of energy*, and consequent paucity of tone, and inaccuracy in expression result from the *concussions arising* at *the key-surface.* Such concussions swallow up Energy intended to produce tone;—molecular-vibrations of the key-surface and finger-surface taking the place of the desired movement of the key itself.

d): *We are debarred from gradually obtaining momentum* in the whole mass of the key-lever and hammer; since the hammer instantly quits its seat on the hopper, when the key is really struck,—with the consequence, that sympathetic (or beautiful) quality of tone is impossible of attainment.

e): *A tendency towards percussion at the string-surface* supervenes, in place of the intended movement of the whole body of the string; which again implies loss of power, and loss of tone-beauty.

f): *Unreliability in the case of rapid reiterations* of the same note. This is due to the fact that the key will "wobble" if the finger-tip rapidly quits its surface. As the key in question may not have fully come to rest before its depression is again required, this induces uncertainty in enunciation, often amounting even to non-repetition of the note.

g): *Impossibility of availing ourselves of the repetition-device:*
We can only make use of this refinement of touch,—which gives us the option of very rapidly reiterating a note at its softest, the so-called "Bebung,"—provided we retain the finger-tip on the key in question, and keep the latter depressed almost (though not quite) to its fullest extent.

h): *Unnecessary muscular fatigue;* due to the improper application of energy as before-described.

i): *Risk of overworking the muscles*, and inflaming the tendons;—owing to the incessant jarring, arising from the blows against the key-surface.

j): *Finally*, it debars us from truly *using*, directing or "aiming" the key into sound. For if we hit at the key, we are compelled to think of the surface-concussion as the thing aimed at; whereas, as the sound does not appear until the key is almost fully depressed, it is to that point—the sound-beginning—that our muscular-effort should be directed. The result being again, loss of power and beauty of tone, and besides that, inaccuracy and haziness in RHYTHM.

It is however difficult to decide whether such "Key-striking" is the most fell disease, or whether there is not a worse one still—in the shape of KEY-BED SQUEEZING!

PART III.

KEY-TREATMENT FROM ITS MUSCULAR ASPECT.

CHAPTER XII.

PREAMBLE:

SYNOPSIS OF THE MAIN MUSCULAR FACTS.

§ 1. THE "muscular aspect of Key-treatment" at once brings us face to face with the most important problems dealt with in this work, and concerning which there exists generally the darkest ignorance and the most vicious teaching.

This is mainly owing to the fact, that the necessary CONDITIONS of muscular activity and in-activity (which form our only means of influencing the Key) do not by any means correspond to the visible movements that accompany such conditions; and that these required actions and cessations are therefore not discoverable through the eye; indeed, the eye in this case often proves quite misleading.

These required conditions will often, however, be unconsciously provided by the muscularly gifted, if they have grasped the facts dealt with in the last Part; that is, if they have either consciously or unconsciously realised the Requirements of the Key.

The study of Part III. should therefore not be pursued until the fundamental facts of Part II. have first been thoroughly mastered.

As there are many who have not yet arrived within measurable distance of many of the unfamiliar truths and theories here advanced, much reiteration is found desirable, in order to bring the various arguments into juxtaposition. The few who do not need such incessant repetition, must therefore here (as elsewhere) bear with the author, for the sake of the less-advanced student and beginner.

For the same reason it is considered desirable to particularise somewhat more fully even in this Preamble. Such being the case, it will be well for the student constantly to refer to this comparatively broad outline of the muscular aspect of our subject, when studying the subsequent chapters of this Part.

§ 2. Coming now at once to the consideration of the muscular means at our disposal for key-depression, we find that there are available THREE sharply defined MUSCULAR COMPONENTS or agents:

The *First* of these components is a down-activity (or exertion) of the Finger; this exertion sets energy free at the finger-tip against the key, but this same exertion also *bears* UPWARDS *against the knuckle of the hand* by recoil, with an equal degree of energy.[1]

The *Second* of the components referred to, is an activity (or exertion) of the Hand; this acts downwards upon the knuckle, and consequently by recoil, also acts *upwards*—in this instance against the Arm at the Wrist-joint.

The *Third* component involved, is Arm-weight; this is set free by *ceasing* the activity of the muscles that otherwise support the arm; and the weight of the arm is consequently left free to be borne by the hand at the Wrist-joint.[2]

All Touch is built up from these three muscular-compo-

---

[1] This fact should at once be thoroughly recognised and mastered,—that we cannot exert muscular-force in any direction with full effect, unless we provide a *basis*, firm enough to take without flinching the recoil that supervenes with equal force in the opposite direction.

[2] This manifestation of Weight may (when necessary for extremely loud effects) be supplemented by a very slight down-activity of the arm itself, thus ultimately bringing into requisition the weight of the Shoulder, and even that of the Body. The Body itself must, however, never be exerted against the keys, it must always be allowed to remain a purely inert mass of reserve Weight.

nents; for it is from their combination in an infinite variety of ways (presently to be described)[1] that the short-lived Muscular-Conditions that are the means of consummating each individual act of key-depression, or Tone-production arise.

§ 3. These three components of Touch, should moreover be recognised as dividing respectively into a DOWNWARD and an UPWARD manifestation of Energy. These two apparently antagonistic manifestations of Energy can be summed up as "Weight" and "Muscular-exertion," and these two elements *meet at the Wrist-joint;*—where they may balance, without evincing any movement.[2]

§ 4. As all muscular-exertion at the Pianoforte is thus shown to act by recoil *upwards* against the Wrist (and in extreme cases upwards against the shoulder) and as it is only *exertion* that can give us a positive muscular-sensation, it follows, that the SENSATION accompanying all correct Touch, must always convey the impression *of work done* UPWARDS,—and not downwards, as one might at first sight be inclined to suppose.

Touch, in a word, resolves itself ultimately into an act of *levering* more or less weight upon the key during descent.

§ 5. Every muscular exertion employed in playing, must moreover be given with perfect freedom, or absence of restraint. That is, there must be no *contrary* exertion of the same part of the limb. However strongly we may wish to urge any particular set of muscles into activity, we must under no circumstances permit this exertion sympathetically to prompt the *opposite* set of muscles into action. If we do, it will infallibly prevent our attaining any accuracy, either in tone-amount, kind or quality; and it will consequently destroy all accuracy and subtlety in Expression; it will besides prevent our attaining any true Agility.

[1] *Vide* §§ 8, 9, and 10, and *Chapters XVI., XVII. and XIX.*, etc.
[2] EXERTION (derived from Finger and Hand activities applied against the key) causes an *upward* tendency, felt at the Wrist-joint, although it does not necessarily occasion any movement there.
WEIGHT (derived from *Lapse* in muscular-activity, lapse on the part of the arm-supporting muscles) on the contrary causes a *downward* tendency at the Wrist-joint; but not necessarily exhibited as an actual movement (or fall) of the arm.

KEY-TREATMENT; MUSCULAR ASPECT.

§ 6. It has been pointed out that no movement need necessarily arise from the combination of the two different manifestations of Force described.[1] A movement of some portion of the super-imposed limb is however bound to ensue, *the moment the key gives way* under the energy thus brought to bear upon its surface. This movement may take the form either of Finger-movement, Hand-movement, or Arm-movement;—these we term respectively Finger-touch, Hand-touch (so-called "Wrist-action") and Arm-touch. Which of these three movements shall ensue, is purely determined by the RELATIVE balance existing *during the moment of key-attack* between the three Muscular-components previously described, and whence all Touch is derived.

ARM-TOUCH (*i.e.*, Touch, accompanied by arm-movement) results, when the lapse in arm-support sets free more energy than can be fully supported by the degree of finger and hand activity employed at the moment against the key. Arm, hand, and finger will in this instance simultaneously descend with the key.

HAND-TOUCH (so-called Wrist-touch) results, in the same way, when the total conditions of arm, hand, and finger, show a slight excess on the part of the hand-activity, which latter then prevents the Arm and Finger from showing any movement.

FINGER-TOUCH results, when it is the finger-activity that slightly outbalances the other two elements; *i.e.*, when the finger-activity is slightly greater than the activity put forward by the hand, and is also in excess of any weight set free by lapse on the part of the arm-supporting muscles.[2]

§ 7. Variety in the QUANTITY of tone—the distinction between *forte* and *piano*—depends on the fact that we can em-

---

[1] *i.e.*: Force derived from the *Activities* that bear *upwards* by recoil against the Wrist, and the Arm-*Inactivities* that produce a *down*-stress there.

[2] It is of course understood, that those portions of the limb *not showing any movement* must not come into operation *until the key-surface is reached*. That is: In Arm-touch there is only Arm-lapse, *until* the key is reached, when the other two components begin to act. In Hand-touch, Arm and Finger do not change their *condition* until the key is reached. And in Finger-touch we have only finger-*action* until the key is reached.

ploy the three Muscular-components *either to their full power, or not*, as we wish; this being optional equally in the case of Finger, Hand or Arm movements.

To sum this up: the *amount* of tone depends on the *degree* of energy with which we employ the three components of muscular-condition during key-descent; while the actual *movement* shown (whether that of the Finger, Hand or Arm) depends on the *relative balance* existing between these three at that crucial moment.

§ 8. Variety in Technique—Technique adapted for all the multifarious requirements of an artistic performance, Technique suitable respectively for slow and heavy passages, or for passages of extreme Agility and lightness, and for that great family of contrasts that comes under the heading of *Tone-Quality*, all this variety depends on the option we should possess of COMBINING the aforesaid three muscular components of Touch in divers ways; of which combinations *three* stand out so saliently as to deserve the title of *Species*.

Distinctions merely in Movement (such as Finger, Hand or Arm touch) sink into insignificance beside the radical and cardinal distinctions in Technique that arise from these just-mentioned differences in Muscular Application.

AGILITY itself, for instance, depends on the fact, that we *need* not employ all three Muscular-components simultaneously. Instead of combining all three against the key (during descent) we may employ the Finger and Hand activities alone without calling Arm-weight to our aid; or we may even employ the Finger-activity alone, without using either hand-activity or arm-weight.[1] It is this last-mentioned form of Technique that gives us the fullest measure of extreme Agility.[2]

---

[1] N.B.:—We must always keep clear in our minds the distinction between the *Activity* of a limb, and its Motion,—since Activity (or Exertion) does not by any means necessarily imply a *movement* of that portion.

[2] We find indeed that the possibility of our attaining a high degree of Agility, directly depends (as does the attainment of Quantity and Beauty of tone) on our implicit obedience to (and discrimination between) the particular laws of muscular combination and co-ordination here described. This discrimination and obedience we may attain either unconsciously (by the haphazard process), or by a conscious exertion of the will, when we know what it is that has to be muscularly learnt.

§ 9. So that we may at once better understand the nature of these three main principles (or Species) of Muscular-Combination, or *Touch-formation*, let us particularise a little further :—

First Form (or Species) *of Combination :* The Arm gently supported by its own muscles, floats over the key-board; while the Hand, inactive, merely lies lightly on the keys at surface level. Work of key-depression is consequently here entirely relegated to the Finger, without aid either from Hand or Arm. Tone, limited to the "brilliant" type, can also be but small in quantity;[1] while Finger-movement is alone available. Permits, on the other hand, the attainment of the extremest grades of Agility or Velocity conceivable—provided we strictly adhere to the law of accurate *cessation* of work at the moment of sound-emission (§ 13) and provided we do really enact this first form of muscular combination,—finger-use only, combined with a passive hand, and absence of all arm-weight or force.

Second Form (or Species) *of Combination :* The Arm is supported as in last, while key-depression is wrought by Finger and Hand exertion,—unaided therefore by arm-Weight. Permits far less extreme Agility than the first combination. Tone-quality is here still restricted to the more aggressive (or "brilliant") types, but tone-quantity is less limited.[2] Hand and Finger movements alone available.

Third Form (or Species) *of Combination :* All three

---

[1] As the hand's activity does not here intervene to transmit the recoil from the finger, the elastically-supported arm is here also debarred from bearing any measure of this recoil; and as the mere weight of the lax hand is insignificant, it follows, that the tone-amount thus available can be but small; and being entirely "initiated" by the finger, that it must also be thin in character, *unless modified by other means.*— *Vide* §§ *10, 11, and 12;* also next note.

[2] The quantity of tone is still somewhat limited, since finger and hand have only the *elastically*-supported arm (an insufficient basis) to act against. The quality of tone is limited for the same reason;—since there is no arm-weight set free, we cannot "initiate" tone by Weight (§ 10) but can do so only by Muscular-initiative—with its more sudden effect upon the key.

Quality may, however, be influenced in some measure (*as in all three forms of combination*) by the choice that is left us, between "flat" and "bent" finger-attitude. *Vide* § *12.*

components are here brought to bear upon the key during descent.—Offers fullest scope both as regards quality and quantity of Tone (*Vide* §§ *7 and 10, etc.*) and it may take the form either of Arm, Hand, or Finger movement —Arm, "Wrist" or Finger "touch." Speed is however limited, owing to impossibility of providing the required arm-release and its cessation (individually directed to each sound) beyond a soon-reached limit of re-iteration.[1]

§ 10. Variety in QUALITY of tone, mainly depends on the fact, that when we do employ the element of WEIGHT (third Species therefore) we then have the option of prompting the complete combination of Weight (arm-release, etc.), and Muscular-exertion (Hand and Finger activity) into operation against the key, by "willing" the employment of *either* of these two Elements, while the remaining Element then comes into operation automatically,—*i.e.*, in response to the one we have "willed."[2]

In this way, we are able to apply the Weight we use, either *suddenly* or more *gradually* to the key (during descent), and it is in this way that we can influence the key either suddenly or gradually into the particular Speed required.

Touch, thus initiated by muscular-*exertion* (with its more or less *sudden* key-descent) tends to make the tone-quality more or less aggressive or harsh; whereas Touch, initiated by

---

[1] While this form of muscular-combination is therefore only available when the speed required does not exceed a comparatively slow gait, it is nevertheless the only form that will enable us to obtain the full measure of good tone permitted us by our particular physical-endowment, since this combination will alone allow us to utilise the whole weight of the arm (and shoulder even) as a recoil-breaker, or basis for the work of the finger and hand. We must be careful not to confuse this short-lived use of Arm-weight, with the slight but *continuous* release, required for Tenuto and Legato. *Vide* § *15.*

[2] In other words: We may start or INITIATE the act of tone-production either by "willing" the finger and hand into Exertion, or may do so by "willing" the arm-supporting muscles into Lapse; and we can rely on reflex-action to complete the remainder of the required muscular-act, provided, of course, that we have formed the necessary mental-muscular co-ordinations, or Habits. Arm-lapse is in the first case given in automatic-response to the willed exertion of the finger and hand; while finger-and-hand Exertion is in the second case given in automatic response to the willed Lapse of the Arm-support.

a partial or complete *lapse* of the whole arm (either incipient or actual as to Movement) furthers a more gradual increase of speed during key-descent, and therefore tends to make the tone-quality more carrying, round, full, sweet and singing; a tone-quality, which, when sufficiently thus marked in character is called " sympathetic."[1]

§ 11. The divergencies of Tone-colour that thus result from this difference in the locality of the initiatory-act are in fact so great, as to warrant our classifying all Touch (from the Artist's point of view) into two primary grand divisions, or contrasting Sub-GENERA, which may conveniently be termed *Muscular-touch* and *Weight-touch* respectively.

To particularise still further, and to sum up this matter:

In the *first* of these two Genera—Touch initiated by Muscular-action, the complete muscular-conditions required for the particular note, are to be prompted into being, by our *willing* into action the depressing muscles of Finger and Hand; Weight, when required, is here to be called into play by a release of the arm, given in automatic-response to the recoil experienced at the Wrist.

In the *second* of these two Genera—Touch initiated by Weight, it is on the contrary Weight-release that must be *willed* for each key's descent; it is therefore the weight of the free-set arm (with its potential or actual fall) that must here automatically prompt the fingers and hand into the (slight) exertion necessary,—an exertion necessary to *prevent* this said weight from fall-

---

[1] The reason why this difference in *the locality of the muscular-initiative* causes respectively sudden or gradual application of Weight, is: that in the *first* case, the total-effect is more immediate upon the key, because the initiatory-step is here taken by the part of the limb CLOSEST to the key—the finger-and-hand element; whereas in the *second* case, the total effect reaches the key far more gradually, because the initiatory-act (in the form of a potential or actual fall of the Upper-arm) is here FURTHEST removed from the key; time is hence consumed in the second case before the response on the part of finger-and-hand fully takes effect, while the elastic medium here provided between the force set free (the arm) and its point of application (the key) also materially delays the transmission of the full effect.

ing at the wrist and elbow without taking effect upon the key.

§ 12. Variety in TONE-QUALITY, while it thus mainly depends upon the locality of the initiatory-prompting (forming the difference between "Muscular" and "Weight" Touch) is moreover much enhanced in its distinctive effects of "brilliant" (or aggressive) key-attack, and "Melody" (or sympathetic) key-attack, by a further element of contrast in muscular-application at our disposal: This arises from the option we have of applying the finger against the key in two diametrically opposite ways,—differences in FINGER-ATTITUDE which moreover bring in their train two relatively opposite conditions of the Upper-arm or Elbow.

These latter contrasts in muscular-attitude have been recognised by many, as "Hammer-touch" and "Clinging-touch" respectively, or as the French have it: "*Avec attaque*" and "*Sans attaque.*"

In the *first*, or "hammer-touch" variety, which we will term the BENT-FINGER attitude, or "Thrusting attitude," a greatly curved or bent position (like the hammer of an old-fashioned percussion-gun) is assumed by the finger when it is raised as a preliminary to the act of tone-production. The finger in this case un-bends (or un-curves) slightly, in descending towards and with the key; the nail-joint however, remaining vertical throughout. The Elbow has to take the brunt of the slightly backward tendency of the recoil that arises in this form of touch from the *thrusting* action of the finger against the key. The Upper-arm must therefore here be supported with a forward *tendency* (but not movement) towards the key-board, so that this forward-tendency at the Elbow may serve to counteract the recoil-thrust of the finger experienced at the knuckle and elbow.

In the *second*, or "clinging" variety of touch, which we will term the FLAT-FINGER attitude (or "Clinging-attitude") a far less curved position is assumed by the finger as a preliminary, and it may indeed be almost unbent or "flat." Exertion is in this case almost entirely restricted to the *under*-tendons of the whole finger. The key is moreover reached (and moved down) with but little change from this flatter or straighter position, and its involved muscular-attitude. As the *clinging* action of the finger in this instance tends to drag the Elbow towards the key-board, this tendency must be counterbalanced by allowing a sufficient lapse to supervene in the supporting-muscles of the Upper-arm. Such release of the upper-arm tends to drag the elbow away from the key-board and thus balances the pull of the finger; whilst the additional weight thus set free, materially helps to drag the key down.

The first kind of finger-attitude (with its correlated upper-arm conditions) is exceedingly less *elastic* than the second.

When the most sympathetic quality of tone is required, we must therefore choose this second (flatter) attitude—with its elastic Knuckle and Wrist, and consequent furthering of *gradual* key-descent, and must employ this in conjunction with Weight-touch,—touch initiated by lapse in arm-support.

§ 13. The importance of CEASING the muscular-act the moment its mission is accomplished, is the next point for consideration. As the act of providing Energy (in its various forms) against the key is required solely for the purpose of inducing speed in key-descent, it follows, that we must *cease applying* such Energy the moment this operation is completed—the very moment that the "sound place" is reached in key-descent.[1]

Unless we do thus time this cessation accurately, some of the force intended to induce key-descent (or sound) will instead be received by the key-pads,—with the inevitable result that our technique will be clumsy and inaccurate, and true Agility and Staccato will be equally impossible, as well as all *accuracy in tone-response*—accuracy in "Expression."

[1] *Vide Part II.*, §§ 4 and 5, *Chapter X.*, *page 71* ; §§ 6 and 7, *Chapter XI.*, *page 80* ; and § 4, *Chapter VII.*, *page 50.*

All force employed *to produce tone* (whether obtained from Muscular-action or from Weight-release) must therefore cease the very moment that Sound-emission begins.[1]

To enable us to provide this cessation with accuracy, we must (as already pointed out) *listen* for this moment,—thus guiding our muscles by our Ear.[2]

§ 14. Now it is evident that STACCATO must result from the Tone-producing operations thus far considered, provided the law of accurately-timed Cessation is strictly adhered to, and provided also, that no Arm-weight (however slight) is meanwhile permitted to lapse continuously upon the keys. For the key *will rebound*, and will even take up with it the superincumbent finger and hand, provided the latter lie on it in a perfectly loose and inactive condition the moment they have *completed* their necessary action.[3] Whence it will be borne in upon us, that there must be *another* operation, to be performed in conjunction with the key-depressing one, if we would produce any effect other than Staccato:—

§ 15. TENUTO (and Legato) we shall thus find, demands, that

---

[1] The *cessation* of Weight is induced by calling into re-activity the arm *supporting* muscles. In this connection it is important to note, that such resumption of work on the part of the arm-supporting muscles *must not* be prompted directly by the Will, but that such resumption must instead be prompted *automatically;*—that is, it must occur in response to the *cessation* of the fingers' and hand's activity against the key; a cessation timed (as so constantly insisted upon) at the moment that tone-production is individually completed for each sound.

Our arm-supporting muscles must therefore here be called into action much in the same way that those of our legs would be (by reflex-action), were the chair we happened to be seated upon, suddenly to collapse under us.

[2] As this insistence on ATTENTION may to some seem exaggerated, it may be as well to call to mind the expression of intensest concentration to be observed on the faces of the great artists during performance;—a concentration of mind amounting to complete self-effacement!

We can observe it even in the case of a mere acrobat about to perform his "turn"; his face exhibits an almost painful expression of attention and concentration. Now, if such mental energy is required for the performance of a purely acrobatic feat, how much more intense must be the mental-force that is required, when we have not only a series of most subtle and delicate *acrobatic* feats to perform, but have in addition to *choose* these, so that the most perfect expression of our Musical-feeling shall be accomplished!

[3] There is a peculiarly sharp Staccato, in which such rebound of the key (with its over-lying limb) is *helped* by a slight "drive" or "kick-off" against the key-bed.

we must *rest continuously* on the key-board, with sufficient weight to compel the implicated fingers to retain their keys depressed, while we must besides this operate against each key *individually*, to induce its proper speed.[1] *Vide: Chapter XI., § 14, page 85.* Also: *Chapters XV. and XVII.*

Such RESTING should for obvious reasons be no heavier than will just suffice to fulfil its purpose. Its degree of ponderousness should be determined by the degree of resistance the key itself offers to depression *at its softest* speech,—for the amount of weight required to overbalance the key must obviously also suffice to prevent its rebound.[2]

This necessary weight is obtained by relaxing the *whole* arm from the shoulder, relaxing it sufficiently but no more, than will just overbalance the key into descent. The weight thus obtained *continues* resting on the key-bed to the end of that note, in Tenuto; or in the case of Legato, on the key-board until the phrase is completed.[3]

§ 16. LEGATO is obtained by the use and intervention of successive fingers during the *continuance* of such act of Resting—a Resting, light and yet heavy enough to compel *some finger or other* to continue a supporting-action of the superimposed Weight.[4]

---

[1] We find indeed that the tone-production in all Tenuti (and Legati) of greater tone-amount than pp is as short-lived as in Staccato; and we might say, that all such Tenuti and Legati therefore *contain* a perfect staccato-production,—although the equally required *accuracy in cessation* is as it were *hidden* from the Ear in Tenuto and Legato,—hidden by the continuous aural effect arising from the continued depression of the keys beyond the first moment of tone-emission, a continued depression caused by this slightly heavier "Resting."

[2] Except in the case of certain very percussive-legato touches, etc., when slightly more weight than this is required to prevent the key-rebound, and consequent staccato effect.

[3] We must be most careful to understand at once, that this light continuous Resting of the arm—the Tenuto and Legato Basis—*is quite irrespective* of what besides this is done to provoke Tone. We may indeed apply the full force of the finger and hand to the key *during its descent*, or may even apply the *full weight* of the arm (and shoulder) during that tone-making operation (third species of combination), and yet this light continuous Resting must go on undisturbed between the strong impulses thus delivered to the key (during descent only) to provoke the full tone.

[4] There is however an exceptional form of LEGATO, which does *not* depend on such Resting-weight. In this case, we apply a slight (a very slight) *con-*

Such legato-compelling weight must in this case be *transferred* from finger to finger. This transfer must be effected to each successive key at the moment that its deflection is desired to *commence*, if we would obtain that effect of perfect continuance between sound and sound (without smudge) which constitutes the perfect Legato (*Vide* § 15, *page* 86, *Chapt. XI*.). The transfer of weight is therefore made from the bottom of an already-sounded note, to the *top*—or surface—of the note next to be sounded.[1]

If Super-legato (legatissimo) is required, then such transfer must be effected a little later than just described, so that the transfer of the weight may be delayed until the next key has already reached its full depression ; thus causing the desired overlapping of the sounds.[2]

---

tinuous exertion of the Hand alone, in place of the usual arm-release ; while the arm here remains self-supported, as in Staccato. The fingers are therefore here again compelled to transfer a *slight* continuous pressure from key to key. Such gentle exertion of the hand, since it acts upwards by recoil against the Wrist, thus after all brings the necessary arm-weight to bear continuously upon the key-board, but does so in a rather more uncertain fashion than when the fingers and hand respond to actual and continuous release of the arm.

This "artificial" Legato, as it may be termed, is suitable for Legato inflections of short duration ; and when *added* to the usual *natural* Weight-release-legato, forms a convenient means of inducing passing SUPER-LEGATO (Legatissimo) inflections. It can also be applied in certain rapid passages, when these are taken *forte*. In such cases, we must, however, be careful that the finger-impulses used are ample to *prevent* such continuous hand-pressure from really reaching the key-beds ; otherwise Agility, and all else, will be materially checked. The act of Running forms a good simile, when extra weight or pressure is thus carried in a rapid passage ; for the body carried either by the legs or the fingers, is in both cases *kept floating off the ground* by the rapid re-iterations of the jump-like acts performed respectively by the fingers, or the legs.

[1] This transfer in weight-supporting duty, from one finger to another (in unbroken continuity of weight) is effected exactly in the same manner that the weight of our bodies is transferred from leg to leg in the act of gently walking,—walking without any stamping or rolling-about. That is : each successive finger's gentle weight-supporting action must be automatically *prompted* by the WILLED LAPSE in the preceding finger's duty. If we wish to produce a *pianissimo*-legato, we must indeed be most careful not to permit ourselves to think of USING (or "putting-down") the finger that is to sound a note, but must on the contrary direct the preceding finger *to give way* at the right moment. In this way we shall feel the preceding finger and its note as it were merged into, and *become* the new note.

[2] A very slight increase in resting-weight may also be desirable in this case; or, we may instead employ the "artificial" legato-influence described in the Note[4] to § 16.

I

§ 17. Variety of Touch-method under Legato and Tenuto is as manifold as it is under Staccato.[1] It is indeed even more so: for the un-aided Resting provides us in addition with a *ppp* tone-production—without any assistance from an "Added-impetus," (§ 18) individually directed to each key.[2]

§ 18. We shall now be prepared to accept the following concept, viz.: that ALL TOUCH is in its nature COMPOUND—with one solitary exception, the *ppp* Tenuto and Legato.

Touch, we find, implies a dual conception and act. This duality consists of a *Resting* on the key-board which is continued parallel with each musical phrase, and an *Added-impetus* which is directed to, but which *ceases* with the consummation of each and every key-depression,[3] and which is therefore discontinuous. In other words, we have two distinct, yet co-existent acts and conceptions,—an act of Resting, interspersed with another act, that of individually supplying Energy to each key, sufficient to move it in the manner dictated by our musical conscience.

---

[1] We should notice, that Finger and Hand have in addition both to be *slightly* but *continuously* active in Tenuto and Legato, so as to ensure the retention of the keys beyond the moment that sound-emission commences.

[2] Here it is well to recapitulate the sources of the main tone-contrasts, which are therefore equally available both under Legato and Staccato: The energy required to provide tone greater than *ppp*, may be drawn either (a) from Finger alone, or (b) from Hand and Finger, or (c) from Arm-weight released behind both. When arm-weight is included, then we can at will render the result of this combination more sudden or less sudden in its effect upon the key, as we direct either Finger-and-hand Activity or Weight release to *start* each act of tone-production.—A contrast between aggressive and sympathetic tone-quality which we can moreover intensify, by employing either the *thrusting* or the *clinging* attitudes of the Finger and their correlated Upper-arm conditions; which latter again, by their diversity in elasticity, so materially influence the resulting tone-quality.

Such resulting differences in tone-amount and quality, can moreover be accompanied either by movements of the Finger, Hand, or Arm, or those of Rotation.

[3] Excepting always the single case of *ppp* Tenuto or Legato, where Resting and Key-depression are synonymous.

Touch, in a word, is found to consist of these two simultaneous operations, the one continuous with the duration of each phrase, and the other intermittent, discontinuous, and lasting only during the space of time consumed in key-descent, and *lasting therefore never longer than in the most abrupt staccatissimo;* —the latter being an act accurately "aimed" to cease the moment our ear perceives the transition from Silence to Sound.[1]

§ 19. STACCATO itself indeed forms no exception to this dual conception of the act of Touch. For we must remember that all our playing (artistically considered) becomes mere un-reliable guesswork *the moment we forget to judge key-resistance.*

We are hence forced to the conclusion that all Touch, including Staccatissimo, must contain this element of Resting, or else its correlative (or substitutionary-parallelism)—the resumption of "key-contact" (the resumption of the sense of key-resistance) as a preliminary to each tone-production.[2]

§ 20. We here again find the teaching of Chapter XI. re-enforced; viz., that the difference between Staccato and Tenuto (and Legato) is determined solely by the weight of this Rest-

---

[1] This "aiming" applies to each individual note in a slow succession of notes, but it becomes (like the act of Resting) merged into a "general impression" and "general direction," in the case of a rapid succession of notes.

[2] *Vide* Chapter XI., §§ 10, 11, *and Note to* § 11; also, §§ 16 *and* 17; Appendix to Part II., Note X., "*Key-hitting;*" also ditto of "*Supplement.*" Consideration of the requirements of the key proved to us, that we must not attempt to *hit* the key into sound, since this would debar us from realising the resistance it offers to movement; with the consequence, that we could not in this case judge with certainty the degree of force required to depress it at the required Speed, and required *angle* of Speed-increase during descent, that would compel the resulting tone-quantity and quality to correspond with the Music under interpretation. As a corollary, we also found, that Key-contact must take the form of a continuous Resting upon the key-board, continuous, or at least always resumed before each key-depression; such coming to "rest" upon the key, and the realisation of its resistance, not necessarily entailing an act discontinuous from that of the ensuing actual key-depression.

Staccato may therefore also be said to "contain" the opposite element—the element of Legato!—In so far, that we must continuously *rest* upon the keys in Staccato as well as in Legato; the only difference being, that we must rest *more lightly* in the case of Staccato than in the case of Legato or Tenuto; —for we must be careful, in Staccato, not to rest more heavily on the keys than they will bear *without* being thereby influenced into depression.

ing,—two distinct degrees of it being optional. The basis for Staccato being a Resting that must not be heavier than the keys will bear *without* giving way, while the basis for Tenuto and Legato is a Resting slightly heavier than the last,—sufficiently heavier just to overbalance the key into descent.[1]

§ 21. There remains to be considered that single exceptional form of touch, which is SIMPLE in structure, and not COMPOUND like the rest. This we have in fact already considered, for it is obtained by employing alone (without the help of any "added-impetus") the form of Resting that is the basis of all Tenuti and Legati. We therefore here have a Touch-mode that does not consist of two co-existent conceptions and operations, inasmuch as there is here *no difference* between the muscular-conditions that determine key-depression, and those that obtain *after* the consummation of each descent; for the conditions that serve for key-descent do in this single instance continue un-altered after the completion of the act of Tone-production.

This touch forms the only true absolute *pianissimo*, and as we have seen, it is also contained (as Basis) in all Tenuti and Legati.[2] Moreover, while this *weighed*-pianissimo touch forms one of the most beautiful (and so far, most rarely employed) effects of which our instrument is capable, it at the same time forms the *simplest* touch-method of all; and logically, it should therefore be mastered before any of the others.[3]

The muscular-conditions here required, are: we must allow the WHOLE arm[4] to become slightly but sufficiently *un-supported* by its muscles to enable the weight, thus set free, precisely to out-balance the weight and friction

---

[1] To re-state the case once again:—The Resting may occur upon the key either in its un-depressed or in its depressed condition. Of these two forms of Resting, the *first* cannot by itself at all induce tone-production,—such light resting at the surface-level of the key-board here only serving to enable us to locate the keys, and to discover the extent of their inertia; whereas the *second* form, although heavy enough to contribute towards making sound, should nevertheless not by itself be employed to induce sound beyond the *softest* degree. [2] Vide "Supplement," No. III., "On Pianissimo Playing."
[3] Vide Appendix to Part III., Note XI., "The 'Foundation-Touch' fallacy." Vide also "Supplement," No. III., re *pp* playing.
[4] *Fore*-arm weight only in "Bent-finger" technique.

PREAMBLE, PART III. 117

of the particular key implicated.[1] Such weight must therefore be set free in automatic response to the resistance the key is *felt* to offer; and no further weight must be set free the moment the key is felt to sink down.[2] The very softest sound the instrument is capable of uttering, will in this way be attainable with absolute certainty from each key,—even when the keys vary in their resistance, as they mostly do.

§ 22. Beside these main facts of muscular condition, there are several subsidiary ones that must be understood. Chief among these, is, the principle of FORE-ARM ROTATION:

The rotary exertions and especially the rotary *lapses* of the fore-arm, play a very important part in Technique. Unfortunately such necessary changes in the state of the fore-arm remain practically invisible,[3] unless deliberately made visible by exaggerating them. The consequence of the normal invisibility of this rotary-adjustment is, that many players never discover its necessity, and its far-reaching influence technically for good or evil.

Constant changes in the state of the fore-arm's rotary Release and rotary Support are imperative, if the fingers at opposite sides of the hand are to be equally " strong ";—*i.e.*, if the little finger and the thumb are to have equal successive apportionments of weight (or

---

[1] The muscular combination used is the *third*,—§ 9.

[2] The weight thus more or less to be set free, must be that of the *whole* arm; lapse only in the support of the fore-arm will not at all serve the purpose. Moreover, the note must be produced solely " by weight-lapse "; the slightest muscular-initiative on the part of finger or hand, will inevitably provoke failure. We must also entirely rely on the key itself to prompt the amount of weight set free,—we must as it were *trust* ourselves to the see-saw-like end of the key. In a slow passage, this prompting is derived from the individual resistance of each key; in quick passages, as usual, it is the general impression of key-board-resistance that serves the purpose. Slight *crescendi* are also available by slightly fluctuating this resting-weight; but we must remember that we dare not increase such resting-weight greatly, as this would lead to loss of agility and clearness of enunciation, and above all, to *inaccuracy* of Tone.

[3] Excepting in a comparatively rarely employed form of touch, the so-called " Side-stroke,"—a touch performed by an actual *tilting* of the hand from side to side.

resistance) to act against, when one of these fingers is applied against the key. Weight must be *released* rotarily towards the little-finger side of the hand, when the little finger is required to work effectively against its key;—a rotary lapse of the fore-arm, that must be precisely reversed, when we wish forcibly to employ the thumb. In the same way, we have rotarily to *support* the thumb-side of the hand, when we wish to employ a finger at the opposite side of the hand alone; and we must reverse the process, when the little-finger side of the hand has to be held off the key-board.

Moreover, not only does EVENNESS of touch thus depend upon accuracy in the constantly changing rotary-adjustment of the fore-arm; but it is again upon this class of adjustment that we have mainly to depend when we desire to make a tone *prominent* at one side of the hand.

§ 23. Other subsidiary actions are as follows:—

a): Horizontal movements of the Hand and Wrist; which render easy the turning under and over of the thumb and fingers, and thus enable us to connect without break the various groups of fingerings of which passages are built up.

b): Side-to-side movements of the fingers themselves, which enable us to reach notes situated within a short range.

c): Slight rotary movements of the Upper-arm, which help us (in conjunction with a certain hidden raising or lowering of the fore-arm) to execute rapid skips *within the radius of about two octaves*, without any lateral displacement of the Elbow, and which consequently allow us to execute such skips not only with celerity, but with relative certainty.

d): A slight lowering and raising of the Wrist-joint, which enables us to reach alternate black and white keys in octave and chord passages, without any fore-and-aft displacement of the Elbow; thus obviating the otherwise more cumbrous movements of the whole arm, forwards and backwards.

Finally (e), there are the side-to-side movements of the Upper-arm itself, which give us the whole range of the key-board; enabling us to take the most extensive skips. Such skips, depending as they do in this case on a lateral movement of the whole arm, cannot however be taken at the relatively high speed of skips taken by the Forearm.—*Vide* (c).

§ 24. Having thus glanced at the whole subject of the Muscular-aspect of the subject, we must in the next Chapters consider the various details somewhat more fully.

CHAPTER XIII.

THE LINK BETWEEN KEY AND MUSCLE—OUR SENSE OF KEY-RESISTANCE.

§ 1. We found, when studying the key's requirements in Part II., that for every shade in tone-difference demanded from the key, the latter exacts a difference in the application of Energy applied to it. The key's requirements in this respect differ with every individual instrument, and differ even with the various portions of the same instrument; and they vary again during the course of each key's descent—during its short life as a tone-agent.

Hence it becomes abundantly clear, that we must have an absolutely sure and ready means constantly at our disposal, which will enable us to determine the precise degree of energy required by the key, if our Execution, Technique, or Tone-production shall be serviceable for any really *artistic* purpose; and that we must not here, at the very fountain-head, depend on mere surmise or guesswork.

Our first step, before proceeding further, must therefore be thoroughly to understand how and by what MEANS we can with certainty be apprised of the key's exact requirements for the particular tone-inflection of each and every individual act of Tone-production—or key-deflection.

§ 2. Since its wants vary practically with each note, it is

evidently upon the Key itself that we must in the first instance rely for this necessary information. This notification the key offers us, through its ever-varying change in RESISTANCE.[1]

§ 3. We are consequently forced to accept the following precept, and it forms probably the most important rule of all the rules of Technique :—

That all the muscular conditions (both of action and of inaction) required for key-deflection, must be given strictly in answer to the *felt resistance* of the key itself, and that we must therefore CONSTANTLY WATCH KEY-RESISTANCE, before and during descent.

This may be formulated by saying, that we must always muscularly watch the key-*surface*; or better still, that we must watch for the point (of resistance) at which the key *will give way*—in short, the *giving-way-ness* of the key.[2]

§ 4. The medium through which we thus become aware of key-resistance is our *muscular-sense* and its co-operatives, which may appropriately therefore be termed our RESISTANCE-SENSE.[3]

---

[1] For Key-resistance we must of course not mistake key-*bed* resistance, but the resistance the key offers *before* it will move, and *during* its descent.

[2] In a word, we must constantly "*weigh*" the key as a preliminary to using it; for we can no more hope *to use* the key accurately without such constant preliminary weighing of it, than we can expect to use the Racket, Cue, etc., successfully, without a similar preliminary judgment of their weight, immediately before each "stroke."

The teaching of LESCHETITZKY, and others, that every finger must (in most passages) *be in contact with every key before deflection*, forms a recognition of this truth. In such teaching, this takes the form of insistance on the finger being *in position* on the key beforehand—several keys (whole fingering-positions) being even thus "prepared" before their depression is due.

We shall presently find (*Vide Chapter XV.*, "*The Concepts of Touch*") that such insistance on "position" is unnecessary and cumbrous, as the element of "RESTING" (when understood, and carried out) compels such preparatory positions unconsciously and more naturally.

[3] The term Muscular-sense (or Resistance-sense) as applied here, is one of convenience. It is not considered expedient to go more into detail. Enough, that the term is here intended to embrace the senses pathologically distinguished as "muscular-sense," "pressure-sense" and "muscular-sensibility." Our object here is merely to insist on the necessity *physically to feel* key-resistance before and during key-descent, since the application of muscular-judgment in this sense forms the main distinguishing feature between *certainty* and *un-certainty* in Technique and Expression. There are many no doubt who have never realised that they possess such a sense, and it would be interesting to pursue the matter more minutely. Such a course would however,

It is by means of this alone, that we can be adequately reminded of the ever-varying Resistance exhibited by the key—if we watch it.[1] And it is this Sense that may therefore be said to forge the LINK which in correct Touch brings our muscular-system and our mind into such intimate connection with the key, as to cause the latter to seem a *continuation* of our finger-tip, so that our very flesh-and-blood seems to end only with the Hammer-felt.

§ 5. We find, that the resistance the key thus offers, is felt to be greater in direct proportion to *the speed* we wish to impart to it. *Vice versa*, if we wish to provoke a key into the production of a large tone, we must try to make the key *resist us greatly*—during descent. For if we have succeeded in that, then we may feel assured that the Tone-result is large, even should we be unable to judge the result by our ears—owing to the faulty acoustics of the room, or other cause.[2]

§ 6. This required muscular-judgment of the key is derived individually from each key in slow passages. In quick passages it is on the contrary derived from the *general sensation*

merely confuse the ordinary student at this stage, and divert his attention from the main issue. Besides which, the precise relationship and even nature of these senses still remains somewhat obscure, and is debatable ground.

[1] This reminder may be accomplished either consciously or unconsciously to ourselves.

[2] The application of Muscular-attention to key-resistance therefore, not only enables us to gauge the degree of resistance the Key offers *before* it will move at all, and the point when it will give way *at its softest* (*Vide Part II., page 80, § 8*); but it also enables us to judge the opposition the key offers against moving at any *higher* grade of speed, and *increase* of speed during descent. Whence we realise, why it is by such means alone that we can with certainty be prompted to deliver the requisite Energy, and increase of it during descent, mutually demanded by Key and Musical-sense.

Seeing how much indifferent execution (and un-musicality therefore) results from its non-application, it is impossible to over-emphasise the necessity of giving a keen, unswerving, and ever-present attention to the Key by means of the Resistance-sense during Performance, in conjunction with the outer ear.

It is true, that a certain grade of rough execution can be accomplished without such careful attention in this way :—a degree of un-musical (because colourless) execution that may content the musically un-educated, or those who do not consider the Pianoforte to be really a "musical" instrument !— Or it may content the *artistically* uneducated,—such as are able to derive ear-gratification from rough, oleograph-like mis-reproductions of musical works—performances not far above the coarse *de*-musical tinkle and clatter of the barrel-piano !—that curse of our English lanes and by-ways, and which even pollutes the air of moor and lake !

of resistance the key-board offers as it is being rapidly traversed —and used; the impression made by the separate key-units being in the latter case *blended* into a general-impression. Such general-impression varies in accordance with the variation in resistance the keys offer, both at surface-level, and as they are being deflected either at great speed or at little speed, and suddenly or gradually.

§ 7. As so much depends on a correct understanding of this matter, it is advisable to attempt a clearer definition of Muscular-sensation or Resistance-sensation as here implied:

What is mainly meant, is the sensation that arises when a muscular-exertion made by us meets with a check or resistance opposed to it—a sensation therefore, that is aroused by something *conflicting* with our muscles.

The sense we desire to enlist, cannot hence be aroused unless some muscle is exerted, for it cannot be aroused unless there is something in conflict with a muscle[1]. Nevertheless, although it is by means of muscular-exertion that the sense of key-resistance is excited, yet very little exertion will suffice to stimulate the Sense. The resistance which the key is able to offer *at surface-level* without giving way (when the hand lies loosely upon it) is quite enough to cause the sensation; which is here caused by the infinitesimally gentle work done by the fingers in supporting the hand, thus loosely and inactively lying upon the keys.[2]

---

[1] A proper realisation of the fact, that the sensation in question arises owing to a muscular-exertion being *opposed*, has important bearings educationally beyond those just considered. We shall presently find, that resistance to muscular-effort may arise within the limb itself,—caused by the "contrary" muscles coming into action along with the necessary ones. The presence of resistance, the sense of conflict or impediment *within the limb* itself (and therefore *not* derived from the key) should hence instantly warn us that we are not fulfilling the law of "*Relaxation of all un-needed muscles*," and that we are therefore not playing with the ease and freedom that might be possible.

[2] The sensation can moreover be materially intensified, without impairing the loose-lying condition of the hand (as required in Staccato and Agility passages for instance) by *slightly wedging* as it were, the front two phalanges of the finger between the key-surface and the light superincumbent weight of the hand. This is a muscular-subtlety, but it is one that is of great use artistically, since it greatly improves one's assurance in light running passages, both in staccato and quasi-legato.

THE LINK BETWEEN KEY AND MUSCLE. 123

§ 8. We must moreover, not mistake another sense for the required Resistance-sense, and that is the sense of TOUCH, properly so-called. This last, the sensation of mere contact with a smooth or rough surface, is quite distinct from the more *ponderous* sensation of Resistance.[1]

The sensation of Touch itself, is however also useful in playing, for it helps us to locate the exact place occupied by the key in space.

The point is, that we must not rest satisfied with realising key-surface merely by this sense of contact or touch, but must besides realise the key's actual resisting-powers.

§ 9. The intimate relation that exists between this attention to Key-resistance and MUSICAL-ATTENTION itself, is perhaps the most striking fact of all in this connection. For if we watch key-resistance as here insisted upon, we shall also find ourselves *compelled* to give Musical-attention. We give this as a direct result, the moment we bring our minds to watch key-resistance, since it would be purposeless to do so without at the same time considering *for what purpose* and *at what moment* that key is *musically required*. Our musical-judgment is consequently stimulated to decide what quality and quantity of tone is at that moment required, and hence again, our attention is instantly and acutely drawn towards COLOURING; and we are thus forced to rely upon the dictates of musical Feeling, Contour and Shape. (*Vide the Table, page 40, Part I.*)

In a word, we cannot judge what the key requires muscularly, without immediate reference to the requirements of Musical-sense. (*Vide also § 12, of next chapter.*)[2]

---

[1] The sensation of Touch seems to be derived from numerous nerve-ends distributed under the skin; these enable us as it were to count or measure the protuberances that form roughness of surface.

[2] To sum up, although it may be granted that a certain degree of rough playing is attainable without such attention, yet the elements of artistic-playing (refinement and subtlety of Expression, and *certainty* in it) must remain impossible of attainment without " Key-judgment through the Resistance-sense "—the act of Resting, and an equally un-swerving attention through the outer-ear; and an unfailing use of the player's musical conscience. For does not Artistic-execution, in short, imply, a Technique that enables us faithfully to portray even the subtlest promptings of our musical-imagination and judgment?

RECAPITULATORY

a): Part II. demonstrates that each and every sound-colour—both of quality and quantity—depends on the way we *move* the key during each short-lived process of descent.

b): The requirements the key exhibits, differ therefore with each difference in sound-kind—sound-shading or inflection.

c): It follows that we must precisely adjust our efforts to meet these constantly varying requirements.

d): Our only means of judging what these are, is through watching the Resistance the key itself offers us, before and during each descent,—the " giving-way point " of the key.

e): It is only by employing our "*Resistance-sense*" (the Muscular-sense and its co-operatives) that we can be apprised with certainty of these inexorable requirements of the key.

f): This sense hence forms the *Link* between the key-board and ourselves.

g): It is not enough to use merely the sense of Contact or Touch, we must insist on feeling the actual *resistance* the key offers to our muscles before and during descent.

h): So intimate will the connection thus formed be, that finger and key will appear as one to us;—the whole leverage-system, from shoulder to hammer-end, will seem as one living lever to us.

i): Certainty, both as to Notes and as to Expression, can alone be secured in this way.

j): In slow successions of notes, each one is to be thus individually felt and judged. In quick passages, the separate units are merged into one general sensation and judgment of the key-board.

k): Attention to key-resistance also compels *Musical-attention*: for we cannot muscularly *judge* the key as to Tone and Time, unless we have a sound in our mind, exactly dictated by our Musical-feeling at that moment.

CHAPTER XIV

On key-contact:

THE NATURE OF THE IMPACT OF THE FINGER AGAINST THE KEY.

§ 1. In the last chapter the fact was insisted upon, that to enable us to obtain certainty in execution and beauty of tonal-effect, we must constantly observe the actual resistance the key offers us, ever-varying as this is, and only to be known and gauged through being physically felt.

The corollary is, that key-hitting is demonstrated to be as undesirable a mode of bringing the Finger-tip into contact with the key, when considered from its muscular aspect, as it was proved to be fallacious when considered mechanically in Part II.; for it is obvious that such mode of contact would render impossible the intervention of our "Resistance-sense," and would therefore prevent any direct judgment of the key's requirements, as well as any accurate exemplification of our musical feeling. As the key-hitting hypothesis has thus been found untenable, from the muscular as well as from the instrumental standpoint, let us now describe more precisely how the Finger-tip should reach the key.

§ 2. Our object being to obtain beauty and accuracy as to tone, we must be careful to reach the key, *practically without percussion or concussion;* i.e., we must reach it with no greater force than it can bear *without giving way* under the actual impact. Not even in fullest *forte* is there any real occasion to make the finger-tip impinge upon the key with more force, than could be borne with impunity by one of those glittering balls of thinnest glass, so much in evidence at Christmas. When beauty and accuracy of tone is a consideration, key-attack should therefore always take the form of *a gentle fall* of the finger-tip upon the key, no matter whether the Finger alone is to move, or whether the Hand and Arm are to move with it. On reaching the key in this comparatively gentle way, we are able intimately to "take hold" of it as it were, before its actual depression commences; and we are thus able to *feel the weight* of the tool we mean to use, as demonstrated to be so necessary in the last chapter. See Notes, pp. 185, 145.

Instead of really hitting the keys down—as is so often done by mistake—we must, even in the most forcible passages, try thus to "take hold" of the keys and weigh them, before using them. It is this difference in the *beginning* of the act of tone-production that constitutes much of the difference between the production of a really large and beautiful tone, and that of a harsh, ear-splitting unmusical noise, of no carrying power.[1]

§ 3. This comparatively gentle fall of the Arm, or Hand, or

[1] Although it may at first sight seem incredible that such careful contact should remain possible even in the quickest and loudest passages, yet not only is this possible, but it becomes perfectly easy, once we have formed the necessary habits both of body and mind. As already insisted upon, all our playing must remain mere "fluking," until such habits have been formed, and we are consequently able to use the key with certainty,—until each musical desire for a tone-shading at a precise moment can be *automatically* supplied through the co-operation of the muscular-system, prompted by an almost *unconscious* employment of the muscular-sense through the key's varying resistance.

A performer, whose habits of key-attack allow him to produce perfectly good qualities of tone, and who therefore proves that he never really does merely hit the keys down, may nevertheless find it difficult to realise, that that which he for years regarded—and may be cherished—as key-"striking," is not really that at all; but that his key-attack consists on the contrary of a compound action, made up of an easy movement to the key, and a subsequent tone-making effort,—subsequent, though in unbroken continuity with the preliminary descent of the limb. In fact, sensibility to Beauty of Tone often unconsciously prevents the adoption of real hitting, although the performer may fancy he does hit, and is even an ardent advocate of that mischievous practice. Perhaps such an one might possibly be cured of his faith in it, by having demonstrated to him the appallingly harsh and yet poor tone that results, when a chord is in reality (and not in fancy) *struck* down by, say by a twelve-inch descent of the arm.

It is moreover true, that it is indeed one of the hardest technical tasks to obtain the fullest *forte* in combination with beauty of tone, requiring as this does considerable energy, but delivered gradually. Much of the difficulty is however enhanced, from the mistaken idea that it is "force" that is needed, no matter how applied!

The moment we recognise that the key must be taken hold of, and used *only* "*to*" *the tone*, that moment our tone will commence to grow in beauty, resonance, and power. It is worth trying for, for how rare are the Pianists that exhibit real beauty in their *fortes!*

Finger upon the key-board, should in character be as far removed as possible from a muscular-*exertion*, *i.e.*, the limb should not be *put down* upon the keys, but should instead be allowed to subside, lapse or sink down upon them,—the descent upon the key should arise rather from *omission* than from *commission* of exertion.

§ 4. It is only when we actually reach the key, and derive from it the necessary information as to its needs, *that the actual process of tone-production can be said to commence*—the process of *pressing the key into motion*.

§ 5. This however does not imply that the process of reaching the key, and the process of depressing it, must needs be separate. On the contrary, this *felt* contact with the key's surface (preliminary to its depression, whence arises the necessary preliminary physical judgment) *need not occur any appreciable time* before the key's depression is started, and it will in this case seem to melt into the latter; proving indeed indistinguishable from the act of key-moving, except under the severest analysis.[1] That is, the comparatively slow preliminary descent of the limb to the key-surface, may be at once succeeded —and *without break in the continuity of the descending movement* —by a great increase in speed-production, when the key's resistance is encountered. Thus, in good Touch, the complete movement of the limb may form a *continuous* acceleration, from a preliminary well-raised position, down to that place in key-descent where our hearing apprises us that the act of tone-production is complete. The latter part of the descent—with the key—being however accomplished at a far greater ratio

---

[1] This, owing to the fact that reflex-actions can be so prompt in their nature as to defy our witnessing the action of stimulus and its response. The act of reaching the key, and the ensuing act of carrying the key down, will hence *appear* as one act, when the requisite *habits* of Mind and Body have been formed,—the habits that will cause us automatically to supply the energy the key demands under each particular circumstance.

We must however take care deliberately to supply both the act of key-depression and its preliminary, until such required habits of co-ordination of Mind and Muscle have been successfully attained. It is only eventually, when key-judging has practically become an automatic habit, and from the rapidity with which such judging is then effected, that we may permit ourselves to *seem* to plunge down upon the keys with finger and arm.

KEY-TREATMENT; MUSCULAR ASPECT.

of speed-*increase* than the earlier part of the descent, *i.e.*, before the key was reached.[1]

§ 6. On the other hand, contact with the key *need not be deferred until the last moment*. On the contrary, it may be accomplished some time before the key is due to be provoked into movement. In quick, light passages, several fingers may indeed be thus ready beforehand. In fact, it is in this way that that "general judgment" of the key-board (rather than of its individual units) is brought about which forms the distinctive mode of applying the Resistance-sense in rapid passages, as already indicated in the last chapter.[2]

§ 7. In illustration of the mechanically immeasurably superior effectiveness of the correct Touch-method (that almost always *presses the key into movement*) over mere key-hitting, the following two experiments should be made:

Raise the hands, thumb upwards, and bring all the finger-tips of both hands into gentle contact, either bending the fingers or not; the hands and fingers together thus roughly assuming the figure of a horseshoe.

For the first experiment: Draw one finger of one hand as far back as possible—exactly as in "lifting" the finger well at the key-board. From this "raised" (but in this case really laterally-moved) position, endeavour to *strike* the opposite finger with all possible force. The unexpected feebleness of the result attainable in this way, will then no doubt surprise many.

For the second experiment: After once more placing all the finger-tips in contact, and now *without* any preliminary drawing-back, let one finger of one hand give the opposite one

---

[1] The descent of the limb through the air prior to the key being reached, is therefore not really very rapid, compared to the speed the Key has to attain just before Tone-emission is reached,—although the visual impression of a blow may be conveyed. This arises merely from the circumstance, that such movements of the Arm, Hand and Finger are quicker than can readily be followed by the eye, even in the case of the softest note.

[2] *Vide Chapter XIII.*, §§ *18 and 19, page 115*. Judgment of the individual units also becomes a less pressing matter in rapid passages, owing to the strong part then played by the Memory; for the exact impressions of Key-resistance experienced, can here remain vivid from note to note; also, the judgment can here be stimulated by the *other* fingers at work in such close propinquity, both as to Time, and as to nearness on the key-board itself.

(already in contact with it) a sharp *push* or *shove-off;* the nature of this push or shove being not a long-continued squeeze, but a sharp, almost merely momentary action, analogous to such as we should employ in assisting a person to *swing*.[1]

The far greater measure of Energy thus so easily brought into operation against the opposite finger, sufficiently demonstrates the true method of muscularly creating Motion in the Pianoforte-key.

§ 8. Energy, thus correctly applied to the key, still admits of the difference between a comparatively Sudden and a Gradual key-depression; for we can direct this application of energy to occur either suddenly, or with any desired degree of *insinuation*.

It will be explained in the later chapters of this Part *how* this difference can be wrought muscularly; for it depends on distinct and relatively opposite conditions of Arm and Finger. We shall then also have to consider *whence* the requisite energy is muscularly derived.

Meanwhile, when we desire a harsh effect, there is no reason why we should not permit Key-contact slightly to approximate towards an actual Stroke.[2] Such harsh effects are however comparatively rarely called for in Music.

§ 9. Players do often moreover deliberately employ such harsh sounds (produced therefore almost by a stroke) under the misapprehension that these harsh sounds are " effective." Now there is no doubt that such over-sudden key-attack does cause much commotion of a kind *close to the instrument;* such noisy clatter nevertheless sounds merely thin and wiry at some little distance from the instrument, since it does not " carry ; " and it therefore by no means conveys to the audience the per-

---

[1] In both forms of this experiment or demonstration, it is essential not to move or exert the *opposite* finger—the one attacked either by blow or by push-off. This opposite finger should be left quite passive, otherwise the experiment will be vitiated.

[2] We must remember, that if we do allow it to approximate too closely to a blow, we shall risk loss of Energy through concussion at the key-surface. In any case, such approximation at once reduces our *directive*-power over the key. True, a little inaccuracy as to tone-kind is not so noticeable in a *forte* passage as in a *piano* passage. Such lapse in " key-judging " however often leads to the note not being sounded at all, in the case of the softest passages.

K

former's intention of a "grand clashing effect"; for the tone cannot under such attack sound really *full*.[1]

Unmitigated clatter, it is true, may itself occasionally be appropriate,—such effects can be found in French Music especially; just as the Cymbals, Triangle and Gong find their place in an Orchestra. But do not let us mistake "the Kitchen utensils" for the Trombones and Tubas!

§ 10. We must moreover constantly adjust ourselves to the particular kind of instrument under our fingers. When we have to deal with a heavily-felted hammer, much more *driving* (not hitting) is permissible and even desirable than when our finger is armed with a more naked hammer.

We must remember, that while an over-felted hammer does certainly in a measure *hide* bad (harsh) key-treatment, it renders "brilliancy" extremely difficult of attainment. The comparatively hard hammer (as hammers should be) on the other hand renders soft and sympathetic tone-production practically impossible for those who have not mastered the elements of correct Touch. Those, however, who have done so, delight in the "hard" hammer, since it gives them far greater range of tone-quality; for they know how to obtain the sympathetic effects when desired, by supplying the requisite Elasticity of attack, through the proper Arm, Hand and Finger conditions; such therefore require no false elasticity mechanically forced upon them by an over-felted hammer.

§ 11. It is desirable that the limb-movements by which the key is reached, should be as ample as commensurate with comfort. This applies particularly to *forte* passages, and applies equally, whether the movement accompanying tone-production be that of the Finger, Hand or Arm.

In brilliant passages, played *forte* with the "Bent" finger, a full curving of the finger upwards (before use) is beneficial,

---

[1] The case is precisely analogous to that of a badly-produced voice. This often seems to be of huge volume in a small chamber, and may make one's ears ring with it. Yet it has no effect when placed in the Concert-room. While a well-produced Voice, and perhaps in reality a much smaller one, may sound far less forcible (compared to the badly produced one) in the small room, but will in the larger space tell out immeasurably better;—even at its softest "filling" the large room to its remotest corners.

—such curving upwards meanwhile leaving the nail-phalange almost vertical.[1]

Such preliminary "raising" must however under no circumstances be permitted to induce stiffness; nor must exaggerated importance be given to such raising, otherwise it will tend rather towards the destruction than towards the acquisition of an easy responseful Technique;—and it will tend rather to impede *and even maim* the performer, than to assist him. (*Vide Appendix to Part II.*, "*On key-hitting,*" *etc.*)

A sufficient lifting of the fingers is beneficial, not because of the reason so often ignorantly ascribed, viz.: that the finger may then "the better hit or strike the key"; but it is beneficial, because we can then better control the finger muscularly, can be more sure that it is *free* when it reaches the key and descends with the latter; and it is advantageous above all things, because we can thus better *discriminate between* finger and finger—can better realise *which finger* we are directing against each key, a point which undeniably has a happy influence towards "playing clean." Ample movements (when practicable) are also advantageous, because they are more *healthy* for the muscles concerned than are constantly recurring small and forcible movements; and it is also mechanically an advantage, to have the portion of the limb that executes the movement *under weigh* before the key is reached, especially when it is the huge mass of the arm; since we then overcome the mere inertia of the limb before we reach the key.[2] In

---

[1] *Vide Part IV.*, "*On Position*"; *also* § *12 and Fig. 6, Chapter XVI.; and* § *12, Chapter XVII.*

[2] The small space available at the Pianoforte, during which it is possible effectively to apply muscular-exertion to the key—during its short descent of only about three-eighths of an inch, is, with its rapid reiterations, very cramping for the muscles concerned. This, as in Gold-beating, in Penmanship, and other pursuits demanding small rapid movements, is apt to lead to muscular-complaints, and even to deterioration, unless *counteracted* by ample, although otherwise not necessary movements.

It is moreover more easy to direct—or to *aim*—with a limb already under muscular-movement, than when the application of Energy has to be made without any preparatory movement.

Besides this, as already pointed out, it is an advantage to have the Arm, or Hand, or Finger already *under way* when the key is reached, since we then have only to start the Key and String into movement, instead of having also

such case we must however be careful to guard against concussion supervening. Manifestly, the slower the passage, the more easy is it thus to well raise the limb sections concerned in such preparatory and *subsidiary* movement, since we then have more time to do so. Conversely, it is also undesirable to insist upon an exaggerated and unnecessary lifting of the Finger, Hand or Arm, when the passage is rapid. The labour involved in making rapidly reiterated movements of the *same* portion of the limb, may then prove so irksome as to defeat the very object in view—Ease and Certainty of Technique. It may even prove physically disabling, if persevered in.[1]

It is indeed best never to allude to any "raising" or "lifting" of the living levers concerned, as it may lead to the introduction of *contrary* exertions. Far better is it, to induce such amplitude in the preliminary movement, by speaking and thinking of "*playing the keys from a distance,*" and with ease. For if we think of reaching the keys from a slight distance, the preceding lifting will be done unconsciously, and in this case probably without any straining either during the ascent or during the subsequent descent.[2]

§ 12. Two comically opposite and contradictory fallacies have arisen in direct consequence of a hazy and but partial realisation of the two truths here enunciated,—(*a*) the truth,

to start to overcome the *inertia* of the motionless limb. This applies particularly where Tone-production is accompanied by movements of the larger limb-sections, such as the Fore-arm or the whole Arm.

It is therefore well thoroughly to elevate Arm, Hand, or Finger, during the preparatory bringing of the finger-tip over its key when there is time to do so, although we must not subsequently use our limbs like bad hammers.

Perhaps here it is well to protest against the exaggeration of such movements, when prompted by mere purposeless affectation; also against the temptation of employing them for the sake of their sheer muscular satisfaction as violent exhilarating exercise;—a motive that, it is to be feared, is at the bottom of much of the enjoyment of both player and audience, in those "general kick-ups" of which most Pianists must at times plead guilty.

[1] Cases of "smashed wrists," etc., are mostly directly traceable to the physiological ignorance of teachers, who insist upon a superfluous degree of hand movement in rapid wrist-passages. The reiterated shocks thus given to the tendons must be terribly severe, the moment the slightest "stiffening" is permitted. Tendons could not withstand such maltreatment for any length of time, were they even of steel.

[2] *Vide Appendix, Part III.; Note XII.,* "*Exaggerated Finger-lifting.*"

ON KEY-CONTACT.

that the real act of Tone-production should not be started until the key is met and felt, if beauty of tone is a consideration; and (*b*), the truth that a plentiful preparatory movement of the limb is both helpful and healthy :—

Thus the fact that all good tone-making must *commence at the surface of the key*, has been misinterpreted into the Dogma that " every note must be played from the *surface* "—in the sense, that neither Finger, nor Hand, nor Arm *dare be lifted off the keys during performance!* Certainly this forms a less baneful fallacy than the one, where the plentiful preparatory raising of the limbs (which conduces towards freedom and ease in key-attack) has been misinterpreted into doctrines of exaggerated limb-raising, especially so of the Finger, arising from the mistaken impression, that the further off the key, and the more strenuous such raising, the better should one be able to hit or "strike" at the key—like a boxer![1]

§ 13. We now see that accuracy in transmitting our musical feeling to the hearer, depends in the first instance on insisting on a proper Key-contact; one that is not really percussive, since this will permit us to judge key-resistance constantly during performance, as shown to be necessary in the last chapter.

To repeat once more: If we do thus make contact in the proper way, we can judge how much force is required to set the key into that *slowest* motion, compatible with merely sounding the note, and we can then judge how much *more* force will be required for any higher grade of sound;—watch-

---

[1] We see, that both these opposite so-called "systems," "schools," or "methods" of Touch rest on a basis of—perverted—truth, in common with many other doctrines and superstitions.

It is only too obvious how such misconceptions have arisen : The executive (and therefore artistic) success of Artists great and small, is correlative with their closer or looser adherence to these two vital laws of execution. Adherence to these laws causes certain *appearances* to accompany such good playing in a more or less marked degree. As it is easy to observe mere appearances, it was concluded that if one only succeeded in insisting upon such movements, that the good results would then also be attained ; hence hasty generalisations and "theories" quite contrary to the facts. Obviously, one should first have waited to analyse the *facts* of key-treatment, instrumental and muscular, that enabled these successful artists to produce their effects ; thus one would inevitably have deduced their true *modus operandi.*

ing the "giving-way" point of each key like this, implies our using our musical judgment for each of the keys thus used;—this we cannot do, unless we are also at the moment conscious of the *course* the Music is taking. As our mind is thus kept vividly on the course of the work under interpretation, through the supreme necessity of pre-conceiving what each sound *should be* (as to Time and Tone), we thus find ourselves employing our musical sense (and attention) to the fullest of its particular capacity.

The difference between playing notes *musically unconsidered*, and notes thus properly *musically considered*—vividly considered *because of the necessities of the key*, proves nothing short of marvellous to those previously unaware of the true form of musical attention,—the main distinction between "unmusical" and "musical" playing.[1]

RECAPITULATORY

a): The finger-tip must reach the key with but little percussion.

b): The preliminary *fall* of the limb upon the key-surface, should be free from perceptible exertion; it should arise rather from Relaxation.

c): It is not until we reach the key, that we can *commence* the act of *pressing it into motion,*—the act proper of tone-production.

d): The act of reaching the key, and the act of setting it into motion, need not necessarily be separate; the two may coalesce into an unbroken descent.

e): Contact, may, on the other hand, be made some time before the note is required; several notes at a time may thus be previously felt, in certain rapid runs.

f): The difference between Sudden and Gradual depression of the key should mostly depend on the *condition* of the muscles during the subsequent operation.[2]

g): Harsh sounds do not carry; hence they do not sound so full and "grand" a little way off, as they seem to do close to the instrument.

[1] § 9 of last chapter should here be re-read.
[2] That is, it should depend upon what we do *during* the operation of tilting the Key into sound.

b) · Contact, and subsequent key-treatment, must be modified according to the softness or hardness of the hammer; a soft hammer requires more "driving" for the brilliant effects, while a harder hammer requires greater *elasticity* in the limb itself for the sympathetic effects.

i): Every key *should be reached* from as great a distance as conveniently possible; this so, that the movement towards (and with the key) may be *as free as possible;* and so that we can the better *individualise* each finger in the quicker passages.

j): Amplitude in preparatory movement must not be insisted upon in very rapid passages, as it may lead to stiffening, and worse—even muscular damage.

k): Proper Contact with the key, is the first step towards Accuracy in Expression.

CHAPTER XV

THE CONCEPTIONS OF TOUCH ARISING FROM CORRECT KEY-CONTACT AND DEFLECTION ;—THE TWO CONCEPTS AND ACTS, OF "RESTING" AND "ADDED-IMPETUS."

§ 1. We must now go a step further, and endeavour to realise how the requisite muscular-conditions can be prompted by the brain, since it is only through mental-impressions stimulated by Feeling that we can direct our muscles for artistic purposes. To enable such prompting to be given, there must be definite ideas or conceptions which the mind can grasp. We must have definite and correct concepts of the act of "Touch"—in the Pianistic acceptation of that term ;—definite concepts of the *muscular* aspect of Key-treatment.

§ 2. If the propositions and arguments of the last chapters have been intelligently followed, we shall now be prepared to accept the conclusion, that all correct Touch is *dual* in nature, and that it consists of two main acts,[1] and concepts therefore:

[1] It is important to remember in this connection, when we attempt to describe the *components* of an Act or Thought, that this necessarily becomes disintegrated in the process. Hence, if we wish to fulfil such description, we must build up these disintegrated components *into one single* Act or Thought.

136 KEY-TREATMENT; MUSCULAR ASPECT.

I): **An act of "Resting,"**—a resting on the keys, an act more or less directly *continuous* during each musical phrase;

II): **An act of Key-deflection, or "Added-impetus."**—The act of delivering Energy individually to each key, for the purpose of its descent into Sound; an act co-operative therefore with the act of Resting, but consisting of Energy only momentarily *added* to such Resting—added to each key, during its descent only, and *ceasing* the moment that sound is reached.

That is: Our whole mental-muscular attitude towards the key-board technically, resolves itself ultimately into a conception embracing these two acts; and it is by more or less consciously *directing these*, that we are able to fulfil the promptings of our musical Sight.

§ 3. Let us review the grounds upon which this dual conception of Technique is based:—

a): Part II. proved to us (*Vide page 85, §§ 14–17, chap. XI.*) that Tenuto demands that the key must be *rested upon* sufficiently heavily to overbalance its weight and friction, thus preventing its rebound when Tone-excitation has been completed; and that the key-*bed* should not be rested upon more heavily than to fulfil this purpose.[1]

b): We also found that such weight, continuing to rest upon the key-*beds* beyond the moment of the completion of the act of tone-production, may be transferred from key to key, and that the effect of *legato* can thus be induced.

c): Moreover, we found, that such act of continuous Resting might be even *lighter* than it is in Tenuto or Legato, and that the effect of *staccato* would thus be

---

[1] The keys must not be rested upon more heavily *during the interspaces between the successive acts of tone-production* than is necessary to induce Legato. *Slight* increases in the Resting-weight are nevertheless permissible for the production of slight *crescendi*, in the case of *pp* "weighed-touch," etc. Such slight increase of Resting-weight also becomes desirable in very loud passages, especially when these are given with *sudden* tone-production. The Resting-weight would otherwise here not suffice to prevent the rebound of the keys. Nevertheless, weight thus used for Resting, must never (even in such forcible passages) be allowed to approximate to the energy (or weight) actually used upon the keys *during* descent to create *forte*; else the passage will inevitably "stick" and sound "dead." (*Vide Appendix, Part III. Note XVII.*)

THE CONCEPTS OF TOUCH.

induced. For the resting weight is in this case incompetent to *prevent* the key from rebounding, provided the tone-producing impetus given to the key is meanwhile accurately ceased. The key, in thus rebounding, will also carry up with it the finger-tip lying on it, and we shall thus find our "Resting" occurring *at the surface level of the keyboard*, instead of at the depressed level, as in Legato.

d): The transference of such Resting therefore takes place from key to key at *surface*-level in Staccato; whereas in Legato it occurs from the *depressed*-level of one key *to the surface level of the next*.

e): The necessity of "Resting" was re-enforced in the last chapter, where we found that besides the physical ones there are also muscular reasons why a *non-percussive renewal of the contact between player and keyboard* is essential, if beauty and certainty in tone-result are a desideratum.

f): It is only in finger-passages that this contact between player and keyboard is really *continuous* as a Resting. In Hand-Touch ("wrist") passages and in Arm-Touch passages we find an admirable equivalent in the ever-recurring gentle resumption of key-contact; which thus creates a ZONE of resistance, felt at the surface-level of the key-board.

g): As the lighter form of Resting [1] does not by itself serve to create any sound whatever, it is also clear that we must here *add* Energy to each individual key to cause its deflection,—an Addition that must cease to exist the moment that tone is completed, and which must therefore be provided independently of the Resting.

h): Again, it follows, that a similar "Added Impetus" (as it may conveniently be termed) is also essential during each individual key-depression, when we require a Tenuto or Legato of *more* tone-quantity than absolute *pp*. For the resting, although in this case heavier than

[1] The Staccato form of it, which is also required for all Agility passages.

in Staccato, is nevertheless by itself only competent to depress the keys *at their softest*. And we dare not continue on the key-*beds* the force here employed *during* key-descent, as this would militate against our *aiming* the intended Energy, and as this would in any case form waste of power.

i) : Finally, we see that it is only when we take Tenuto or Legato in its softest or "weighed" form, that we require no "Added-impetus." For the act of Resting here suffices, alone, to overbalance the key into sound; and since this same muscular-act here continues unchanged when key-depression is reached, the key remains in its depressed condition. The act of Resting and that of key-deflection are therefore in this solitary instance identical. This being so, Pianissimo-Tenuto or Legato constitutes the only SIMPLE form of Touch, muscularly; while all other touches are COMPOUND, containing as they do both the " Resting " and the "Added-impetus."

§ 4. The *first* point all this serves to re-enforce upon our attention (and it cannot be too strongly impressed) is : that all passages, no matter whether they are Staccato or fully Legato, must be conceived as *a series (or string) of* DISCONTINUOUS *muscular operations* against the key-board, individually provided, directed and ceased for each of the sounds that form the passage ;—the solitary exception being *pp*-tenuto (weighed-*pp*) or *pp*-legato (weight-transfer-touch).

The second point is, that we must conceive these distinct and separate muscular-acts (for each sound) as being *accompanied by a continuous act of light resting* on the keys. Such Resting being *continuous* during each phrase in Finger-passages, and in the form of a constantly resumed Contact in the case of Hand (Wrist), and Arm touches.[1] This Resting being moreover, in the case of Staccato, not heavy enough to depress

---

[1] That form of Staccato, where hand and arm seem to bound right off the key-board, may at first sight appear to be a contradiction of this general principle. It is however no more so than is the detached ejaculation of words

the keys, nor heavy enough therefore to keep them depressed; here serving merely to remind us *whence* to commence the tone-producing stresses—the key-surface;[1] whereas, in the case of Tenuto or Legato, the Resting is slightly *less light*, being here sufficiently heavy to depress the keys and to keep them depressed.[2]

In other words: all touches (always excepting *pp* Ten. or Leg.) consist of a series of *discontinuous* operations against the individual keys,[3] in combination with a *continuous* one against the key-board. That is: we have a series of short-lived impetuses delivered to the individual keys, simultaneous with an act of Resting, continuous during each phrase, and which is somewhat more or less light, according as the desired result be Staccato or Legato.

Or, finally, we might define Touch as consisting of an act of a refutation of the general principle, that our phrases are spoken "in one breath."

The Staccato *rebound* of a limb *during the course of a phrase*, forms quite a distinct conception from that final (and more permanent) floating-up of the arm, which is more or less inseparable from the act of ending a phrase.

In the quicker passages especially, such rebounds of the limb are *unbrokenly* followed by its re-descent, until the completion of each act of phrasing, and the sensation of continuous "Resting" is here therefore very distinct, in spite of the flow of rebounds.

This matter will become clearer, when we learn to recognise (*Vide Chapters XVII. and XVIII.*) how such apparent rebound of the limb right off the keys, is in reality a muscular lifting, strictly consequent upon (and automatically prompted by) the *rebound of the key itself*.—For it is not in this case an act of wilful affectation, as it is often however observed to be in the case of those who endeavour to ape the merely *visible* evidences of good, free execution.

[1] The rebound of the key and finger, in extreme Staccatissimo, may be assisted by a slight driving-off action against the key-beds, analogous to the act of jumping or kicking.

[2] Unless we accept this dual interpretation of the Act of Touch, we shall be reduced to a still more complex one, the only alternative: we shall have to conceive each individual "note" as being (*a*) preceded by an individual act of key-weighing, (*b*) the process of depression, followed by (*c*) an individual act of resting on the key-bed in the case of Tenuti or Legato, or a "lifting" off of the limb, in the case of Staccato. And while this triple conception would fail to embrace *that sense of continuance* between the notes of a phrase that characterises correct key-treatment (and would therefore not be in accord with facts) it would meanwhile prove insuperably complex.

[3] This fact, that the true aspect of all Technique (except *pp* Ten. or Leg.) consists of a series of *discontinuous* operations, is perhaps the most important of all the facts connected with Tone-production. Agility remains impossible unless this is thoroughly grasped (consciously or unconsciously) and all other technical accuracy as well as expression remains equally unattainable.

KEY-TREATMENT; MUSCULAR ASPECT.

Resting, *interspersed* with a series of added Impetuses; the determining influence as to sound-*duration* being the level at which the Resting occurs; and the determining influence as to *sound-kind*, being the form taken by the Added impetus.[1]

§ 5. Such correct conceptions of Touch teach us indeed to regard the key *at its top-most level* (and during depression *to* Sound) as the Object, or resistance, against which to apply ourselves in producing tone; thus at the same time forbidding us to regard the key-*bed* as that object. We learn indeed, that we must endeavour to feel the key *as solid as possible* at its surface-level, whilst avoiding that sensation so far as possible when the key is depressed.

In a word, we must learn to depress the key solely for the sake of obtaining Sound,—and not at all for the sake of the mere *muscular* satisfaction of impinging against the key-bed.[2]

§ 6. The reason why the incipient player so rarely consciously, or unconsciously, discovers the fact of the discontinuity of the muscular operations in playing, is to be attributed to the circumstance that the Ear itself is so misleading in this particular respect.

This is not to be wondered at, when we remember, that all legato passages and phrases (and velocity passages too) form CONTINUOUS aural effects. Such continuous impression on the ear must hence almost inevitably suggest, and lead to, a

---

[1] In fact, as already pointed out, one may say, that all Tenuti and Legati include—embrace—or contain—in their performance (muscularly) a *staccatissimo* for each note!—since each act of tone-production must always be concluded as sharply as in an actual Staccatissimo,—no matter whether the key is, or is not, subsequently retained by the state of the continuous Resting obtaining at the moment.

Conversely, we may say: that all Finger-*staccato* passages do also contain an element muscularly akin to that required for Legato!—For we here still have the element of Resting, although it must in this instance be light enough (at the surface of the key-board) not to compel the fingers to retain their keys depressed beyond the moment that the separate acts of tone-production have been completed.

[2] One's primeval ideas of the key-board are thus totally reversed: Instead of imagining (as most of us do at first) that we have to deal with a *flimsy* surface and a solid key-bed, we must force ourselves to recognise that surface as being heavy and ponderous and potent, while nought but (un-solid) *sound* should be reached at the bottom-level:—a solid surface "with holes for the sounds to come out."

continuous muscular stress upon the key-board, unless such muscular wrong-doing is corrected by knowledge or unconscious experience; knowledge, that individual muscular acts are required for *each* of the components of such continuous aural-effect.[1]

§ 7. We will then take it as established, that the process of Touch (or Tone-production) is muscularly a *dual* or *compound* one, excepting always in the solitary case of *pianissimo* Tenuto or Legato, which latter is therefore the only *simple* Touch-kind. In applying these concepts *directively* in performance, all we therefore have to do, is to see to it (*a*) that the Resting is REAL, and of the kind required; and (*b*) that the Added-impetus is also of the kind required, and above all things, that this latter is " accurately aimed "—TIMED—to cease at the moment of its consummation in Sound."[2] In short, we must more or less consciously *choose* the requisite *kind* of Resting and kind of Key-deflection, and must insist that the first is real, and that the latter is accurately " aimed " by the Ear to the time-spot musically due. (*Vide Note XIII, Appendix to this Part*, "The province of automaticity.")

§ 8. This consummation and ending of the muscular-act in

[1] In other words: the very fact of the aural effect being continuous, will tend to prevent our discovering that the production of each individual unit of a passage should form an almost instantaneous operation,—separate and individual for each note, even in the most rapid, and in the most connected passages.

In the case of most other instruments, we find that the aural effect and the muscular operation do coincide as to continuity. At the Pianoforte, on the contrary, *the moment we permit such aural prompting to induce continuity in the muscular stresses employed* (excepting in *pp* Ten. and Leg.), *that moment all ease in technique vanishes*, and passages become blurred to extinction.

Hence the necessity to insist on mastering the conception of Touch, as consisting of a dual act: of " Resting " and " Added-impetus,"—however difficult it may seem at first to do so.—This will however become easier, when we have studied the later chapters, dealing with the " actions and in-actions," etc.

[2] We must remember, that we can and should be conscious of the place where sound begins, in each separate key-descent during a slow passage; but that such " aiming " must be transformed into a " general impression " in the case of rapid passages,—a general impression of Place (near the key-beds) where the whole *row* of individual finger-impulses culminates. In the latter case, it is a *continuous* Place to which the timed-units of the passage are aimed, —it is somewhat like driving a furrow along the key-depth, a furrow of carefully *uniform depth*, and not too deep!

Sound, we must realise as the *deed* itself of tone-production—the Note.

"Aiming" in its Pianoforte sense, we now see means, that we must *finish* each Key-depression at the moment the sound is musically due to commence. Our sense of rhythmical necessity is thus translated into a physical reality;—musical Imagination and physical Execution that moment merge or coalesce into one Identity; and we see again how it is on the common ground of RHYTHMICAL-DEFINITION, alone, that they unite.[1] (*Vide Part I., Chap. V.*)

§ 9. We learn moreover this important fact: *that we must conceive and undertake the production of each sound at the pianoforte* BEFORE *the moment it is musically due;* since it is at this moment that the production of the sound must arrive at completion.

That is, if we wish to play in time, we must *begin* the process of making each note sufficiently before the time its completion is due, to allow us to feel and depress the key in the right way.[2] In a singing passage this involves quite a perceptible lapse of time, owing to the very gradual form of production there required. Unless this fact is appreciated, it often leads to an unconscious "spreading" between the hands.

§ 10. Here it will be well to give a series of pedagogic definitions of the nature and duties of the various forms of Resting and Added-impetus. These definitions at the same time form the "Recapitulatory" of this chapter.

---

[1] Chapter XVIII, "The Muscular Tests," deals with the forms of Muscular-testing that provide the means of our ensuring the acquisition, and subsequent constant application, of these two essentials of Technique—the reality of the Resting (or Key-weighing) and accuracy in "aiming" the consummation and cessation of the key-deflecting impulse.

[2] The experience is here somewhat akin to that of production on the Trombone, where, owing to its slow speech, the actual commencement of the act of production has to be timed somewhat before the moment the sound is required.

RECAPITULATORY, AND DEFINITIONS

a): Touch consists of two concepts, and acts:
        (*a*) a " Resting,"
        (*b*) an " Added-impetus."

b): The act of Resting is analogous to that of *breath-control* in Speech, and Song. Phrasing is mainly made evident through the continuance or discontinuance of this element of Resting, or its equivalent.

c): The act of Resting is *continuous* during each phrase in all finger-passages, whether these be Legato or Staccato. It is also in a sense continuous even during " wrist " and arm passages.

d): We may " rest " upon the key-board in two distinct ways:—

    (1) We may do so with weight no greater than the keys will bear *without* their being thereby depressed. In this form it is the Basis of *staccato*.

    (2) We may do so, with slightly more weight, sufficient just to *overbalance* the key into descent, and thus to provoke its softest sound. This forms the basis of all Tenuti and Legati.

    In the first case we rest at the *surface-level* of the key-board; in the second case we rest at the *depressed-level* of the key-board.

e): The non-percussive renewal of Contact with the key-board forms an equivalent to the first-named form of the Resting.

f): The *first*, or lighter form of the Resting (at the surface-level of the key-board) keeps us informed *where* the key is in space, and of the degree of resistance it offers to movement; so that we may know *whence* to commence the stresses needed for tone-production, and their required intensity.

Such Resting, unaided, is incapable of creating tone; the Added-impetus is therefore here required in any case to form the tone.

g): The *second*, or heavier form of Resting (at depressed key-level) includes the first. It compels the fingers to retain their keys in a depressed condition, as required for Legato and Tenuto, and it gives us besides the same information as does the Surface-resting.

h): This *second* form of Resting should outbalance the key with no more weight than will just suffice to overcome the friction and inertia of the Key and String. This Resting, unaided, is competent to produce soft sounds; and it forms the sole means of obtaining the true, absolute *pp*.

But when *greater tone-amounts* than *pp* are desired, an Added-impetus is also here required, just as in the Staccato form of the Resting.[1]

i): Such "weighed" *pp*, moreover forms the only *simple* form of Touch; since it consists of but one act—that of Resting.

j): All other forms of touch are *compound*, for these require the co-operation of the Added-impetus with the Resting.

k): The muscular-difference between Staccato and Tenuto consists therefore in the *difference of level* at which the Resting is accomplished. Such difference in level depends upon the slight difference in the Weight continuously resting upon the key-board. The heavier form of the Resting compels the fingers to continue working against their keys, *beyond* the completion of each individual act of tone-production; while the lighter form permits them to rebound with the key.

l): Legato consists of a sequence of *complete* Tenuti. The Resting is here transferred from finger to finger;—the transference being in this case effected from the bottom of a depressed key, to the *surface* of the key whose deflection we intend to start; whereas in Staccato, the transference is effected entirely at the surface-level of the key-board.

m): As all forms of Staccato, Tenuto and Legato (except absolute *pp*) require the Added-impetus to form the tone, we must be careful that Energy, thus applied for tone-production, is promptly and completely *ceased* when sound is reached.

---

[1] It is permissible to induce *slight* increments of tone beyond *pp* by means of slight increases in the transferred or "passed-on" Resting-weight. This for instance is appropriate in many of the gentle, but swiftly swirling arabesques or *cadenzi* of Chopin and Liszt.

THE CONCEPTS OF TOUCH.

n): Both Tone-quantity and quality (except *ppp*) depend on the form and application of this Added-impetus. It is the source of all colouring.

o): Touch consists therefore of a *continuous* Element (the Resting) which determines Duration; interspersed with a *discontinuous* Element (the Added-impetus) which determines Sound-kind.[1]

p): In playing, we must hence be careful (*a*) to select the *right* kind of Resting, and to see that this is *real*; and (*b*) that the Added-impetus is accurately "aimed" to culminate and cease with each sound-beginning, and that it is muscularly of the required kind.

[1] A Synopsis follows in tabular form.

NOTE as to §§ *h* and *i*.—Refer to Note III, *On Pianissimo Playing*, in "Some Commentaries on Pianoforte Technique; a Supplement to 'Act of Touch' and 'First Principles.'"—(Longmans.)

TABLE

TOUCH
Consists of:—

THE RESTING The continuous Element		THE ADDED-IMPETUS The dis-continuous Element
Is coexistent with the duration of each phrase or sustained note: Either absolutely continuous, as in all finger passages, or of *resumed* continuance, in Hand and Arm passages.		Lasts only during the moment of key-deflection, and ceases instantly with the emission of sound, no matter what the kind of tone.
FIRST, OR LIGHTER FORM, at key-surface only, is **The Basis of all Staccati.**	**SECOND, OR HEAVIER FORM,** at key-bed; includes the first form, and is **The Basis of all Tenuti and Legati.**	Required to produce the sound in all *staccati*; also in all Tenuti and Legati of *greater* Tone-amount than pp.
Not heavy enough to depress the key; hence permits the key to rebound on the conclusion of the act of key-depression.	Suffices to depress the key *at its softest*, and to retain it depressed.*	Its many-sidedness permits all tone-differences both of Quality and Quantity. The various forms consequently required of it, are described in the Chapters that follow.
	(a) Tenuto, and all degrees of Duration less than that, down to staccato.	*(b)* Legato, when the Tenuti are transferred from finger to finger.	

* The Resting and the Added-impetus are hence identical in ppp-Tenuto or Legato, which thus forms the only simple form of Touch.

CHAPTER XVI.

THE NATURE OF THE LIMBS EMPLOYED, AND THEIR MUSCULAR EQUIPMENT.

§ 1. The Limb, from finger-tip to shoulder, consists of four main sections in the shape of four *levers*, which we can employ either separately or in conjunction; these are:

    a. **The Upper-arm**—from Shoulder to Elbow.
    b. **The Fore-arm**—from Elbow to Wrist-joint.
    c. **The Hand**—from Wrist to the Knuckle-joint; and
    d. **The four Fingers and the Thumb**; the fingers commence at the Knuckle, and each consists of three little levers, termed the *phalanges*, of which the first one (nearest the Hand) is the Knuckle-phalanx, the second the Middle-phalanx, and the third the Nail-phalanx. The thumb also consists of three little levers, but instead of commencing at the Knuckle-joint like the fingers, its movement arises close to the wrist-end of the hand.

§ 2. Each of these four sections of the whole limb is provided with its own set of muscles; thus giving us more or less independent use of each section.[1]

§ 3. The whole limb can also be raised at the shoulder, in-

---

[1] In this way we are enabled to raise Finger, Hand, Fore-arm, or Upper-arm, either independently or conjointly.

dependently of any action or inaction on the part of any portion of the limb itself.[1]

§ 4. The muscles that energise the limb are not necessarily found upon that portion of the limb to which they give movement. While they are attached (by tendons or otherwise) to the part of the limb they serve to move, they have their "origin" on an adjoining portion, or even on a portion next again removed.

§ 5. Thus we find, that the movements of the hand are caused by muscles attached to the fore-arm and upper-arm; and that the fore-arm derives its attached muscles from the upper-arm and shoulder; while the muscles moving the fingers spring not only from the hand itself, but also from the fore-arm and upper-arm. It is also well to note, that the muscles that raise the upper-arm, pull it forward or drag it backward and rotate it either outwards or inwards, are placed on the shoulder-blades and on the chest and back;—and it is the raising (or forward-acting) muscles of the upper-arm which we must *relax*, if we wish to obtain the free weight of the upper-arm, as required in playing.[2]

[1] Although such movement is not required in playing, yet we must be careful also to train these raising-muscles,—so that they may when required be left *lax*.

[2] Such general ideas as to the location of the various muscles is of some value, since it may prevent our misunderstanding the muscular-effects required when we try to cause some portion of a limb to act, or to remain lax. For example, if we wish to "release" the Fore-arm, unless we are aware that the muscles concerned are not at all on the fore-arm itself, but are instead on the upper-arm, we may in our ignorance endeavour to create a muscular-change *inside* the Fore-arm itself; and the result would probably then be a dead-lock, since such misplaced attention would certainly tend to cause a stiffening of the limb, and would thus prevent the very effect desired.

It is however quite possible to be over-zealous in this direction. Beyond a merely rudimentary understanding of the locality of the muscles, and the principles of their action, we cannot derive therefrom much direct or practical help. Firstly, because we cannot directly induce a particular piece of flesh to contract or relax, although we may know it to be the implicated muscle. Secondly, because the use or disuse of even a portion of a limb, involves usually far too complex a set of muscular co-ordinations to be thinkable, even if we had the power to "*think*" a muscle, which we have not,—for it is only through remembrance of the sensations that accompany particular muscular changes, that we can learn consciously to direct such changes. Besides this, there are muscles that have quite opposite functions, which are in many cases

THE LIMBS EMPLOYED. 149

§ 6. The Fingers are not only furnished with muscles that enable us to move or exert them upwards and downwards, but they are also provided with others by which we can move them from side to side.

§ 7. The Hand is similarly provided.[1]

§ 8. The Fore-arm and the Upper-arm are similarly and separately endowed with muscles that will provide movements or exertions directed either upwards or downwards, or sideways.

§ 9. The Fore-arm can moreover be applied *rotarily*. That is, it can be partially rotated on its own axis, and can thus be exerted and relaxed in a rotary direction,—a twisting action that appears to arise at the Elbow-joint.[2]

Fore-arm Rotation, besides the actual movement, has a far more important function; since it permits us both to *equalise* and *un-equalise* the effect of Hand-force upon the fingers.—It enables us to support the *opposite* side of the hand off the keys, when the thumb or little-finger is engaged against them; and by employing the *release* at either side of the hand (and arm), it also enables us to provide Weight behind either the little-finger or the thumb, when these are required to act energetically;

---

so closely placed together anatomically, that it requires some dissection to separate them. It is therefore futile to attempt to learn much, by watching the actual muscular-contractions that accompany exertion or movement.

What is required, is knowledge of the mechanical effects required *from the various portions of the limbs*—the leverages and stresses that can be induced by the living levers actuated by such muscles. These mechanical effects, we can formulate as Thought, through sensation;—it is the *activity* or the *in-activity* of the living lever which results from the desired muscular-conditions, which we can think of, and can therefore learn to direct by the intervention of the Will.

[1] Here it is interesting to note that the four chief muscles that energise the Hand, giving it both its vertical and horizontal powers, serve the double purpose. Situated on the fore-arm, their tendons cross the wrist-joint, and are inserted into the hand close to its wrist-end. They can either be paired so as to enable the hand to act upwards or downwards; or they can be paired to act in couples on either side, thus enabling the hand to give those side-to-side movements of itself or the wrist-joint, required to help the thumb when "turning under," and the fingers when "turning over."

[2] Rotation of the Fore-arm—the act of pronation and supination—is really a twisting and un-twisting of the bones forming the Fore-arm. It is this twisting action that makes it seem as if the Fore-arm were rotated on a pivot at the Elbow, although there is no actual rotation at that point.

thus not only equalising the effect of the thumb and little-finger, but also giving us the option of rendering either side of the hand more powerful for the moment.

§ 10. The Upper-arm is somewhat similarly provided. The twisting in this case arises at the Shoulder-joint. This helps to give us that fan-like movement of the Fore-arm, that allows the hand to sweep across the key-board to a considerable distance, while the Elbow itself remains stationary.[1] This enables us to take "skips" within a range of about two octaves with a certainty and a rapidity that would be far less easy of attainment, if not impossible, with a compound movement of the *whole* arm.

§ 11. Coming now back to the Fingers, we find that they have this peculiarity: that they can be moved or exerted in *two quite distinct ways*; for we find that they can be exerted either *outwards*, or *inwards*, during their downward action against the key;—or the difference might be described as either "forwards" or "backwards."

It is imperative thoroughly to distinguish between these two completely opposite *attitudes* of the Finger,—the difference between the *thrusting* (or *bent*) attitude, and the *clinging* (or *flat*) attitude:—

§ 12. The THRUSTING attitude of the finger implies, that it *un-bends* (un-folds, or expands) as it descends upon and with the key; the nail-phalanx here remains practically *vertical* throughout both the upward and the downward movement; while the finger assumes a more closely *bent* position the higher it is raised, preliminary to the act of tone-production. *Vide Fig. 6, next page.* The CLINGING attitude implies, that the finger *tends*, in descending, to fold in upon the hand, somewhat as in the commencement of the act of grasping; all three phalanges of the fingers here act equally in the same

---

[1] The Upper-arm bone rotates on its own axis, rotation taking place at the shoulder-joint, so that the hinge-shaped joint with the fore-arm faces alternately a little outwards or a little inwards. As the fore-arm is in a position almost at an obtuse angle with the upper-arm during performance, the fore-arm with the hand is therefore carried from side to side, the level being maintained by slight accessory up and down adjustments of the fore-arm itself.

direction; while the finger assumes a more *flat* (or straighter) position, the higher its preliminary raising. *Vide Fig. 7.*

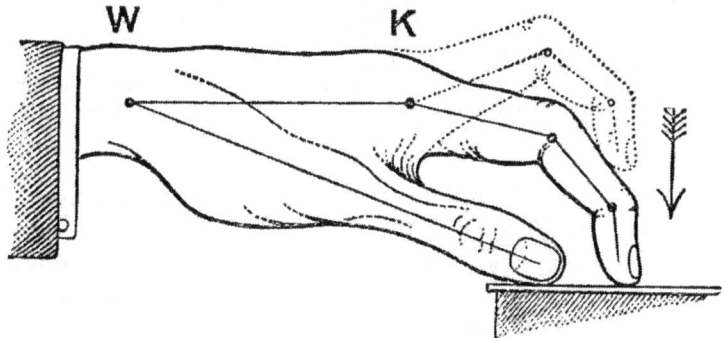

Fig. 6.—The Thrusting (Bent) Finger-attitude.

The position is with depressed key; the dotted lines exhibit the index-finger fully raised.
W is the Wrist, K the Knuckle.

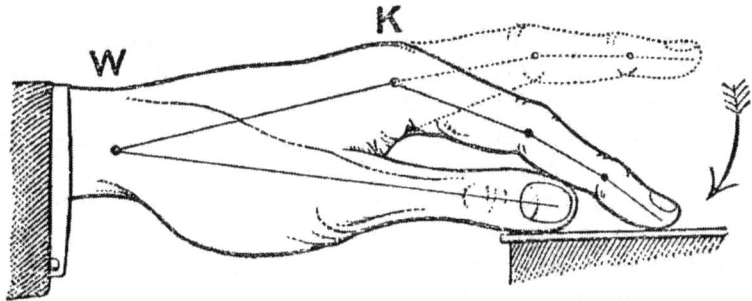

Fig. 7.—The Clinging (Flat) Finger-attitude.

The position is with depressed key; the dotted lines exhibit the index-finger fully raised.

The above two figures are designed to exhibit the two opposite Finger-attitudes employed in playing. They consist of differences in movement and action, and they demand totally opposite *conditions* of the Upper-arm.

The actual *Position* assumed by the Wrist-joint and Knuckle may vary rather considerably, without interfering with the due operation of these two opposite sets of Muscular-conditions:

The main point with the Thrusting-attitude, Fig. 6, is, that the Knuckle must be sufficiently high to allow it easily to take the *thrust* of the fingers;— wherefore some teachers bend the fingers very fully and hold the Knuckle exceedingly high with a low-dropped wrist.*

The Clinging-action (Fig. 7) even admits of the Wrist-joint being either

---

* *Vide,* for instance, the excessively high Knuckle (with dropped wrist) as illustrated in VON MELASFELD'S "Die Hand des Pianisten;"—Leschetizki Method.

held quite high, or of being dropped below the level of the key-board,—provided no running passage be attempted in the latter case. It also admits of the finger being as much curved with full key-depression as in thrusting-action—but such contracted position in this case modifies the tone-character from that resulting from the fully "flat,"—and "elastic" finger.

The main difference to be noted by the eye, is, that when the finger is *well-raised* as a preliminary, it is much curved in the first attitude, whereas it is almost fully opened-out in the second.

These points will be further elucidated in the next chapter, and also in Part IV., "On Position."

§ 13. As already indicated, besides having the power independently to move either the whole limb or a portion of it, we also possess the option of exerting the muscles that serve to actuate such movement, *without any actual movement arising* from such exertion; the attached limb instead exhibiting force or stress in one direction or the other:

In this case there will be *no visual evidence* of any Exertion or Lapse of it, and the only proof that there has been any change in muscular-condition will be in the force or stress exhibited against either some outside object (such as the key) or against some other portion of the same limb.

It so happens, that the most important Actions and In-actions required in tone-production are precisely the ones that are thus "hidden" for want of resulting *movement*, and it is these very ones that require the most careful direction when learning to play.[1] We see therefore why it is so much more important to study Condition, than the merely resulting Position of the limbs concerned.

§ 14. Absence of visible result from Exertion or Lapse of it, may arise from several causes:

    a) Movement may be prevented from resulting from Muscular-exertion, by causes *outside* the limb; this will happen if the resistance opposed to the free end of the limb is greater than the force exerted by it.

[1] To teach and acquire these "hidden" muscular-changes, they must (as already pointed out) be first demonstrated visually, *i.e.*, *as movements*; after having been thus learnt, the same muscular-changes must then be slightly modified, thus eventually inducing them without the accompaniment of the non-required motion.

THE LIMBS EMPLOYED. 153

b) Movement may fail to arise, owing to contrary and balancing exertions, or the WEIGHT of *other portions* of the limb.

c) Movement may be impeded or prevented, by exertion of the *contrary* or *opposing* muscles of the *same portion* of the limb.[1]

§ 15. This last alternative has a most important bearing on the muscular aspect of technique. It must therefore be considered more closely :—

Let us clearly understand, that for every muscle or set of muscles designed to produce movement or stress, we are also provided with an opposite muscle or set of muscles, that enables us to execute the opposite movement or stress by means of that same section of the limb.

§ 16. It follows, that if opposite sets of muscles are *equally* exerted, that the two balance, and that there will be no movement as a result of such exertion, and also no effect upon any outside object, such as the key. The only effect being, that the limb (or portion of it affected) becomes " set " or rigid for the time.

[1] Thus, we may exert the finger, or the hand and the finger together downwards, against an un-giving surface, and no movement will arise unless the exertion exceeds a certain limit ; and if it exceeds such limit, an upward movement of the knuckle and wrist-joint will arise by recoil. Understanding how such upward recoil arises from the downward action of the finger and hand against a surface, we can also realise how such upward recoil can be *prevented*, by allowing the supporting muscles of the *arm* to lapse sufficiently ; for the Weight thus set free will bear downwards at the wrist, and will thus prevent the recoil there. In thus preventing loss of energy by recoil, our fingers will consequently act more effectively,—for instance against the keys during descent.*

Moreover, we can also understand, how the exertions of a limb can be either partly or completely *nullified* as regards application against an outside object, such as the key, if we permit the *opposite exertion* to be made along with the desired one—if, in making the exertion that serves to provoke the desired movement or stress, we also at the same time make the exertion that produces the opposite effects. This we can illustrate, by holding an arm raised, and "stiffening" it ; for the stiffening is purely owing to the conflict between the two opposite sets of muscles, each nullifying the other's influence. We see the same apparent loss of energy in the "tug of war,"— when two parties of athletes pull on a rope in opposite directions, with hardly any visible effect either one way or the other ; the energy applied by one party being almost or completely counteracted by their opponents.

* *Vide* next Chapter for details on this point.

Such *tendency* towards rigidity is indeed bound to ensue, however slightly the opposite muscles are allowed to act. The latter must therefore remain perfectly quiescent, if we would obtain the best effects from our muscular efforts against the keys.

§ 17. It is imperative to bear in mind, that there can be no real "STIFFNESS" either of Finger, "Wrist" or Arm, except from such conflicting action of the muscles themselves. Excepting, of course, in those rare cases of stiffening disease, such as rheumatism or gout, or other physical abnormality.

All "stiffness" vanishes under normal circumstances, when we succeed in employing the required muscles only, and no others.[1]

Hence the excellence of the doctrine of EASE. Ease—absolute freedom from all restraint in the muscular actions employed at the Pianoforte,—or in any other athletic pursuit.

§ 18. Hence also, if we would learn to play with freedom and ease, the *first step* muscularly, is, to learn to separate or isolate all muscular activities from their opposite ones—giving as complete relaxation to these opposite ones as possible.[2]

As already insisted upon, inexpertness in this respect, absolutely prevents the attainment of all certainty and subtlety of technique of every kind,—including tone-variety, control of

---

[1] Provided, also, that we carefully cease all unnecessary action, the moment the sound appears in key-descent.

[2] The "Tonicity" of the muscles, as it is termed, sets a pathological limit to such relaxation; for an extremely slight residuum of tension probably remains in all muscles, even when we leave them as passive as we can.

No doubt it is owing in part to the slight *variations in degree* of this element of Tonicity—variations depending directly on our bodily health and nervous state, whence that daily, nay, hourly, variation in technical-power arises, which every player experiences more or less—often to his confusion and exasperation! Here however, we must always remain at the momentary mercy of our Body, and surrounding circumstances; as we must in that other essential matter, that of *Musical-attention*, given fully, will-lessly and under emotional-stress—so often consecrated and sanctified under the name of "Inspiration." We can nevertheless help ourselves greatly in both these matters, once we recognise the *immediate* cause of our perhaps but momentary inefficiency :—

Knowing that Relaxation, that Ease is essential—as essential indeed as Musical-attention or "Listening," knowing this, we can even when not muscularly "fit," nor "inspired," still succeed in forcing ourselves into a condition of Mind and Body, at all events somewhat less un-fit.

THE LIMBS EMPLOYED. 155

sound-entry (Time) and also that facility in Agility, to which the all-embracing term Technique is so often limited.

Such Isolation of the muscular exertions from their opposite ones, certainly comes more easily to some than to others. Those who easily learn it—to whom it "comes naturally," in popular parlance—are indeed *muscularly* gifted for the Pianoforte, and for any other musical instrument; especially if they have in addition *large* muscles,—a good "Piano-voice" in a word.[1]

§ 19. This passivity of the opposing muscles we can teach ourselves by a direct method :—

In this case, we must first learn to recognise the muscular act *we wish to omit*. This we can do, by first allowing that act to induce a movement of the limb-section it is attached to, and *noting the sensation* which arises from such act,—a sensation that can be intensified by applying such act against an object outside the limb, of sufficient power of resistance—a table for instance.

Having thus learnt to recognise the muscular-sensation that accompanies the *action* of those muscles *which we desire to render passive*, we can then proceed to teach them this desired habit, by seeing to it, and insisting upon it, that the sensation that accompanies their activity is *omitted* when we employ that opposite movement of the limb (or stress by means of it) which we wish to render free and unrestrained.[2]

---

[1] Here it is well to repeat, that such talent is, however, not at all necessarily accompanied by a *musical faculty*, any more than the latter is a necessary concomitant of the possession of a good vocal-apparatus ; while the converse is also true,—for a bias towards Music does not necessarily bring in its train those valuable muscular-talents, that render the acquisition of Technique so much more easy of attainment.

[2] An actual example of the general principles to be pursued, will make this clearer : To free for instance the required downward act of the Hand (" wrist-action " so-called) from being opposed and rendered " stiff " by the raising muscles of the hand, we must first learn to recognise the particular muscular-sensation that will *warn* us of our wrong-doing. This we may do, by simply raising the hand as stiffly as possible, and carefully noting the accompanying stiff sensation, which we have to avoid in playing ; and following this experiment with a free movement of the hand. Or : we may place the back of the hand under the ledge of a table, and exert it *upwards* against the table, first pressing the knuckle thus against the table by the hand, and afterwards sub-

The Studies, or Exercises in *Muscular-Discrimination*, that form Part V. ("Relaxation") of this work, will here be found useful; for these are designed to supply the opportunity for such direct study of all the main muscular acts required in playing.

§ 20. *To sum up :*

We must learn to segregate the exertions that will enable us to move one finger independently of another, and each either in the "thrusting" or the "clinging" attitude, and in any direction sideways; also the Upper-arm from the Fore-arm; and the latter from the Hand. And while we can thus mentally separate one portion of the limb from another, we must also be able to isolate each separate exertion from its related *opposite* exertion.

We must first learn to recognise these differences; must then fix them in our memory, and subsequently form such discriminatory-powers into physical habits. Always remembering, that without perfect practical passivity of all contrary-muscles, it is quite impossible to direct the required exertions with that complete nicety and mastery that is imperative for *artistic* playing.

RECAPITULATORY

a) : The limb employed in playing consists of four main portions, four levers:—the Finger, the Hand, the Fore-arm and the Upper-arm.

b) : Each portion or segment is individually provided with muscles; we can therefore control each portion separately—both as to exertion, and as to lapse of it.

c) : The finger can be exerted in two completely different

stituting the back of the fingers, to be thus pressed upwards by the hand. The sensation accompanying this upward action of the hand (the one to be avoided) should then be compared with the sensation arising from a free action of the hand downwards against the table.

It is advisable not to employ much force in such trials or experiments; there is no occasion to do so, and it may even prove harmful.

Exactly similar procedure will teach us to avoid a restrained (or "stiff") action of the fingers.

THE LIMBS EMPLOYED.

ways;—the Bent or *Thrusting* attitude; and the Flat, or *Clinging* attitude.[1]

d): Exertion implies muscular-action. For every exertion we are able to make in any direction, we are also provided with muscles to provide the *reverse* exertion.

e): Exertion of a muscle leads to a visible result—motion of the limb-section to which it is attached, only when there be nothing to prevent such motion.

f): Four quite distinct effects may hence result from a muscular-exertion:—

(1) It may lead to an actual *movement* of the portion of the limb to which it is attached;

(2) It may cause that limb-section to *bear* against some outside object,—such as the Pianoforte key;

(3) Or may cause it to bear against another portion of the *same* limb;

(4) Lastly, if allowed to act in sympathy with its *opposite* neighbour, it will deter that muscle (or set) in its work; thus leading to the work being done un-freely, or even inducing for the time a total stiffening or rigidity of the involved portion of the limb.

g): The isolation of each set of muscular impulses from its opposite set, is hence the first and most important step towards acquiring a correct Technique; since any inexpertness in this respect causes a "stiffness" of Finger and Wrist, etc., that infallibly precludes accuracy either in tonal or in rhythmical result.

h): RELAXATION—Ease, derived from the omission of all unnecessary muscular-exertion (in conjunction with accuracy in its application to the key), forms the main secret of all *easy* and therefore accurate Playing.

[1] *Vide Figs. 6 and 7, page 151.*

CHAPTER XVII.

THE MUSCULAR ACTIONS AND INACTIONS CONCERNED IN THE ACT OF TOUCH.

The nature of the Muscular-Operation. § 1. The nature of the muscular act by means of which the necessities of Key-treatment are fulfilled, may at its broadest be defined as an ACT OF LEVERAGE.

All good touch implies a levering of Weight upon and against the key,[1] to induce the latter to move.

This act of leverage must be almost entirely fulfilled by the Finger and Hand.

§ 2. The Weight thus brought to bear upon the key, is that of the ARM.

When more Weight is required than that of the Arm alone, then we must employ that of the Shoulder, bringing it to bear upon the keys through the leverage exerted by certain of the arm-muscles, in addition to those of the finger and hand. The WEIGHT of the Body itself may ultimately thus be requisitioned.

The leverage-principle nevertheless remains unaltered,—any muscular-force, correctly employed in the act of tone-production *must invariably act upwards* against Weight.

Exertion produces an Upward-stress. § 3. To amplify this:—The consequence of the Finger acting downwards with its tip against the key, is, that it bears *upwards* (by recoil) with equal force against the knuckle of the hand.[2] Similarly,

---

[1] That is, Leverage against Weight,—leverage against the key, with a Basis for this leverage consisting of Weight, to prevent waste of Energy by recoil.

[2] That is, the finger bears *upwards* against the Knuckle with the same degree of force, that its tip is exerted against the key.

As some of my readers may not be aware of the inevitableness of the law of recoil—the law that action and re-action are equal, I will quote the following from GANOT, "Physics," translated by Atkinson, § 39 :—"*Reaction is always equal and contrary to action : that is to say, mutual actions of two bodies on each other are always forces equal in amount and opposite in direction.* This law is perfectly general, and is equally true when the bodies are in motion as well as when they are at rest."

THE ACTIONS AND INACTIONS. 159

the consequence of the Hand acting downwards upon the Finger at its knuckle-end, is, that the Hand also equally bears *upwards* (with its Wrist-end) against the Fore-arm. We thus find, that the Finger and Hand bear upwards against the ARM (at the Wrist-joint) when we play, just as our legs bear upwards against our bodies in walking up (and *down*) stairs, or as in cycling.

The ultimate foundation, or Basis, for the Fingers' and Hand's work against the key, is moreover seen to consist of Arm-weight,[1] sometimes supplemented by Shoulder-weight, or even Body-weight.[2]

Body-weight not Body-force. § 4. For the extremest *forte* effects, we thus find that it is the PASSIVE Body which serves as an ultimate reserve of Weight, and it of course forms an inexhaustible reserve.

Now it is extremely important that we should at once fully recognise and grasp the difference between correct and incorrect muscular-condition in this connection:

The exertion employed to impel the key into a high rate of speed, however great, must never exceed a *tendency* to force the shoulders and body *upwards;* such upward tendency being the recoil-result of the leverage exerted upon the key (during its descent) by the finger, hand and arm.[3] That is, we must not permit ourselves to force the finger and hand down *by using the muscles* of the Body and Back, in place of such proper levering against a *passive* body.

Or, in other words: Although the leverage exerted against the keys, may, when sufficiently great, *tend* by recoil to bear the body upwards by the shoulder, yet the body itself must nevertheless remain absolutely passive—loose, and lax; and

---

[1] *Vide Appendix to Part III., Note XIX.:* "*Arm-weight.*"
[2] This "bearing upwards against Weight" applies equally, whether the arm is released, or not, at the moment of key-depression; and it applies still, when we occasionally have to assist arm-*weight*, by having recourse to a slight activity of the arm itself—as light activity that is mostly confined to the fore-arm; the arm, in its turn, bears still upwards,—against the loose-left Shoulder, or the Body itself.
[3] Needless to add, we must not allow this recoil to cause any actual upward *movement* of the shoulder.

we must never be tempted to *push forwards and downwards* upon the finger and hand by any actual exertion of the body itself.[1] (*Vide also, Appendix to this Part, Note XVI.,* "*Incorrect v. correct Finger-technique.*")

The accompanying sensation.
§ 5. Since the exertions employed are almost entirely provided by the finger and hand, and since it is only Exertion which we can appreciate as muscular sensation, it follows that the sensation accompanying the employment of finger and hand exertion (against arm-weight) must be felt to be *upwards;*—and not downwards, as might be imagined.

Moreover, as the action of the finger and hand is in the nature of a levering of weight upon the key, the sensation conveyed may also be said to resemble a *stepping-up on to the keys,* to induce their descent. For the muscular act resembles that of stepping upstairs, and also that of bearing against the cycle-pedal with our legs.[2]

[1] This radical difference between good and bad action, should at once be made plain to every beginner, even the child-beginner. This can easily be done by means of the two following experiments, which should be repeated as often as necessary:
Experiment I: Place the fingers upon the key-board in an easy chord-position, without sounding the notes. Now force the arm and hand both forwards (towards the instrument) and downwards by means of the Body and Back; and we at once perceive the nature of the iniquitous "Body-squeezing" process, so common a fault.
Experiment II: Place fingers as before, but now leave the body perfectly passive and lax; and while insisting upon this condition, endeavour to raise the body from its seat, by means of the leverage exerted upon the keys by the fingers and hands, and the consequent stress upwards by recoil against the shoulder. N.B.: No *actual* raising of the Body is possible, nor should it be attempted. The exertion in the *direction* indicated is all that is required. In the *first* case, we shall feel as if *acting downwards;* in the *second* case, the sensation will unmistakably be felt to be *upwards* against weight.
It should be insisted upon, that the first attitude will assuredly compel the appearance of most of the faults (including stiffening and squeezing, etc.) which it should be our constant endeavour to avoid in learning Technique; whereas with the *second* attitude, our Technique *may* at once be on the correct lines, although even then it will not necessarily be so, unless we also fulfil the many other necessary rules of procedure.

[2] True, when we are in a hurry, it may seem that we "strike" the stairs with our feet; but this is not really so, unless we do so as naughty children, and "stamp" upstairs! We certainly do not "strike" the cycle-pedal!—most carefully indeed do we guide our feet to "take hold" upon it, to propel ourselves.
It is also true, that both in the case of the stairs, and the cycle-pedal, a

THE ACTIONS AND INACTIONS. 161

Three main muscular-components.
§ 6. Seeing that we have to deal with Finger-exertion, Hand-exertion, and Arm-weight (and its co-operatives) as the main sources of Energy by which to set the key into motion, we now realise that all Touch is built up of these THREE MAIN MUSCULAR-COMPONENTS.

We should carefully bear this in mind, for these three muscular-components (or elements) of force, can be applied to the key, combined in a great variety of ways. In fact, these modes of application can again be classified, as coming under *three main principles of combination*, forming THREE SPECIES OF TOUCH-FORMATION, or construction, viz.:

I.): Tone produced by exertion of Finger alone, with passive Hand and Arm.

II.): Finger and Hand both exerted against the key, with passive Arm.

III.): Arm-weight (etc.) combined with the Finger-and-hand exertion.

In forming or constructing the Act of Touch, a thorough understanding of these different modes of combining the Elements of force at our disposal is essential; for it is of the highest practical utility both to Teacher and Performer, in acquiring and applying a true Technique—a Technique that will serve the Artist. A separate chapter—(Chapter XIX.)—is therefore devoted to a fuller exposition of these points.

Arm-weight employed in two ways.
§ 7. To render the arm effective for its purpose as a Basis, we may employ it in either of two distinct ways:[1] (a), We may *support* it gently by its raising-muscles; or (b), we may leave it *un-supported* during the act of Tone-production.

"PRESSURE" does occur during the moment of propulsion; and in this sense, and this only, should "pressure" be experienced against the Piano-key. For we must be careful to understand, that such "pressure" will not serve the purposes of Tone-making, unless it exists between finger-tip and key *only during the short period* that the key is being brought under way, and is moving. As so often here insisted upon, all force exerted against the key *beyond* the moment that the latter reaches Sound is futile,—excepting only that very minute residue required to detain the key depressed in Tenuto and Legato.

[1] Unless such Basis or Foundation is supplied, energy will be lost at the Knuckle or Wrist by these giving way *upwards*, when we apply the finger-tip against the key.

M

In the *first* case (when the arm is gently and easily supported by its proper muscles) its inertia becomes available as the necessary basis for the Finger and Hand to act against; a basis sufficient for certain light touches, but insufficient where any large volume of tone is required.

In the *second* case (when the arm is left momentarily *un-supported*, or "relaxed" during the crisis of Key-descent) its whole weight may become available behind the finger and hand,—thus rendering possible large volumes of tone of a perfectly beautiful and un-forced character.[1]

Two sources of Energy, meeting at Wrist.

§ 8. We perceive, moreover, that the Energy required at the key-board is, broadly speaking, derived from TWO SOURCES; that is: (a), from *activity*—the exertion of the Finger and Hand, and (b), from *passivity*—the weight of the Arm and Shoulder set free. Further, we should now recognise, that these two sources of Energy MEET AT THE WRIST-JOINT, there manifesting themselves: (1), as an Activity *upwards*—derived from Finger and Hand; and (2), as a passive Weight there tending *downwards*.[2]

Quantity of sound depends on Total amount of energy.

§ 9. It is from the *sum-total* of the energies derived from these two sources, and thus set free against the key during its descent, that directly arises the total QUANTITY of tone for each note;— the particular grade of tone-quantity depending on the particular sum-total of such Energy.

Quality of sound mainly determined by the locality of the Initiatory force-component.

§ 10. The QUALITY of the resulting tone on the other hand depends primarily on the fact, that the tone-production may be INITIATED by *either* of these same two sources of Energy, viz.: either (a), by Arm-lapse, or (b), by the Finger's and Hand's muscular activity. They thus form the distinction between WEIGHT-TOUCH and MUSCULAR-TOUCH.

[1] The sensation of a *Loose-left* Arm must be still paramount, even when it is itself employed to "lever" Shoulder-weight upon the keys; for the *raising*-muscles of the arm should remain perfectly lax, even when we are employing its *down*-muscles to lever or bear-up against the Shoulder from the keys during their descent.

[2] Finger and Hand thus act *upwards* at the Wrist against the Weight of the

THE ACTIONS AND INACTIONS. 163

To describe these two GENERA of key-attack more fully:

a): We may *start* the muscular-operation required during the short space of Key-descent (or Tone-excitation) by "willing" the Arm-supporting muscles to LAPSE;—in this case, the finger and hand must automatically undertake the duty of supporting the Weight thus set free upon the key, doing so in response to the sensation of weight *felt* to be left un-supported.

b): We may, on the contrary, *start* the process of Tone-excitation, by "willing" the muscles of the Finger and Hand to ACT. In this case, *when required*, we may also add Arm-weight, through lapse on the part of the arm-supporting muscles; but this lapse will, under these circumstances be given in answer to the need for a firm Basis, felt at the Wrist-joint; for such need arises when Hand and Fingers act vigorously as in *forte*,—owing to the recoil upwards being equal to the force manifested against the key, as already pointed out.

§ 11. The tone-contrasts resulting from this difference in treatment are as follows:

Tone initiated by Muscular-lapse—by Weight, tends towards an un-percussive, singing, and *sympathetic* quality, strongly possessing the characteristic of "carrying power." These qualities it owes to the fact, that the full speed of the key's descent is here attained *gradually* rather than *suddenly*.

Tone, initiated on the contrary by Muscular-activity (that of the Finger and Hand), tends towards a percussive, sharp, aggressive, *brilliant* quality, possessing comparatively little fulness or carrying-power.[1] Reference should here be made to Fig. 4, Part II., Chapter XI.; §§ 12 and 13.

---

arm; while the latter is for this purpose either left *un-supported* by its muscles to the desired extent, or is instead gently *supported*—when only a fraction of the weight becomes effectively available. (*Vide Figs. 8 and 9, page 151.*)

[1] The reason why this difference in the *locality* of the Initiative forms the main muscular difference between Brilliant and Sympathetic Touch, is, that in the one case the application of Energy to the key is more *Sudden*, and in the other case more *Gradual*. That is: If we start the tone-production by activity of the Finger and Hand, the energies set free are more immediately transferred to the key-surface; and, are therefore translated into more sudden key-descent

Quality of sound influenced also by difference between Clinging and Thrusting attitude.

§ 12. The distinction between Sympathetic and Brilliant tone-qualities depends, further, on those two opposite relative conditions of the Arm and Finger, from which result the CLINGING and THRUSTING Finger-attitudes already alluded to in §§ 11 and 12 of last chapter.[1] That is, apart from the difference in tone-quality wrought by finger-and-hand Initiative, as against that wrought by weight-release Initiative, the distinction between "*sympathetic*" (full) tone, and "*brilliant*" (thin) tone, may be further enhanced by the optional employment of the FLAT finger-attitude, as against that of the BENT finger-attitude.

These two opposite attitudes of the finger, available, seem at first sight but a slight distinction, but they also bring in their train completely opposite attitudes of the *upper-arm*.[2]
For this reason they give rise to two diametrically opposite kinds of technique:

In the first case,—that which enhances "Sympathetic" tone-tendency—the Finger is applied in a comparatively

than if we start the tone-production by *lapse* of arm-support. In the latter case, the finger's and hand's supporting activities are given but in response to the promptings of the inauguratory arm-release, hence the energy takes longer to accumulate on the key, and thus induces that more gradual descent of the key which is associated with un-percussive tone.

We shall have no difficulty in grasping this matter, if we bear in mind the *duplex* nature of the muscular conditions required for all tone,—consisting as these do of the Weight of arm *versus* Muscular-activity of finger and hand. (*Vide* § 8.) If we do this, it becomes easy to realise that either of these two elements may *start* the process of tone-production, although *both* are more or less needed for its consummation.

The difference in general tendency of the muscular-attitude between sudden and gradual tone-production, may here be compared to the difference between mounting and descending a stair: Our legs support our bodies in both cases; but in the one case, there is "muscular-initiative," as it were; for in mounting, we have to do more than merely support the body. Whereas, in descending, we *omit* the exertion of our nether limbs just sufficiently to permit of a gentle descent of our body—one step at a time, and without percussion!

[1] *Vide Figs. 6 and 7, Chap. XVI., p. 151.*
[2] We shall find on closer investigation, that the true *cause* of the difference between "bent" and "flat" finger, is not to be traced to the difference in the finger's action, but rather to the difference in Condition of the Upper-arm or Elbow. In other words, it is owing to the last-mentioned fact—the fact of the Arm being either held supported forwards, or instead tending to hang loose, whence originates the finger's thrusting or clinging action, respectively. (*Vide Chap. XIX., § 20.*)

THE ACTIONS AND INACTIONS. 165

"FLAT" position. Its action here is, that it *clings* to the key, and tends to draw the Elbow towards the key-board. This *tendency* of the Elbow to be drawn forward by the finger's folding-up action,[1] must, however be prevented from actually taking place; it must be counterbalanced by a sufficient (and but momentary) lapse of the Upper-arm; such lapse being allowed to supervene at the proper moment during the act of key-depression.

In this way, the finger's *forward* pull upon the Elbow is so neutralised by the *backward*-tending Weight of the Upper-arm, as to cause these two forces together to act in a perfectly VERTICAL direction at the Wrist and upon the key; creating there the sensation of *verticality of application;* and not necessarily evincing any actual backward or forward movement of the limb during key-depression.

In the second case,—that which makes for brilliancy and sharpness of tone, the Finger is applied in its fully curved or "BENT" position. In this instance, its *tendency* is to *thrust* against the key, and therefore (by recoil) it also tends to thrust the Elbow away from the key-board. Any actual movement, or thrusting-back of the Elbow, must also here be prevented; this is accomplished by exerting the Upper-arm itself forwards, doing this however *very slightly*,—indeed not more so, than will just serve to neutralise the finger's backward-thrust. In this way, we here again obtain perfect *verticality* in the application of the force; such being one's experience at the Wrist-joint, and indeed also at the key itself. (*Vide Appendix, Part III., Note XV.:* "*Flat v. bent Finger-attitude.*")

These interactions of Exertion and Weight may become clearer by referring to the following two Figs., on the next page:

[1] The finger, in this case, *acts as a whole*,—all three segments of it in the same direction. It remains also almost straight during the process; while it feels like a mere rubber-stick or rope—as the arm does in hanging from a horizontal-bar;—a sensation very different from that derived from the legs in their *thrusting* action when mounting stairs.

166 KEY-TREATMENT; MUSCULAR ASPECT.

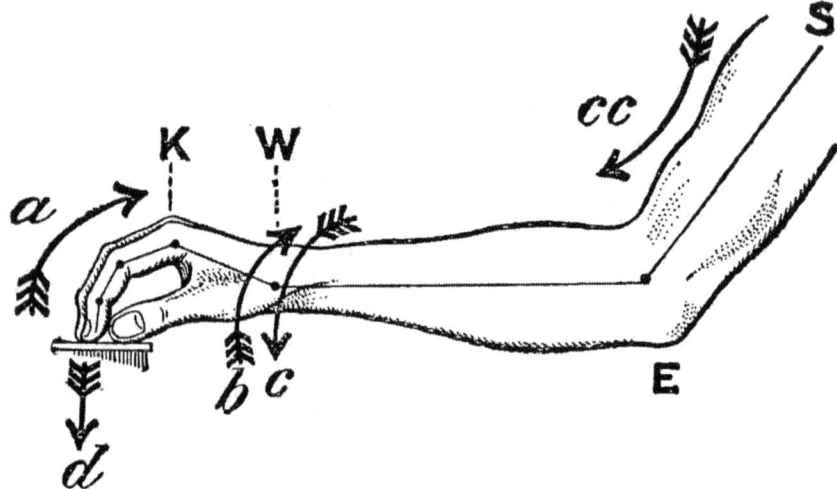

Fig. 8.—Description: * The arrows in the above, represent the directions in which the forces tend during BENT finger-attitude.

a and *b* denote the direction of the energy resulting by recoil from the *thrusting* action of the finger and hand against the key, and manifesting itself upwards and backwards respectively at the knuckle and wrist joints.

c and *cc*, the energy that balances this, derived from arm-weight and force.

K is the Knuckle; W the Wrist; E the Elbow, and S the Shoulder.

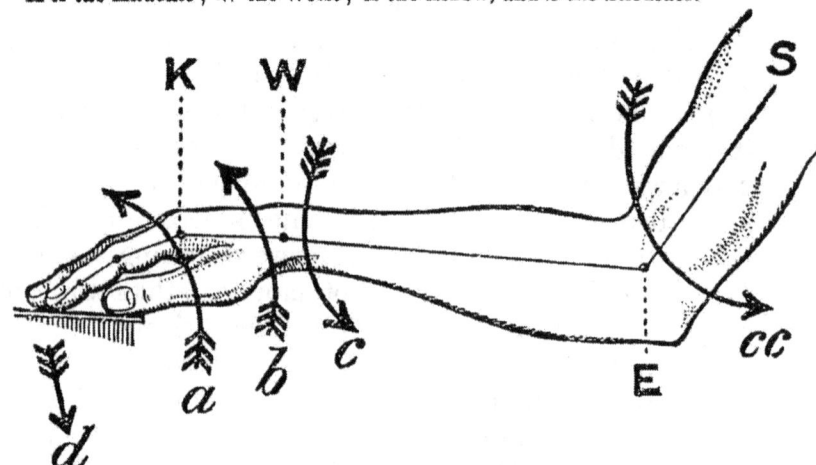

Fig. 9.—Description: The arrows denote the tendencies during FLAT finger-attitude.

a and *b* denote the direction of the energy resulting from the finger and hand *clinging* to the key, and how it manifests itself as an upward and forward-drawing stress at the knuckle and wrist.

c and *cc*, the direction in which the energy tends, that is set free in this case at the elbow and wrist, and derived from Arm-weight through its release.

d, in both Figs., shows the direction of the total Energy-result,—*vertical* upon the key during its descent, and slightly dragging, in Fig. 9.

* In Fig. 6, page 151, the Bent-finger was shown with the wrist-position almost as high as it may be; in the above figure, the lower position-limit is illustrated. On this point, the various "Methods" differ completely as to their Dogma. The fact is, that the precise position adopted should vary in accordance with variety in hand-conformation. (*Vide Part IV.*, "*On Position.*")

THE ACTIONS AND INACTIONS.

The difference between these two attitudes might also be expressed thus:

With the Bent-finger attitude, the whole framework of arm, hand and finger *tends to unbend* from its normal position; whereas with the Flat-finger attitude the general tendency is precisely in the opposite direction.

This can easily be made clear, by exaggerating these tendencies and stresses of the limb into actual movements of it,—although such movements are not required in actual performance at the instrument, and are even to be deprecated.

Fig. 10 is an attempt to show this experiment, and its interactions, on paper:

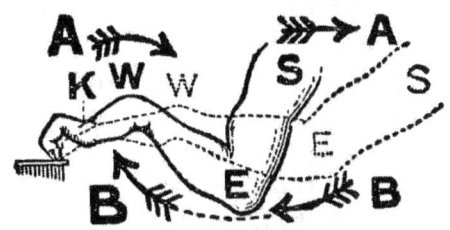

Fig. 10.—Description: Above Fig. represents the arm, hand and finger, in as fully doubled-up a position as it is possible to place them.
 In the case of Bent or Thrusting finger, the whole framework (from finger-tip to shoulder) will tend to *unbend* from such position to the one shown in dotted outline; —power to be derived from the finger and hand.
 In the case of Flat or Clinging finger, the tendency is, on the contrary, to *contract* from the fully extended position (in dotted outline) to the fully bent one.
 The arrows at A suggest the direction of force in thrusting-attitude; whereas those at B denote the direction in Clinging-attitude.
 Both positions are greatly exaggerated, to show the result of the required tendencies. Figs. 6 and 7, page 151, and Figs. 8 and 9, page 166, should be studied in conjunction with this experiment.

In making this experiment (and for the time exaggerating into visible movement those actions which in actual playing should be mere tendencies and stresses) we must be careful that these movements *are not caused by any action of the arm itself.* The movement must in both cases be wrought only by the action of the finger and the hand. In illustrating the Thrusting attitude, it is therefore the finger and hand, thrusting against the keys, that must thrust the arm away backwards; and in the case of Clinging-attitude it must be the finger and hand that must *draw* the arm towards the key-board.

The thumb does not show these divergencies of attitude so markedly as do the other fingers, and it does so in a slightly different fashion. This minor point will appear more clearly under "Position." (*Vide Part IV.*)

The difference in Elasticity is the reason of the difference in result.

§ 13. Let us for a moment consider *why* these divergencies in treatment further the difference between sympathetic and brilliant tone-effects:

The *flat* or *clinging* finger (with its correlated "hanging" upper-arm) reduces the whole system of finger-hand-and-arm into its *most elastic* condition;—a disposition favouring therefore a *gradual* transmission to the key of the full amount of Energy employed,—with its resulting gradual key-depression and more sympathetic (or unpercussive) quality of tone.[1]

The *bent* or *thrusting* finger (with its correlated *resisting* upper-arm, or elbow) on the contrary, places the whole limb in an inelastically standing condition upon the keys;—a disposition of the material therefore calculated to cause *direct* transmission of the full energy to the key;—with its resulting sudden depression of it, and consequent more brilliant tone-quality.[2]

---

[1] The part that Elasticity plays in promoting beauty of tone, has already been dimly recognised by many. Some have gone no further than to suppose that the difference is wrought by bringing "the more fleshy part" of the finger into contact with the key. Others have gone somewhat further, and have recognised that the finger itself is more elastic when it is applied in the "flatter" position; while they have not succeeded in recognising the function of Arm-weight, nor the supreme necessity of ceasing "pressure" the moment that tone has been reached in Key-descent. In a recent work (FRANKLIN TAYLOR, "Technique and Expression," page 10) we read for instance: "to produce the most musical and singing quality, it is necessary that the finger, however firm the pressure, should be in an elastic condition, and it is therefore important that every joint of the finger and hand, and even the wrist, should be kept loose, and should yield slightly with each pressure of the finger-tip." We now see, however, that it is the *whole* limb (from the shoulder) that becomes elastic if we employ Upper-arm Weight-lapse; the main cause of difference in tone-quality being the condition of the Upper-arm, or Elbow. For if the upper-arm *tends* forward, not only are elbow and finger more rigid, but the weight of the upper-arm cannot then be set free; and conversely, if the upper-arm hangs on to the key during descent, it will preclude our obtaining brilliance when we desire it, as we cannot then give a thrusting action of the finger.

[2] We observe that a "thrusting" finger demands a corresponding forward-tending Elbow:

This is all very well so long as *no very large* quantity of tone is required.

Knuckle-joint action, its importance.

§ 14. It is imperative thoroughly to understand the duties of the three Finger-phalanges, respectively in "flat" and in "bent" attitudes, and the precise nature of the contrasts here evident:—

The main point is, that it is the *knuckle-phalanx* (the portion of the finger next to the hand) that must do most of the actual work, both in clinging and thrusting attitudes. This portion of the finger must be exerted downwards upon the front two joints (and therefore upwards by recoil at the knuckle) no matter whether the two front joints are straightened out (as in clinging touch) or whether they are pointing downwards (as in thrusting touch).

The essential difference between the two Attitudes is therefore to be found in the action and resulting position of these two front phalanges,—(a), if these two phalanges are used in the comparatively vertical position, they thrust backwards in taking the down-force of the knuckle-phalanx behind them;—the action of the whole finger being here analogous to that of the leg in getting up from a chair, or in cycling, or in mounting stairs. Whereas (b), if we leave these front two joints almost straightened out, or with but a slight clinging action, then the whole finger makes the arm cling to the key;—an action analogous to that of the hand and arm when clinging to a horizontal bar.

But if we adopt this form of technique or "FORWARD TOUCH," as it may be termed, for a really full *forte* chord, then we shall find that the result is an exceedingly hard, sharp and disagreeable effect. An effect perhaps not objectionable to us if we are accustomed to its ugliness, but most objectionable when we have discovered that the instrument can give something better.

The fault is, that instead of doing as we should do, and allowing Arm-weight, and when necessary Shoulder-weight or even Body-weight to come upon the key—instead of "levering" Weight upon the key during its descent,—instead of the arm and shoulder being left free, so that finger and hand can "lift" this weight upon the key—instead of a perfect looseness of Body—in a word, instead of WEIGHT-TOUCH, we here as it were *wedge* the arm in between key and shoulder. The arm, in thus wedging itself against the keys, drives almost straight back against the shoulder,—and not *upwards* practically, as in Weight-touch. The consequence is, that the muscles of the body and back are compelled to resist this drive *backwards* by in turn driving the body itself forwards against the key.

Such rigid, real "down-arm" force (or Body-force) thus viciously employed in *fortes*, proves absolutely fatal to beauty of tone; although it forms a ready means of obtaining plenty of noise without much thought or care.

The fault of relying upon the two front phalanges.

§ 15. It is well to be urgently warned against the fatal fault so often connected with the flatter and clinging finger-attitude, a fault, which, when once formed is probably more difficult to eradicate than any other, viz.: the exertion of the two front portions of the finger with *more* force than the knuckle-portion.

In this case, the two front phalanges *pull inwards* towards the body, while the knuckle-phalanx remains almost passive; —causing the finger to feel quite helpless and weak.[1] This is owing to the exertion of the finger *not being vertical* upon the key as it should be—in the direction of the key's descent, but instead taking the form of an ineffective pull, or even backward rub. Such touch might aptly be dubbed "Key-tickling" instead of Playing. Fig. 11 exhibits an exaggerated view of this faulty tendency:

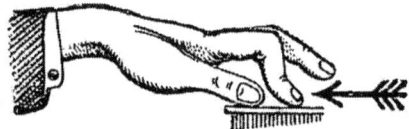

FIG. 11.—Faulty action of the *two front phalanges* of the finger, showing the result of these being exerted with greater force than the Knuckle-phalanx—which should be the main *working*-lever of the finger.

In correct "flat" finger-touch action, the two front phalanges should on the contrary be left comparatively passive, or almost completely so in fully sympathetic tone;—and it should always be the strong knuckle-phalanx (the one next to the hand) that provides the work of "levering weight" upon the key.[2]

---

[1] The opposite fault is also occasionally met with, viz.: a *thrusting* finger (and arm) with a perfectly *straight* position! It forms a most inconvenient and ungainly Touch-method, with a most ugly tone-result.

How Finger-action should be shown.

[2] The nature of Finger-action, in both its forms (and Hand-action also, in fact) is best made clear by *inverting* the hand, and laying it flat upon the table, or upon one's knee, and practising the following three exercises:

Procure a small weight of a few ounces—or use the partial weight of the other arm, transmitted through a finger or pencil. Let this weight rest upon the Knuckle-phalanx of one finger of the inverted hand, and close to the *middle-joint end* of this phalanx. Now raise the weight by means of this phalanx; support and balance the weight thus for a few moments, meanwhile

THE ACTIONS AND INACTIONS. 171

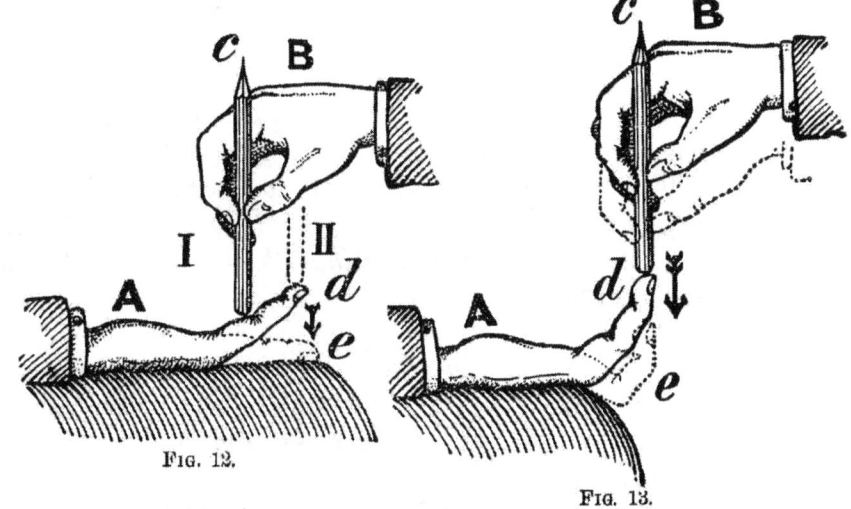

FIG. 12.

FIG. 13.

FIGS. 12 AND 13.—DESCRIPTION: A exhibits the learner's hand, lying inverted upon his knee. B the teacher's hand, its weight and energy being supported through the pencil *c* by the learner's finger *d*.

To instruct and exercise the Knuckle-phalanx alone, the pencil or weight should be placed as at I in Fig. 12. To instruct and exercise the finger as required for *clinging* attitude, the pencil should be placed as at II (dotted outline) in Fig. 12. While for the *thrusting*-attitude the finger and pencil should be as in Fig. 13.

If a weight is used in these exercises, it should be allowed to slide freely up and down between the fingers of the other hand, or the teacher's. If the weight is that of another arm (transmitted through a finger or pencil) then one should be careful that the resistance given be not too great; otherwise harm might be done.

---

taking care *not to move or exert the two front phalanges of the finger in question.* Then, suddenly *cease* this supporting exertion, and thus allow the weight to fall with the finger. Repeat this process several times. *Vide Position 1 of the pencil in Fig. 12.*

Next, place the weight (or finger, or pencil) on the soft tip of the working finger; and proceed again to lift, balance, and subsequently to let fall the weight with the finger. The two front joints are meanwhile to be left almost limp and inactive, and the position of the whole finger should therefore remain straight, while the work of lifting is to be done by the knuckle-phalanx itself, which should act precisely as in the first experiment. *Vide Position II of the pencil in Fig. 12.*

We have thus practised the action of the "flat" or *clinging* finger, and we must now study the action of the "bent" or *thrusting* finger in the same way:—

This is done thus: Bend the two front phalanges into the proper position—with nail phalanx vertical, and after placing the weight or pencil on the tip of this experimental finger close to its nail, now proceed again to exercise the finger in lifting, balancing and then suddenly ceasing to support the weight. *Vide Fig. 13.*

Having in this way learnt and practised the proper action of the Knuckle-

KEY-TREATMENT; MUSCULAR ASPECT.

§ 16. From the foregoing we obtain the two following practical rules for obtaining the respective extremes of Sympathetic and Brilliant tone-colours:

(a): *For extremely sympathetic-quality, we must allow the* flat *finger-attitude (with its hanging elbow) to co-operate with Weight-initiative; while* (b) *for extremely brilliant-quality we must on the contrary allow the* bent *finger-attitude with its forward-tending elbow to co-operate with Muscular-initiative.*

The distinction between Finger, Hand and Arm touches.

§ 17. We now come to the distinctions in touch-method respectively termed Arm-touch, Hand-touch (so-called "Wrist-action") and Finger-touch.

We shall now be prepared to realise that these are by no means the distinctions radically of KIND which they at first sight appear to be. For the movement of the Arm, Hand or Finger, visible during Tone-production, results from a merely *slight excess* on the part of one or other of the components of the complete muscular condition requisite (and different) for each particular kind of tone. It is the SUM of the arm, hand and finger *conditions* (which creates the particular muscular operation), that determines each tone-kind; whereas the distinction as to mere movement (be it that of the Arm, Hand, or Finger) depends on the fact that *one* of these components slightly outbalances the other two.

We therefore also perceive, taking the particular set of muscular conditions that produces any given kind of tone,[1] that such particular muscular-operation (with its resulting tone-shading) can be accompanied *by a movement of either the*

---

phalanx, both in the clinging and thrusting attitudes, the next step to take is, to repeat the whole proceeding at the Piano, with the hand returned to its proper un-inverted position; and while fulfilling the same changes of action and in-action, seeing to it, that the knuckle-phalanx still executes most of the work—of key-depression. Subsequently, we must then learn to *time this work accurately to cease* the moment sound-emission is reached in descent.

[1] Some muscular-combinations are however only available as Finger-touch and Hand-touch; while there are also a few available only as Finger-touch.

Finger, Hand or Arm, without materially affecting the tone-result.[1]

Arm-touch. § 18. Thus we find that:

(a): ARM-TOUCH (tone-production accompanied by Arm-*movement*) results, when there is a state of *balance* between the three components that form the complete muscular-operation against the key, during the latter's descent,—a state of balance between the Arm, Hand and Finger conditions.

For these three portions of the complete limb will in this case retain their relative positions towards each other during the act of key-descent; and the visible product must therefore be: a movement of the whole arm.

Hand-touch. (b): HAND-TOUCH (Wrist-touch)[2] results when Hand-exertion is slightly in excess of Arm-release and balances finger-exertion during key-descent. Hand-*move-*

[1] In a word, we find, that those differences in muscular co-ordination of Action and In-action ("Muscular-combinations") which are respectively required (a) to cause each possible difference in sound result; and (b) to give us command alike over ponderous passages and agility-passages, are *practically invisible*. And it follows, that those other differences, which are so strikingly exhibited to the Eye as MOVEMENT—of the Finger, Hand and Arm, are as nothing when compared to these *invisible* differences, just mentioned.

[2] Hand-touch is often mis-termed "Wrist-action," although the wrist cannot *act*, since it is merely a hinge. Finger-"action," and Arm-"action" are also most misleading terms. Finger-action, for instance, would seem to imply, that the finger is alone "active."—Whereas we have learned, that from finger-*movement* alone no tone can possibly result beyond a quite soft and springy one, *without the additional intervention of Hand-activity* to lever weight against the key,—while this latter addition need also not necessarily imply hand-*movement*.

Arm-"action" is also a peculiarly infelicitous term, since it must infallibly suggest to the unwary, an *active* "pounding" done by the arm. Especially so, as the beautifully free arm-movements of a great Artist (resulting from a more or less complete lapse of the arm-supporting muscles) are very likely to convey to the uninitiated eye, the impression of a real hitting-down of the keys by *down*-activity of the arm;—than which there can be no greater sin against the laws of tone-production, nor any, more far-reaching in its consequences.

Wrist-action, anyway, is a complete misnomer; for if Touch accompanied by Hand-movement is to be thus styled, then surely to be consistent, we should speak of Finger-movement as "Knuckle-action," and of arm-movement as "Elbow" or "Shoulder" ACTION.

The idea, however, really meant to be conveyed, is not at all that of "action" in the sense of work, but merely that of movement. Hence by so-called finger, hand (wrist) and arm "actions," are meant tone-excitations *accompanied* respectively by movements of those portions of the whole limb. Now, as the whole of the main *conditions* of the arm, hand and finger are

ment must obviously here be the product, for the slight excess of hand-exertion will suffice to prevent the Arm from falling (if it is muscularly-lapsed), while the finger-exertion (as it is not in excess of that of the hand) will only suffice to retain the finger in its relative position towards the hand.

Finger-touch. (c): FINGER-TOUCH results, when it is the finger-exertion that slightly (but sufficiently) outbalances that of the Hand, and of any Weight that may be set free by arm-lapse during Key-descent. For the slight excess of Finger-energy will here prevent both Hand and Arm from showing any movement, and Finger-movement hence becomes the only visible product.[1]

Vide, also appendix to this part, Note XVI., "Incorrect v. correct Finger-touch."

To sum this up: *The conditions of Arm, Hand, and Finger obtaining for any particular quantity and quality of tone remain practically identical, no matter whether these conditions exhibit arm, hand or finger movements as a result. Diversity of movement is quite a subsidiary difference, since it is simply the consequence of one of these components being very slightly in excess of the other two.*

The relative sensations of Finger, Hand and Arm touches. § 19. It is well to note in this connection, that when we move the finger only, the sensation resulting therefrom seems as it were to stop at the knuckle,—for the finger seems to thrust up against the Knuckle. When we employ hand-touch ("wrist-action") it appears as if we played upwards against the Wrist. Similarly, in employing only a movement of the fore-arm;[2] we find that the sensation may be described

clearly identical for each different tone-kind, no matter whether these conditions involve a *slight* excess on the part of one or other of the three components of the muscular-act, it follows, that it must prove far less misleading, if we choose the neutral term of "TOUCH." This nomenclature has therefore been adopted in this work.

[1] In speaking of "Finger-touch," do not let us forget that the term merely signifies, an act of Tone-production accompanied by a *movement* of the finger; and that this does not preclude our employing all three muscular components, when desirable. All three *Species* of Touch-formation can indeed be applied as "Finger-touch." (*Vide* § 6, and *Chapter XIX.*, on *these points*.)

[2] *Vide Note 2 to next paragraph,—next page.*

THE ACTIONS AND INACTIONS. 175

as being *upwards* against the Elbow; and likewise, if we employ a movement of the whole arm, and use the full "Piano-voice" we possess, the sensation seems upwards against the Shoulder,[1]—always "upwards," by recoil from the key.

Arm, Hand and Finger movements, when appropriate.

§ 20. Judicious choice between Arm, Hand and Finger touch (or movement), for each particular passage is of considerable importance. It is the actual speed of the passage that should in the main determine such choice.

Thus: ARM-touch (movement either of the whole arm, or of the fore-arm only) is the most appropriate to choose for a slow succession of chords or detached notes; in the same way that the most natural mode of picking up any object, when we are not in too great a hurry, is to move the arm towards it.[2]

Not only are slow successions of single notes and chords thus performed by arm-touch (*i.e.*, key-depression accompanied by arm-movement), but the beginnings practically of all phrases are performed in the same way; and this is done *whatever the nature of the touch* selected for the rest of the passage. The reason for this selection is, that it is more simple and easy thus to move the whole arm (or fore-arm) when there is time to do so, than *first* to move the arm towards the key (or other object) and then to commence *another movement* in taking hold of, and moving it.[3]

[1] When the whole arm moves with key-descent, we must remember to avoid making a mistake, similar to one already warned against; that namely of using the down (and backward) *muscular-exertion* of the UPPER-arm. The keys should not be pulled down by a backward exertion of the upper-arm; on the contrary, the backward *tendency* at the elbow (forming Clinging-touch) should be wrought solely by allowing the upper-arm to lapse.

[2] For certain passages, that prove too fast for a movement of the whole arm, and for which nevertheless it is not desirable to use Hand-touch, we may adopt a movement of the *fore-arm* only—a movement of the arm from the Elbow. This fore-arm movement may nevertheless be accompanied (when desirable for "thick" tone) by lapse in the support of the Upper-arm,—in which case we employ the Weight of that portion of the limb, without however showing any motion of it. If we do not employ such weight-lapse (of the upper-arm) then the touch becomes of the "forward" or "thrusting" description, with its less full, and more aggressive tone-character.

[3] Non-apprehension of this fact, is at the root of much absurdity in the choice of touch. This arises from prejudice against "using the arm too much," etc.; and it causes stilted movements of the hand and finger.

The absurdity of such prejudice becomes apparent, when we remember,

KEY-TREATMENT; MUSCULAR ASPECT.

HAND-TOUCH (Wrist-touch) becomes imperative, when the passage is too quick to permit of the reiterations of arm-movement. For the hand is a much shorter lever than the arm, and it therefore admits of far quicker repetition of its movements. The speed-limit, when Hand-touch becomes imperative in the place of Arm-touch, is quite definite for each player. The speed at which Arm-repetitions become laborious (and even impossible) to the individual, should in fact be carefully noted.

FINGER-TOUCH becomes essential, when the speed required is still greater. For even the shorter Hand-lever becomes cumbrous beyond a certain limit of speed, and the shortest-lever, *i.e.*, the Finger will then alone avail.[1] Finger-movement is also compulsory for all true Legato passages, whatever the *tempo;* since Legato can only be obtained by continuously carrying the Tenuto-form of the Resting from note to note, through the interposition of the successive fingers.

---

that *no note can be played above* mezzo-forte, without bringing the Arm-element into operation,—employed as it has to be either as an elastic, and then only partially effective Basis, or employed as a weight-providing component, *i.e.*, to its fullest effect, by the momentary omission of its own muscular support.

Granted, it is right to object to Arm-*movement*, when the speed in note-repetitions exceeds that which can be conveniently executed by moving so long a lever; and granted also, that no prejudice against arm-movement can possibly be too strong *when* the *said arm-movement signifies* ARM-FORCE *badly applied!*

[1] The Flat-finger attitude permits of a refinement of action and movement suitable for extremely rapid (and delicate) passages, such as are occasionally to be met with; as for instance in Chopin's Berceuse, with its sound-waftings—mere breaths almost—of bare-laid Emotion. In such case we move only *the front two phalanges of the finger;* the knuckle-phalanx being hardly moved at all. The motion of the finger is here altogether of the slightest description, just the depth of key-depression in fact. It indeed forms the solitary exception to the necessity of Knuckle-phalanx movement and exertion, so much insisted upon, which, in all other finger-touches should be paramount not only as to movement, but also as to *action*. As already pointed out (*Vide* § 15 *and its note*) movement and action are very cramped and ineffectual when restricted more or less to the front two phalanges. Therefore, excepting in the particular gossamer-like finger-touch here referred to, we must always remember that it is the strong knuckle-phalanx that must be relied upon to do most of the finger's work and movement;—just as the thigh of the leg is the most important factor in walking and cycling.

Combination-movements. Circumstances tend to modify the rules here given, since certain kinds of tone are more easy of attainment with a particular kind of movement.[1]

Although it is undesirable, and even impossible to move the longer levers in the quicker passages, yet this does not debar us from moving the shorter levers in the slower passages. There is in fact no reason why we should not at times employ a movement of the hand, or even of the finger, in quite a slow passage—the latter movement being indeed imperative when dealing with a Legato.

The movements of the arm, hand and finger may also at times be found desirable *in combination*. Thus, we may find passages suitable for a combination of finger and hand movement; or, a movement of the arm along with that of the hand.[2]

Choice of muscular-combination far more important than choice of movement. § 21. Of far greater importance however than choice of limb-movement, is choice of MUSCULAR-COMBINATION—the particular choice of muscular-*conditions* that will induce the right quantity and quality of tone—the choice also in this respect that will permit our attaining the full measure of required agility. As already noted in § 6, consideration of this all-important matter, the consideration of the *Three Species of Touch-formation, or construction*, is deferred until Chapter XIX. (*Vide also, Note to § 23.*)

Arm-weight—how obtained. § 22. We have elicited (§§ 2, 6, 7, 8 and elsewhere) that the use of Arm-weight is required for the "Added-impetus" during the moment of key-descent when the tone is to be full and round; and that we require it also in a slight and continuous form, for that second

---

[1] Singing-tone itself for instance is usually *far more simple* to obtain, when accompanied by a movement of the whole arm ;—although it can quite well be obtained, accompanied only by a movement of the hand or of the finger.

[2] As good examples of Finger-hand touch (finger and hand both moving) might be cited: The left-hand single-note staccato passage after the first octave subject, of Chopin's C-sharp minor Scherzo ; and the left-hand staccato from the *Allegretto* of Beethoven's Sonata in E flat, Op. 31. Some players would also for instance find the octaves of the same Chopin Scherzo more convenient as an example of Arm-hand staccato, than as one of pure Hand-touch.

kind of "Resting," which, while being ponderous enough to create *ppp*-sound unaided, also forms the Basis of all natural Tenuti and Legati. It is therefore obviously essential, that we should be able to obtain Arm-weight with certainty; since all beauty and fulness of tone, and ease in Legato, directly depend on our facility in this direction. Hence the following details:

To set Arm-weight free: we must relax (or cease acting with) the muscles that serve to move, or retain, or support the arm *upwards*.

Now (a), the arm will *rise*, if we exert these muscles sufficiently,—and the exertion will be hardly noticeable, it is so easy; while (b) the arm will remain gently and lightly supported off the keys, if we exert these muscles slightly *less* than will thus suffice to raise the arm; whereas (c), only if we *cease* acting with these same muscles (or relax them still further) will arm-weight be set free; for only then will the arm become limp and ready to fall, which it will in fact do, unless it is at that moment supported at the wrist by the fingers and hand upon the keys.[1]

It is important to notice, that the release required, is not that of the Fore-arm alone—a mistake often made—but that it is the whole arm (from the shoulder) that must be released. And as the muscles involved are partly situated on both sides of the shoulder and chest, it follows that the sensation of their exertion (and cessation of such exertion therefore) is not experienced in the arm itself, but is on the contrary felt to proceed from muscles situated upon the body—across the shoulders. Lapse in arm-support is hence felt as Shoulder-release.

The warning is also necessary, that mere *movement* of the

[1] No movement of the arm will ensue, if we do thus support the loose-left arm at the wrist through such reactions of the finger and hand activities against the key, although we shall feel the full benefit of the released weight during tone-production.

The amount of weight will of course be in direct proportion to the extent that the arm-release is complete or incomplete; while the operation of this weight must, as so often insisted upon, *cease* instantly when sound is reached.

arm can very easily be mistaken for release of it. The arm can nevertheless be moved downwards with a hardly appreciable amount of restraint, and yet be *in a totally unfit condition* for either full or beautiful tone; for unless the arm is really released, and is moreover released *in answer to* the key's felt resistance, failure will assuredly result.

In short, the movement of the arm, resulting from a real release, is perfectly free from all sensation of work done, and can be realised as a distinct *lapse* or cessation of work.

Those who do not naturally employ un-restrained muscular-actions (*Vide* § *23*), find it exceedingly difficult to give these necessary arm-releases; but unless they succeed in this, it is hopeless to endeavour to improve their tone-production.[1]

---

[1] Those, for instance, who have been accustomed to employ their arms in a "held" instead of released condition during *forte* touches, find it exceedingly difficult to hit upon the requisite condition of the limb,—unused as they are to such conditions of it in conjunction with a comparatively forcibly-acting finger and hand.

The main difficulty is of course the mental one: Such performers, to obtain the small and bad tone they have succeeded in obtaining, having formed the vicious habit of making violent exertions (either against the key-beds, or against their own muscles) find it an exceedingly difficult problem, to mentally disassociate a big tone from such huge exertions.

To remedy this, they must learn to realise (as above insisted upon) that quite a large tone can be obtained by means of that which feels like a *lapse* (or absence) of all exertion. For that is undoubtedly the sensation uppermost during the production of a really "full" tone, produced as this should be, by the supporting muscles of the arm being made to *cease* their activity during the moment of key-descent. If these muscles are relaxed, the arm lies as loose as it does when we lie down in an easy chair. And it must be realised that it is this *lax* arm which has to be supported upon (or levered on to) the keys by the finger and hand;—their exertion against the key *while the latter* is moving supporting the freed Weight at the Wrist-joint, by recoil.

To secure such required absence of arm Down-force (with its concomitant Body-force) a good lesson is as follows: Obtain a chair with an almost straight back to it; sitting rather closer to the instrument than in the usual position, one should lie well back against this support, thoroughly resting the full weight of the body against it. The body-muscles (the forward-driving ones) being now fully relaxed, the body no longer offers muscular *force* forwards against a backward-forcing arm. We shall therefore find ourselves strongly tempted to adopt unconsciously the desired touch-method, *i.e.*, Arm-weight *v.* Finger-and-hand exertion,—the Weight-touch form of tone-production. I have known this device effect its object almost instantaneously on subjects who have had years of wrong habit behind them in this direction. But of course, it will even then take time to form such newly-learnt manipulations into a strong *habit*.

Curiously enough, some of the greater Artists have been observed deliberately to lie back in their chairs when commencing a slow movement;—probably an unconscious action found provocative of the required more sympathetic tone.

180 KEY-TREATMENT; MUSCULAR ASPECT.

Where there are wrong habits of long standing in this respect, the first steps towards the employment of Weight-release in playing, had best be undertaken *away from the instrument*, with its faulty mental-muscular associations.[1] For it is easy to realise that the arm will fall of its own weight, if we only cease to support it by its own muscles, when the acquired faulty key-board-associations do not prevent our doing so. And having succeeded in this first step, it then becomes comparatively easy to realise, that the key also can be carried down by a similar *lapse* in arm-supporting work.

The question of opposing-muscles. § 23. As regards the required EXERTIONS of the Finger and Hand, it has already been insisted upon (Chapter XVI., §§ 13-15) that every muscular-exertion employed must be free from all *contrary exertion*; otherwise we cannot hope to play either with ease, or in response to our wish. It is therefore imperative, that we learn to direct the exertion of each set of muscles, without permitting the opposite set to act in sympathy with these required ones.[2]

To ensure this, we must eradicate *all sensation of restraint* during any of the movements required during performance. Every movement towards a key, or with it, must be kept perfectly free from any sensation of resistance *not directly*

---

[1] The *freedom* of action discussed here and in the next paragraph, and all the other main *muscular discriminations* required for tone-production, can be directly studied, taught and practised as to their fundamental principles, away from the instrument. The means of doing this, are indicated in Part V.,—"RELAXATION; Exercises in Muscular-discrimination," which see.

[2] Much bad playing, with bad tone-production as its cause, no doubt arises in the case of elementary students (young children and others) from the difficulty experienced *in distinguishing between* Mental and Muscular effort.

Mental effort is found necessary, and the hazy perception that an effort of *some kind* is required, leads consequently to the making of a general *muscular*-effort,—not a muscular-effort directed towards some particular key, during its descent only, and at a definite time, but an effort taking the form of muscular contractions all over the body, similar to those that supervene when one is startled.

Stiffening thus caused, cannot be corrected by talking of tone-production. It can only be cured, by making clear its true cause—the want of discrimination between the exertion of Will to concentrate, and muscular-exertion.

Vide Chap. XVI., § *15*, *on the cause of stiffening, etc.*

THE ACTIONS AND INACTIONS. 181

attributable to the resistance of the key itself, before and during its descent.

This rule cannot be too strongly insisted upon.[1]

The cessation of Weight.
§ 24. It is not enough to be able to set free Arm-weight when thus required for the "Added-impetus," but we must also be able to *cease* (or omit) such manifestations of Weight, the moment we have completed the act of tone-production. For unless we can, and do, thus "cease" the weight used, it will come to bear upon the key-beds; in which case it will greatly impede our attempts at Agility, and will also vitiate our AIMING of the Added-impetus, and will in this way preclude our obtaining the musical effects we intend.[2]

The process by which Weight is made to cease manifesting itself against the key, is, by calling the supporting (or "raising") muscles of the arm into operation. Evidently, therefore, if Weight is to be accurately directed to tone-consummation, it follows that the required *lapse* on the part of the arm-supporting muscles must not only be accurately *ceased* the moment the key reaches the point where Tone arises, but that the process must also at that very moment be reversed into an arm-sustaining action. Since these arm-sustaining muscles must commence to act at the very moment that the *down*-muscles of the finger and hand must *cease to act* (in response to our hearing the beginning of sound), it is clear that it would be almost impossible for us directly to "will" the arm-muscles in question into action. We could not accurately enough time

---

[1] In speaking of the muscles and "Contrary" muscles, it is well to repeat, that it requires the co-operation and co-ordination of many muscles to produce some of the apparently most simple actions. (*Vide Note to* § *5, Chap. XVI.*)

[2] For it manifestly constitutes a case of bad "aiming," when the energy intended to induce Tone, reaches the pads under the keys instead. And we must remind ourselves that such bad aiming not only effectually prevents all Agility, but also strongly militates against accuracy in Tone-response (accuracy in the correspondence of the deed to the wish), and renders a natural Staccato impossible, and finally makes the muscular-act of performance a vast labour instead of a delight.

This rule, as to the cessation of all energy used for key-depression, obviously applies as much to the energy derived from Weight, as it does to the energy derived from the finger and hand exertions.

them to do so; and we must therefore under no circumstances attempt to prevent Arm-weight from reaching the key-beds by directly "willing" these raising-muscles into action.

These muscles must, on the contrary, be taught to act practically by reflex-action; we must be able to rely on their acting *automatically* in response to the arm being suddenly "left in the lurch" at the wrist-joint, owing to the *well-timed cessation of the finger and hand exertions against the key* the very moment that tone-production is completed. That is: if we accurately time the exertions of the finger and hand to cease the moment that sound is reached, then the arm will be felt to be suddenly left *un-supported* at the wrist, and the arm-raising muscles will then (unconsciously to us) be induced to *re-take* charge of the arm (to prevent its falling) as before the commencement of the particular "Added-impetus" in question. Weight will consequently at that moment cease to bear upon the key,—and will leave the latter either free to rebound (and thus cause Staccato); or if the Resting is sufficiently cumbersome, will at all events relieve the key of all weight excepting that slight residue required to retain it depressed, for Tenuto or Legato.

To sum this up: *We shall only obtain a satisfactory result, when the arm is caught-up by its muscles* in response to the sudden failure *in its support at the Wrist-joint, arising from our willing the hand and finger to cease their action against the key.*[1]

The question of Legato v. Staccato. § 25. We have recognised (*Vide pp. 85, 111, and 136, etc.*) that the physical difference between Staccato and Legato is the amount of weight allowed to rest upon the key before *and after* each individual act of key-depression;—that such "Resting" may occur either at the surface-level or at the bottom-level of the key;—that the key

[1] The muscles will act far more promptly in this way, than if the action is *directly* willed by us; just as our legs will act far more promptly, in response to reflex-action, than in direct response to our will. For instance, the action of rising from our chair in direct response to our will cannot be executed with the celerity with which it is accomplished by reflex-action, in the event of the chair suddenly collapsing under us.

will rebound and form Staccato during the continuance of the "Surface-resting," provided we cease each "Added-impetus" accurately at the moment of sound-emission; and that Tenuto will arise, if the Resting is on the contrary ponderous enough to overbalance the key into descent, since the implicated fingers are in this case compelled to continue their work (to the extent of the Resting-weight) *beyond* the moment of sound-emission.[1]

There remains to be considered (1) how the effect of Rest

---

[1] Besides the *passive* Staccato here considered,—a Staccato induced and assured (a) by insisting on the continuous Resting-weight being so attenuated as *not* to compel the fingers to continue working beyond the moment that sound is reached, and (b) by insisting on accurately timing the cessation of each finger's action; besides this natural Staccato, there is also a forced kind,—a Staccatissimo, in which the key-bed is as it were "kicked" against by each finger.

While the *raising*-muscles of the finger and hand are not required in the natural Staccato, we find that in this "kick-off" Staccato they do come into operation in a slight measure. But even here, they must under no circumstances be directly *willed* into action. If we do try to "will" the raising of the limb, we shall only succeed in causing stiffness in its action. This is owing to the fact, that the raising-muscles must not commence to act, until the very moment that the *down*-action of the limb is completed, with the beginning of sound; and it is impossible for us *will-fully* to time the raising muscles with accuracy, at the very moment that the downward ones cease their work. Hence the raising-muscles must here again be taught to act only in strict *response* to the suggestion and impetus *derived from the rising key itself in its rebound.* We must therefore only think of "kicking" against the key-bed—an act analogous to the one of jumping, and the raising-muscles must act in automatic response to the felt rebound of the key; and coming thus into operation automatically, these will do so at the necessary moment. It is in this way that should be obtained this more rarely used, sharp and acrid form of Staccatissimo; and it is immaterial, in rising off the key, whether it is the finger, the hand, or the arm that is driven up.

The sharply accented initial staccato note, characteristic of a good Mazurka theme, may be cited as peculiarly appropriate for the application of this "kick-off" Staccato, and it can also be applied to staccatissimo running passages of an incisive nature. As it can be formed into an excellent test for the employment of finger-and-hand force *without* the faulty arm-force, this matter will be more fully dealt with in Chapter XVIII., "The Tests," etc.

Moreover, besides the natural Legato, determined by the continuous (although light) Resting-weight, there is also an "artificial" form of legato, occasionally suitable, which does not thus depend on Weight-release, but on an artificially-continued application of hand-exertion. This has already been described in the "Preamble" to this Part,—Note 4, page 112, and it will be further discussed presently. (*Vide Appendix, Part III., Note XVII. Vide also Note 4 to § 27, page 185.*)

ing is obtained, muscularly, and (2) how the transfer of it is effected, muscularly.

Staccato-resting, how to be obtained.
§ 26. The first or *lighter* form of the Resting (the Surface-resting, required for Staccato and Agility) is induced by keeping the Arm *supported* by its own muscles, so that practically none of its weight reaches the key-board in a continuous form.[1]

One is very liable to allow this complete and continuous self-support of the arm to lapse more or less ; and we must be particularly aware of this danger, since the slightest weight of the arm, left continuously on the key-board, will infallibly wreck all Staccato as well as extreme Agility-passages.

The arm, while it must thus be *adequately* supported off the keys in Staccato and Agility, must nevertheless not be held in the least degree stiffly ;—on the contrary, it must as it were *float* over the key-board. The weight employed for this lighter form of the Resting, is therefore not Arm-weight at all, but merely the weight of the Hand. For this purpose, the hand must remain quite passive, and must lie loosely upon the keys. It may indeed be described as *hanging* from the arm at

---

[1] The Resting we must remember, should be *felt to be continuous* during each phrase, even when it is not directly transferred from note to note, as it is in all Finger-passages—both staccato and legato. This applies for instance even in the case of a high-stepping "wrist-touch," where the hand is well raised off the keys preparatory to each sound-excitation : for the general impression of the *normal* attitude during each phrase must even in this case be that of a continuous resting on the key-board, and it must not seem, as if the normal position *were the raised one.*

The latter idea is often used in teaching, but it is a doctrine that must be condemned as most mischievous. It implies a form of touch hardly ever appropriate ; and it of course necessitates a *continuous tension* of the "contrary" muscles for the time.

This doctrine of the *up*-held hand, as the normal position in Hand-touch— a "hand springing back from the key" cannot indeed be too strongly condemned. For it directly insures (a) *stiff* and clumsy performance of the act of key-depression ; (b) risks inflamed tendons ; and (c) reduces all playing to mere "fluking," since it prevents our judging with certainty *where* the keys are actually located, and the degree of resistance they offer to depression.

It must be repeated, that we can only obtain Certainty of technique, when proper key-contact, or Resting, precedes the act of key-depression ;—a preliminary act, we remember, that need not be separate from the ensuing act of key-depression, and which may, in the case of Velocity-passages, even merge into a mere general impression of key-board surface-resistance, felt to continue apparently during each phrase.

THE ACTIONS AND INACTIONS. 185

the wrist-joint,¹ while the fingers gently support it on the keys at their surface-level. Its weight, while thus adequate to render the contact between finger-tip and key sufficiently intimate for Staccato, etc., will not cause the keys to remain depressed, provided we are careful to insist on "aiming" the work of each finger to cease accurately, as each sound is reached.²

Legato-resting, how to be obtained. § 27. The second, or heavier form of the Resting (at bottom-level of the keys, as required for Tenuto and Legato) is, we have learnt, identical with the down-*weighed* key of absolute *pianissimo* touch (p. 145). Muscularly it should be induced by a slight lapse in the self-support of the arm. The *whole* arm must participate in the release in question, but this release of arm-weight must of course not be greater than will just serve to overbalance the key into descent. In other words: the whole arm must be released from the shoulder, just as it has to be for the momentary weight-release of the "Added-impetus,"³ but in this instance continuously, and only to the extent the key is *felt* to resist depression at its softest. And as we have already learnt, it is the *giving-way* of the key that tells us how much weight is needed to encompass this, while that same amount of weight also manifestly suffices to retain the key depressed with the least waste of power, both for Tenuto and Legato.⁴ Legato

---

¹ The fact, that the hand thus lies on the keys (or "hangs" from the wrist-joint), should not be understood to imply that the wrist should be placed in a higher level than the hand itself. Freedom it is, that should be striven for.
 This freedom we should often make sure of, by sliding the hand off the keys, and seeing whether it *drops* over the edge.

² The sensation of *contact* with the key derived from such mere passive Resting, can however be considerably intensified, if we add to the Resting a slight clinging action of the two front phalanges of the fingers, causing them individually to contract and lock upon their respective keys at surface-level by their nail-phalanges. Such attenuated "clinging" must however in this instance be so slight—so infinitesimal—as not in the least to call the Upper-arm into responsive Lapse—as in a true "clinging" touch, else the tone would be influenced, and the Staccato ruined. Such slight nail-joint-clinging to the key, if properly executed, will however much enhance our confidence and security in certain soft Agility-passages, enabling us to give them with far more evenness than could be otherwise attained.

³ *Vide* § 22, *Arm-weight, how obtained.*

⁴ It is obvious that the finger and hand must *act* very slightly more in the heavier form of the Resting than in the lighter form, as a slightly heavier weight has to be supported continuously in the latter case. But such exer-

can only exist in the *finger-touch* form of all the Species, as already pointed out in Chapter XV., for there is no other way of producing that actual transfer of light weight that causes the effect.[1]

Weight-transfer, its muscular-aspect. § 28. We have learnt how a Pianissimo-tenuto, such as was considered in the last paragraph, can be transformed into a *ppp* Finger-legato, by causing the light weight thus resting on the key-beds, to be transferred from key to key. Now one should be careful to insist, that such transfer of weight is effected by directing each weight-supporting finger in turn to *cease* its gentle task; and that such cessation be timed to occur at the moment when the next key is desired to *commence* its descent. The finger already in contact with this next note will in this case be *automatically* prompted into activity,—prompted into supporting in its turn the continuous weight of the act of Resting.[2]

tion of the finger and hand (for the purpose of Resting, in both its forms) is so slight, as to be hardly noticeable, even when specially watched for. Any exertion, beyond this degree, felt against the key-beds, can therefore safely be assumed to be caused by some inaccuracy in the Conditions that should obtain during touch of any kind. Slightly more weight than is ordinarily required for Tenuto and Legato, and *pp* Weight-touch, can however under exceptional circumstances be "carried along" with impunity in Finger-passages. Such slight *extra* Weight is required for certain Over-legato passages and the "artificial" or "pressure" Legati, already referred to. Moreover, as already pointed out, a similar increment or weight can also be applied for certain *heavy* Staccato-passages.

These exceptional matters receive further attention in the Appendix to this Part, Note XVII. "Certain exceptional forms of Legato and Staccato, and the slightly heavier Resting thus transmissible." (*Vide also Notes to* §§ *25 and 27.*)

[1] Hand or Arm Legato, does not exist, properly speaking; for there cannot be more than a mere approximation towards Legato, when the hand itself actually rises with the key, and thus allows the damper to fall before the next key has begun to descend, unless the Pedal is used. So-called Legato by means of Hand and Arm-movements, is therefore necessarily but a *close sequence of Tenuti,* each one distinct for each note, in spite of the general impression of Resting on the key-beds that accompanies such touches;—an impression derived from the continuous series of Restings there accomplished after the completion of each individual tone-production unit; and owing also to the key-board-surface not being quitted between the sounds.

[2] Weight is thus suddenly as it were "left in the lurch," and it is this sensation which should by reflex action prompt the new finger into its necessary action. As already pointed out (Preamble to this Part, page 113, Note 1) we have an excellent analogy in the act of *walking,* when quietly fulfilled. For the transfer of the Resting-weight from finger to finger, is accomplished precisely in the same way as the weight of the body in walking,—the lapse in the sup-

THE ACTIONS AND INACTIONS.

An automatic and perfect Legato is thus secured, owing to the ascending and descending keys passing each other at the right moment.

The sensation accompanying the Transfer. § 29. Coming now to the sensation that accompanies correct transfer of the Resting-weight. As we here cause the new finger to act, not by directly "willing" it into action, but on the contrary, by timing the *cessation* of the preceding finger's support of weight, we find as a consequence, that the sensation, so far from being an active one, is on the contrary *passive* in character. That is: the act of transference is felt rather as a *lapse* in exertion than as an exertion,—the transfer seems to "do itself," since it is accomplished without our willing any added-effort at the moment. The weight is also felt to pass-on from the bottom of one key, to the *top* (or surface-level) of the next. The general sensation being, that each note seems successively to "become" another note, just as in vocal tone-production. Indeed, the idea of separate and detached acts of tone-production does here in a measure become blurred over,[1] owing to this sensation of one finger *giving way* to the next finger in causing the new note; thus creating a continuity in sensation, while inducing the continuity in sound.[2]

PP - Weight-touch accompanies all Tenuti and Legati. § 30. We now realise more clearly, how this same act which forms *pianissimo*-tenuto and legato, does also accompany ALL Tenuti and Legati, however much their tone-amount or quality may differ from this Basis. That is: the Resting which causes Tenuto and Legato is practically never more ponderous than that which causes the softest "held" note, no matter what may meanwhile be the nature of the Added-impetus—that portion of energy communicated to the key porting-activity of one leg prompting the other to undertake its duty. The analogy would be perfect, if we were walking on a series of trap-doors, which gave way to us at every step. Some of the old organs were indeed blown on this principle, by the blower alternately stepping from one to another of a pair of bellows. The treadmill is another instance of the same principle of allowing the lapse of weight to induce movement.

[1] In *pp*, it is *entirely* blurred over.
[2] In a rapid passage the impression is thus produced, of a train of up-springing keys behind one, in one's progress across the key-board.

to move it into sound, and which gives us our tone-varieties.[1]

Rotary-adjustments of the Fore-arm.

§ 31. Evenness of Touch (and un-evenness at will) depends greatly upon the proper *condition* of the Fore-arm in its ROTARY aspect;—upon the condition of the Fore-arm's rotary activities and inactivities, with their influence upon the hand in a *tilting* direction.[2]

It is only by accurately adjusting these rotary possibilities of the fore-arm to the needs of each finger (and each particular tone-character) that Energy can be transmitted (either equally or un-equally as desired) to the Thumb and Little-finger sides of the hand. Such adjustment of the fore-arm's condition enables us muscularly to support either side of the hand *off* the keys when required; it enables us to set free weight at either side; and it enables us even to provide muscular force in a rotary direction; while all these adjustments of Condition may moreover be accompanied either by an actual tilting movement, or not, as is deemed desirable. Thus:—

The fore-arm's rotary *activities* should be equally adjusted, when weight is required equally at both sides of the hand.[3] But when *one* side of the hand is left without any finger to support it upon the keys, then that side of the hand must be sustained by the fore-arm tending to *rotate upwards* with it. Such fore-arm rotation must be reversed when that side of the hand has to serve as a foundation for a finger's action against the key.

It is in this way, that we owe *evenness* of touch to the fore-

---

[1] As has already been insisted upon in Chapter XV. ("The Concepts"): the act which causes us to retain the key at its bottom-level after completion of the act of tone-production (in Legato and Tenuto), should never be more ponderous than in the softest tenuto, although we may have depressed the key with fullest force; so that in the case of *forte*-legato for instance, we have to provide an act of continuous Resting, just heavy enough to compel the down-retention of the successive keys, interspersed with forcible but *short-lived* acts of key-depression, which latter must cease with the moment of sound-emission, and which will thus leave the gentle Resting unaffected between-whiles, and no different than for *ppp*. Also *vide* Note on p. 145 and "Supplement," Note No. III.

[2] Refer to § 9 of last Chapter, and "Supplement," Note No. I.

[3] Except the slight residue of *activity* required to keep the hand in its playing position, palm downwards.

arm's rotary tendencies; and also owe to it, the power of making notes "stand out" at either side of the hand at will.

Fore-arm Rotation-touch.
§ 32. Production of tone, as noticed above may be accompanied by an actual tilting or rolling movement of the hand,—in connection with a partial rotation of the fore-arm itself. These adjustments of the fore-arm, at other times invisible, are then rendered visible. Such movement has been termed "Sidestroke" by some of the German teachers. A far less objectionable term for this variety of movement is however found in "ARM-ROTATION-TOUCH," which, while describing it more accurately, also eliminates the word "stroke"—so objectionable when applied to any form of Touch.

§ 33. Rotation-touch, like all other kinds of touch-movements, may be wrought either by Muscular-initiative, or by Weight-initiative. (*Vide* §§ *10 and 11.*) That is, the visible tilting movement of the hand may result either (a) from a rotary down-*activity* of the arm upon that particular side of the hand, causing that to out-balance the finger under it; or (b) it may result, by applying a rotary *lifting*-exertion at the *other* side of the hand, which will cause that side to tilt upwards, while setting free weight at the tone-producing side—owing to *lapse* of the supporting muscles on the latter side. Obviously, the first form will tend towards "Muscular-initiative," with its more aggressive tone qualities, while the second form will tend towards "Weight-initiative," with its more sympathetic tone-qualities.

Horizontal adjustments of Wrist.
§ 34. Another important muscular-adjustment, is that of the Hand and Wrist-joint, in the HORIZONTAL (or lateral) direction:—

Successive *fingering*-positions [1] can only be linked together without break and unevenness, by lateral movements of the Thumb and Hand. To enable these to be amplified and unimpeded, we require lateral *freedom* of the Wrist-joint, and actual

---

[1] By "fingering-position," is meant a group of notes that can be reached by the fingers of one hand, without the intervention of any "turning under" or "over" of the thumb and finger.

movements also of the Hand and Wrist from side to side—in a plane with the key-board. This freedom can only be attained, by leaving such amplifying movements of the Hand and Wrist absolutely unrestrained—free from all contrary exertions. In this way they will enable us to give the fullest scope to the Thumb in turning under the fingers, and to the fingers in "passing over" the thumb, and will also facilitate the passage of a longer finger over a shorter one in passages of double notes. They moreover help us to reach notes otherwise too far apart to come easily under the hand; and enable us to play widely laid-out chords (by spreading them) which at first sight appear to be extreme "extensions." [1]

Lateral freedom of the wrist-joint can only be attained by learning to discriminate between the muscular-activities that move the Hand to one side (horizontally) and those that move it to the opposite side. For unless we leave the opposite set of muscles to the required ones practically *passive*, restraint, with all its accompanying evils, will supervene during the required adjustment.

There are two kinds of movement requiring this horizontal freedom, and they seem at first sight quite distinct; for in one case (*i.e.*, when the fingers are passed over the thumb), it is the hand that moves; whereas in the other case (*i.e.*, when the thumb is passed under a finger that is stationary on its key), the wrist-joint itself moves, carrying with it the fore-arm.

The *same* set of muscles should however be employed for both these apparently dissimilar operations; that is: the

---

[1] Perfectly un-restrained mobility of the Hand from side to side, is required during the performance of the notes comprised within fingering-positions that embrace sounds beyond the extent of an octave; with most hands, such lateral movement is indeed required even *within* the limits of an octave.

It is a very ordinary misconception, that such groups of notes, covering much key-board space, should be "STRETCHES," although they do not have to be sounded simultaneously. Widely laid-out harmonies should in fact never be regarded as "stretches" or extensions at all, unless they have actually to be sounded together. What is imperatively required, is, that all the implicated fingers be *successively* brought over their respective keys *by the lateral movements of the hand and wrist here considered*, and that this "preparation" over each note is effected, as it always should be, *before* the actual depression of each key is commenced.

THE ACTIONS AND INACTIONS.

muscles that move the *hand* from side to side are the ones that should be employed in both cases. Thus :—

When the thumb rests on a key, it acts as a pivot, and the hand itself then moves obviously enough, since its finger-end is here free to do so.

When, however, one of the *other* fingers has to sustain a note, and the finger-end of the hand is therefore unable to travel, then the *other* end of the hand (the Wrist end) has to move instead. In the latter case, we have two pivots—(a) the finger-tip upon its note, and (b) the Elbow; and while these two pivots do not move, the wrist is moved laterally by means of the hand-muscles in a plane with the key-board surface.[1]

The sensation of rotary and lateral freedom.

§ 35. If we fulfil these two last requirements, *viz.:* perfect adjustment and freedom of the Forearm rotarily (§ 31) and perfect ease in the hand and wrist motions that assist the turning under and over of the fingers, we shall experience the sensation of always *being ready*—of always feeling VERTICAL—over every note before it is used, or played.

Now, it follows, that if we insist on not playing *unless we do experience this sensation* of verticality, then we may also assume, that we are fulfilling these two extremely necessary requirements. And it is in fact only in this way that we should urge these muscular details into operation during the performance of a piece of music.[2]

---

[1] When the wrist-joint itself thus moves from side to side, with a quiescent Elbow, we find that this also implicates a slight *rotary* movement of the UPPER-ARM, thus allowing the fore-arm to move slightly from side to side at the wrist in following the hand.

[2] For it would be undesirable, during the actual performance of music, to allow our attention to stray towards the personal accomplishment of muscular-conditions, however necessary these are.

To do so would take our thoughts off Music. And we must always remember when we have to deal with Music, that our business is (a) to watch Key-resistance, and (b) to pre-conceive the time and tone-place of each note —for the sake of the phrase,—and the work—under performance. (*Vide Table, page 40, Part I.*) To insist on a general impression of "verticality" does not detract from such necessary intention technically and musically; but to allow ourselves at such time to think of the details of "Rotation" and

192   KEY-TREATMENT; MUSCULAR ASPECT.

The triple-aspect of Wrist-freedom. § 36. Here is the place to sum-up the elements that make for a FREE WRIST—that desideratum striven for by teachers of all schools, old and new. For we shall now be in a position to realise, that freedom of the wrist-joint implies freedom in three distinct aspects:—

 I. Vertical freedom.
 II. Lateral freedom.
 III. Rotary freedom,—really that of the Fore-arm.

 a): *The wrist must be perfectly mobile vertically, even under the strain of the severest forte passage,*—nothing must be allowed to militate against ease of Wrist, in an upward and downward direction, however forcibly the hand and finger may be momentarily applied to the keys during their descent.[2]

 b): *The wrist must be perfectly unrestrained horizontally, under the same conditions;*—the hand (and wrist) during its movements from side to side, as well as during its position when quiescent at either point, must also be perfectly unimpeded in this plane.[3]

 c): *The hand (and the wrist and fore-arm therefore) must be equally unrestrained in a rotary or tilting direction:*—The hand, whether actually tilted or not during the act of tone-production, or exerted without movement in either direction rotarily or not, must be likewise un-restrained in this respect.[4]

"Horizontal adjustment" would probably do so. And this warning applies to all the rules of Technique in performance.

We must indeed give close attention to the acquisition of the required facilities, but we must study them at their proper time—while we are *learning* to play. On the other hand, the moment we wish to apply ourselves to the actual performance of a musical-work, we must strive to give our supreme attention to Music itself, through the necessary key-attention; and the laws of Technique must then be enforced semi-automatically, or entirely so. For it is obvious, that unless we succeed in this latter respect, we shall not be able to exhibit our musical perceptions untrammelled by the *means* of Execution, any more than we can freely converse in an unfamiliar language.

[1] Excepting those few, who by advocating the "rigid wrist," thereby prove themselves incredibly ignorant of the very first physical principles of all Technique.

[2] *Vide* §§ 8, 23, 26, etc., also *Tests, Nos. I. and III., Chapter XVIII.*
[3] *Vide* § 34.
[4] *Vide* § 31.

THE ACTIONS AND INACTIONS.

In short:—

The Wrist can only be said to be "really free" when it is felt to be equally un-impeded in all three of these aspects.[1]

Fore-arm skips.
§ 37. Skips within the compass of about two octaves are executed by movement of the fore-arm alone. This horizontal or lateral movement of the fore-arm is fan-like in character, the Elbow forming its axis. With a quiet elbow, it allows us to perform such skips with great celerity and yet with comparative certainty; our muscular-memory enabling us to do so, since this movement is simpler and less cumbrous than that of the whole arm. The Elbow should in such cases be placed *midway between* the two notes forming the skip, preparatory to taking it, as the elbow would otherwise have to move.[2]

Upper-arm Skips.
§ 38. Skips that are too large to be convenient for this fore-arm movement, must be taken by a horizontal (or lateral) movement of the Upper-arm itself;—a side-way movement of the Elbow, away from the body, or back towards it.[3]

Because of the clumsiness of this movement and because of its unreliability, such skips are found far more "risky." Skips, beyond the compass of two octaves, are therefore not often required at a *tempo* so fast *that the eye cannot direct them;* and being so uncertain of execution, they should therefore also not be written beyond that speed-limit.[4]

---

[1] During Practice, the greatest care should be taken to ensure this three-fold freedom, by constantly testing the mobility of the Wrist, as indicated in the next Chapter, and in Part V.—"On Relaxation."

[2] Such movement of the fore-arm with the elbow as an axis, is not at all so simple muscularly as it appears. As already pointed out, in the last Note (page 191) of § 34, this movement is really formed by a combination of Upper-arm *rotation* with supplementary vertical movements of the Fore-arm. The rotation of the upper-arm alone, would take the fore-arm off the key-board plane; this upper-arm rotation is therefore here modified (or "corrected") into a horizontal movement of the fore-arm, by slightly employing the latter's raising-muscles, or allowing these to lapse, as the case requires.

[3] Refer to last Chapter, § 10.

[4] Such passages have however occasionally been written, not in ignorance, but deliberately for purposes of acrobatic display—the interest centring purely in the performer's knack of reaching the right keys in spite of difficulty and risk.

o

KEY-TREATMENT; MUSCULAR ASPECT.

Lateral adjustments of the Fingers.

§ 39. Small lateral movements of the fingers themselves, also help to bring them over their respective keys. To these movements, which are so perfectly obvious to the eye, no further allusion need be made, except to point out, that they should be as un-restrained as all the other motions required in Technique, and that no greater extensions should be made by their means than is really necessary.[1] The behaviour of the thumb in this respect, will be found explained under "Position"—Part IV.

Muscular-discrimination, its acquisition.

§ 40. Consideration of the Actions and Inactions explained in this Chapter, will enforce the conclusion, that we must acquire muscular *discrimination* in very definite directions, if we wish to learn to play with Ease and Certainty. These discriminatory-powers may be acquired either un-consciously, or consciously:

We can acquire them unconsciously, if we experiment persistently enough at the key-board—and may succeed, if we possess exceptional powers of Ear, muscular adaptability, memory of Sound (especially as to quantity and quality) and memory of muscular-sensations.

Few possess all these powers, and fewer still possess them all in an exceptional degree. Even amongst artists there are few, who attain to easy Technique in all its branches.

The far quicker and more certain way to acquire this necessary muscular skill and perceptiveness, is therefore to use the Reason, as already suggested in Part I. By using our reasoning-faculty, we can easily learn thoroughly to understand exactly what is required of our limbs in each and all of the various forms of Touch. Understanding this, we can then with assurance deliberately and directly proceed to *teach* our muscles to fulfil each of the required conditions, thus gradually but surely teaching our Muscular-memory, and forming correct habits.

To render this task easier, a list of the most necessary Muscular-discriminations required, is here appended.[2]

---

[1] *Vide Note to* § *34, on page 190.*

[2] Studies and exercises, mostly for use away from the instrument, will be provided in Part V., as already explained.

TABLE

OF THE MAIN MENTAL-MUSCULAR DISCRIMINATIONS REQUIRED TO ENABLE US TO FULFIL THE CONDITIONS OF ACTION AND IN-ACTION EMPLOYED DURING THE ACT OF TOUCH.

I. *Ability independently to leave lax—unsupported by their respective muscles* :—

a) The *Hand*,
b) The *Fore-arm*,
c) The *Upper-arm*,
d) The *Shoulder*,

so that we shall be able to set free their Weight as required, independently of any downward exertion of the finger or hand.[1]

II. *Isolation of the Finger's down-activity (or exertion) from that of the Hand*—ability to exert the finger against the key, independently of any *exertion* downwards of the hand.[2]

III. *Isolation of the Hand's down-activity from that of the Arm*—ability to exert the hand downwards behind the fingers upon the keys, even to its fullest extent, without permitting any down-activity of the Arm.[3]

IV. *Freedom of the Finger's action*—isolation of the finger's down-exertion from its opposite exertion—freeing the finger's down-exertion from the upward one.[4]

V. *Freedom of the Hand's action*—isolation of the hand's down-exertion from the upward one.[5]

VI. *Discrimination between the Thrusting and the Clinging application of the Finger against the key*—with its correlated alternative, either of *forward-supported* or *lax-left* Elbow and Upper-arm.[6]

VII. *Freedom in the rotary-adjustments of the Fore-arm*—

—a) ability to leave the fore-arm *lax* in a tilting direction towards either side of the hand,—both fifth-finger and thumb sides.

—b) ability to *exert* the fore-arm rotarily in either of these directions.[7]

[1] §§ 2, 3, 4, 6, 7, 22.
[2] § 6, etc.
[3] § 6, etc.
[4] § 23, also last chapter.
[5] § 23, also last chapter.
[6] §§ 12–15, also last chapter.
[7] § 31.

VIII. *Freedom of the Wrist and Hand horizontally—*
—isolation of the muscular act that moves the hand to one side laterally, from the act that moves it in the opposite direction; required to assist the thumb in turning under, and the fingers in turning over.[1]

IX. *Ability accurately to time the cessation of the down-exertion of the Finger, employed during key-descent—*
—ability to "*aim*" this exertion, so that it may culminate and cease at the moment of sound emission.[2]

X. *Ability accurately to time the cessation of the down-exertion of the Hand, employed during key-descent—*
—ability to *aim* the hand-exertion, so that it may also be directed by the ear, like that of the finger.[3]

XI. *Ability accurately to time the cessation of* WEIGHT, *employed to produce tone—*
—ability to time the application of any Arm-weight employed for the creation of key-descent, so that it may culminate and cease at the moment of sound emission.[4]

XII. *Freedom in the movements required of the Finger, the Hand, the Fore-arm and the Upper-arm in bringing the finger-tips into place over their required notes, antecedent to the act of key-depression—*
—freedom in the lateral, or side-to-side movements: (a) of the Fingers and Thumb, (b) of the Hand, (c) of the Fore-arm, with the elbow as a pivot, and (d) of the Elbow and Upper-arm itself.[5]

---

[1] § 34.
[2] §§ 24 and 28, *vide also* "*The Added Impetus,*" *last chapter.*
[3] § 24, *vide The Added Impetus, last chapter.*
[4] A cessation that must be caused, by the arm-supporting muscles acting in strict response to the timed *cessation* of the up-bearing action of the finger and hand against the arm at the wrist, during the act of key-depression.[*]
[5] §§ 24, 37, 38, and 39.
[*] § 24 and last Chapter.

RECAPITULATORY

a): The Act of Touch implies levering weight upon the key, to cause its deflection.

b): This leverage-power is obtained:

1) by exerting the Finger,
2) by exerting the Hand in conjunction with the Finger.

c): When the finger is exerted against the key, it bears upwards by recoil against the Knuckle of the hand, and with equal force.

d): The hand, when it is exerted, bears downwards upon the finger at the knuckle, and it likewise bears upwards (by reaction) with equal force—against the Arm at the Wrist-joint.

e): At the Wrist-joint, these two combined forces meet the weight of the Arm; and it is therefore the Arm that forms the Basis for the operation of the finger and hand against the key.

f): The arm may be employed for this purpose in two distinct ways:

1) It may be *self-supported* by its muscles.
2) It may be left *un-supported* during the action of tone-production.

g): Arm-weight, if insufficient for extreme *fortes*, may be supplemented by a bearing-up against the Shoulder. The weight of the Shoulder and even of the Body itself thus forms the ultimate Basis, or Foundation. Body-*force* must never be employed instead.

h): All sensation, during the Act of Touch, must invariably be *upwards*.

This is so because all the work done reacts upwards against Weight—thus producing a stepping-up against the Knuckle and the Wrist, and even against the Shoulder in extreme cases.

i): There are therefore *Three Muscular Components* from which we can construct the Act of Touch, viz.:

    1) Finger-exertion,
    2) Hand-exertion,
    3) Arm-weight, and its co-operatives.

j): These three components divide, broadly, into two distinct kinds—Exertion and Weight. The two opposite *elements* thus recognised, meet at the Wrist-joint. Exertion, there bearing upwards, meets the downward tendency of Weight.

k): The total *quantity* of tone (loudness) depends on the total amount of Energy used against the key during its descent, and obtained from these two sources.

l): The *quality* of the tone mainly depends on how we *start* this combination of Exertion and Weight against the key, viz.:

    1): If we want tone of a beautiful quality, we must start the combination by Weight (*i.e.*, by Arm-release); for the key is then more gradually driven into Speed.

    2): If we want a tone of a brilliant, aggressive, or sharp quality, we must start the combination by Exertion (of the finger and hand); for the key is then driven more suddenly into Speed.

We thus obtain two completely different *genera* of Touch—"Weight-touch" and "Muscular-touch."

m): The Tone-quality is further influenced by which *attitude* we adopt of the Finger and Upper-arm conjointly. There are two opposite attitudes:

    1) The *Clinging*, or *flat*-finger attitude.
    2) The *Thrusting*, or *bent*-finger attitude.

The Clinging-attitude makes for beauty of the tone,—the *singing*-quality, with its carrying character; because the whole limb is here in its most *elastic* condition.

The Thrusting-attitude makes for brilliancy and aggressiveness, with its "short" Tone-character; because the whole limb is then in a more rigid condition.

n): To use the Clinging-attitude, we must leave the Upper-arm more or less relaxed during the moment of tone-production; thus causing the Elbow to tend to hang on to the fingers. Weight thus set free permits the finger to cling to the key to the necessary extent.

The finger, in thus tending to drag the Elbow towards the keyboard, should be used *as a whole,*—all three joints nearly straight or "flat."

o): To use the Thrusting-attitude, we must on the contrary support the Upper-arm—more or less forwards. This permits the finger to thrust against the key to the necessary extent, the thrust being taken by the Elbow.

The finger, in thus tending to thrust against the Elbow, is used in a very rounded (or bent) position, and it tends to *un-bend* towards and with the key; the nail-joint remaining almost upright. The action is like that of the leg in walking upstairs.

p): Most of the work done by the finger, should be derived from the part of the finger next to the knuckle—the knuckle-phalanx, *i.e.:* The part of the finger next to the knuckle (or hand), is the part that should do most of the work.

This applies equally in "flat" and "bent" attitudes.

q): The action of the finger, in both attitudes, is best understood at first, by turning the hand palm upwards, and lifting a weight by the tip of the finger.

r): If we require the most sympathetic tone, we must combine Clinging-attitude with Weight-initiative. Remembering that the slightest "putting-down" of the key, will destroy the desired result.

s): If we want a sharp incisive tone (sacrificing carrying-power) then we must combine the Thrusting-attitude with Muscular-initiative.

t): Finger-touch, Hand-touch ("Wrist-action") and Arm-touch, are terms *not* referring to the action or otherwise of the three various parts designated. They merely refer to *movements* of those parts, respectively. Whether an actual *movement* of the

Finger, Hand or Arm accompanies key-descent, depends purely upon *which* of the three components provides slightly more Energy. Thus:

> 1): Finger-touch (or movement) *may* involve the operation of all three of the muscular components—finger-exertion, hand-exertion, and arm-weight. Or, finger and hand exertion may alone be used; or, the finger-exertion alone.
>
> 2): Hand-touch (or movement) *must* involve finger-exertion, and *may* also involve arm-weight.
>
> 3): Arm-touch (or movement) *must* involve exertion both of the finger and the hand, accompanied by Arm-lapse.

u): Choice of movement is chiefly determined by the actual speed of the passage; *i.e.*: It is the actual speed of the passage that mostly determines which part of the limb we must move:—

> 1): Arm-movement (or touch) should be employed when the passage is sufficiently slow to admit of it.
>
> A more or less slight raising of the whole limb off the key-board renders the act of phrasing clearer. The first note of a phrase is therefore nearly always played by arm-descent.
>
> 2): Hand-movement (or touch) must be chosen, when the notes succeed each other too quickly to be conveniently played by arm-touch.
>
> 3): Finger-movement (or touch), as it provides the shortest lever, must be chosen for passages beyond the speed-capacity of Hand-touch.
>
> 4): Finger-movement (or touch) is however also employed for slower passages, and even for the slowest. This, because we can only obtain a true Legato through the intervention of the fingers, thus enabling us to transfer the second kind of Resting from key to key.

v): Choice of Touch-*formation* (the Muscular-combination employed during the act of key-depression) is however even more important than choice of Touch-movement.

There are three main forms of such combination; forming Three Species of Touch-formation or construction:

1): Finger-exertion alone, with passive Hand and self-supported Arm.

2): Hand-exertion behind the Finger-exertion, with self-supported Arm.

3): Arm-weight (etc.) released in conjunction with the Finger-and-hand exertion.[1]

w): The weight of the arm, thus required for the "Added-impetus," is obtained by omitting its self-support for the time.

The *whole* arm must be released from the shoulder (to the necessary extent), not the Fore-arm only. Movement of the arm, is moreover no guarantee that it is really descending of its own weight.

x): Arm-weight thus employed in the form of "Added-impetus" during the act of tone-production, must cease to bear upon the key the moment sound is reached; but we must not cause this cessation, by trying to lift the arm off the keys. On the contrary, the arm must be made to resume its self-support *automatically*. This it will do, if we "leave it in the lurch," at the Wrist, by promptly ceasing all work of the finger and hand against the key, the moment that sound is reached.

y): The continuous weight required to form the second (or slightly heavier) kind of "Resting," upon which depends the effect of Tenuto and Legato, is obtained in the same way: A very slight release of the *whole* arm suffices; not dis-continuous as for the Added-impetus, but here continuous, and no greater than just sufficient to overbalance the key into descent.

z): This same process also forms the absolute-*pp* Weight-touch.

[1] This all-important matter, the muscular-construction of the act of Touch in its Three main Species, and the Varieties of these, is more fully dealt with in Chapter XIX., which see.

To obtain it, we must be careful really to weigh the key down by such arm-release, and not in the least to *put* it down by muscular-initiative.

aa): True Legato, we found, is only possible in finger-passages;[1] for the Tenuto form of the Resting (or *pp* Weight-touch) must here be transferred from finger to finger during the continuance of each phrase.

This transfer should be effected by timing the *previous* finger to cease its weight-supporting activity at the moment that the next key's descent is required to *commence*. Thus the new finger is compelled to take up its duties automatically in response to the weight being "left in the lurch" by the preceding finger.

bb): Without any Added-impetus, this forms *pp* Transfer-touch. Here again we must be careful not directly to influence the new finger's depression; we must instead insist on the previous finger giving way at the right moment.

cc): The following facts will now be clearer:—

Pianissimo Weight-touch[2] accompanies *all* forms of Tenuto; —since all tone beyond *pp* must be supplied by one of the multifarious forms of the Added-impetus.

Pianissimo Weight-transfer touch, in the same way accompanies all Legati of greater tone-amount than *pp*.

Tenuto and Legato of *more* tone than *pp*, hence consist of *pp* Weight-touch or Weight-transfer-touch respectively, with a tone-making operation *added thereto* for each note—the Added-impetus, the latter as short-lived as in Staccatissimo.

dd): For the first (or Staccato) form of the Resting, the weight of the hand alone is sufficient. For this purpose, the hand must lie quite loosely upon the keys. Tone, of whatever kind, must of course be obtained by employment of the Added-impetus in one of its many forms.

ee): Invisible adjustments of the Forearm are constantly required in a *rotary* or *tilting* direction, to ensure Evenness of effect from all the fingers; and also to enable the fingers at either side

---

[1] Except by intervention of the Damper-pedal. Chap. XV., etc.
[2] Already considered in Chapter XV. *Vide* also Ref. on p. 145.

THE ACTIONS AND INACTIONS.

of the hand to pronounce their notes prominently. These adjustments enable us to support either side of the hand off the keys when required; and enable us also to influence either side with more force or weight when that is required.

ff) : This forms *Rotation-touch*, when such adjustments are allowed to become visible as a tilting movement of the hand.

gg) : Lateral movements of the Hand and of the Wrist itself are also required to ensure Evenness. Without such movements, it would be impossible to connect without break or jerk the various fingering-positions out of which passages are formed. These side to side movements (whether great or small) must be absolutely unrestrained.

hh) : Rotary and lateral freedom of the Wrist enables one to feel always "ready" over every note beforehand.

ii) : Purely Vertical freedom of the Wrist-joint itself must be insisted upon, besides this rotary and lateral freedom. Only in this way can a really free Wrist be ensured.

jj) : *Per contra* : if we always insist on feeling *ready* and *vertical* over each note, before attempting its production, we shall fulfil these three conditions of freedom of the Wrist—laterally, rotarily, and vertically.

kk) : To enable us to reach closely adjacent notes, slight lateral movements of the fingers themselves suffice.

ll) : To enable us to take larger skips, but such as do not exceed about two octaves in extent, we must use lateral movements of the Forearm, with the Elbow as the apparent pivot. These are mainly induced by a partial rotation of the Upper-arm.

mm) : For still larger skips, the whole arm, from the shoulder, must move sideways. Such large skips however become exceedingly uncertain, if attempted beyond a comparatively slow speed.

nn) : Muscular - discriminations in very definite directions have thus been proved requisite. These should be studied in the Table annexed to this chapter.

CHAPTER XVIII.

THE THREE CHIEF MUSCULAR TESTS REQUIRED DURING PRACTICE AND PERFORMANCE.

§ 1. Three deductions of extreme importance are borne in upon us, after careful consideration of the muscular acts and in-actions discussed in the last chapter and the preceding ones. We shall perceive that good Technique must greatly depend upon close obedience to three salient laws: (a) efficiency in the Resting, (b) efficiency in accurately aiming and ceasing the energy required to move the key, and (c) efficiency in actively employing both Finger and Hand (the Exertion elements) without any non-intended application of the down-muscles of the Arm.

There are many more requirements to be fulfilled, but these three undoubtedly assume supreme importance.

§ 2. For this reason it is necessary that we should constantly *test* ourselves muscularly, both during Practice and during Performance, so that we may ensure the fulfilment of these three supreme requirements. . . . This we can do by adopting THREE MUSCULAR TESTS as they may be termed. These Tests, we shall find if we observe closely enough, are indeed adopted—unconsciously for the most part—by all those artists who have learnt to succeed technically.

§ 3. We shall be convinced that such "testing" is really necessary, and is not merely a matter of personal habit or idiosyncrasy, if we consider for a moment the necessities of other vocations. Thus we find, that the Bank-clerk does not trust to his eye, in spite of his years of experience, whether he has to count out £500 or merely five sovereigns,—he makes sure of the amount by using his fingers or his scales. The chemist is not satisfied unless he possesses the best scales and tests obtainable. Even the domestic cook of the better class, is learning rather to depend on actual measurements than on mere " rule of thumb." . . . In fact we find that a striving after accuracy by Test obtains everywhere.

We find it in all athletic avocations. The expert thrower weighs his ball consciously or unconsciously whilst aiming his throw; the tennis-player does likewise with his racquet, and the cricketer with his bat. Again, the billiard-player does not essay to propel his ball, until he has carefully tested both *weight* and direction of his cue, for he does not bring his implement into contact with his ball until he has *tested his cue and his arm,* by swinging his cue several times backwards and forwards towards the ball.

In the same way, if we desire to estimate the weight of an object, we do not merely hold the latter at arm's length. On the contrary, *we balance it;* that is: we test *our arm* to see whether the exertion we are employing (to sustain that object) *is freed from any contrary exertion*—is freed from exertion of the contrary muscles; for experience has taught us that we cannot estimate the weight of an article unless we first eliminate any confusion in sensation arising from such contrary exertion. We therefore unconsciously move the article in question a few times, slightly upwards and downwards; and thus, by alternately using slightly *more* force, and then again slightly *less* force than is actually required to support the weight, we are by this means enabled to gauge the exertion required with great accuracy, and hence derive the exact sensation of weight (or resistance to our muscular effort) caused by the object thus tested.[1]

Exactly in the same way, must we constantly *test* our muscular-conditions while engaged at the Pianoforte,—so that we may be able to estimate each key's resistance accurately, and may also be able to employ our muscles unfettered by their opposing ones,—in a word, that we may play *with freedom.*

[1] If we have sufficient experience and a good muscular *memory* we shall also then be able to say how this sensation compares with those we have derived from previously tested *accepted standards* of Weight—lbs. and ozs.

§ 4. Such testing must be unremitting, during the practice-hour, as well as during an actual performance.

The Learner needs it, that he may gradually learn to discern between correct and incorrect application of energy. The Adept needs it, otherwise he cannot expect the instrument to respond either with accuracy or with certainty to his musical feeling and judgment.

But the difference between Adept and Learner is, that the former need not *show* the means of testing he is compelled to adopt, since the slightest and almost unnoticeable movements will suffice in his case—tests and reminders here accomplished more or less *unconsciously*, we must remember. Whereas in the case of the Learner, whose discriminatory-power, muscularly, is as yet weak, and who therefore requires far more salient tests to assure himself that he is doing right, such tests have for a time to be made with exaggerated movements, if they are to serve their purpose. Such exaggerated movements must subsequently be gradually reduced to the smallest limits compatible with due efficiency; and they must of course be formed into almost unconscious habit.

The three most insidious faults, preventing successful Technique. § 5. The most common and ever-present tendencies towards faulty Technique lie in the following three directions: (1) a tendency towards *restrained* muscular-action, which vitiates efficiency in Resting, (2) a tendency towards unpromptness in *ceasing* the muscular-conditions required during key-descent, which vitiates the aiming of the Added-impetus, and (3) a tendency towards unclear *discrimination* between the necessary Exertion-element and the Weight-element.[1]

Whence we see how necessary it is, as already forecast in § 1, that we should test for efficient Resting, for accuracy of Aim in using the key, and for the elimination of Arm down-exertion.

---

[1] This last fault means an imperfect separation or isolation of the Finger- and-hand down-exertions from Down-arm force and Arm-lapse; for it is so difficult to learn to act downwards with both finger and hand (quite forcibly as we sometimes have to do) whilst nevertheless leaving the ARM down-action muscles quiescent.

The three tests required take the following shape:—

The *First* of the Three Tests constantly required.   § 6. To enable us to be sure of RESTING properly, and by that means to be sure of accurately feeling the degree of resistance the keys offer us, we must *insist* that our fingers and hands are used against the keys *whilst perfectly free from contrary* (or raising) *exertion.*

The required test must therefore in this case be identical with that slight up-and-down movement we employ, when we unconsciously test any other Weight, by *balancing* it.[1]

At the Pianoforte, however, such balancing of the arm seems different to the eye. This is owing to the fact that the finger-tips must remain lying on the keys whilst the testing is done. The arm, slightly moving up and down, raises merely *the wrist-joint,* whilst the hand nevertheless remains passively lying on the keys without depressing them.

We cannot be sure that we are leaving the "up" muscles of the hand passive, and the arm unrestrained, and that we are experiencing key-resistance (plus arm-weight), unless this gentle up-and-down swaying of the Wrist-joint *does not in the least influence* or alter the exact sensation of Weight experienced at the finger-tips.

A similar test can be employed for the finger-muscles: In this case it takes the form of an alternate gentle rolling-up and unrolling of the fingers themselves; their tips not quitting their original places on the keys, and without any raising or lowering either of the Wrist or Knuckle joints. The arm here as it were merely rolls and unrolls the fingers, without in the least altering the sensation of weight experienced at the finger-tips, and without causing these to slide on the keys.

The "up-tendons" of the fingers are proved to be passive, only when this sensation of weight here again remains unaffected by the testing-movement.

§ 7. To teach us and to remind us to CEASE with precision the muscular-conditions that cause key-descent the moment that

[1] *Vide the third paragraph of § 3 of this chapter.*

sound-emission is reached, we must test for this cessation at the place where Muscular-action and Weight mostly come into conflict, in their respective *upward* and *downward* tendencies:—

<small>The *Second* of the Three Tests.</small>

As the muscular-force exerted against the key is mainly that of the finger and hand, and as this by recoil bears upward against Arm-weight—meeting the latter at the Wrist-joint, it follows, that *it is at the Wrist-joint* that we can best become cognisant of the conflict between these two elements of force during key-descent, and can also best realise their disappearance or cessation.

It also follows, if we *suddenly cease* the muscular activity employed,[1] that the Wrist-joint itself will then be suddenly left unsupported—that it will be left "in the lurch," as it were, and will consequently commence to fall, unless it is promptly (and automatically) caught up by the up-muscles of the arm.

To test accuracy in Cessation therefore, all we have to do, is, to weigh down an easily-gripped chord, etc., and the instant the tone-production of the chord is completed, to allow the *wrist itself to drop*, while the keys are nevertheless left free to *rise*; for if we succeed in ceasing all action of the finger and the hand (and Weight too) at that moment, then there is nothing to prevent the key from rebounding, in spite of the descending arm.

It is in fact just here that we can obtain *proof* whether we have or have not accurately "aimed" our added-impetus. For we only have such proof, provided the keys are found *to rebound freely* (producing an absolute Staccato) in spite of the fact that the fingers remain lying on their respective key-surfaces, and in spite of the fact, also, that the Wrist (and Arm therefore) is allowed actually to descend past the level of the key-board, for the purpose of this test.

Unless we thus succeed in accurately ceasing all Force and Weight (excepting the slight weight of the resting hand), the keys will fail thus to rebound. And if they fail to rebound,

[1] The activity or exertion of the finger and hand against the key.

the sound will be continued, instead of being Staccato, as intended.

We must moreover insist on *not pulling the hand up*, it is the key that must rebound and carry up with it the hand.[1]

Before practising this "Aiming-test," one should always practise merely *balancing* the keys, *without sounding them at all.* This balancing should be precisely analogous to the balancing of any other weight. The whole arm from the shoulder with the key to its hammer-end, should be slightly swayed up and down, until arm and key seem thoroughly to belong together. Having established (and re-established) this intimate connection between arm-weight and key-weight, all subsequent use of the key starts from this basis, and is thereby rendered infinitely more certain.

The *Third* of the Three Tests. § 8. To teach us and to remind us of ARM-FORCE ELIMINATION (which is the main secret in the attainment of Agility, etc.) we must again have some means of testing ourselves, so that we may in some measure be certain we are not forcing the arm down upon the fingers, when we desire either Finger-activity unaided, or aided by Hand-force alone behind it.

This test we can obtain, by allowing the Arm to be as it

[1] To make the test as useful and searching as possible in the Practice-room, it is preferable to employ *Weight-touch* as here directed, rather than *Muscular-touch;* employing it first in absolute *pp*, and afterwards in full *forte;* but always taking care to employ the weight of the Upper-arm, and not merely that of the Fore-arm. One should *weigh* the chord down, and yet leave the keys free so that they actually *rebound* on the completion of the act of tone-production, and thus form the natural Staccato. In this way we compel ourselves to cause the key to attain its speed as *gradually* as possible, and yet insist on accuracy and suddenness of cessation (or "aim") of the muscular-operation. The test can nevertheless be practised with Muscular-touch occasionally. The Wrist will however in this case not "drop past" the keyboard, but it will instead tend to fly up, at the conclusion of the act of tone-production. This, owing to the fact, that brilliant (or passage) touch implies the thrusting finger-attitude, with a forward-tending upper-arm; and it is this slight exertion of the upper-arm that tends in this case to drive the wrist forwards, and afterwards upwards.

STACCATO, thus accurately executed, in fact forms the best practice and test for accuracy of tone-production of all kinds : for the key cannot rebound (and thus create Staccato) unless the tone-producing stresses are successfully timed to cease at the right moment,—a moment that is the same both in Staccato and in Tenuto or Legato. Even the dullest Ear can detect with-

P

were either *driven* off, or *floated* off the key-board at the end of a little run or arpeggio undertaken for the purpose.

That is, we should play a short run or arpeggio, and the *last finger used* (say the little finger or the thumb) must then as it were kick against the key-bed. The arm is meanwhile to float with such exceeding lightness over the keys that this "kick-off"[1] will suffice to *start* the arm in an upward direction;—and the arm being thus started, it can then automatically "take the hint" and continue its journey, assisted herein by its own raising-muscles, the arm and hand thus rising together a considerable distance off the keys. Since the *initiative* of this "kick-off" of the arm has however been given by the finger (or hand and finger), it will—and should—seem to the performer, as if this rising of the arm were entirely due to the impact against the keys.

This test should be made both in *forte* and in *pianissimo*. In the first case, it causes a forcible accent with the end-note, and the arm seems forcibly driven up into the air. In the second case, no accent need result, and the arm then seems almost to float upwards.[2]

In both cases, the test can be considered properly fulfilled, out much difficulty or much effort of attention, when the tone itself does *not* instantly cease—is not accurately cut short—on emission; whereas, it demands a comparatively fine ear, and fine muscular-sense, both considerably trained in listening and perception, *easily* to recognise when effort has been prolonged beyond the requisite moment in the case of Tenuto or Legato; and that the effort has consequently been mis-spent on the key-beds, and has rendered the tone harsher in quality. As Legato (of more tone than *pp*) is but an accurately produced Staccato, with the Resting altered to the slightly heavier form, it follows, that any accuracy gained through the practice of correct Staccato, must also improve our tone-production in Legato.

Hence also, it is probable, that in spite of accepted doctrines to the contrary, it is best for most students to learn Staccato *before* Tenuto or Legato,—provided that the Staccato is done naturally, as here insisted upon, and is not made an exhibition of Up-muscle work of the finger and hand, as so often erroneously taught.

We must perceive, that Legato only *appears* "more easy" at first, because faults in production are not so glaringly obvious in Legato as they are in Staccato to the un-initiated.

[1] A "kick-off" or jumping action, delivered by the finger alone, or by the finger and hand in combination for the more forcible form of the Test.

[2] Both forms of this Test,—"kick-off" and "float-off," should moreover be practised in two ways:—*firstly*, with whole arm rising, from the shoulder; and *secondly*, with fore-arm alone rising.

only when the cessation is so timed as to permit at the crucial moment an actual *rebounding of the key* from its bed,—forming the effect of absolute *staccatissimo*. No "willed" raising of the arm will in the least serve the purpose, although it may appear to be almost the same thing to the onlooker, and it is often thus faultily imitated from a public performer's doings.

§ 9. Other muscular Tests are also desirable :

Chief amongst these are two (a) for ROTATION-FREEDOM, and (b) for LATERAL-FREEDOM of the Wrist. We should constantly test for freedom in both of these directions during Practice, and also even during Performance. *Rotary-freedom* of the forearm can be tested at the key-board, by allowing these adjustments, as they occur, to induce (for this purpose of testing) an actual slight *but perfectly free* tilting of the hand to either side. This tilting may be displayed during the act of key-depression, and after its completion.

Lateral-freedom of the wrist and hand is best tested when at the key-board, by allowing the horizontal adjusting-movements of the hand and wrist *to be continued* (for this purpose) *beyond the moment* that the finger has reached and has played its key. That is: the necessary horizontal (or lateral) movements may be exaggerated as a Test, so that the key is as it were depressed "en passant"—the lateral movement continuing perfectly freely during the act of key-depression, and after this is concluded.[1]

§ 10. As the proper accomplishment of all such tests (including the three already discussed) appertains rather to the pedagogic, than to the explanatory side of the Art of Tone-

---

[1] For instance, it is generally found difficult to execute CHOPIN'S chord study in E flat, No. 11, Op. 10, with the required lightness and grace. The difficulty however vanishes for the most part, the moment we really succeed in leaving the wrist perfectly unrestrained not only *rotarily*, but also *horizontally*. This we can ensure, by compelling the horizontal movements to be free, by thus insisting on the relaxed movement continuing beyond the moment that the top note of each chord is reached.

In fact, one might formulate it as a general principle, that we can test all the actions required in the act of touch, by *continuing* the necessary movements beyond the moment they are required for that act, but continuing them perfectly freely and *freed*—one might say in a "passive" fashion.

All dead stops of the limbs employed, invariably suggest and create Stiffness.

production, further explanations and instructions concerning them must be deferred to Part V,—"Relaxation"—Muscular Discrimination Studies, where they find their proper place.

RECAPITULATORY

a): Knowledge of what constitutes correct muscular action and in-action at the Piano, proves that three points of muscular efficiency are of paramount necessity:

b):
> I. We must learn to *rest* properly on the keys, by leaving our fingers and hands free from contrary exertion, when they are applied to the keys.
>
> II. We must learn accurately to *time* the culmination and the *cessation* of the energy we apply to move the key.
>
> III. We must acquire the power to *use* our fingers and hands quite independently of any downward-acting arm-force, and even independently of arm-weight.

c): We must *test* ourselves constantly during Practice and Performance, so that we may ensure compliance with these paramount necessities.[1]

d): The Three Muscular-tests required, are as follows:

Test I. To ensure proper Resting, and use of the Muscular-sense; by freeing the finger and hand from contrary-exertions; two Exs.:—

1): Employ a slight up-and-down balancing movement of the arm at the Wrist; the hand to lie loose, and the fingers to remain in contact with their respective keys. See to it, that no alteration occurs in the Weight resting on the keys, which must remain at their surface-level.

---

[1] As these tests form preventives of wrong-doing, they should invariably be practised the first thing every day.

THE THREE CHIEF MUSCULAR TESTS. 213

2): Roll and unroll the fingers by means of a forward and backward movement of the arm and hand, while the finger-tips remain unaffected thereby, both as to position and as to the Resting-weight, as before.[1]

Test II. To ensure proper "aiming" of the Added-impetus; accuracy in Tone-production:—

Play an easy chord (preferably by "weight" or clinging-touch[2]), and accurately *cease* all action of the finger and hand the moment that Sound is reached, so as to allow the Wrist to *drop* in consequence. The weight used, must also disappear in consequence of the cessation of its support at the wrist. The keys will thus be able to *rebound* of their own accord, in spite of the finger-tips resting on their surfaces, and in spite of the descending wrist and arm.[3] See to it, that the resulting *staccato* is absolute, both when practised *pp* and when practised *ff*.

Test III. To ensure elimination of Down-arm-exertion, and independence of the finger-and-hand exertions, even from arm-weight:—

Play a short run or arpeggio, and drive the arm off the keys, in accenting the last note; using a kind of kick against the key-bed, delivered for the purpose by the finger and hand. The key to *rebound* (forming *staccatissimo*) and to seem to drive the arm into the air.[4]

This, also to be practised *pianissimo*, without the final accent. The arm, in this case seems to *float* upwards, instead of being driven off.

[1] Any alteration in the degree of Weight forms presumptive proof that contrary-exertions have been permitted; so does any forward or backward sliding of the finger-tips on the key-surfaces. No alteration occurs in either of these respects, if the contrary-muscles of both Hand and Finger are left as relaxed as they should be.

[2] N. B.—The weight required for "Clinging-touch" must be obtained by release of the *upper* arm.

[3] If practised instead with "forward" or thrusting-touch, the wrist will not fall, but will rebound upwards—but the fingers must nevertheless remain on their respective keys, with the rising keys under them.

[4] This test should be practised in two ways: (a) with the whole arm rising in the air, and (b) with the fore-arm alone, thus responding to the rebound of the keys.

e): Rotary and lateral freedom at the Wrist, should also constantly be *tested* for. This, by allowing the resulting movements to continue during the moment of key-depression and beyond that moment. Both kinds of movement to be perfectly free from all restraint.

CHAPTER XIX.

THE THREE SPECIES OF TOUCH-FORMATION:

THE THREE CHIEF PRINCIPLES OF MUSCULAR-COMBINATION, AND THE ENSUING VARIETIES OF KEY-ATTACK.

Knowledge and Choice of Touch-formation; its extreme importance.

§ 1. However important the choice of appropriate *movement* may be—the choice between Arm, Hand, and Finger touches, it is far exceeded in importance by the exercise of that Technical judgment which is required in quite another direction, as already pointed out.[1] For each particular passage differs in its technical requirements, and it is therefore supremely necessary that we should choose the most appropriate *muscular-combination* (or construction of touch) for each,—be it a singing-passage, or one of brilliance, —a slow one or a quick one,—be it light or ponderous in tone-character.

We must now look more closely into this matter; for it completes our practical knowledge of the manner in which all touches are formed. Such knowledge will enable us: (a) at once to construct each kind of touch-formation from its muscular constituents or components;[2] (b) it will enable us to

---

[1] *Vide chapter XVII.*, §§ *6, 21, and Note to* § *28.*

[2] We found, in Chapter XVII., that the Energy employed against the key consists of *three* muscular constituents or components, *viz.:* Finger-force, Hand-force, and Arm-weight with its coöperatives. It is owing to the fact of these muscular-components being available under various forms of combination, that we owe the possibility of all those divergences of Key-attack, with their consequent Tone-varieties, that form the principal Means of Expression at the Pianoforte, and enable us also to select the muscular-conditions suitable respectively for slow, and for rapid transit across the keys.

THE THREE SPECIES OF TOUCH-FORMATION. 215

teach others to do this; and finally, (c) it will enable us to select the appropriate technique for each passage.

The three main Principles of Combination. § 2. The first step to take, is, to learn thoroughly to recognise the nature of these main principles or forms of Combination, under which the physical components of Touch are available, with the particular advantages and drawbacks peculiar to each combination. We learnt in Chapter XVII. (§ 6), that there are *three* such Principles of Combination (or principles of Touch-formation) to which all others are subordinate. These, we found, are as follows:

> **First Species of Touch-formation:** Finger-activity alone, with loose-lying Hand, and self-supported Arm.
> **Second Species of Touch-formation:** Finger-activity with Hand-activity behind it, and self-supported Arm.
> **Third Species of Touch-formation:** Finger-and-hand activities, with relaxed Arm-weight (and its coöperatives) behind them—*i.e.*, with Lapse in the self-support of the Arm momentarily added.[1]

[1] We must remember that the phrase "Arm-lapse," as used in this work, merely signifies a lapse or failure on the part of the arm-supporting muscles, and that this does not necessarily entail *any actual movement* of the arm itself.

Here also, the warning must again be reiterated, not to confuse those two distinct ideas and acts, (a) the MOMENTARY lapse in arm-support required to assist each individual key-descent in Species III., and (b) the slight but CONTINUOUS lapse in arm-support required to induce the natural Tenuto and Legato.

Let us in fact always remember, that the difference between Staccato and Tenuto (or Legato) depends on the *continuous* state of the arm during each phrase,—depends on whether the "RESTING" is so light (owing to the entire absence of arm-weight) as to permit the key and finger to rebound after each individual tone-production; or whether it is instead *slightly heavier* (owing to the slight but continuous lapse in arm-support); the resting being in the latter case sufficiently heavy to compel an attenuated residue of *action* on the part of the finger and hand *beyond* the moment that each individual act of key-depression is completed, thus compelling the keys to remain depressed. And we must recall, how such light continuous resting of arm-weight on the keys, is perfectly independent in thought and action, from those short-lived lapses of the arm which are individually directed for the consummation of Tone, in the form of the "Added-impetus."

Moreover, we must be careful, not to permit this *continuous* slight arm-lapse (required for Legato) to VITIATE the act of *aiming* those momentary (though full) releases of the arm, required for the Added-impetus during *forte* Legato and Tenuto. Nor must we, on the other hand, lose sight of the continuous arm-*support* required during all Staccati, even when we happen in addition to employ those full, but "momentary" arm-releases required to render the Staccato *forte*. In short, we must not allow such momentary

These three different ways of building up the muscular-operation against the key cause the greatest possible fundamental differences in the Act of Touch, muscularly considered; and the term Species is for this reason applied to them.[1]

§ 3. Whichever one we employ of these three Species of muscular-operation, it must only be applied to the key *to induce its descent;*[2] and it must therefore always be recognised as a form of the "Added-impetus." Being an Added-impetus, it must also therefore *cease* to exist as such, the instant that sound is reached.[3]

Staccato and Legato, equally applicable to all three Species.
§ 4. All these three Species of the Added-impetus, it is clear, can be either Staccato, Tenuto, or Legato. They will be STACCATO, if we employ, in conjunction therewith, the lighter form of the Resting—for the keys will in this case be free to rebound, provided we accurately "aim" the cessation of such Added-impetus. Whereas, the same Touch-formations will be TENUTO, if we employ instead the slightly heavier form of the Resting. And they will be LEGATO, if we transfer such Tenuto-resting from note to note. (*Vide Chapters XV. and XVII., etc.*[4])

---

arm-lapses to affect the idea of *continuity* in arm-support required during Staccato,—a continuity only broken during the momentary life of the "Added-impetus." These points have been fully dealt with in Chapters XV. and XVII.

[1] These differences are indeed far more distinct and radical, when muscularly considered, than those differences (a) in mere *movement*, respectively termed Finger, Hand, and Arm touches, which are so obvious to the eye; and those differences (b) in Duration (Legato and Staccato) which arise from the two opposite forms of the Resting.

[2] Always excepting the solitary instance of *ppp* "Weight-touch," when Resting and Added-impetus are synonymous.

[3] Again, we realise the importance of distinguishing between the act of *adding* energy to the key *to move it*, and that other act: the act of Resting, which co-exists independently of such Added-impetus.

[4] Here we must again urge the student never to lose sight of the fact, that our Tone-making impulses must always *cease* as accurately as in the extremest Staccatissimo, no matter how Tenuto or Legato a passage may be owing to the employment of the *second* or heavier form of the Resting; thus always keeping in view the "Warp and Woof" nature of all Touch,—and of which rule, *ppp* "Transfer-touch" forms the solitary exception.

It is also instructive to note, that we may regard Legato *of greater tone-amount* than such *ppp*-transfer-touch, as being a *combination* of the last-named continuous touch with *a series of key-speeding impulses*, staccatissimo in themselves as to duration, but which may take the form of *any* of these three Spe-

Staccato as well as Legato, may moreover under any of the Species be either of the "inward" or "outward"-acting type—according as we employ either the flat or the bent-finger attitudes.[1] While we have the further option of either "passive" or "active" Staccato,—for we may passively permit the key merely to rebound, or may actively assist this, by a slight kicking action against the key-beds, this active form being necessarily accompanied by a more aggressive tone-quality.

§ 5. To particularise somewhat more fully, we will now consider each of these three forms of muscular-combination separately, and will take them in reversed order:—

The Third Species of Touch-formation. **Finger-force and Hand-force, and Released Arm-Weight:**—Since all three muscular-components are here employed against the key during its descent, this Species offers us the option of all possible varieties of both tone-quantity and tone-quality,[2]—including the extreme antitheses of *Forte* v. *Piano*, Muscular-touches v. Weight-touches, or Passage-touches v. Melody-touches.

§ 6. For the same reason[3] it also follows, that we may, in producing any of the varieties of this Species, optionally employ *movements* either of the Arm, the Hand, or the Finger; *i.e.*, this Species may optionally take the form either of Arm-touch, Hand-touch ("Wrist-action") or Finger-touch.[4]

§ 7. This Species, however, bears this disadvantage: that the actual speed, or transit across the key-board—Agility, is

cies of key-attack in question, or their Varieties; for the co-existence of a transferred continuous Weight, will transform these staccato-*executed* Added-impetuses (whatever their Species) into a continuous aural-effect. In short, do not let us forget, that the *ppp*-transfer-touch is the accompanying Basis of all natural Legati; and that it underlies (as the legato-forming element) the loudest Legati; and that the loudness must arise solely from a muscular-act, which, added to such transfer-touch, is as sharply defined and short of duration as in the shortest-lived sounds.

[1] For further details on these opposite ways of quitting the keys in Staccato, *vide* Part IV.
[2] *Vide Chapter XVII.*, §§ *10–12*.
[3] *i.e.*, The reason, that all three of the muscular-components here participate in inducing key-descent.
[4] Fore-arm Rotation-touch is available, in addition.

considerably hampered and circumscribed. This, we must remember, is owing to the fact, that Arm-weight (thus momentarily employed) must be individually supplied for each key-descent, and must be *ceased* each time that sound is reached;—as we should otherwise make the passage "stick," and obtain a tone quite different to our intention. For we must again recall, that the alternate release and subsequent "catch-up" of the arm, takes an appreciable time to accomplish, and that we cannot therefore employ this *third* Species, with its full tone-possibilities, beyond the speed at which we can reiterate these opposite conditions of the Upper-arm.[1]

§ 8. While this form of muscular-combination is therefore only available, when the speed required does not exceed a comparatively slow gait, it is nevertheless the only form that will allow us to obtain the *full* measure of good tone permitted us by our particular physical endowment; for this combination alone will permit us to utilise the whole weight of the relaxed arm and shoulder as recoil-breaker (or Basis) for the operations of the finger and hand against the key during its descent.[2]

§ 9. While Species III. thus offers us the opportunity of obtaining the fullest tone-amounts, this combination may with

---

[1] In short, Speed or Agility is here absolutely limited by the degree of swiftness with which *the lapse and subsequent re-activity of the arm-supporting muscles* can be reiterated. Some of the broader Finger-passages of BEETHOVEN, for instance, are however by no means too quick, to debar their being treated under this species of Touch-formation,—of course under its "finger-movement" aspect. It also follows, that a properly dignified interpretation of such passages (as so obviously desired by the composer), must necessarily be impossible to the pianist, whose Touch-repertory—or Tone-palette—does not include this particular form of Key-manipulation. *Vide* also, remarks as to *third* and *second* Species, in connection with Beethoven, to be found in *Note XVII., Appendix to this Part:* "*Certain exceptional forms of Legato and Staccato.*"

[2] We must reiterate that we are here discussing the "Added-impetus." The condition of the Arm, described above, does therefore not preclude a slight (and continuous) modification of it, to induce the form of "Resting" required, respectively for Tenuto and Legato, or for Staccato. For Legato-resting, the arm would not be *quite fully* "self-supported"; whereas for staccato, it would be fully self-supported *so far as the "Resting" is concerned;*—but this CONTINUOUS state of slighter or greater support, does not affect the general question of the arm's condition for the purpose of the Added-impetus—of tone-production. The Note (*on page 215*) to § 2, might here be referred to with advantage.

equal facility be employed for the production of *lesser* tone-amounts, down to the least. For we can supply this combination (of Arm-release with activity of Finger and Hand) in a measure so slight—it can be minimised to such an extent—that the total effect upon the key need not exceed the amount necessary just to overbalance it into descent; thus forming the true *pp* by "Weight-touch," provided we are careful to eliminate all Finger and Hand *Initiative*.[1]

[1] Let us recall, that this absolute *pp*, both in its *tenuto* or *legato* form (the "Passing-on" or "Transfer-touch"), moreover forms the solitary exception there is to the rule, that " all tone-making impetuses must cease at the moment that tone is consummated "; for we must, in this solitary instance, *continue* on the key-beds the Weight employed to overbalance the key into its softest descent.

The Nature of Glissando. Here is the place to point out, that the GLISSANDO is only another and even *simpler* form of this very "transferred Weight-touch." In this case the Weight that is to overbalance the key is applied through the back (the nail) of one finger; and the weight having reached the bed of the first key, and sounding it, this weight is then drawn along the key-board by a horizontal arm-movement. *Glissando* demands, that one or more phalanges of the finger (or fingers) employed, must be left in so gently elastic a condition, as to enable that portion of the finger to act the part of a ratchet, when the superincumbent gentle weight is drawn across the key-board. The phalanx or phalanges in question, must be sufficiently tense to permit of their supporting the Weight used *without bringing the nail too flatly* upon the keys. For unless the nail is sufficiently upright to form about *an acute angle* with the key, we cannot use it to surmount the successive keys in the required wedge-like fashion. But there must be no greater tenseness of the finger than will only just barely suffice for this purpose. Any greater tenseness, or the slightest arm-*force* applied, will inevitably jam the fingers immovably against the key-beds.

Glissando is therefore identical with the *ppp*-weight-transfer touch; and it even forms a most valuable and instructive channel through which to acquire the latter much-required touch; the only difference being, that in the latter case the transfer has to be effected through a sequence of fingers, in the place of the solitary one, used as a ratchet. *Crescendi*, of a limited nature, are practicable in both the Glissando and *ppp*-Transfer-touch, by permitting slight increases to supervene in the resting and transferred weight,—a *continuous* weight, we must remember, in this solitary case, *without* any Added-impetus. But such increments in continuously-resting weight must be but slight; and they must of course be accompanied by correspondingly slight increases in the gentle finger and hand forces applied.

A subtle variation of Species II., which forms a hybrid between Hand and Finger movement, is applicable to extremely rapid Octave-passages, such as in the Coda of the last movement of the "Waldstein" Sonata. Such passages cannot be easily performed *glissando* on the modern Piano. This hybrid touch can, however, give an almost identical effect. In it, all movement is almost entirely restricted to a movement of the fingers—to the extent of the key-depth. An extremely light glissando-like resting of the arm is thus caused to mount the successive keys, almost as in the true glissando.

§ 10. The reason why this kind of touch-formation offers us *all varieties* of Tone-*quality*, as above referred to, lies in the fact, that we here alone have available those two so clearly contrasted forms of touch, respectively termed Weight-touch and Muscular-touch.

We must recall, that this combination includes Arm-release and Muscular-exertion of Hand and Finger, and that we may therefore start (or "initiate") the whole of this combination into operation against the key in either of two ways—as we have learnt in Chapter XVII., § 10, etc. That is: we may directly prompt either of the two implicated elements into use— either the element of Weight, or the element of Exertion, when the remaining element will automatically respond to the other's initiative. In the first case—Weight-initiative—we have the conditions that make for "sympathetic" tone-colour; whereas in the second case, we have those that tend towards brilliancy.[1]

§ 11. Meanwhile, we have the option of that additional Quality-influence, the contrast between "flat" and "bent" finger-attitudes, which helps those differences between beauty and harshness of tone respectively.

The Second Species of Touch-formation.

§ 12. **Finger-force and Hand-force against a Self-supported Arm.**—When greater Agility is required than is possible under the *third* species of Touch-formation, then we must sacrifice the element of Arm-release (or Weight), and we can consequently in this case only rely upon the remaining muscular-components (the Hand and Finger exertions) to fulfil the work of key-depression: thus forming the second Species of Touch-formation.

The arm is in this case to be supported by its own muscles

---

[1] To repeat: We may *will* the lapse in Arm-support, and permit the Finger and Hand to act purely in response to the weight thus set free, when their action will serve to lever this weight upon the key, and thus prevent its dropping down past the key without influencing the latter. Or, we may instead prompt the Finger and Hand into activity, and allow the sensation of recoil (experienced against the Wrist-joint) to cause the Arm to be sufficiently released in response, to prevent any loss of energy.

THE THREE SPECIES OF TOUCH-FORMATION. 221

gently, elastically, and certainly not stiffly, so that the arm as it were floats along the key-board, and thus *carries* the loosely lying hand and fingers towards the desired notes, which, being reached, are then depressed by the combined action of Hand and Finger.[1]

§ 13. As there is here no question of Weight,[2] it follows that the tone can only be *muscularly initiated* (§ 10) when this touch-formation is employed, and that the tone-quality is consequently here restricted to the sharper (or "brilliant") kinds, modifiable only by the contrasts between the thrusting and clinging Finger-attitudes.

§ 14. The quantity of tone is also far more limited than in the previously-described combination, for the only Basis now available for the finger and hand to act against (or from) is the self-*supported* arm; and this implies an *elastically* supported weight, and therefore one that cannot offer much resistance or basis.[3]

§ 15. As the arm-element is not used, it also follows, that our choice of *movement* is limited to that of the Hand and Finger, and that we are in this Species limited to Hand ("Wrist") and Finger touches.

§ 16. There is, however, this compensation, that we can under these circumstances get over the ground a great deal faster; *i.e.*, that a far higher grade of Agility is here open to us, provided we obey the ever-present rules in this case, (*a*) of

---

[1] It is suggestive of the required free condition of the Wrist, to say, that "*the Wrist-end of the Hand must be carried by the Arm.*" For it is certain, if the *wrist*-end of the loose-lying hand is "supported" by the arm, that the latter is then also *supported off* the key-beds.

[2] That is, in other words: there is here no muscular-*inflection* (or change) in Arm-condition *for the purpose of key-descent* or Tone-production. This, we must remember, does not preclude that slight but *continuous* Lapse in Arm-support, which gives us Tenuto and Legato.

[3] As this might be misunderstood to imply that the arm should sometimes *not* be in an "elastic" condition, it is here necessary to recall the fact, that a gently self-supported arm is necessarily in an elastic condition, owing to the elastic nature of muscle and tendon; the self-supported arm is thus "elastic" in the sense, that being in a state of balance, it can afford but little resistance to the recoil (or reaction) experienced from finger and hand, on their acting against the keys. Whereas the whole available arm-weight becomes serviceable for a basis behind finger and hand, when the arm is left momentarily unsupported.

222 KEY-TREATMENT; MUSCULAR ASPECT.

thus really supporting the arm (and not allowing it to influence key-descent by any change in itself) and (*b*) the rule of accuracy in ceasing the muscular-actions employed the very instant that sound is reached.—These two Rules (*a*, as to the supported Arm, and, *b*, as to the accuracy in Cessation) must indeed be unflinchingly adhered to, if we wish to master the problem of true Agility—and of Staccato.[1]

The First Species of Touch-formation. § 17. **The First form of muscular-combination,** *finger-force alone, against a continuously loose-lying hand, and self-supported arm:*—When a still higher grade of Agility is required than is attainable under the last-described combination, then we must forego exerting even the hand, and must in this case restrict all activity absolutely to the single remaining muscular-component here alone available—that of Finger down-exertion.

The arm merely floats over the key-board in this instance, and it again "carries the Wrist-end of the Hand," as in the touch-formation last considered.[2]

The hand itself must meanwhile lie passively on the keys, supported thereon by the fingers, which must be individually exerted against their keys, either from a previously raised

---

[1] There is this further Rule in the case of both Hand and Finger touches at extreme Speed, especially when the same keys have to be repeated:—*In such cases it is undesirable that the finger-tips should leave the surface of the key-board at all.* The keys must be permitted merely to rebound with the finger or hand, and that is all; the finger-tips meanwhile—throughout the passage—must remain firmly upon the key-surface, or key-board surface.[*] Extreme rapidity indeed becomes almost impossible in the case of Hand-touches, if the Hand is actually raised *off* the keys;—it takes time to do so, and *uncertainty* results, owing to the impossibility of re-feeling key-resistance under such rapid "tapping" of the key-surfaces. The consequence of committing this fault, is, that the keys are felt to "wobble" under the hand, during repetition. This sensation arises owing to the key, when suddenly quitted, *giving slight oscillations before coming to rest*,—unless the fingers remain on the keys to prevent this occurring.

Very rapid Hand-touch passages, whether quasi-legato or really staccato, must therefore be executed with "finger-tips close to the keys,"—causing one to experience a sensation of continuous contact, since the fingers remain on their keys when repeating them, and *slide* from one key to the next in other passages.

[2] Again we must caution the reader, not to be confused by the slight (but *continuous*) divergence from this complete "self-support" of the arm, required to provide the slight, but continuous weight for the natural Tenuto and Legato.

[*] To enable such firm contact to be maintained without militating against the lightness of the "Resting," refer to *Note 2 of § 26, Chapter XVII., page 185.*

position, or from a less-raised position, as deemed expedient.

§ 18. Since the hand's activity here no longer intervenes to transmit the recoil of the finger from Knuckle to Wrist, the elastically-supported arm is here also debarred from bearing any measure of this recoil. Now, as the mere weight of the hand (now alone available) is insignificant, it follows that the fingers cannot here receive much Basis for their operations against the keys; whence it also follows, that the tone-amount available under these circumstances can be but very small, while its quality must of necessity, as in the second Species, belong to the "harder" type, since it is modifiable only by the difference between the "thrusting" and "clinging" attitudes.[1]

Passages played lightly enough to admit of Species I., are, however, modifiable in their tone-quality, by employing the legato form of the Resting, in conjunction with this species of the Added-impetus. That is, we may combine with *this form of the Added-impetus* (Species I.) the "passing-on" (or "transfer-touch") form of the *Resting;* and as the whole tone-amount of this combination is not large, we shall thus obtain the sympathetic tendency of the latter's Weight-influence; for this will here make itself strongly felt, owing to the small sum-total of the tone resulting from the combination.[2]

§ 19. On the other hand, this form of combination offers us the great advantage, that we can by its means attain any degree of Agility or VELOCITY which it is possible to conceive,—up to the highest degree in fact, at which we can direct the Rhythm

---

[1] Under this Species, the tone cannot, however, really reach "hardness," owing to the small tone-total available, and the quality hence remains merely thin.

Quality-contrasts derived from "thrusting" and "clinging," are moreover for the same reason reduced almost to *nil*, so far as the Ear is concerned; although it is still important to have both modes of finger-attack equally at command.

[2] Alone, the "passing-on" touch is necessarily sympathetic—being entirely "weight-initiated." Alone, the Species I. of the Added-impetus is necessarily "short" (except for its flat-finger modification)—being muscularly-initiated. But by combining these, we obtain a certain range of subtle tone-modifications; which prove very useful, since they are available under stress of Velocity.

by means of our *automatic* counting-capacity.[1] (*Vide Appendix to Part I.: Note II.,* "*On Rhythm,*" *page 42.*)

To attain such lightning-like velocities, however, requires implicit obedience to the two laws previously enunciated: (a) that we must carefully exclude all Arm-weight (and of course all arm and body-force!) and Hand-activity; and (b), that we must *cease* each finger's activity so promptly, as to permit the key to *rebound.* It is of no use merely to allow the key to rise, it must be permitted really to rebound instantly.[2]

The reasons that should determine the choice between "flat" and "bent" finger.

§ 20. Understanding what constitutes the very material difference between the *third* Species of touch-formation and the other two Species,[3] it will now also be clearer to us why the "bent" finger attitude becomes imperative for certain passages, and the "flat" finger for others. Rapid passages, to be played *forte* with brilliance, demand the use of the "bent" finger.[4] We shall discern the reason for this, if we consider for a moment, what it is that really *causes* the difference between the "thrusting" and the "clinging" attitudes:

The cause is not to be found, as might be imagined, in the total difference of the muscular action of the implicated fingers. On the contrary, such difference in action, is itself *but a result.* For it is *the variable condition of the Upper-arm,* that induces the finger to act thus differently. That is: (a), if the Upper-arm tends to hang loose at the moment of tone-production, then the finger is *compelled* to cling to the key; whereas (b), if the Upper-arm does not thus hang loose, then it is supported or "held" in a more or less decidedly *forward*-tending direction; and the finger is in this case *compelled* into a thrusting action.

[1] Such light velocity-touch has often been aptly described as the "pearling" touch.

[2] A passage, taken at great speed, consequently appears to the player, as *a trail of up-springing* keys in the wake of the fingers as they rush along. We observe also, that the Staccato form of the Resting is the required one.

[3] *i.e.,* the presence or absence of Arm-weight.

[4] Many of the more rapid passages of BEETHOVEN have thus to be played "bent-finger." For instance, the passage commencing bar 52 of the first movement of the "Appassionata," must have all the non-accented notes played "bent" finger and second Species of touch, while for the accented notes we must add the arm-element in its "forward" variety.

THE THREE SPECIES OF TOUCH-FORMATION. 225

We know how this influences tone-quality. We must now also recognise, that herein lies the reason why we must choose "bent" finger, if we would be free to run rapidly across the key-board while *playing forte*. For the moment we allow the *Upper*-arm to lapse, that moment we have the *third* Species, which, we have learnt only permits velocity up to a very limited point—owing to the necessity, that Weight must here be separately lapsed for each note in *forte*, as it will otherwise bear continuously on the key-beds, with disastrous results.[1]

Hence, as we cannot *individualise* weight-lapse beyond a certain speed-limit, we are compelled to *support* the Upper-arm at greater speeds; and this at once compels the finger to assume its *thrusting* action, and with (what should be) a more fully bent position. Moreover, should we make the mistake to employ the *flat* (or clinging) finger forcibly, *while supporting the arm* (second Species therefore), such forcible action of the finger would then tend after all to drag the upper-arm weight on to the key-board, with the same laming effect as before-mentioned. For it is obvious, since the clinging-finger furthers *graduality* in key-attack, that it will in the same measure render prompt cessation less easy.

Sympathetic effects are on the other hand impossible, except with the clinging attitude, and this must then be employed with its drawbacks as to tone-amount when taken at speed.[2]

The Permits to Agility. § 21. Here it is useful once again to sum-up the true nature of the muscular-difficulties to be surmounted, if we would possess absolute Agility:—
(*a*) We must be able to produce the *second* Species of touch-

[1] Except when Weight is used continuously, as it may be, in very soft passages—in the form of the "passing-on" or "transfer" touch.
[2] Most of Chopin's passages indeed require the "flat" finger. It is even probable that Chopin himself never understood the "bent" finger,—hence his supposed "weakness" on the Concert-room platform—probably in *forte* finger-passages. On the other hand, to attempt to play some of his more strenuous passages with "flat" finger on a modern Pianoforte, would render them dull, clumsy, and uncertain. On the horns of such a dilemma, all we can do for such passages is to use a technique probably not intended by the composer (the "bent" finger),—as we should otherwise not obtain the contrasts and climaxes he undoubtedly did intend beyond everything else. (*Vide Note to* § 25.)

formation; which means, that we must be able to apply finger-and-hand force against the key (quite violently if need be), while nevertheless not exerting the arm downwards. (*b*) For the higher grades of Velocity, we must be able to supply the *first* Species of touch-formation, and must therefore here be able to discriminate also between *down* Finger-force and *down* Hand-force, so that we can employ the former without also employing the latter.[1] (*c*) We must moreover be able to employ both these two Species under the "bent" (or thrusting) attitude of the finger and its concomitant Upper-arm condition. (*d*) Meanwhile our attention to the series of *Sound-beginnings* must be alert and ever-present, so that we may succeed in directing the finger-and-hand exertions to *cease* their work at the very moment of sound-emission.[2] . . . . A timing, we must

---

[1] All sensation of activity or exertion *seems* in such touch *to reach no further than the knuckle*. The moment the sensation of exertion reaches the end of the hand at the wrist-joint—underneath, that moment all *extreme* agility is rendered impossible, for we are then *using* the Hand—are in fact probably employing Species II. instead of the intended Species I. Refer also to *II.* and *III.* of the Table of Muscular-discriminations appended to Chapter XVII.

[2] The truth will here become clearer to us, how all extreme Agility-key-treatment must as a matter of fact be purely STACCATO. Owing, however, to the extreme speed employed, the Ear cannot detect any Staccato, since the "damping" of the instrument cannot be prompt enough to permit any actual separation being exhibited between the sounds, when they occur in such close succession. In practising such passages slowly, it is therefore futile to practise them Legato, since the attainment of the desired speed depends so materially upon the accuracy of their Staccato production.

The process of performance may even at times take the form of rows of light "kick-offs" against the key-beds, as alluded to in Note XVII., Appendix to this Part. But we must in this case be cautious not to allow the slightest continuous weight (or pressure) to reach the key-*beds;* else the keys will be unable to rebound, and our RUN will as certainly be impeded; in short, the Resting must here be entirely at the key-board surface. Such *resilient* passages, as before said, are indeed perfectly analogous to the act of running with our legs; for the continuous light weight used (that of the hand, etc.) is as it were kept floating in the air (or at the surface of the key-board) by the quick reiteration of "kicks" (or jump-like actions) delivered against the key-beds.

In Species II., we may even permit a slight modicum of *continuous* arm-release to take effect behind the finger and hand, provided the passage is taken at a full *forte* and sufficiently fast, and yet not too fast. For the combined kick of the hand and finger will here be sufficiently forcible to cope even with such additional continuous weight, and will be able to prevent this from actually reaching the key-*beds*. And while this slight extra weight will have no ill effect on our Technique if successfully thus carried at the key-board sur-

THE THREE SPECIES OF TOUCH-FORMATION. 227

remember, not *individually* willed for each separate note in the case of great Agility, but instead willed as groups of Rhythm, and as a general (but precise) impression or realisation of key-board DEPTH.[1]

In short, we may say: that Agility depends *firstly* on our insisting on the ELIMINATION of Arm-force, and Weight, while either using our fingers and hands conjointly, or using the fingers alone for key-descent; and that it depends *secondly*, on accuracy in *cessation* of the force used.[2]

Muscular-discrimination must be systematically taught and practised.
§ 22. We realise indeed, more and more, that Agility itself, as well as the power of obtaining any particular Tone-amount or Tone-quality at will, ultimately depends on an unconscious or conscious *discrimination of the Muscular-causes that will provoke the effects;* thus re-enforcing the argument, that a systematic teaching and acquisition of these Muscular-discriminations should form the first steps in learning to play. Such discrimination-exercises, indeed, form the only logical, natural, and direct way of acquiring the Basis of a good Technique.[3]

face, it will enhance our tone-possibilities in this kind of passage, owing to the extra Basis thus provided for the vigorous but short-lived actions of the Finger and Hand against the Key during descent.

[1] *Vide Note to* § 7 *of Chapter XV.*

[2] Here it is well to point out, that it is an unconscious lapse of Arm-weight which so often vitiates not only our Agility, but also our Staccato, and even Pianissimo. If we reflect for a moment, we shall see, that *to hold the heavy weight of the arm suspended over the keys* (as it should be in such Touches) and not resting instead on the key-beds, must necessarily become very fatiguing when continued for a length of time. Hence, as the arm tires, we are apt unconsciously to allow it to lapse upon the keys more or less;—and we then wonder why our fingers seem so lame and tired.

The student should make the experiment, of holding his arm supported in front of him (away from the key-board) for some considerable time, and thus satisfy himself of this lurking danger to his Technique.

[3] Moreover, it must now be clearly manifest to us, how appalling an absurdity it is (indeed, it seems criminal, once these facts are understood) to give Technical Exercises, or Studies, or Pieces to old or young students, *without first giving them those absolutely necessary directions as to what are the habits they should form* BY MEANS OF SUCH MUSCULAR PRACTICE, and insisting upon attention to such directions during Practice. Without such directions, the unfortunate student (if he is conscientious) will try to learn "somehow" to sound the notes of such Exercises, etc.,—and he will meanwhile be sure to acquire countless wrong muscular habits—habits, to break which, will subsequently demand his keenest will-power, perseverance, and enthusiasm.

228   KEY-TREATMENT; MUSCULAR ASPECT.

General Directions as to Choice of Touch-formation.
§ 23. We shall also now be able to realise why it is, that in our choice between these three Species of Touch-formation, we are compelled to bear in mind (either consciously or unconsciously) the particular advantages and drawbacks of each; and that the speed required, and the tone-quality and quantity required, are the determining influences in such choice.[1]

The following general broad principles of application, are appended for the guidance of the student, as it is at first difficult to use one's reasoning power in this direction:—

§ 24. For passages of Agility, we must understand that we are limited to Species I. and II., and for *fortes*, to the Bent-finger form of these Species.[2]

When the speed is considerable, but not too excessive, we can employ Species II., and we then have at our disposal the benefits it confers in the way of considerable tone-compass; but for extreme speeds we cannot employ even Species II., but are restricted to Species I., with its extremely narrow possibilities in tone-amount, and variation of it.[3]

---

[1] The result of our failing to keep these facts constantly before us, will render us liable to commit errors of judgment that will preclude our obtaining due expression of our musical feeling, and will meanwhile cause us to play unrhythmically, owing to the difficulty of our progress across the keys. For instance, we may try to play an Agility *forte*-passage with Species III., which will have the effect of rendering such passage exceedingly laborious to us, or even impossible.—Or, wishing to play a *forte*-passage, we may employ Species I., when we shall probably ascribe our failure to "want of strength," etc., that will not permit of our obtaining any tone beyond the thinnest and smallest!—Or, again, when we want a full singing tone, not understanding the precise muscular conditions under which alone it can be obtained, we may select Species II., and consequently will find ourselves unable to obtain anything beyond a sharp brilliant effect!—Or, we may even select the correct Species— Species III.—and yet fail to obtain a true *cantabile*, owing to our not insisting on Weight-*initiative*, in coöperation with the *flat* or clinging finger-attitude!

[2] For Agility, we are limited to these two Species, except in the case of the *softest* Tenuto and Legato passages, when that exceptional touch, the "*passing-on*" touch (or Transfer-touch) is also available under the conditions of full Agility. (*Vide* § 9 *and its Note.*) This exceptional touch-form has already often been referred to as the only true *ppp*-touch. As it is, in its "transfer" form, perfectly well adapted for *Agility* passages, we shall find that it is as such often suitable for those gossamer-like embroideries of CHOPIN, etc.

[3] We must moreover bear in mind, that the slight *continuous* Weight, required to induce Legato, *must not be employed* when we require the full ex-

THE THREE SPECIES OF TOUCH-FORMATION.

Quality of tone under either of these Species, is, however, slightly variable by means of the contrast between Thrusting and Clinging finger-attitudes.

§ 25. For passages of *full* tone,—tone, of full amount and thick quality, and tone of small amount but of thick quality—we are restricted to Species III. But we must bear in mind, as already insisted upon, that this Species is only available up to a very definitely limited speed. Beyond that speed, really full tone remains a physical impossibility; and if we nevertheless attempt to apply its muscular-conditions beyond those speed-limits, we find such passages will at once become "difficult" and laborious, if not completely "sticky" and unclear.

All *cantando* passages must be performed under this Species. The *bent* finger may be employed for the harder-toned *forte*-passages; but when a real *cantando* is required, we must have recourse at least to the Weight-*initiative* form of this Species. Moreover, to ensure the true subtle *cantabile*—such as CHOPIN nearly always demands for his melodic matter, we must, in addition to Weight-initiative, insist upon the coöperation of that fully elastic condition of Finger, Hand, and Upper-arm, implied in the "*clinging*" finger-attitude.[1]

§ 26. As already pointed out in § 4,[2] all three species of touch-formation are equally available under Staccato and Legato; the difference depending merely upon which of the two kinds of Resting accompanies these forms of the Added-impetus.

We must, however, bear in mind, that the Resting *must*

---

tremes of Agility these two Species render possible. Even such slight weight will then prove an encumbrance, and will detract from our Agility-power.

As insisted upon in the second Note to § 21, extreme Agility-technique must really be *staccato* in its execution; although to the ear the sounds are merged into an unbroken succession.

[1] Unless the performer has this fully "sympathetic" *cantabile* in his repertory, it is a piece of sheer vandalism for him to attempt to play CHOPIN, for instance. Chopin-playing must indeed remain hopeless of attainment, until the performer is able to produce all shades of sympathetic (un-sudden) key-attack,—in Staccato as well as in Legato, in Pianissimo as well as in Forte. It is an experience worthy of Purgatory, to be compelled to hear a performer crunch through poor Chopin, with one of those brick and mortar tone-productions affected by some who nevertheless fancy themselves to be Pianoforte-artists! *Refer also to second Note to § 20; page* 225.

[2] *Also vide second Note to* § 21; *page* 227.

remain at the key-*surface* in all passages of considerable **Agility**,—although the effect is not necessarily Staccato at these speeds.

§ 27. We must also note, that all three alternatives of *movement* (Arm, Hand, and Finger "touches") are available under Species III.; while with Species II., we have only two such alternatives—Hand and Finger-touches; while lastly, Species I., can only show Finger-movement.

The question of Order of Study. § 28. As to the order, in which to learn the various touches, it is generally found easiest to acquire the muscular-combinations of Species III. as *Arm-movement* in the first instance, applying them to single chords and notes; then proceeding to the acquisition of the same tonal and muscular-effects under their Finger-touch form; and lastly under their Hand-movement form.

Species II. is, on the contrary, best learnt first as Hand-movement. When the touch-formation has been thoroughly mastered, it is easy to substitute Finger-movement in place of the Hand-movement first learnt.[1]

§ 29. Even in these cases, however, much must be left to individual idiosyncrasy,—the needful thing being, to learn that first, which is least unclear at the time. The same rule in some measure holds good as to the question, whether *Passage*-touches or *Cantabile*-touches should be first acquired.

Personally, I am inclined to think that Singing-touch is the best first step for most people. In its softest aspect, it is muscularly the simplest touch of all. And once the important truth has been recognised, that a tone can be produced apparently by sheer "Relaxation," it will become comparatively an

---

[1] The Finger-form of this Species might indeed be described as consisting of Hand-touch ("Wrist-action") *without the Hand-movement;* for the individualised activity of the hand here provided behind each finger would indeed induce Hand-movement, were the latter activity in excess of the finger-activity used at the moment,—as it should be, if we wish for the finger-touch. Probably, it was this touch-combination, that unconsciously suggested to CHOPIN the desirability of "practising finger passages with 'wrist-touch.'" It undoubtedly is beneficial to do so, when the end in view is Species II., in its Finger-touch form.

THE THREE SPECIES OF TOUCH-FORMATION. 231

easy matter subsequently to learn to *support* the arm during tone-production. But although this seems the logical course, we have as teachers to deal with human beings, and the only way to deal with such, especially in their younger stages, is to seize the opportunity which any glimmering of intelligence or bodily-aptitude offers us, and to start the whole sequence of touch-learning from that point of vantage.[1]

Caution necessary when studying Muscular-conditions. Music, through Key-movement, the ever-present Purpose.

§ 30. Here it is as well once again to remind both Student and Teacher, that we must be careful, while striving to acquire the necessary muscular facilities, that we do not meanwhile forget to *use the Key*, and thus ultimately forget the very Purpose of such muscular facility — the Musical-result! That is: while striving to employ the correct *muscular-means* that will enable us to obtain any required tone, we must always insist on *directing* such muscular operations solely to the production of Sound *by means of* the Key; and directing them not only to a sound, but to a definitely desired kind of sound, and above all things to a definitely desired Time-spot for its beginning;—in short, we must always have Music as our ultimate Aim. Meanwhile we must also remember, that it is only by means of such Purpose in Time, that this can be accomplished; since Purpose in Time is as inseparable from the act of Tone-production as it is from Music itself—if there is to be success; and that our conception of a musical work can only become translated into Performance, by means of the *grip* that Time-definiteness offers us.[2]

We must therefore constantly bear in mind how important it is, for us to LISTEN with vivid alertness for the beginning of each sound (for the moment where " silence changes into sound ") so that we may be able accurately to direct the culmination of each *correct* muscular act, and its prompt cessation

---

[1] As every human being differs more or less from his fellows, we must insert the thin edge of the wedge of Knowledge, wherever the outer cuticle of Non-knowledge is least dense. To endeavour therefore to lay down strict laws of procedure in such matters is sheer folly, worthy only of an exaggerated Militarism.

[2] *Part I., Chapter V.*

and reversal; meanwhile seeing to it, that this accurately aimed culmination and cessation of the muscular-operation against the key, is also compelled accurately to synchronise with a (consciously or unconsciously) selected moment in Time and Tone.[1]

Moreover, it is necessary to insist that this rule also applies with equal force, when we are studying merely single sounds or chords, during the process of acquiring the art of tone-production; for it is here equally essential for us to have a definite moment of Time in our mind—to which to direct the speed-culmination of each key-descent, as we shall otherwise be meanwhile forming wrong habits of Attention.

RECAPITULATORY

a): We have learnt[2] that the three muscular-components available (Finger-force, Hand-force, and Arm-weight with its coöperatives) can be applied to the Key, under three main Principles of Combination, forming three distinct Species of Touch-formation:

Description of the Three Species of Touch-formation:

b): The First Species consists of Finger-force alone acting against the key during descent; while the hand is passive, and the Arm self-supported.

The Second Species consists of Hand-force acting in conjunction with the Finger against the key during descent; while the Arm remains self-supported.

The Third Species consists of all three components, operative

---

[1] In a word, we must always recall the rule enunciated in Part I., *viz.*, that we must listen *both outwardly and inwardly* for each sound-beginning, so that it may arise in strict response to the imagined place in Time and Tone dictated by our musical intellect and feeling. For it is alone by such means—through accuracy of Rhythm, that we can make definiteness of purpose evident in our performance,—alone in this way, that our playing can become "living," and not mere unmeaning note-strumming.

[2] Chapter XVII., § 6.

THE THREE SPECIES OF TOUCH-FORMATION. 233

against the key during descent; Finger and Hand force being supplemented by Arm-weight, etc.

How these Touch-formations are used:

c): To produce the 1st Species: the Arm must remain fully but elastically supported by its own muscles, and while the Arm thus floats over the key-board and supports the Wrist-end of the loose-lying Hand, the sound must be produced solely by the Finger's action against the key; such Finger-action ceasing the moment that sound is reached.

d): To produce the 2d Species: the Arm-condition is the same as in the last, but the Hand must here act behind the Finger during key-descent: both Finger and Hand accurately ceasing to act, the moment that sound is heard to begin.

e): To produce the 3d Species: we have to add Arm-weight behind the Finger and Hand, the latter acting as in the other Species. Such lapse in Arm-support must reach its climax at the moment of sound-emission, and it, as well as the finger-and-hand actions employed, must disappear at that very moment.

The forms of Movement available:

f): The Third Species can be employed either in the form of Arm-touch (arm-movement), or Hand-touch[1] (Hand-movement), or as Finger-touch (Finger-movement); all three forms of movement being available in this Species, since it contains all the three muscular-components.

The Second Species can only be employed either in the form of Hand-touch or as Finger-touch, since the Arm does not here change its condition during the act of tone-production.

The First Species is only available as Finger-touch, since neither Hand nor Arm should here show any change of condition during key-descent.

The speeds at which the Species are available:

g): The Third Species can however only be used, when the speed of the passage does not exceed a certain rate;—the speed

---

[1] "Wrist-action."

being restricted by the limit beyond which we cannot give the necessary repetitions of Arm-release.¹

The Second Species permits far greater Agility, while——

The First Species offers no physical limit to speed, beyond the mental difficulty of keeping the passage " in hand."

The contrasts of Tone-*quantity* available :

h) : The Third Species offers us the whole range of Tone, from the very softest to the loudest and fullest, owing to the presence of Arm-weight.

The Second Species cannot procure us so much Tone, as the Hand and Finger here have only the self-supported (or suspended) Arm as a Basis.

The First Species only renders a very small quantity of Tone available, since we here have only the slight weight of the loose-lying Hand as a Basis.

The contrasts of Tone-*quality* available :

i) : The *Third* is the only Species, under which all varieties of Tone-*quality* are available. For it is owing to the inclusion of Arm-release, that we can under this Species *start* the act of Tone-production either by Weight-release or by Muscular-exertion. ²

The Second and First Species only permit " Muscular-initiative." No "singing" tone can therefore be obtained through them.

j) : All three Species can moreover be somewhat modified (either towards Beauty or towards Harshness) by selecting either the flat (or clinging) attitude, or the bent (or thrusting) attitude.

k) : To obtain fully "sympathetic" *cantabile* or *cantando*, we must combine the Clinging-attitude with the Third Species, in its Weight-initiative form.

---

¹ Such alternations of Arm-release and renewed self-support, are, we must remember, not necessarily shown as arm-*movements*.

What may be considered a Variety of this Species, is, however, also available in full-speed passages, provided we do not attempt to obtain more tone than a *piano*—provided, therefore, that it takes the form of "transfer" (or "passing-on") touch. In this form it is also available as a GLISSANDO.

² We must remember that with "Weight-touch" the tendency is towards beauty of tone, while with "Muscular-touch" it is towards hardness, harshness (or asperity) of quality.

Bent finger, 2d Species, compulsory, for rapid *forte* passages.

l): We moreover now discern, that the Clinging (or flat) finger, requires some measure of Upper-arm release. This incapacitates this form of touch for *rapid* passages, when these are required *forte*.

For rapid *forte* passages, we must therefore use the self-supported arm (Second Species) with the thrusting (or bent) finger in combination with it.[1]

m): The secret of Agility, hence, is found to lie in the self-supported arm; and combined with it, the thrusting finger, when the passage is *forte*. Accuracy in ceasing the action *at* sound, is a law that meanwhile bears no breaking.

The contrasts in Duration, how available:

n): All three Species of touch-formation are Staccato, provided we insist meanwhile on the Act of Resting being sufficiently light;—so light that the arm is continuously in a state of complete self-support; and provided we are also careful to time our *actions against* the keys to *cease* so accurately as to permit these to rebound.[2]

o): All the Species can be transformed into Tenuti, by merely changing the Resting into a slightly heavier form, the arm (as to its *continuous* condition) being here not quite so fully supported as in Staccato.

p): All the Species can moreover be transformed into Legati, by transferring such Tenuto-form of the Resting from key to key.

The danger of forgetting to think of Sound, when learning new muscular habits:

q): In endeavouring to acquire correct Muscular-conditions, we must meanwhile never lose sight of their Object, *viz.*: to *move* the Key *for the sake* of Music.

---

[1] The clinging-finger, would in rapid *forte* passages, tend to dull the passage by dragging the Upper-arm on to the key-beds.
[2] We must recall that the *Continuous* condition of the arm, here implied in the Resting, does by no means preclude our using the momentary lapses required in Species III., to form the Added-impetus.

To succeed in this, we must remember to watch the key unremittingly, both before depression—for its weight, and during depression—for the Place where tone-production culminates and ceases. We can moreover only ensure our doing this, by remembering to watch TIME.

We must therefore insist on judging not only how, but *where* each note should sound. Thus, only, can we hope to learn to employ Technique solely for a Musical Purpose.

r) : The following Table should now be studied.

TABLE SHOWING RELATIONSHIP BETWEEN THE THREE SPECIES OF ADDED-IMPETUS, MOVEMENT, AND THE RESTING, Etc.

THE ACT OF ADDED-IMPETUS:

—— required during the moment of key-descent for all tone-making, except *ppp*-ten. and leg., and *always as short-lived as in staccatissimo*:—

	FIRST SPECIES.	SECOND SPECIES.	THIRD SPECIES.	
	Momentary finger-exertion alone, with lax hand and self-supported arm.	Momentary hand-exertion behind the finger-exertion, with self-supported arm.	Momentary Arm-weight release behind finger-and-hand exertion.	
			(a) Weight-initiated.*	(b) Muscularly-initiated.†
MOVEMENTS AVAILABLE:	Finger-touches only.	Finger-touches and Hand (Wrist) touches.	Finger-touches, Hand-touches, and Arm-touches.‡	
FINGER-ARM ATTITUDES AVAILABLE:	{(a) The "flat," or Clinging — — — helps towards sympathetic quality. {(b) The "bent," or Thrusting — — — helps towards brilliant quality.			
(A): The *Staccato* Basis, at Surface key-level :—	{ Hand-weight only, — — — insufficient to depress keys, or to retain them depressed.			
(B): The *Tenuto* or *Legato* Basis, at Depressed key-level :—	{ Arm-weight §, sufficient, unassisted, to induce key-descent for *ppp*-tenuto and legato.			

THE ACT OF RESTING:

—— required continuously during each phrase :—

* Makes for thick tone.   † Makes for sharp tone.   ‡ Including arm-rotation touches.   § The *whole* arm, slightly released continuously.

CHAPTER XX.

ENUMERATION AND CLASSIFICATION OF TOUCHES.

§ 1. To facilitate the understanding of this matter, we must first once again briefly review the whole ground of Muscular-facts and Touch-construction. Enumeration of the main kinds of Touch follows; while Classification naturally ensues during the course of this Enumeration. After giving a Recapitulatory and Summary, several Tables are appended, exhibiting Enumeration and Classification from different points of view.

Constant re-statements of the same facts are here involved, so that each successive point may be complete in itself so far as possible. As already pointed out, although this must prove tedious to many a reader, nevertheless it is essential for the sake of the ordinary student.

Any Enumeration and Classification of Touches may at first seem to be an impossible achievement, when we see how endless are the possible varieties and their modifications.[1] The task nevertheless becomes quite feasible, if we keep in view the *natural divisions* that Touch falls into,—owing to the Three Species of Muscular-construction described in the last chapter.

Duly bearing in mind these and other fundamental and radical distinctions, the whole problem, so far from being com-

---

[1] Happily there is no limit to the possible combinations and gradations of Touch, any more than there is to the combination-possibilities of Melody, Harmony and Rhythm, otherwise we should have to agree with JOHN STUART MILL, and, finding our Art to be miserably "limited" and ' finite," give it up in despair.

plex, becomes one of extreme simplicity; and our understanding of it, as well as *its practical application to the key-board*, will then be found perfectly clear and easy.

The result, when brought down to figures, may at first glance seem alarmingly complicated and impracticable; but no such difficulty is found in actual practice. There is none, provided we always, both as Students and as Players, keep in view the few main *and simple* facts which explain the derivation of all this complicated array of possible Touch-varieties;—varieties that give us all options of tone-quantity and quality, and varying opportunities for Agility.

We will therefore first recall these general main facts, and then briefly reconsider the Three Species of Touch-formation, and their potentialities:

§ 2. These MAIN FACTS, we must remember, can be summed up under the following heads:—

    a) *The Resting*—the continuous Element, in its two forms of Staccato and Legato-Basis.

    b) *The Added-impetus*—the short-lived key-moving act.

    c) *The Three Species of Muscular - combination* (or Touch-formation) under which the Added-impetus can be given.

    d) *Weight-initiated Touch*, and *Muscularly-initiated Touch*—those two great distinctions which respectively make for Beauty and Harshness of Tone.

    e) *The Clinging and Thrusting Attitudes*, which further influence Tone towards the Sympathetic and the Unsympathetic respectively.

§ 3. The THREE SPECIES of TOUCH-FORMATION, we must remember, are as follows:—

    I.) *The First Species*, implies a self-supported Arm, and loose-lying Hand; the sound being obtained solely by the action of the Finger.

II.) *The Second Species*, implies a self-supported **Arm**, while sound is produced by the conjoint action of the Finger and Hand.

III.) *The Third Species*, implies the employment of all three muscular components against the key, during descent; *viz.*, Arm-weight release, in conjunction with Hand and Finger-activity.

§ 4. We found Species III. to be the most important, because, containing the element of separate Arm-release for each individual key-descent, it provides us with those radical differences in Tone-*quality* which we have termed respectively: "Weight-touch" and "Muscular-touch,"[1] and which are entitled to rank as Sub-genera. This Third Species is the most important, also, because it offers us all three alternatives of *Movement*,—*i.e.*, movement either of the Arm itself, or of the Hand, or of the Finger; and because it moreover gives us the largest range of Tone-*quantity*—ranging from the softest to the loudest possible.

§ 5. Species II. and I., while they neither give us the great Quality nor Quantity-contrasts of Species III., nevertheless offer us the advantage of easy progression across the key-board, and they are therefore both entitled to be called "Agility-touches."

Species II., moreover, is more important than Species I., since the former (depending as it does both on Finger and Hand-force for key descent) offers us some considerable range of Tone-quantity, and the alternatives of Hand and Finger-movement; whereas, with Species I., we are restricted to the movement of the Finger itself, and to a very scant variety in Tone, as we only have finger-force to depend on.

§ 6. To complete this review of the derivation of Touch-variety, we must refer to the fact that any of these Species, and Sub-genera, can appear either under the "Thrusting" (Bent-

---

[1] We must recollect that Weight-touch is so called, because the complete combination (of Arm, Hand and Finger) is herein brought into operation through Arm-release initiative; whereas Muscular-touch is thus called, because the complete combination is here, on the contrary, started into operation by the muscular-*action* of the Finger and Hand.

ENUMERATION AND CLASSIFICATION. 241

finger) attitude, or under the "Clinging" (Flat-finger) attitude. A fact which at one step doubles our number of Touch-varieties.[1]

§ 7. There is, however, one kind of Touch not included in any of these Species, which is nevertheless perhaps one of the most important of all, *and that is the ppp-Tenuto or Legato Weight-touch*.[2]

This exceptional form of touch, we therefore classify as a tone-producing form of the Act of Resting itself; in fact, as the "Second form of the Resting,"—a Resting continued at key-bed level, and which is the Basis of all Tenuti and Legati.

§ 8. Being here again brought face to face with those two Mental-muscular Concepts which together form the foundation of all true Technique—the "Added-impetus" and the "Resting," we are also reminded that it is merely the slight difference in the weight of the Resting, that constitutes the cause of the distinction between Staccato and Tenuto or Legato.[3] We are reminded, too, that if the Resting is heavy enough to take the key down, it is also sufficiently heavy to retain the key depressed; and that if we desire the natural Staccato effect, our resting must be even lighter than in the former case; *i. e.*, it must then exist without the slightest vestige of Arm-weight.[4]

§ 9. Having thus reviewed our material, we can now proceed

---

[1] We also have the further alternative, that nearly all these Touches may be accompanied by the *rotary-movement* of the Fore-arm (or *rocking* of the Hand), termed Rotary-touch, in place of the more usual movements of the Arm, Hand or Finger.

[2] *ppp*-Tenuto or Legato "Weight-touch" might be classified as a very light form of Species III., were it not that we have applied the term "Species" to those short-lived muscular acts which last only during key-*descent*. This exceptional form of Tone-production, on the contrary, *continues* to be of the same muscular-status, *beyond* the moment that the act of tone-production is concluded; and it is therefore identical with that continuous act of Resting on the key-board, which in its second form constantly attends the individualised acts of Key-speeding during Tenuto or Legato.

[3] In addition to the wide range of contrasts that here opens out, in the shape of natural Staccati and Legati, we also have those subsidiary contrasts in this direction obtained from the "driven-off" Staccato in its many aspects, and that artificial Hand-induced Legato which has sometimes to be employed.

[4] The reminder is here again necessary, not to confuse this continuous or continuously-resumed *status* of the Resting (and its Arm-conditions) with those *discontinuous* and rapidly alternating conditions of the Arm that obtain during the moment of key-descent in Species III.

242   KEY-TREATMENT; MUSCULAR ASPECT.

to the desired Enumeration, at the same time exhibiting the natural Classification of Touches. Under such Classification, Touch first of all segregates into the two primary Divisions of *Staccato* and *Legato*,—with the "Resting" either at Surface or Depressed level of the Key-board. Under each of these Divisions we then have the three aspects of *Movement*; *i.e.*, Finger-touch, Hand-touch, and Arm-touch. As Finger-Movement is available under all the Three Species of Muscular-combination (or Touch-formation), and as Hand-movement is available under Species II. and III., and Arm-movement only under Species III., we then finally discover the number of the main Varieties available under each.

ENUMERATION OF TOUCHES.

DIVISION I.—Staccato.

The act of "Resting" is here at the Surface-level of the Key-board.

No greater weight must here rest continuously on the keys than these will bear without depression. The Arm must therefore be in a state of continuous (or continuously resumed) Self-support.

§ 10. **Finger-staccato Touches.**

There are eight distinct Varieties of Finger-staccato, as follows:

The sound-inducing Impetus may be produced: (a) by Finger-exertion alone, (b) by Hand-exertion in conjunction with the Finger;[1] and (c) by Arm-weight in conjunction with both. As the latter Species of touch (the *third* species) can exist as either of the two Sub-genera: (a) Weight-initiated touch, or (b) Muscularly-initiated touch, it follows that this gives us *four* kinds of Touch. As all these four can exist either under the "Thrusting" (bent) attitude, or the "Clinging" (flat) attitude, this raises the complete number of Finger-staccato touches to *eight*.[2]

---

[1] Do not let us confuse Touch-*construction* with mere Movement.

[2] DRIVEN-OFF Staccato. As the *muscularly-initiated* Staccati can be rendered more prompt (and aggressive in tone-character) by assisting the other-

§ 11. Hand-staccato Touches.

There are Six distinct Varieties of Hand-staccato (Wrist-staccato) touches:

Species II. and III. can both exist as Hand-touch ("Wrist-action") if we permit the Hand-activity slightly to outbalance the other muscular-components. Species II. (Hand acting in conjunction with the Finger) will thus give us two kinds of Hand-touch, since it can appear either under the guise of the "Bent" or the "Flat" attitude. Species III. will give us four more,—since we have the alternative Sub-genera in the shape of initiatory Weight-release or initiatory Muscular-action, with the further alternatives to each of these of "Bent" and "Flat" attitudes; thus raising the complete number of Hand-staccato touches to SIX.[1]

§ 12. Arm-staccato Touches.

There are Four Varieties of Arm-staccato Touch:

A very slight excess of Arm-lapse over the other two muscular-constituents which form Species III. will cause Arm-*movement* to supervene in place of either Finger or Hand movement. As we can start the complete muscular conditions required in Species III., either by Lapse of Weight, or by Activity of the Finger-and-Hand, and as either of these Sub-genera can exist either in the "Thrusting" or "Clinging" form, this shows FOUR to be the complete number of Arm-staccato touches.[2]

DIVISION II.—Tenuto and Legato.

The act of "Resting" is here at depressed level of the keys. The "resting" Weight must therefore be sufficient to over-balance the keys into descent; and it therefore also

---

wise "passive" rebound of the key and its superimposed limb, through the application of a sharp "kick-off," we in this way gain several more or less well-defined additional Sub-varieties of Finger-staccato.

[1] The addition of a key-bed "kick-off" or "drive-off" offers us, as in the case of the Finger-staccato touches, a further series of Touch-modifications or Varieties.

[2] The "Driven-off" Staccato gives us, in the case of Arm-movement, four additional well-defined Sub-varieties of Touch.

suffices to retain them depressed beyond the moment the act of tone-production is complete.

The Arm-sustaining muscles must therefore here be in a state of continuous (or continuously resumed) slight lapse.[1]

§ 13. **This second form of the "resting" we have recognised as being itself a Tone-producing agent.**

Employed alone (*i.e.*, without any "Added Impetus") it gives us the softest sound obtainable from the instrument, and at the same time forms *Tenuto*. Such Tenuto, transferred unbrokenly from key to key by the fingers, thus forms Legato. It is also the Basis of all other Tenuto and Legato touches, however loud, or brilliant, or sympathetic they may be. It moreover forms the only *simple* form of Touch; and it can be accompanied either by Arm-movement, Hand-movement, or Finger-movement.[2]

It can also be employed as a tone-*quality* modifying agent, when it is combined (in the form of weight-transfer-touch) with the light finger-touches of Species I. For its weight influence (making for sympathetic quality) can here make itself felt, owing to the fact that the muscular-initiative influence of this form of the Added-impetus is too light to prove overpowering. (*Vide* § 17, *Chapter XIX*.)

§ 14. **Finger-tenuto and Legato touches.**

There are Ten distinct Varieties of Finger-tenuto (or Legato) touches, as follows:

To begin with, we may obtain sound by the unaided "Resting" itself,[3] and as we may employ either the "Thrusting" or the "Clinging" attitude, this gives us *two* Touch-varieties.

---

[1] We must recall that the appearance of this slight degree of Arm-weight must be *continuous* during each musical Phrase or Sentence, or must else be unremittingly resumed during such musical divisions.

[2] As before explained, it is the only form of *simple* touch; since there is here *no change* in the muscular conditions existing *during* key-descent and *after* key-descent,—for the conditions that cause the tone, and the conditions that cause Tenuto and Legato are here identical; whereas in all other touches (Staccato as well as Legato) we are obliged to have a separate set of muscular-conditions to provoke each tone,—separate from the conditions that give us the "Resting" either at key-surface or key-bed.

[3] When transferred from note to note, in the form of Legato, this kind of key-attack forms "Transfer-touch" or "Passing-on touch."

ENUMERATION AND CLASSIFICATION. 245

The remaining eight varieties are obtained by *adding* to this "second form of the Resting" *any of the previously enumerated eight* FINGER-STACCATO *forms of Tone-production,*—or forms of the Added-impetus. That is: We may combine an Added-impetus with this act of Resting, and this Added-impetus may be in the form of *any of the three* Species of Touch-formation;—while the third Species is moreover available in either of its Sub-genera;—and all of these again, either under "Bent" or "Flat" option.

Thus we find that the complete number of Finger-touches available as Tenuto (or Legato) is TEN.[1]

§ 15. Hand ("Wrist") tenuto touches.

There are Eight Hand-tenuto touches:

The "Resting" unaided (as simple "weight-touch") provides two varieties, since it can be applied either in "Bent" or "Flat" attitudes.

Then, again, we may add to this Tenuto-element any of the six previously enumerated forms of Hand-*staccato* tone-production. Thus we have the option of the *third* Species of Touch-formation in either of its Sub-generic forms, and also the *second* Species, while we have the further option of giving any of these three, either in the "Bent" or the "Flat" modifications; thus showing the full number of Hand-tenuto Touches to be EIGHT.[2]

---

[1] In addition, we can obtain the "artificial" legato, as previously explained, by employing a *continuous* but very slight exertion of the *Hand* and *Fingers* (or "pressure") in the place of the usual slight Arm-weight. This is occasionally applicable, and, as before noted, it is by its means that we should obtain those short-lived slight extra "pressures" required during momentary *inflections* of Legato and Super-Legato, or Legatissimo.

[2] We often hear of "Wrist" or "Arm *Legato* touch." This, however, is merely a term of convenience, as already pointed out. For it is obvious that no true Legato can exist apart from Finger-touch (or movement) except through the intervention of the Damper-pedal.—Without the Damper-pedal we can only approximate towards Legato in Hand and Arm touches, by insisting on making the successions of Tenuti as close as possible.

The term "*Semi-legato*" is a similar misnomer when physically considered. The Duration-effect in question should be termed *Semi-tenuto;* for it is obtained by discontinuing each of the successive Tenuto effects before the appearance of each new note.

§ 16. Arm-tenuto touches.

There are Six varieties of Arm-tenuto:

The "Resting" itself supplies two varieties, since we can apply it to the keys either under the "Thrusting" or the "Clinging" form.[1]

We owe the remaining four Varieties to the fact that the *third* Species can be applied either as Weight-touch or as Muscular-touch; and that both of these Sub-genera can again appear either under the "Bent" or the "Flat" Finger attitudes; thus completing the full number, SIX, of Arm-tenuti.[2]

§ 17. Rotary Touches:

Most of the touches so far enumerated are (more or less conveniently) available as Fore-arm Rotation-touches, or so-called "Side-stroke" touch. They are transformed into such, by permitting the ever-present adjustments of the Fore-arm-rotation to manifest themselves as an actual rocking movement of Hand and Fore-arm; these adjustments being in this case slightly in excess of the other muscular-components of Touch, and this rocking movement therefore here taking the place of the more usual movements of the Finger, Hand, or Arm.

As the appropriate application of Rotary-touch is comparatively rare, it is undesirable to encumber this page with a minute enumeration of the possible Varieties of this kind of touch; especially as such differentiations depend on precisely the same causes as in the case of all other touch-formations.

---

[1] We must remember that simple *pianissimo* Weight-touch takes the form of Arm-movement when the Finger and Hand are insufficiently exerted to support the gently (and but slightly) relaxing Weight of the *whole* Arm,—and the Arm itself in consequence sinks down with the key. Arm-movement forms the best (and usual) mode of applying this simplest of the Touches, in slow successions of notes or chords.

[2] The Student must here once again be warned, clearly to keep in mind the difference between that *continuous* (or continuously resumed) slight arm-lapse which constitutes the act of Simple-touch (and is the Basis of all Tenuti and Legati—in the form of the *second* kind of "Resting") and that *other act*, a MOMENTARY lapse of the Arm-supporting muscles,—a lapse that may be complete, and may even have Shoulder-weight and Body-weight behind it, but which act is only *added* to give the necessary impulse to the key in the larger Tone-forms; and which ceases to exist with the very moment of Tone-emission.

§ 18. While we thus find that there are 42 main kinds of key-attack that can be enumerated, it by no means follows that it is either necessary or even desirable that we should keep these distinctions in view when playing.   On the contrary, the less we are compelled to think of these distinctions the better—provided we do correctly produce and apply them.[1]

Certainly, in learning to play, we must at first employ them consciously—purposefully; but we must also gradually learn to employ them more and more unconsciously, until at least Musical-suggestion will itself suffice to prompt them into operation.   Moreover, in thus, as it were, gradually losing sight of these mechanical (but necessary) distinctions, we should do so in their natural order of importance;—the less easily misused and less important actions being hence the first to reach almost unconscious (but correct) application.

It is well, therefore, in this connection to bear in mind, that *Movement* (the distinction between Finger, Hand, and Arm touch) is the least important thus muscularly considered; that the difference in *Resting* (the difference between Legato and Staccato Basis) comes next; and that the distinctions formed by the Bent and Flat Attitudes and by the *Three Species of Touch-formation*, on the contrary, are the most important, especially as the third of these brings with it the distinction between WEIGHT-touch and MUSCULAR-touch.

Even the Artist must ever remain careful to use good judgment in these last respects when he is "laying-out" a work for study.

The distinctions between (a) the Three Species of Formation, (b) Weight *v.* Muscular touch, (c) Bent *v.* Flat finger, hence always remain burning questions, whether we think of them under this actual nomenclature, or think of them as undefined *Means* towards the attainment of real music.

[1] In any case it is not Phrases that have to be kept in view, but Facts that must be realised and made into Habit through Practice.

RECAPITULATORY AND SUMMARY.

a): Enumeration and Classification only become possible (and easy) if we bear in mind the main facts of Touch-construction, *viz.*:—

1): The Resting.
2): The Added-impetus.
3): The Three distinct Species of muscular-combination, or Touch-formation; and
4): The two great distinctions thence elicited:
    I.): *Weight*-initiated Touch.
    II.): *Muscularly*-initiated Touch.
5): The Distinction between Clinging and Thrusting attitudes.

b): To attain our present object, we must review some of the potentialities of these Elements:

1): The *Third* Species of Muscular-combination (or Touch-formation) alone offers us (because of its two Sub-genera) the option both of Muscular-initiative and of Weight-initiative; the other Species being necessarily Muscularly-initiated.

This *Third* Species, as regards movement, can be exhibited either as Finger-touch, Hand-touch, or as Arm-touch.

2): The *Second* Species only offers the option between Finger-touch and Hand-touch.

3): The *First* Species can only be obtained as Finger-touch.

4): The *Thrusting* and *Clinging* muscular-attitudes tend to qualify *all* Touch towards the Brilliant type and towards the Sympathetic type, respectively.

5): The *whole* of these Tone-producing Elements can be applied either under the *first* (Key-surface) form of the Resting, or under the *second* (Key-depressed) form of the Resting:

In the first case the effect is STACCATO; and in the second case it is TENUTO, and the latter can, moreover, in the case of Finger-touch, be transformed into Legato.

6): The *Second* form of the Resting, applied by itself to the key (without the assistance of any Added-impetus) forms the true *pp*-tenuto or Legato—*pp* Weight-touch or Transfer-touch.

It is identical with the muscular-combination, Species III., and can therefore exist either in the guise of Finger, Hand, or Arm-movement.[1]

c) : Enumerating the forms of Key-attack thus reviewed, we find there are :—

I.) : *Eight* distinct kinds of Finger-staccato; and *ten* kinds of Finger-tenuto, or Legato.

II.) : *Six* forms of Hand ("Wrist") staccato; and *eight* forms of Hand-tenuto.

III.) : *Four* forms of Arm-staccato and *six* forms of Arm-tenuto.

d) : These 42 well-defined modes of Key-attack, meanwhile each offer us a greater or smaller range of Tone-quantity and quality, and of Speed-possibility, respectively, according to their construction, as demonstrated in the previous chapters.

e) : Subsidiary modifications are :—

1) : An additional set of touch-forms, exhibited as Fore-arm Rotation-touch, sometimes advisable, and available under most forms of touch-construction.

2) : The " Kick-off " Staccato influence ; capable of being added to all the enumerated forms of Staccato.

3) : The " Artificial " form of Legato, induced by slight and continuous pressure of the hand and fingers, in place of the usual heavier form of the Resting.

f) : All these distinctions need not be consciously kept in

---

[1] This Resting, when applied in conjunction with a 1st Species Added-Impetus, subtly modifies the latter's tone-quality.

view, once we have mastered their application. But we must more or less remain conscious of those few *main principles* recalled in §§ *a* and *g* of this Recapitulatory.

g) : From the Artist's point of view—and the Student-*colourist's*[1]—Classification must therefore needs take the following aspect:

Div. I. : **Weight *v*. Muscular-initiative.** } Forming the distinctions of tone-*quality* : roundness *v.* hardness, or Sympathetic *v.* Aggressive.
Div. II. : **Flat *v*. Bent Finger-arm Attitude (Clinging *v*. Thrusting).**

Div. III. : **The Three Species of Added-impetus-construction** .... } Giving various options of tone-*quantity*, and Agility-powers.

Div. IV. : **Key-surface *v.* key-bed Resting** .... } Forming the distinctions between Legato and Staccato.

and lastly,

Div. V. : **Finger, Hand, and Arm-touches.** } Forming the distinctions of mere movement.

h) : The following three Tables should now be referred to.

---

[1] Without *Colouring*, Piano-playing is reduced to mere strumming.

TABLE I.
ENUMERATION-SUMMARY.

Movement.*	The Resting:		The Added-Impetus: Muscularly-started, makes for Hardness; Weight-release started, for Roundness.	The Bent or Flat Attitude:	Enumeration Totals.	
	1st form.	2d form.			Staccato.	Legato or Ten.
	Insufficient to depress keys—The Basis of STACCATO †—enables one to feel the key surface-resistance.	*Sufficient*, un-aided, to depress keys at their *softest*—The Basis of *Tenuto* and *Legato***—serves also to show us Key-resistance, and helps tone to the *pp*-extent.		The Thrusting Attitude helps to modify Quality towards *Brilliance*. The Clinging Attitude helps to modify tone towards the *Sympathetic*.		
FINGER-Touches:			*First* Species.		*Eight* Varieties.	*Ten* Varieties. ‡‡
			Second Species.			
			Third Species: *Weight*-initiated.			
			Third Species: *Muscularly*-initiated.			
HAND (Wrist) Touches:			*Second* Species.		*Six* Varieties.	*Eight* Varieties. ‡‡
			Third Species: *Weight*-initiated.			
			Third Species: *Muscularly*-initiated.			
ARM-Touches:			*Third* Species: *Weight*-initiated.		*Four* Varieties.	*Six* Varieties. ‡‡
			Third Species: *Muscularly*-initiated.			

* Rotation-touch is also occasionally required. † The Staccato can be helped in promptness by the key-bed "kick-off" or drive-off.
** An Artificial Legato is occasionally required—formed without a heavier Resting, and with a slight hand-pressure instead. ‡‡ We have two touches obtained from the Resting, *alone*: since it gives us a Ten. or Leg. pianissimo, while this can be given in either Bent or Flat attitude.

TABLE II.
CLASSIFICATION, No. I.

DURATION (STACCATO AND LEGATO) AND MOVEMENT HERE FORM THE MAIN BASIS FOR CLASSIFICATION.

DIVISION I:

WITH FIRST FORM OF 'RESTING'
(at surface level of the Key-board).
— *STACCATO*.*

Either Thrusting (Bent) or Clinging (flat) attitude :—

	Finger-staccati, 8 kinds.	Hand ("Wrist") staccati, 6 kinds.	Arm-staccati, 4 kinds.
Tone-production induced by :—	(a) Finger activity alone.—First species of touch-formation.	(a) Finger and Hand activity, *second* species.	Finger and Hand activity, and Arm-weight—*third* species: Weight-touch— (i) (Weight-release initiated). (ii) Muscular-touch— (Muscularly-initiated). Under Two alternative Sub-genera.
	(b) Finger and Hand activity— Second species of touch-formation.	(b) Finger and Hand activity, and Arm-weight — *third* species: (i) Weight-touch— (Weight-release initiated). (ii) Muscular-touch— (Muscularly-initiated) Under Two alternative Sub-genera.	
	(c) Finger and Hand activity, and Arm-weight—Third species of touch-formation: (i) Weight-touch— (Weight-release initiated). (ii) Muscular-touch— (Muscularly-initiated). Under Two alternative Subgenera		

* A "drive-off" the key-beds may exceptionally be added.

TABLE II.—Continued.
DIVISION II:
WITH SECOND FORM OF 'RESTING'
(at depressed level of Key-board).
— *TENUTO and LEGATO.**

Either Thrusting (Bent) or Clinging (flat) attitude :—

	Finger-tenuti or Legati, 10 kinds.	Hand ("Wrist") tenuti, 8 kinds.	Arm-tenuti, 6 kinds.
Tone-production induced by :—	(a) The unaided Resting : *PPP*-weight or transfer Touch *Continuous* during note, or phrase.	(a) The unaided Resting : *PPP*-tenuto Touch —*Continuous*.	(a) The unaided Resting: *PPP*-tenuto Touch —*Continuous*.
	(b) Finger activity, alone, added *during key-descent*: *first* species.	(b) Finger and Hand activity, added *during key-descent*, *second* species.	(b) Finger and Hand activity with Arm - weight added : *third* species :— Under Two Sub-genera. { (i) Weight-touch— (Weight - release initiated). (ii) Muscular-touch— (Muscularly-initiated).
	(c) Finger and Hand activity, added *during key-descent*: *second* species.	(c) Finger and Hand activity, with Arm-weight added, *third* species :— Under Two Sub-genera. { (i) Weight-touch— (Weight - release initiated). (ii) Muscular-touch— (Muscularly-initiated).	
	(d) Finger and Hand activity, with Arm-weight added *during key-descent*: *third* species :— Under Two alter-native Sub-genera. { (i) Weight-touch— (Weight - release initiated). (ii) Muscular-touch— (Muscularly-initiated).		

* The artificial (pressure) Legato-influence is occasionally appropriate.

TABLE III.
FINAL CLASSIFICATION.

Tone-quality is here the basis of Classification. It is the one that should be kept in view both by the Performer and Student-Colourist.

DIVISION I. WEIGHT-TOUCH. (Makes for Roundness of tone.)	DIVISION II. MUSCULAR-TOUCH. (Makes for Brilliancy of tone.)
Obtained *solely* under : { (a) SPECIES III, in its 1st Sub-genus—Weight-release initiated, and (b) *Second* form of the *Resting* when employed unaided.	Obtained under either : { Species I, Species II, or Species III, in its 2nd Sub-genus—Muscularly-initiated.
Both Divisions may be further modified, either towards Beauty, or towards Aggressiveness of tone, by the "Clinging" attitude and the "Thrusting" attitude, respectively.	
Both may be accompanied either by : { (a) The STACCATO Basis—The Resting at Surface-level of Key-board ;* or (b) The TENUTO and LEGATO Basis—The Resting at depressed-level of Key-board.†	
Can be exhibited under the following aspects of Movement :**	Can be exhibited under the following aspects of Movement :**

a: Finger-touch.	b: Hand (Wrist) touch.	c: Arm-touch.	a: Finger-touch. Formed either under : { 1st *Species*, 2nd *Species*, or 3rd *Species*, in its 2nd Sub-genus.	b: Hand (Wrist) touch. Formed either under : { 2nd *Species*, or 3rd *Species*, in its 2nd Sub-genus.	c: Arm-touch. Formed under : { 3rd *Species*, in its 2nd Sub-genus.

* Or with addition of "kick-off." † Or with addition or alternative of "Pressure-legato" element. ** Also as Rotation-touch.

CHAPTER XXI

RECAPITULATORY AND SUMMARY

OF THE MAIN CONCLUSIONS OF

PART III

The Link.[1]   1): During the process of learning the requisite Muscular-habits (when we must of necessity pay attention to the muscular-details) we must not permit this to divert our attention from the *instrument's* requirements; these must always be kept supremely in view, and for the sake of the required musical-effect.   That is: Muscular-action must only be thought of—and applied—for the purpose of fulfilling the requirements of the key, and these again solely for the purpose of Musical-result.

2): The key's requirements vary according to each difference in sound-shading dictated by our musical sense. Accurate and musical Technique hence demands that our muscular-efforts must vary correspondingly.

3): We can only insure this correspondence by an unswerving attention to the RESISTANCE the keys offer before and during descent. We must therefore constantly notice the "giving-way point" of the key, even in the case of our employing a considerable movement before reaching it.

4): Attention thus given through our resistance-sense, also enforces Musical-attention and intention; for we find ourselves compelled to refer to our musical-conscience, the moment we endeavour to judge what should be done to each key.

On Key-Contact.[2]   5): It follows, that *Key-contact* must never take the form of a real blow, if we desire musical-accuracy.

[1] For explanation of §§ 2 to 4, refer to Chapter XIII., page 114.
[2] Explanation of §§ 5 to 7, found in Chapter XIV., page 125.

6) : Not only should we therefore reach the key-surface quite easily and lightly; but we must also be most careful to remember, that the required tone has to be made during the ensuing short descending *movement* of the key.[1]

7) : This light fall of the limb upon, and subsequent movement with the key, may either form an unbroken descent, or we may instead bring the finger into contact with the key before the moment its depression is due. But in either case we must, before using the key, insist on feeling its resistance.

Concepts of Touch.[2]

8) : Since careful Contact is so essential, and since Tenuto and Legato further require the operation of a light resting Weight, and as we must nevertheless often apply much energy to the key in addition to this Resting to provoke the key into the necessary tone, it follows that TOUCH consists of the combination of two muscular operations, *viz.* :

a) The act of "Resting," and
b) The act of "Added-impetus."

9) : The act of "Resting" is practically continuous during each phrase, but may differ in its actual weight. This constitutes the difference in Basis between Staccato and Legato.

10) : The "Added-impetus" is applied only for and during key-descent; and it must cease to exist the very moment that tone-emission commences. This law applies both in Legato and in Staccato.

11) : For *Staccato*, the Resting must be no heavier than the key will bear at its top-most level.

For *Tenuto* and *Legato*, the Resting should never be heavier than will just suffice to retain the keys depressed.

12) : The Legato-resting, employed without any Added-impetus, is the only simple form of touch; and thus employed, it gives us an absolute *ppp* Tenuto or Legato.

---

[1] For the act of Tone-production does not really *commence* until we have actually reached the key.

[2] Explanation of §§ 8 to 15, found in Chapter XV., page 135.

SUMMARY OF PART III. 257

13): *Legato* implies a sequence of complete Tenuti, transferred from finger to finger.

14): *Duration* therefore depends on the kind of Resting, while *Sound-kind* depends on the kind of Added-impetus.

The limbs and their muscles.[1]
15): Four distinct living-levers are employed, *viz.:* the Finger, the Hand, the Fore-arm, and the Upper-arm.

16): The finger itself can be exerted in two completely different ways:

    a) The Bent, or *thrusting* attitude, and

    b) The Flat, or *clinging* attitude.[2]

17): By means of attached muscles, we can exert any of these living-levers in many directions.

18): Moreover, for every direction in which we can thus exert these levers, we can also exert them in the opposite direction, by means of opposite muscles.

19): *Stiffness* is induced, when we exert both these sets of muscles simultaneously. We must therefore carefully guard against doing this; for unless we provide every required action and movement with perfect freedom, we shall certainly spoil all our playing.

The Actions and In-actions.[3]
20): The muscular-operation against the key implies leverage on the part of the finger and hand.

This leverage re-acts upwards: (a) against the hand at the knuckle, and (b) against the arm at the wrist.

21): To form the necessary Basis, the arm may be employed in two ways: (a) it may be fully self-supported by its own muscles, or (b) its *weight* may be set free by relaxation, during each act of key-depression.[4]

---

[1] Explanation of §§ 16 to 19, found in Chapter XVI., page 147.
[2] *Vide Figs. 6 and 7, page 151.*
[3] Explanation of §§ 20 to 43 are found in Chapter XVII., page 158.
[4] For extreme *fortes*, in addition to the full use of arm-weight, we may lever the weight of the shoulder on to the key.

S

22): The sensation of exertion is always *upwards* in correct touch, since the required exertions should be mainly derived from finger-and-hand leverage—which by reaction from the keys operates upwards against knuckle and wrist.[1]

23): There are three main *muscular-components*: Finger and Hand down-exertion, and Arm-weight.

24): *Loudness* depends on the total degree of Energy thus derived.

25): *Quality* mainly depends on the locality of the initiatory muscular-component;—*i.e.*: whether we start the act of key-depression by Muscular-initiative or Weight-initiative. The first makes for sudden key-depression—sharpness of tone; whereas the second makes for that gradual attainment of key-speed associated with beauty of tone.

26): *Quality* is moreover modified in these same directions, by the contrast obtainable between the Thrusting and the Clinging finger-attitudes, and their related upper-arm conditions;—*i.e.*: by the contrast between a forward-held, or a backward-hanging Elbow.[2]

27): To obtain the extreme effects of Quality, we must *combine* both of these influences.

28): The most active portion of the finger should always be that next to the knuckle of the hand. This applies equally in Thrusting and in Clinging touch.

29): *Movement*—the distinction between Finger-touch, Hand-touch, and Arm-touch—depends upon which one of the three muscular-*components*[3] is slightly in excess of the other two, during the process of key-speeding (descent).

30): Choice of *Movement* should be mainly determined by the speed of the passage. Finger-movement (Finger-touch), however, can be employed both in quick and in slow passages.

31): Good choice of *Touch-formation*—or Species of touch—

---

[1] The reaction is upwards against the shoulder in extreme cases.
[2] *Vide Figs.* 8 *and* 9, *page* 166; *Fig.* 10, *page* 167; *and Figs.* 12 *and* 13, *page* 171.
[3] Finger-force, Hand-force, and Arm-weight.

is nevertheless far more important, since upon it depends the kind and degree of tone, and our agility-possibilities.

32) : There are three ways of forming or constructing the act of Touch from its three muscular-components. These three muscular-*combinations* are :—(a) *First Species of Touch-formation,* Finger-exertion only, with passive hand and self-supported arm; (b) *Second Species of Touch-formation,* Hand and finger exertions, combined with the self-supported arm; (c) *Third Species of Touch-formation,* Arm-weight employed in conjunction with the exertions of the finger and hand.

33) : Arm-weight, whenever it is employed,[1] must be obtained by releasing or relaxing the arm-supporting muscles. The *whole* arm from the shoulder must thus be relaxed, to the extent required by the key; and we must guard against endeavouring to obtain the required weight from the Fore-arm only.

34) : The slight but *continuous* release of Arm-weight which induces the second (or slightly heavier) form of the Resting— and which forms the basis of all natural Tenuti and Legati, is identical with the act of tone-production at its very *softest.*
To obtain this effect, we must release arm-weight upon the key, until the latter's resistance is just overcome. The consequent sinking down of the key feels more like a passive process than like an active one.

35) : Arm-weight, when applied as an "Added-impetus," must cease to operate against the key the very moment that sound is reached. This cessation must be wrought by accurately timing the hand-and-finger exertions against the key. And it is in response to the consequent disappearance of support at the Wrist that the arm-supporting muscles must be automatically called into action.

36) : Natural Legato arises, when we transfer the second form of the "Resting" from finger to finger. The result is *ppp,* unless we meanwhile add force in some form during key-depression;—*i.e.:* unless we also employ the Added-impetus in one of its numberless forms.

[1] Both in its forms of "Added-impetus" and of "Resting."

37) : Such transfer of the Resting-weight must also occur *automatically*—*i.e.* : in response to the cessation of the *last* finger's supporting action upon the key; this being timed to occur at the moment the *next* finger's key is desired to commence its descent.

38) : For the Staccato-form of the "Resting," the weight of the hand is found sufficient, and this is not ponderous enough to prevent the required rebound of the key.

39) : We must remember that the "Added-impetus" is quite as short-lived in Tenuto and Legato as it is in Staccatissimo.

40) : The fore-arm *Rotation*-element is extremely important. To it we owe our possibilities of Evenness of Touch, and also the power to render notes prominent at either side of the hand. The adjustments in question must therefore be constant, although for the most part invisible.

This adjustment, when it is allowed to become visible as an actual tilting of the hand, is termed *Rotation-touch*.

41) : Lateral freedom of the Wrist and Hand is imperative. Free horizontal movements of the hand are also required to promote evenness, when turning over the thumb and turning under the fingers.

42) : "Wrist-freedom," which is so much desired by everyone, must hence be insisted upon in all these three aspects—the vertical, rotary and horizontal. We can insure such freedom by insisting on *feeling vertical* over each key, before commencing to use it.

43) : Subsidiary points are :—freedom in the horizontal movements of the fore-arm itself, and of the fingers, and of the upper-arm, when bringing the finger-tips over their respective keys.

Muscular Testing.[1]

44) : Three Muscular Tests are essential, so that we may insure our fulfilling the required Muscular Conditions. These tests, which should be practised every day before anything else, are as follows:

45) : *Test No. I.* : —A slight up-and-down swaying of the

[1] Explanations of §§ 44 to 47, found in Chapter XVIII., page 204.

Wrist-joint, while the finger-tips remain lying on their keys; also a rolling and un-rolling of the fingers themselves, while they support a certain proportion of the weight of the hand on the keys. Designed to insure the elimination of all *contrary* exertions from those required from the finger and the hand.

46): *Test No. II.:*—A drop of the Wrist-joint, occurring in response to the accurately-timed cessation of the finger-and-hand exertion, at the moment of sound-emission; thus permitting the keys to rebound while the Wrist falls past them. Designed to secure accuracy in "aiming" the act of Tone-production. This should be practised in four ways: Staccato, *pp* and *ff;* Legato, *pp* and *ff.*

47): *Test No. III:*—The performance of a short, light run, ending in a rebound of the arm off the keys with the last note; practised (a) with the whole arm thus rebounding, and (b) with the fore-arm alone thus rebounding; and practised both with a vigorous bounding-off and with a gentle floating-off of the arm. Designed to insure the elimination of Down-arm-force from the required down-exertions of the finger and the hand.

The Three Species of Touch-formation.[1]

48): All three species can be applied as "Added-impetus" both during Legato and during Staccato.

49): *The First Species* can only be applied through finger-*movement*—"finger-touch." It enables us to provide the highest degrees of Agility, but it offers us only slight possibilities of Tone-contrast.

50): *The Second Species* can be applied both as Finger-touch and as Hand-touch—"Wrist-touch." It enables us to provide greater contrasts in tone-*quantity* than the first species, but agility-power is here more restricted.

51): *The Third Species* can be applied in all three forms of Movement; *viz.:* as Finger-touch, Hand-touch, and as Arm-touch. This species permits us to attain not only the fullest contrasts in Tone-quantity, but also those of Tone-*quality.*

[1] Explanation of §§ 48 to 52, found in Chapter XIX., page 214.

Agility is however still more limited, owing to the rapid alternations of arm-release and re-support here required.

52): We must bear in mind the particular scope (the possibilities and limitations) of these Three Species, when we (consciously or un-consciously) choose the touch-formation for each particular passage; we may otherwise fail to employ the most appropriate form.

Enumeration and Classification of Touches.[1]

53): Enumeration and Classification are possible, if we recall the main facts of Touch-construction. We thus find there are some 42 distinct kinds of key-attack, as follows:

54): *Finger-staccato, eight kinds :*—for we can employ either the 1st Species of touch-formation, or the 2nd, or the 3rd, and the latter in either of its two aspects (either as Weight-touch or as Muscular-touch), and we can employ these four either as Clinging or as Thrusting-touch.

55): *Finger-legato, ten kinds :*—for we have the same options as in Finger-Staccato, and have in addition the option of using the Resting unaided (*ppp* Ten., or Leg.) either under the Bent or Flat finger conditions.

56): *Hand (wrist) staccato, six kinds :*—in the form either of 2nd Species, or 3rd Species under its two aspects, and these again either as Clinging or Thrusting-touch.

57): *Hand (wrist) tenuto, eight kinds :*—the same options as in Hand-staccato, and in addition, the Bent and Flat finger forms of the un-aided Resting.

58): *Arm-staccato, four kinds :*—3rd Species either in its muscularly-initiated or weight-initiated form, and these taken either Bent or Flat.

59): *Arm-tenuto, six kinds :*—the same alternatives as with Arm-staccato, but with the additional ones obtained under the unaided Resting, with either thrusting or clinging key-attack.

60): From the Artist's and Colourist's point of view, Classifi-

---

[1] Explanation of §§ 53 to 60, found in Chapter XX., page 238.

cation is as follows:—*Weight*-touch and *Muscular*-touch; these under *Flat* or *Bent* attitudes; these all under any of the *Three Species* of Touch-formation; these again under the two alternatives of *Resting,* with their Staccato or Legato result; and finally all these under the aspect of *movement*—either Arm, or Hand, or Finger-touch.

APPENDIX TO PART III.

THE "FOUNDATION-TOUCH" AND MONO-METHOD FALLACIES

NOTE XI.—To § 20, Chapter XII. Seeing how great is the multiplicity of radically different Touch-methods available, and that we cannot find any really great Artist who is not compelled to avail himself of the means of constant contrast these different touch-methods afford, to enable him to communicate his Musical-feeling to us; seeing all this, we are inevitably driven to the conclusion, that without this element of "COLOURING" there can be nothing worthy the name of Pianoforte-playing, as already insisted upon in the Preface.

Moreover, as so many of these available touches are of equal importance, it also follows that it must be a gross fallacy to speak of any "foundation-touch." For who will undertake to decide between Melody-touches or Passage-touches—which is the most important? Or between those touch-methods that give us large, full tone-kinds, and those touch-methods that enable us to attain all degrees of Agility?

To suppose that there can be but one "correct" method of touch, or one "foundation-touch," to which all others are subservient, or tolerated ornamental appendages, is as foolish as to suppose that there is but one correct form of using the voice in Speech or Song; or but one colour to paint with! Indeed, it seems inconceivable how such fallacy can have arisen, in the face of the actual doings of the great Artists.

The fact is, there should be nothing in Pianoforte playing akin to the black and white element in the art of delineation. In Pianoforte playing, there is no "drawing to be learnt first, and then painting"; on the contrary, at the Pianoforte we must always be learning to "paint," and learning to paint better every day.

However, teachers and students are liable to make this mistake, if they have not realised that our powers of "Expression" almost entirely depend on *variety* in Touch-method. Otherwise, if they happen after many failures to discover some mode of producing tone, or agility, that proves effective, this success will most probably cause them to fly to the conclusion, that this discovery forms the best, or even sole possible form of correct touch!

Such, led away by the effectiveness of their discovery, often go the same lengths as do the faddists mentioned in Appendix to Part II.—"On Key-striking." Like these, they do not hesitate to close their ears and minds to all outside impressions which are contrary to the ones *they expect;* and they hence fail to perceive that the really great artist does not exhibit any one "method" of production, but that he on the contrary employs all kinds of tone-production—kaleidoscopic in the constant though subtle variety of their contrasts.

We come upon far more debatable—and difficult—ground, when the question arises, in what order should we acquire these innumerable forms of production open to us? For it is obvious we can only learn one kind of touch at a time, although we may at once grasp the general principles that underlie all Touch-acquisition.

Here again we must beware of Method-mania,—that bane of so many Educational systems; that pandering to automaticity, laziness, and lack of initiative on the part of teachers. Indeed, the less "method" there is here in the sense of a rigidly fixed "COURSE OF STUDY" the better for the student.—A fixed course of study resembles the system of having ready-made boots! Not one person in a hundred can thus be properly fitted! Rigid methods are all very well for the rough and ready education required in the drill-room of a barracks, but they should assuredly have no place in any educational system that purposes to impart anything in connection with Art.

The only good system is that which adapts the course of teaching to the individual needs of each and every particular pupil. All have eventually to learn the same things; but the order, and the ways employed, must depend almost entirely on individual needs.

Failure in Art, arises in the main from lack of Imagination and lack of DISCRIMINATION. It is therefore the acquisition of discriminatory power which we must insist upon in connection with our present subject. As regards Touch, we must for instance insist on discrimination between the proper and the improper way of making key-contact, with its intimate corollary, the idea that sound can only be made by means of Key-movement. Discrimination between the two families of Weight-touch and Muscular-touch should also at once be made clear, just as should be the two absolutely opposite attitudes of the Finger and Upper-arm. Having distinguished between these fundamental points of difference,—which involves a preliminary understanding of the three muscular-components whence we derive the act of touch, it might first be expedient to learn to act with the finger alone, with loose-lying hand, and self-supported arm—the first species of touch-formation; subsequently learning to add to this combination the action of the hand—the second species; and finally learning to employ the weight of the arm in conjunction with these two actions, during key-depression—the third species.

But even here, the bias of each pupil must be carefully studied. One's "system" should be, to seize upon the easiest "opening." Perceiving the pupil's inclination to find one point easier to grasp than another, we must if possible start our instructions from this point of vantage, and let the rest of the necessary information unfold itself from that basis—the basis proved easiest to commence with.

But more about this anon. *Vide § 28, Chapter XIX.; § 18, Chapter XX., and concluding chapter of Part IV.*

EXAGGERATED FINGER-LIFTING

NOTE XII.—For § 10, Chapter XIV. Some teachers have actually made the absurd mistake of recommending that "the fingers must be *more raised* the quicker the passage"! This fallacy has arisen from a partial apprehension of the real facts of Touch, and from the experience, that *badly aimed* Tone-production proves more obviously fatal in quick passages than it does in slower ones. For in the quicker passages, if we inaccurately direct the force we employ to produce tone, this will not only lead to inaccuracy of tone-result, but it will in this case also cause the passage to become "difficult" and "sticky";—whereas in correct Agility-touches, the keys will be free to rebound with the fingers. Hazy perception of this fact—that the key must imperatively be left free the moment each tone-making is completed (with its consequent resilient rebounding of the keys *with* the fingers), has therefore obviously misled the aforesaid faulty reasoners to imagine that *the fingers themselves should be sharply pulled away from the keys!*—For this faulty action (that of sharply pulling the fingers up *after* each successive sound) has some analogy to the correct condition, that in such touch the keys and fingers should be felt to *rebound.* It is hardly necessary to repeat, that in such pulling-up action of the fingers, we should in the first place hamper ourselves with an extra and unnecessary action, which extra exertion we should, in the second place, find almost impossible to time accurately—so that it might coincide with the necessary *cessation* of the operation of driving the key down. For we must remember, that in correct touch, all we have to do, is to aim the culmination and cessation of the key-speeding act. In a word, we must see that all our key-moving operations form a sharply defined *aim* to the sound-beginning, and not a merely indefinite un-located impulse against the key—with some added fallacies in the way of up-pulled fingers.

THE PROVINCE OF AUTOMATICITY

Note XIII.—To § 9, Chapter XV. We shall now be in a better position to perceive how the function of Automaticity can help us in Technique. In the Introductory Part it was urged, that Execution must be as "natural" (*i.e.*, as semi-automatic) as a familiar language, before it can become an implement for really artistic playing. Fluent use of a language remains impossible so long as we have to consider the pronunciation of the individual words; and the necessary combinations of muscular effort and relaxation must therefore be automatically or semi-automatically prompted. If, however, we are anxious to convey exact meanings and subtle shades of feeling, or wish to be as intelligible as possible in our utterances, then we must *choose* our word-shadings far less automatically than we do as a rule in colloquial speech. In speaking by means of the Pianoforte keys, the same thing applies. For, although we cannot play fluently until the muscular-*details* of Tone-production can be provided practically in automatic response to the mere wish for a particular tone-colour, yet the *general choice* (and even production) of a particular kind of technique must not become completely automatic, if our performance is not to degenerate into mere automaticity, in the place of really living, "felt" Music-playing. It is here that the true conceptions of Touch can greatly help us. By seeing to it, for instance, that we choose the correct kind of Resting and Added-Impetus, we gain mastery over our muscles and force them to express our musical ideas.

Before we can reach this ultimate stage of facility in execution—when the dictates of our musical feeling directly prompt muscular-action, we must first, however, be content to acquire consciously those details of muscular-attitude that cause each different kind of key-descent. These details we shall proceed to study in the following chapters.—We must first learn by Analysis, what are the constituents of muscular-attitude (or Condition) that will give us each particular tone-result; we can then, by Synthesis, teach ourselves (and others) these required muscular-operations. Having thus acquired the power to provide correct Key-treatment consciously, we must proceed, by constantly using our Ear, to form a strong bond of mental association between these correct muscular-actions (and sensations) and the related Sound-effects, until at last the mere wish for a particular Sound-kind brings automatic response from the muscles concerned. It is then that semi-conscious attention to "Resting" and "Aiming," etc., will suffice.

ON ARM-WEIGHT

NOTE XIV.—To § 3, Chapter XVII. The enormous advantage accruing from the use of the released weight of the Upper-arm and Shoulder, in place of mere brute arm-force, is so patent to anyone who has heard the infinitely superior tonal-result, that no further commendatory words are here required.

The true explanation of the benefit of Weight-use, is however by no means so simple as might be assumed. The explanation is not, for instance, that the greater the weight used, the quicker its descent. For a weight tends to gravitate towards the centre of the earth with the same speed, no matter whether it is an ounce or a ton that is in question!

The true explanation is, that presence of weight behind the finger and hand, enables these to act more effectively against the key than without this Basis. For instance, if we use the supported arm—supported elastically by its muscles, the only resistance which the finger and hand then have behind them, is the mere Inertia of the arm, and the moment this is overcome, the arm will commence to give way upwards. Or we shall have even a weaker Basis, if, we "hold" the arm rigidly. We may, on the contrary, release the arm at the moment that the finger and hand commence to act against the key, and we shall then have the full benefit of that weight as a basis. And we have learnt that we can promote the operation of this Basis either (a) by allowing the arm-lapse to occur *in response* to the finger-and-hand's recoil experienced at the wrist, or (b) by allowing the arm-lapse itself to initiate the tone, in which case, the finger-and-hand activity must occur in response to such lapse; and since this latter combination will (owing to its elasticity) come to bear upon the key in growing measure during its descent, we shall thus have the fullest benefit that can be derived from weight and muscular-action. Meanwhile the fact remains, that the greater the weight we thus have at our disposal to release against the key, the fuller and larger can be the tone. This once again seems to re-enforce the hypothesis, that we do not really lose control over the hammer until the moment that String-deflection is complete; and that it is therefore a fallacy to suppose that the hopper does (in actual tone-production) escape *before* the hammer actually reaches the string.[1] For although it is true that a weight (excepting for friction) falls with the same speed, be it an ounce or a ton, yet the IMPACT produced respectively by an ounce and a ton, differs vastly!

As regards the actual weight of the arm, only half of it is available as free weight at the finger tip, since half the weight is necessarily supported at the shoulder, unless the shoulder itself is also released at the moment of key descent, when the whole weight of the arm may become available. Experiments that were made on a number of male and female subjects, showed the effective average weight of the arm to vary between 3 and 5 lbs., in the case of males, while the female arm proved lighter on an average. In the case of males, an average difference was also observed of about four ounces in favour of the right arm over the left arm. While in one case, that of an exceptionally muscular woman, the effective weight reached 7 lbs. For the valuable experiments made in this connection in the dissecting room, and on subjects under chloroform, I should like to express my indebtedness to Dr. David Hepburn, and Dr. Charles Kennedy, of Edinburgh.

[1] *Vide Appendix, Part II., Note IX., page 39.*

BENT VERSUS FLAT FINGER-ATTITUDE

NOTE XV.—To § 13, Chapter XVII. A few additional words on this subject seem desirable. We have found that the "flat-finger"—with its *tendency* to fold or curl-up, demands a corresponding release of the Upper-arm ; the consequence being, that the Elbow hangs on to the finger, while this in turn *clings* to the key, during the latter's descent. The "bent" finger—with its *tendency* to un-curl or "thrust" outwards, on the contrary, demands that the Upper-arm does not thus hang-on to finger and key, but that it is here more or less supported by its own muscles. The Elbow or Upper-arm, therefore here tends (although but slightly) to *thrust* forwards upon the key. Or we may say, that it is the upper-arm's Condition that in both cases causes the difference in finger Action and Position.

These forward and backward forces, will moreover in both kinds of touch-method be *felt* at the Wrist as a conflict between KNUCKLE and ELBOW, for the two forces should almost entirely balance at the Wrist-joint ; *i.e.*, the direction of the sum-total of force at the Wrist-joint should there be quite *vertical*, as it should also be at the key itself, excepting that slightest of slight tendencies either to thrust or to cling, already alluded to.

The Clinging-touch attitude becomes clearer, if we take care to realise, that the Upper-arm, on its being released, would cause the Elbow and Finger together to *slide* away from the key-board, were it not for the action of the clinging-finger, which, in thus clinging, supports the arm-weight at the Wrist-joint through the hand—from underneath.

This point can be illustrated by taking an open book, and holding it by its outside edge, while the opposite edge rests on the key-board, thus :

The back of the book is consequently not to be directly supported, and it will serve to represent the Elbow. Now, the moment we cease fully to support the book, it will tend to drop, to slide off the keys, and to fold-up (or close) in so doing. The similar tendency of the upper-arm, thus to slip-away from the key-board, may indeed be defined as the immediate *cause* of the fingers evincing their clinging attitude during "sympathetic" touch.

We may be better able to realise these contrasts in muscular-condition, if we call to mind some analogies to be found in other already familiar actions ;—analogies, which, although they form good working ones, owing to their suggestiveness, must not be considered as being exact, physiologically. Thus we find, that the *bent* finger attitude, or thrusting-touch, is somewhat analogous to the action of the LEG, when used in the act of rising from a chair ; or in stepping upstairs, or in depressing the cycle-pedal. From a more or less contracted position, the leg here somewhat *unfolds* in the act of propulsion. The movement of the knuckle-phalanx of the finger here corresponds to that of the thigh. The same attitude of the finger is employed in bringing it upon the violin string. In fact the peculiar action here required, has given a nickname to the muscle most concerned in fulfilling it ; and it is interesting to note, that the tendon from this "fiddler's-muscle" is connected with the under-side of the Knuckle-phalanx, and then passes to the *upper* portion of the front two phalanges ; the muscle itself (one to each finger) lying entirely in the hand. This muscle thus helps to cause the descent of the Knuckle-phalanx, while it at the same time assists the front two phalanges in what is really a *rising* action—relatively to the descending knuckle-phalanx; and the nail-phalanx is thus able to remain erect in spite of the descent or ascent of the rest of the finger.

The *flat*-finger action, or clinging touch, is on the other hand analogous to the action of the ARM, when, extended before us, we employ it to assist us in rising from a chair,—by exerting it downwards upon some object in front of us, such as a table. The manner in which we can help ourselves upstairs by our arms on the bannisters, is another kindred case. So, in some measure, is the action of our legs in walking; for we then employ our leg-muscles differently to what we do in cycling, or when mounting stairs. Hence the sense of relief experienced when we pass from one to the other mode of leg-exertion. And we experience a similar sense of freshness at the Pianoforte, when, after having practised "brilliant" passages, we pass to singing passages, or vice versa;—this, owing to the change involved from "bent" to "flat" finger action.

We can also experimentally suggest this contrast in finger-action, if, when seated upon a chair, we first extend our legs fully in front of us, and try to rise by their help in this "flatter" and elastic condition—although, of course, we cannot really raise ourselves in this case; and then contrast this "flat-attitude," by placing our feet almost under our chair, and rising in this case in the usual manner,—the un-bending of the leg in this instance admirably serving to suggest (although with some exaggeration) the action of the finger against the key, in the "bent" or thrusting- attitude.

IN-CORRECT VERSUS CORRECT FINGER-TECHNIQUE

The Contrast between the Non individualised and the Individualised Finger.

NOTE XVI.—To §§ 4 and 18, Chapter XVII. The distinction here in question, is the one between (a) "stickiness" of finger, with its un-rhythmical passages, and (b) fluency and ease of finger, with its clean-cut, rhythmically definite passages—with every note perfectly "placed" and evenly sounded.

The point that should be enforced, is, that the fault can usually be traced to the employment of defective *muscular-conditions*, which in their turn render it impossible for the sufferer wilfully to direct his fingers in quick passages, either as regards Time or Tone.

The muscular fault in such cases is the one so often here alluded to and condemned,—the use of continuous Arm-*pressure* behind the fingers. It is, we must remember, the most natural fault to make:—We wish to make the key before us move down,—what more natural, than that we should try to induce this by using the muscles of the back, with down-pressure of the arm? If we wished to press down anything in the ordinary course of our existence, we should certainly act thus, and rightly so. At the Piano the temptation to act likewise is commensurately great, and it *must at any cost* be resisted. This tendency must indeed be absolutely eliminated, if we wish to succeed in playing passages with ease, and wish to avoid liability to a sudden and complete collapse of our Technique, when the moment of stress arrives. How often do we find an otherwise admirable performer, suddenly lose all cleanness and fluency of finger! An unduly felted or over-toned hammer is perhaps presented for his use, and being thus prevented from *hearing* what a considerable degree of force he is already applying to the keys, he endeavours to apply more,—and he will then be tempted to transgress the laws of finger-technique, and will permit himself to apply that fatal thing, Arm-pressure, unless the laws of Agility have been fixed into secure habit of mind and body. If these laws are ignored, the passages go from bad to worse, until they become almost obliterated under the more and more laboured progress that ensues upon the key-*beds*, and the performer leaves the instrument with perspiration streaming from him, and feeling as if he had suffered under the incubus of a nightmare.[1]

The fault of all faults to be guarded against is therefore : a continuous PRESSURE exerted downwards upon the fingers by the arm ; a condition of affairs that renders the hand as helpless as if it were a *hoof*, with five prongs attached, instead of fingers. If such pressure is *continuous, and at all severe*, it absolutely stops all movement across the key-board. To help one to avoid this fault, one should commit it deliberately, doing so in a scale or arpeggio; so that its sensation of stickiness may be vividly experienced, and so that its unfailing result, the complete breakdown of all technique may be as vividly remembered.

Less obvious than this *continuous* arm-pressure, is the occasionally attempted correction of it. Many a musician, with even mediocre reasoning power, will soon learn to avoid the *continuous* effort behind the fingers just condemned, since he finds himself thereby deprived of all Agility. But this will not prevent his using the same muscular-combination (*i.e.*, direct down-arm force behind his fingers) when he wishes to play *forte* finger-passages, provided he now carefully *ceases such force* the moment that tone is reached with each key. And many a player's technique never advances beyond this stage, since it enables him to " get along " somehow, and even at considerable speed. Naturally enough, he will fail to recognise his inefficiency technically, unless his ears are sufficiently quick to detect, that other (and better) players are able to play similar passages with greater ease, and with far *more beautiful tone ;*—or unless he some day, by lucky accident, happens to discover the correct technique,—and is able to recognise it as such at the moment.

No, the arm must neither be continuously pressed down upon the fingers, nor may it be " jabbed " down on them for each individual note. There must be none of this, in any shape whatsoever !

The only forms of technique that will permit of the attainment of real Agility, are those two forms in both of which the arm is almost or entirely supported off the keys by its own muscles—the *first* and the *second* Species of Touch-formation ; and, either in conjunction with these, or unaided, the Weight-transfer touch—or second form of the act of Resting.— *Vide Chapter XIX.*

In this connection it behoves us to remember, that the Wrist-joint must ever remain absolutely free and flexible ;—in proper touch there should never be sufficient down-pressure upon it, to prevent its being so. In the *first* two species of technique (where the finger and hand alone act against the key, while the arm remains self-supported) the Wrist-joint is indeed in a condition so elastic, that it is *almost* on the point of being driven off the keys by the rapidly recurring, short-lived actions of the finger and hand against the keys—whence we see the reason for insisting on the constant practice of the *third* of the " Muscular-tests " described in Chapter XVIII. The wrist should consequently feel as if it were *floating in space*, in spite of the perhaps quite vigorous finger-and-hand exertions against the individual keys,—exertions, which must of course be so fleeting, and must be so carefully timed in all Agility-touches as

---

[1] Perspiration does not however arise only from violent and un-necessary muscular-work at the key-board. It is often indeed copiously induced, by the highly-strung, nervous state of an excitable performer.

to vanish before they induce the slightest impeding action against the key-beds.

We can in fact often suggest the correct muscular-attitude here required, by simply insisting upon the Wrist-joint remaining absolutely free,—*free almost to the rebounding point*, as just described, owing to the upward-recoil kicks received by it at each sound-consumption. It is also well to remember, that all action must here seem to *end* either at the Knuckle, or at the Wrist-end of the hand,[1]—such action being there felt as an up-driving one, from the keys upwards against the knuckle and wrist,—and such action being individualised for each sound, and as short-lived as the shortest Staccatissimo always proves the act of tone-production to be in its nature.

CERTAIN EXCEPTIONAL FORMS OF STACCATO AND LEGATO, AND THE SLIGHTLY HEAVIER RESTING THUS TRANSMISSIBLE

NOTE XVII.—For Note to § 28, Chapter XVII, page 186. Slightly more Weight than has been described under the two forms of the Resting, can under certain exceptional conditions be continuously applied in finger-passages, both Staccato and Legato. That is, the fingers can carry such slightly-increased load without harm, provided the speed of the passage is considerable, and yet does not exceed a certain limit ; and provided moreover, that the individual fingers are used with sufficient vigour in forming the short-lived "Added-impetuses" against the keys ;—for the exceptionally vigorous momentary action of the fingers, will in this case *prevent* such additional weight from actually *reaching the key-beds*. The process is analogous to the action of the legs in running : for in this case our body is kept floating off the ground by the rapid succession of jump-like acts delivered against it by the legs—a fact that can easily be demonstrated by Snap-shot camera.

In such exceptional touches, we can therefore employ a slightly increased weight (or slight hand-pressure, as the case may be) borne by the successive fingers, and as it were *kept floating* (away from the key-beds) by the aforesaid sharp, individually-aimed (and ceased) exertions of the fingers. The weight (or pressure) must however never be greater than the fingers can thus keep in a "floating" condition, by the rapid succession of their momentary "kicks" or impacts against the key-beds.[2] Provided the Weight thus carried does not exceed a soon discovered limit, we thus obtain a running form of the "kick-off" Staccato, already described ; this is suitable for certain bright, brisk, but *forte* Staccato-passages.

By a slightly different adjustment of the continuous weight *versus* the briskly stepping finger, this kind of technique can be transformed into a softer but *legato* form, or even into a Legatissimo, such as we often meet with in BEETHOVEN.

The extra weight thus continuously carried, might preferably in this case be provided by a *slight, continuous activity of the Hand and Fingers*, rather than by any extra arm-release. For the slight continuous *pressure*,

---

[1] I have, in this connection often found it very suggestive, actually to touch the ends of the tendons that chiefly serve to draw the hand down against the keys. The "insertions" of these tendons into the hand at its wrist-end, usually form two easily-found slight protuberances at the base of the hand, at its little-finger and thumb side, respectively.

[2] *Vide Note XVI. ; especially the last two paragraphs.*

thus produced by the hand and fingers, levers arm-weight continuously on to the keys at will, and the weight is thus more directly and momentarily modifiable, and more elastic, than would be the case did we relax the arm sufficiently to obtain the full amount of weight necessary to induce the effect of *Super-legato*, for instance. This gentle, added Hand-pressure is therefore particularly suitable to induce the over-lapping of the sounds required in the super-legato inflections of Legato. We here have the "artificial" legato, already several times referred to. To distinguish this from the natural, or Weight-legato, it might be termed a "*pressure*-legato." [1]

No passage should however be attempted in this form of technique unless the speed is ample to admit of such "pressure" being kept in the floating state described, otherwise stickiness is bound to ensue. The cumbrousness of it, also precludes the employment of this form of technique beyond a soon-reached limit of velocity. Now it so happens, that many of the rapid *cantabile* passages of BEETHOVEN do unmistakably demand just this very treatment. It follows, that here we also find the limit of Speed defined for us, beyond which such passages cannot be performed, if we would fulfil the composer's obvious intentions as to Tone. The first part of the Rondo from the "Waldstein" is a case in point. How lamentably often is it attempted at a Tempo, not only faster than Musical-sense commands, but faster than it is physically possible to execute the rapid *cantabile* semiquavers, with the *obviously required thick tone!* Instead of employing (as should be done) the *second* Species of muscular-combination [2] either in its normal (Weight) legato form, or in the artificial (Pressure) legato form here considered, we often hear these beautiful melody-passages SKIMMED through with *first* Touch-species, with its thin passionless tone;—so that the performer may forsooth have the opportunity of making his audience gape at his supposed wonderful Achievement in racing across the keys "at incredible speed!"

Knowledge of the Components of the various touch-kinds, and the respective Speed and Tone possibilities of the three species of formation, will therefore often assist us in determining even the Tempo of a piece.

BEETHOVEN, for instance, rarely, if ever, employs the *first* Species,—indeed, he probably never discovered that trick of modern extreme Agility-passage touch! He mostly requires *second* Species, and often the *third*, with its fullest of full tones, but comparatively low Speed-power. [3]

Besides the possibility of thus producing Legatissimo inflections by slight Hand-pressures, we may also in similar manner produce such inflections by slight pressures, sufficiently continued, but derived *from the fingers* alone. Such un-aided finger-*pressures*, are the ones most suitable for the legatissimo inflections of *light* running passages.

[1] *Vide Preamble to this Part, Note 4, page 112.*
[2] *Vide Chapter XIX., Note to § 7 and § 12.*
[3] *Vide § 6, Chapter XVII., and Chapter XIX.*
Vide, also the *Note*, No. VII of "*Supplement*" on "Artificial" Legato.

PART IV.

On Position.

CHAPTER XXII.

PREAMBLE:

Synopsis of the Main Aspects of Position.

§ 1. Correct Position of limb and body, in nearly all its details, will arise as a necessary consequence, if we adopt the correct muscular Actions and Inactions required in playing.

Readers who have even slightly grasped the truths treated of in the preceding chapters, hardly require to have it pointed out, how deplorable has been the mistake committed by nearly all teachers until recently, in attaching such vastly exaggerated importance to the subject of "Position," as to cause them to place implicit reliance on what has proved a veritable quicksand. Many indeed going so far as to make it into an absolute fetish.[1]

Now although it must be granted, that we cannot play correctly (that is *at our easiest*) unless the chosen positions are also correct—unless they are the most convenient ones, yet it does not in the least follow, that the adoption of "correct" Position, at rest, and during the necessary movements, will in the least ensure our employing those particular muscular-attitudes (or conditions of Activity and In-activity) which alone enable us to fulfil the requirements of the Key for each particular variety of tone.[2]

---

[1] *Vide Appendix to this Part, Note XVIII.*:—"The fallacy of 'Position' worship."
[2] *Vide, for instance*: § 13 of *Chap. XVI.*, page 152.

Bad Position and incorrect Movement no doubt form valuable *warnings*, since they form visible signs that totally inefficient muscular conditions are being employed, or that the desirable ones are being employed not at their easiest. Correct position, on the other hand, unfortunately does not form any guarantee whatsoever that the very fundamentals of Technique are correct,—since it forms no reliable indication either that the muscular-conditions are correct, or that the mechanical-requirements of the key are being fulfilled.

It is necessary to insist on this point, since a degree of importance has been generally attached to Position that is absurdly out of all proportion to its real significance. The fallacy has been, to perceive in Position the CAUSE of good technique; whereas we must now recognise it in its true aspect—and let it arise, mostly, as a RESULT of the correct muscular and mechanical conditions being fulfilled at their easiest.[1]

§ 2. The subject of Position includes the normal positions of the body and limbs when seated before the key-board, with the hands at rest upon the keys, and it also includes the positions that have to be assumed during the execution of the various movements that accompany the individual acts of tone-production, and that precede such. As the subject thus naturally divides into two sections, it will be best to consider its details also in a measure separately.

§ 3. Since our rule must be, to adopt the positions and movements that enable us most easily to fulfil the required muscular-conditions, it also follows that not only are slight

---

[1] Often indeed do we find the unwary hoping to attain good Technique by watching and imitating the *visible* effects exhibited by great players, while they are not in the least discouraged by finding no amelioration of their Technique as a result of such mimicry. Such seem to fancy that Playing depends on the look of it, and not on the sound of it!

This does not signify that we should under-estimate the advantage of hearing a good performance. On the contrary, it may prove invaluable, if we will but use our ears chiefly, instead of our eyes. Musically, it may help to fire our enthusiasm, and technically it may also help us greatly; the example of beauty of tone, of variety in all its subtlest gradations, the evident *ease* with which all is accomplished, may, if we are earnest seekers for musical-success, cause us to experiment until we find ourselves also capable of obtaining similarly beautiful effects from our instrument.

variations of position from the mean allowable, but that they are often an absolute necessity. For there are no two players whose bodily conformation is absolutely identical, whereas the Pianoforte remains an "unchanging quantity" as regards the size of the keys it presents to the player.
Every detail as to the actual or relative size of the finger, hand, fore-arm, and especially of the upper-arm, and of the body itself from the hips upwards, must therefore influence our ultimate choice of easy posture. While there must thus be slight divergences in Position in some directions, there are others however, in which there can hardly be any variation without seriously militating against the mechanical efficiency of the concerned limbs.

§ 4. Here we consequently come to some really important facts relative to Position. But even here, we shall not choose wrongly if we plainly bear in mind those necessities of muscular-action and inaction we have learnt to recognise during the preceding chapters. These points of greatest importance are *three* in number, for unless these are attended to, we shall find it impossible to provide certain of these much desired muscular-conditions at their easiest.

§ 5. First and foremost amongst these, is the one relating to position of the shoulder relatively to the keys, a position depending upon the relative length of the fore-arm and upper-arm. The law being, that the shoulder *must* be sufficiently removed from the keys to enable the arm to be unbent almost into an obtuse angle, so that we can conveniently reach all portions of the key-board, and more important still, so that we can when required, allow the weight of the upper-arm to take effect upon the keys by mere lapse in its support;—an operation that becomes impossible if we sit too close to the key-board.

§ 6. The next point is, when we employ "bent-finger" touch—brilliant or thrusting touch, and are playing the finger for this purpose from a distance, that the finger's position when raised, can then indicate whether or not we shall *be able* to employ the requisite muscular-conditions for this kind of touch. For we shall find ourselves unable to provide these, unless the finger does in a measure unbend towards and with the key in its descent, and unless consequently the finger is started in a position the more curved the greater its preliminary elevation.[1]

For the clinging, or flat-finger touch, we must likewise note that the finger must here be the "flatter" the more we raise it as a preliminary to the act of tone-production.[2]

§ 7. The third point is, that the hand must be so placed in its lateral direction relatively to the keys, as to avoid all unnecessary lateral movements so far as possible, while executing with perfect ease those that are necessary for the convenient passage of the thumb, etc., and for the negotiation of extensions. We here find that the hand and fingers remain in a straight line with the keys during "five-finger" positions; that they remain pointing inwards during scales; that in double-notes passages they point in the direction in which the passage is travelling; and that in arpeggi and in other spread-out passages, while the normal position of the hand is the inward-pointing one (or "wrist outwards"), additional horizontal movements are required of it to bring the fingers properly over their notes.

§ 8. Subsidiary details will receive further treatment in the following chapters; but it may meanwhile be pointed out, that the wrist-level should neither be exaggeratedly low or high, but about level with the fore-arm, an over high position being likely to cause forward-driving from the shoulder. The knuckle of the hand must also be held well away from the keys, and about level with the wrist and fore-arm, or very slightly higher, so as to give plenty of opportunity for the fingers to bear upwards there,—a position which of course is totally at variance with the "knuckle-in" fallacy. Our seat at the instrument should also be always in the centre, sufficiently distant from the instrument, and of such height as to allow the lower part of the fore-arm to be on a level with the keys; since

---

[1] *Vide Fig. 6, page 151.*
[2] *Vide Fig. 7, page 151.*

a lower position will render brilliancy more difficult, although it rather tends to further clinging touches.

§ 9. The finding of correct notes, has so far been regarded as one of the aspects of Position. The previous chapters have nevertheless demonstrated to us that this ground is also covered, by simply insisting on the proper fulfilment of the act of Resting—in either of its two forms; for not only does the act of Resting induce certainty as to Tone (*i.e.*, certainty as to "Expression") but it also furthers certainty in reaching the correct keys.

If we properly fulfil the act of Resting, we can—and must—reach each successive key through muscular-sensation; it follows that we must reach each successive key as a progression laterally *from each preceding key*. We hence realise and execute each sequence of notes, as *a succession of distances* accurately judged from each preceding key; and we thus find, that the act of Resting, conscientiously fulfilled, engenders certainty in Notes, as well as certainty in Tone-kind and degree.

§ 10. Understanding then thoroughly, that correct position is no guarantee whatever that the essential muscular-conditions are being satisfactorily promoted, and that the subject of Position is only important in so far, that inaccuracy in this respect does render it more difficult to provide these correct conditions, the fact nevertheless remains that the study of Position is indeed important, although not so important as has been popularly supposed, and certainly not one of those "short cuts" to the top of Mount Parnassus, so beloved of the amateur reasoner.

CHAPTER XXIII.

THE DETAILS OF POSITION.

MOST of the details of Position have already been fully dealt with in Part III., under the aspect of muscular action and inaction. In addition, it has been pointed out in the last chapter, that there are certain of these details of Position that require careful watching. For the sake of completeness, however, it is now desirable to go over the whole ground from its positional aspect. In doing this, we must not forget, that correct Position should be but the natural result of the fulfilment of the exact muscular-conditions required by correct Key-treatment, and that we must beware of falling into the error of regarding Position, itself, as the cause of correct touch.

Finger-position, vertical aspect.
§ 1. Two distinct positions of the finger, vertically, are available, corresponding to the difference between the Thrusting and Clinging attitudes. This distinction between the comparatively "*bent*" and comparatively "*flat*" finger, should arise directly from the finger's duties relatively to the upper-arm;—the position assumed should occur as the natural consequence of the Elbow *tending* either to lie forwards, or to hang backwards, thus causing the finger either to thrust or to cling.[1] But it is important to pay close attention to the accompanying divergences of position; since incorrect position, here, may actually prevent our using our fingers correctly, muscularly,—although it does not follow that correct action will supervene owing to correct position.

§ 2. These differences in position are not so noticeable, when the finger is depressed, as when it is *raised*. Indeed, the curvature assumed may be almost identical, *when the finger*

---

[1] See Chapter XVI., § 11, etc., page 150 ; Figs. 6 and 7, page 151 ; Chapter XVII., § 12. etc., page 164; Figs. 8 and 9, page 166 ; Fig. 10, page 167; Fig. 11, page 170; and Figs. 12 and 13, page 171.

THE DETAILS OF POSITION. 279

is depressed, unless it is a question of obtaining the more extreme effects of either "brilliant" or "sympathetic" tone-qualities. Whereas, if we require either of these tone-characters very definitely, then the fingers must assume their full distinction in curvature, even with fully depressed key. These distinctions nevertheless always display themselves in a marked manner when the finger is *raised*, especially if it is well-raised; and it is here therefore that we can best study and watch finger-position. And it is moreover in the case of the nail-phalanx and its neighbour, that the distinction in posture is particularly noticeable.

§ 3. IN THRUSTING-ATTITUDE ("bent-finger"), the higher the preliminary raising, the more does the finger tend to bend upon itself. Conversely, it unbends (or tends to open-out) as it falls upon the key, and moves down with the latter. The nail-phalanx is here employed in an *almost vertical position*, which it retains both during the ascent and descent of the finger. Unless we do thus start with a well-bent finger, it will be difficult to attain a really brilliant finger-touch.[1]

IN CLINGING-ATTITUDE ("flat-finger"), on the contrary, the finger straightens out in proportion to its preliminary raising; while it either remains straight during descent, or tends to close upon itself.[2]

---

[1] If we start with a flat finger, we shall, in bringing the finger against the key, either curve it inwards, and thus cause the clinging effect; or, if we try to avoid that, we shall probably jerk the elbow forwards with each finger—a most reprehensible action. Hence, the importance of seeing to it, that Bent-finger touch *starts* bent.

[2] Let us consider these distinctions somewhat further:—The Elbow, when it tends forward, requires the *thrusting* finger to support it upon the key. The finger's duty (during key-descent) is here akin to that of a "flying buttress" (*Vide a, Fig. 14*); the stresses it undergoes and its position approximating to that contrivance. The meeting-point of buttress and wall here corresponds to the meeting-point of the finger and hand at the Knuckle; and the finger naturally assumes its convex position because the force exerted by it is upwards and backwards against the knuckle,—by re-action from the key. The backward-tending Elbow, on the contrary, demands a lax-left

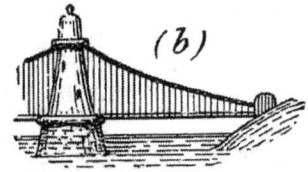

FIG. 14.

280　ON POSITION.

§ 4. We notice that the difference between the two finger attitudes is most shown when the finger is considerably raised off the keys, and we can thus detect certain faults by the eye; such as that of commencing with the *opened-out* finger when "thrusting" or bent-finger touch is nevertheless intended; or the opposite fault, that of "nipping" with the finger, when a round tone is intended.

The very MOVEMENT itself of the finger, in falling towards the key, can moreover in some measure indicate when certain faults of *action* are committed; the finger, for instance, that sins in really hitting its key, goes down like a flash, whereas the finger that is used with intention—"that means to use its key," can usually be actually *seen* to begin its descent

upper-arm, with its corresponding *clinging* action of the finger, to draw weight upon the key—during descent. In this case the finger's duty and condition may be compared to that of the suspension-bridge cable (*Vide b, Fig. 14*). The point where the cable reaches the tower is here supposed to represent the Knuckle of the hand. And although the analogy does not hold good in so far that the cable does *not* support the tower, and also that the finger never really assumes so concave a position as the cable, yet the *tendency* is towards such

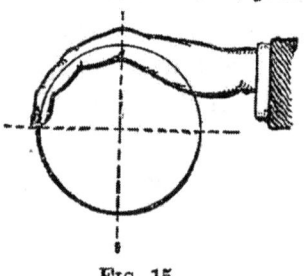

Fig. 15.

concave position,—a comparatively flat (or even completely flat) position the finger is compelled to assume because the stresses of the middle of the finger are here not dissimilar to those we can imagine the cable to undergo.

Comparing the forms of arch exhibited by the finger in these two contrasting capacities, we also find that the arch is far more acute in the case of thrusting touch than in the clinging form. For thrusting-touch, the finger is indeed so greatly rounded, that it forms approximately a *quarter of a complete circle*, from knuckle to tip (*Vide Fig. 15*); while for clinging-touch, on the contrary, the finger forms merely a *small* portion of an immensely larger circle, and the arch being so much weaker, this increases the finger's elasticity.

The arch-form is indeed quite lost sight of, when we require tone really of the fullest sympathetic character. The front two phalanges are in this case left so limp, that the finger completely loses its curve, and may indeed almost turn "inside out," without harm.

In this connection it is interesting to note that CHOPIN evidently often employed the "fully sympathetic touch," for we find eye-witnesses remarking with astonishment, that "he seemed at times to play with his fingers perfectly flat." The singing-touch shape of the fingers is also very clearly expressed in a cast of Chopin's hand in the possession of Mr. E. W. Hennell,—a cast, which I think must have been taken with the hand on the key-board, its position is so natural for the kind of touch most required in the Master's music. (*Vide Note 2, to § 20, of Chap. XIX., page 225.*)

towards the key *quietly*—persuasively, however well-raised it may be to start with, and however loud and quick the passage may be.

§ 5. In flat-finger touch, the fleshy part of the finger (the part opposite to the nail) is brought into contact with the key,[1] whereas in bent-finger touch, contact is made by the very tip close to the nail—the nail itself however not being permitted to touch the key.

Owing to the clinging nature of the flat finger's action, the tendency is also, to draw the flesh towards (and even round) the nail; whereas the thrusting action of the bent finger not only precludes this tendency, but would encourage the opposite tendency (to draw the flesh away from the nail), were it not, that an absolutely vertical application should be insisted upon. (*Refer again to Fig. 6, page 151.*)

§ 6. In bent-finger touch, the fingers should all be nearly equally rounded. In the case of the fifth finger being abnormally short, it may however be used in a very slightly straighter position. It should nevertheless not be used straighter (in this kind of touch) than is necessary to enable us conveniently to reach the key-board with it and the thumb simultaneously.[2]

§ 7. Ample preliminary movement of the finger is healthy, provided it is not excessive, and does not lead to "hitting," and provided there is time for it. Provided also, that such ample raising—or "playing from a distance"—is undertaken solely for the purpose of attaining *freedom* during the subsequent stepping-upon the key, or key-attack. We must be particularly on our guard, lest we fall into the common error of

---

[1] Hence has arisen the absurd fallacy, that the more sympathetic result of "flat-finger" is owing to this "more sensitive" part of the finger touching the key!

[2] The moment the finger is much straightened out, it tends to become more elastic, although we may meanwhile try to insist on its thrusting *action*. A really short fifth finger is hence found to be a considerable disadvantage for brilliant touch, although this is often not discovered by its owner, owing to his avoidance of this finger *during the course* of brilliant-touch passages. And when used at the ends of such passages, the disadvantage is not strikingly obvious, owing to the advantage the finger may then receive in the form of rotation-touch. (*Vide* § *12; Also Note XIX., Appendix to this Part:* "*The straight fifth-finger.*")

allowing such raising, itself, to be looked upon as the object to be attained, instead of its being regarded merely as the accompaniment of free action.[1]

The Thumb. § 8. The difference in attitude (action) exhibited by the thumb corresponds to those of the other fingers, although the visible differences in movement are small.

Thus the thumb tends to unbend in descending towards the key in thrusting touch, and it tends to contract in clinging touch. And although there is a very marked difference muscularly, the resulting difference in movement is (and should be) so slight as almost to baffle the eye.

The thumb should usually form a sufficient angle upwards towards the hand at the wrist, to give it ample freedom of movement, even when it has occasionally to be used under the hand.[2] The thumb should therefore never be allowed to be held contracted against the hand—held tight against the base

---

[1] We must always bear in mind, that if key-attack is to be certain in its musical results, it must commence without much actual *hitting* of the key-surfaces, and that all tone-producing stresses should occur in more or less unconscious response to the resistance experienced from the keys themselves.

Excessive raising of the fingers actually impedes their action. Nothing can be more pernicious than pulling the fingers up until they "kink."

The nail-phalanx should moreover never be permitted actually *to point upwards*—even in the "flattest" touches. This phalanx may reach an almost level (or horizontal) position, when the "flat" finger is raised to its fullest extent,— *Vide Fig. 7, page 151*,—but beyond such level it cannot be raised without vitiating the subsequent act of tone-production. And we see moreover, that this nail-phalanx must remain upright in "bent"-finger touches, both when it is raised and depressed,—the tip of the finger, close to the nail, here continuously pointing towards the key— *Vide Fig. 6, page 151*.

As already animadverted upon, (pages 131, 132) one cannot too strongly deprecate that particular little "corner" in fetish-worship, the "high-raised finger." So far from its being productive of good results, we find it is generally associated with the fallacy, that the *fingers* should act as hammers against the keys—the fact that it is the strings we have to play by means of the keys being quite lost sight of !

"Nearness breeds contempt," is by many people reversed into "Far-ness breeds veneration" (to alter the old adage slightly), and as the doings of the departed are therefore apt to be of greater authority than those of the living, it may be well here to point out, that as regards the finger-action of that greatest of Pianoforte-wizards, FRANZ LISZT, it often seemed (as observed by myself and others) " *as if his fingers hardly moved at all*," his marvellously soft, rapid passages appearing merely to glide along, absolutely without effort,—so " *close to the key-surfaces* " was his technique at such times.

[2] *Vide Fig. 6, page 151.*

THE DETAILS OF POSITION.

of the index finger, as in accompanying Fig. 16. It is a fault that is frequently to be met with, and it cannot be combated too early. More on this point appears under the horizontal aspect of the fingers. *(Vide § 12 of this chapter, and illustration of correct thumb-position, § 13, page 290.)*

§ 9. The movement of the thumb arises near the wrist-end of the hand, whereas the movement of the finger arises at the

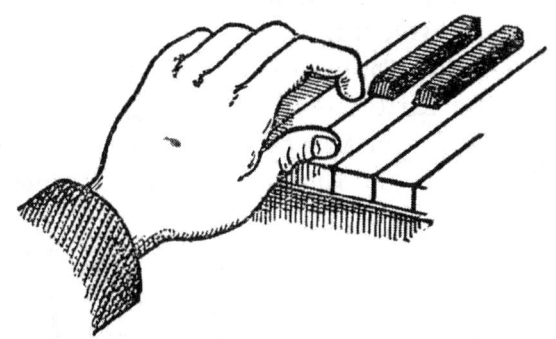

FIG. 16.—Faulty position of the thumb.

knuckle of the hand. That the thumb's movement thus dates further back than that of the fingers, and that its pivot, as it were, is some inches behind that of the knuckle, is a fact often not realised, and this leads to a constrained action of the thumb; the learner trying to bend it vertically in the middle, which of course is impossible.

Finger-position in Hand ("Wrist") touch. § 10. In Hand-touch, the fingers required to touch the keys, should assume their fully depressed condition relatively to the hand, *before* commencing the downward movement of the hand. In rapid passages of this nature, the new finger (or fingers) should take up their position while the hand (and previously used fingers) are ascending from the last played notes;—*i.e.*, the next required fingers should be as it were, "left behind" as the hand rises, so that no movement is required of the fingers during the subsequent descent of the hand.[1]

[1] This trick of allowing the new fingers to assume their depressed position relatively to the hand, during the latter's *ascent*, can be easily acquired, by

284   ON POSITION.

In passages of single notes (or of double-notes, when the extension is small) it is possible to *combine* finger and hand down-movement against the keys; but in passages of extension, such as octaves, this is most un-desirable, as it seems to hamper the free movement of the hand. During the continuance of such passages, the thumb and little finger should remain depressed relatively to the hand once they have been placed in position. The same rules apply to touch accompanied by Arm-movement.

Finger-staccato. §11. Since there are two kinds of Finger-arm Attitude—the Clinging and the Thrusting, it follows that there must be two corresponding kinds of Staccato available.   In the case of Finger-staccato, this dif-

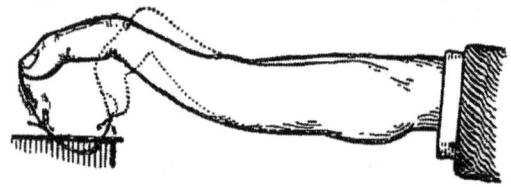

Fig. 17; showing movement of the finger in *flat-finger* (or clinging-touch) *Staccato*.

ference in muscular-action manifests itself in a slight difference in the *return*-movement of the finger—a slight difference in the way the finger rises off the keys. . . . This return movement is continuous with the descent, for the ascent should commence *as a rebound* at the instant that tone is reached.

The consequence is: that in finger-staccato with Thrusting-attitude, the finger bounces back in the *same line* as in its descent,—or it may even tend to drive slightly outwards.

Whereas, in the case of the Clinging-attitude, a slight inward pull of the front two phalanges accompanies the rebound of the finger; and the finger thus assumes a more rounded position as it rises, than before its descent. (*Vide Fig. 17*.[1])

practising the following Exercise :—Execute a free throw-up of the hand (as in the "Third Daily Test"—Page 209) and allow the whole of the fingers simultaneously to recede (or fold) into the hand. I say "allow the fingers to fold," advisedly, for it is of no use doubling them up with effort. There must be absolute freedom in their folding thus during the hand's ascent, and they must seem really to "remain behind,"—so leisurely must be the action.

[1] It is a curious fact, that while certain Piano "methods" have insisted upon the exclusive use of the *bent* finger for all *Legato* passages, they have

THE DETAILS OF POSITION. 285

The explanation of the process is as follows: As all three phalanges are equally exerted in Clinging-touch—or the knuckle phalanx *more* than the others, it follows, when we suddenly cease the finger-exertion, that it is more natural to *begin this cessation* (and consequent recoil) *with the knuckle phalanx;* and the front two phalanges consequently still *slightly continue* their contraction while the key drives the finger up, and prompts its knuckle phalanx into an upward action. The result is, that the finger is more bent at the end of such movement, than at starting; the front phalanges giving a slight fillip inwards somewhat analogous to the similar action of the horse's foreleg.   As all unnecessary movement is always to be deprecated, the inward swing of the fore-part of the finger should never be great—and it is even slightly exaggerated in Fig. 17.

Finger position, horizontal aspect.

§ 12. Looking down upon them from above, the position of the fingers relatively to the keys varies with the kind of passage to be performed:

a) : During *Five-finger position:* When the passage is of the five-finger order, with the five fingers (or fewer) falling on adjacent notes, diatonic or chromatic, *i.e.*, when the notes lie so conveniently under the hand that they can be evenly executed without the intervention of any lateral (horizontal) movement of the hand, then the normal position is: that the *middle-finger* remains in a straight line with its key, and this, no matter where the hand is located on the key-board.

The places where the fingers should reach the keys are in this case such, that with the five-finger position on five adjacent *white* keys, the middle finger reaches its white key close to the *front edge of the black keys*.[1] The other fingers fall upon

also exclusively insisted upon the *flat* finger for Finger-staccato ! It never occurring to the sufferers, that "bent" and "flat" are equally applicable to both Legato and Staccato !

[1] The middle finger should play thus close to the edge of the black keys, because this will permit our reaching the black keys without having to shift our hand and arm forwards and backwards, which clumsy movement would otherwise be necessary. The fingers should therefore normally be sufficiently bent in thrusting-touch, to admit of their reaching the black keys without greatly losing their "bent" characteristics. In clinging-touch, the fingers can

their keys slightly nearer the edge of the key-board, each according to its length—the actual places thus varying with each individual hand. Employing a normal hand *in the bent attitude* — for thrusting touch, it will be found that the *index* finger will be nearly one finger-thickness behind the middle finger, if we look at the fingers sideways; the ring-finger will be half-way between these two points on the key-board; the *little*-finger will come one finger-thickness again behind the index-finger, while the *thumb* will fall into line one finger-thickness behind the little-finger.[1] Thus, taking the dotted lines drawn across the keys in Fig.

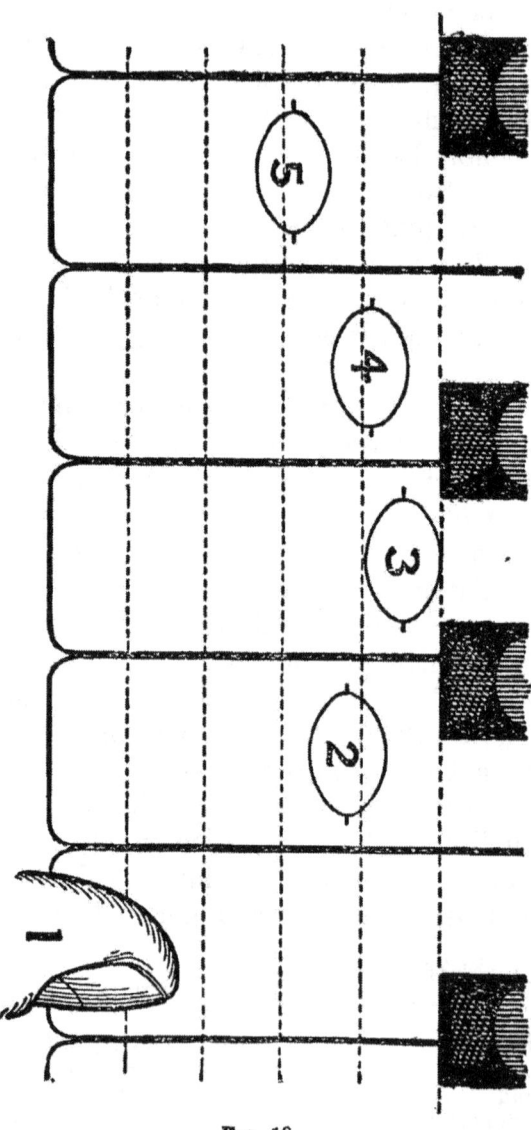

Fig. 18.

always easily reach the black keys with no risk of altering the touch-character. It is for this reason that tonalities with many black keys lie so easily under the fingers for this kind of touch.

[1] The extent to which the thumb should reach on to its white key—its distance from the edge of the key—depends (a) on the length of the thumb, and (b), on the comparative height of the Knuckle and Wrist. The shorter the thumb, the nearer the edge does it naturally fall; while it is brought more on the key the more we *raise* the knuckle and *lower* the wrist.

THE DETAILS OF POSITION.

18 to represent the thickness of the finger-tips, we should approximately obtain the relative results there depicted, taken from a rather large hand,—the result *roughly forming a semi-circle*.[1]

The fingers also naturally fall into this shape, if they are placed round a ball of the exact size that will cause their tips to reach a level line ;—an experiment that also indicates the proper curve of the thumb.[2]

Employing such a normal hand, but in the *flat* attitude in place of the "bent," the middle-finger remains close to the edge of the black keys, as just described, but the other fingers must fall either slightly nearer the edge of the white keys, or further away from it, than in the example given. The particular conformation of the fingers determines the exact place. This, it must be understood, is always the case, since this point will not admit of any hard and fast rules being laid down ; and the example (Fig. 18) is given purely as an illustration of what happens in this particular case, a normally large male hand.

[1] That the fingers should reach the keys all in a straight line, is a fallacy, as already alluded to in § 7, and in Note XIX. of the Appendix to this Part—"The straight finger," which see. It has arisen from the false idea, that unless the fingers reach the keys at the same distance from their edge, thus giving the same leverage, that this will cause un-evenness of touch.—A very pretty theory, and quite correct so far as the leverage-power over the keys is concerned; but it fails to take into account that none of the fingers are *naturally* equally powerful ; and that to make up for this deficiency, so far from placing the little finger and thumb in a line with the other fingers, it would (according to this argument) be better to place them *nearer* the *edges* of the keys. And it altogether loses sight of the fact, that the fingers do individually and instantly adapt themselves to *the constant change of key-leverage* presented to them during performance, if the performer has learnt to be guided by his sense of Key-resistance,—as he should be. Unless we did thus constantly adapt ourselves to the key-board, how for instance could we execute any passage with evenness that lies across and between the black keys ? On the contrary, we find that the fingers instantly adjust themselves to the changed leverage, provided we do employ our muscular-sense and our ear with proper alertness. The practice of all the scales and arpeggi with the *C* major fingering,—which forms such excellent training, and has been termed "levelling the key-board," may be cited as a useful object lesson to those faddists who would endeavour to obtain Evenness by placing all the fingers in a row, no matter how long or short they happen to be !

[2] Such natural position at the key-board is, however, only possible with a normally large hand. An abnormally small or large hand must therefore diverge slightly from this most natural position, since the key-board itself remains unchangeable.

The position given in the figure, is moreover bodily transferred forward, when we require the five-finger position *with the thumb on the black keys.* The line formed by the edge of the black keys must in such case be regarded as the limit of the key-board, and those fingers requiring white keys must reach them as well as they can *in between* the black keys. Moreover, if the fingers are too thick-tipped conveniently to do this, then the hand must be slightly turned either outwards or inwards (as described under *b* and *e*) to enable them to do so.

b): When the passage, on the contrary, demands a lateral displacement of the hand, such as is required to allow the thumb to "pass under,"—as in the single-note scale and arpeggio, then the fingers no longer remain in line with the keys, but are instead placed at an angle with them, the thumb being more or less extended, and the Hand being turned slightly inwards,—or the Wrist outwards,—as already explicitly explained in Chapter XVII., § 34; and further alluded to in § 23 of this chapter.[1] But whichever way we turn the fingers (or the wrist, or hand), the middle finger should remain close to the edge of the black keys, so long as the passage does not require the help of the thumb on a *black* key.

c): *Scale-position:* During the single-note scale, this outwardly turned Wrist (or inward-pointing hand) becomes the normal position for the time, since we should otherwise have to make unnecessary to-and-fro movements of the hand twice during each octave.

d): *Arpeggio-position:* During the single-note arpeggio, not only must the normal position be the same as in the single-

---

[1] In thus turning the hand or wrist outwards or inwards, it should always seem as if the initiative came from the FINGER ;—*i.e.*, it should seem as if the fingers *drew* the hand from side to side, or turned the wrist outwards or inwards; and it is probable that a slight sideway activity of the fingers does really help to encompass such movement of the hand, or wrist itself. Unless the fingers thus *prompt* the movement, we are apt to have a mental putting of the cart before the horse. And not only this, but we are likely to employ the arm-moving muscles for the purpose, which we should certainly not do; for the movement should arise entirely from the side-to-side activity of the HAND-muscles—perhaps supplemented by those of the fingers themselves, as just suggested. *Vide, also, Note to* § *23, as to the turning under of the thumb, etc.*, and also § 24.

note scale (with inward-turned hand and fingers), but the extensions involved in turning under or over, here demand in addition a sufficiently ample horizontal *movement* of the hand or wrist; this *movement* being however provided to an extent no greater than is really necessary to enable the fingers and thumb to reach their notes easily.[1]

e): *Double-notes scales:* For double-notes scales in thirds, the fingers and hands have to be turned in the opposite direction— the hand outwards, or the wrist inwards—when the passage moves from the centre towards the extreme ends of the keyboard. This is to allow of our passing a longer finger over a shorter finger in making the connections between the successive fingering-positions. The reverse rule applies when the passage moves back towards the centre of the key-board, and we can formulate all this, by saying: "In double-notes passages, *the hand must be turned in the direction in which the passage is travelling.*"

f): *Other double-notes passages:* The last mentioned rules apply to all double-notes passages, equally,—including those constructed on the double-note (or quadruple) arpeggio; these latter, however, demand slight lateral movements in addition. In this connection it should be noted, that when we turn the fingers over the thumb, or a long finger over a short one, in double-notes passages, that we cannot then retain both notes depressed their full value. In these cases, it is the thumb or the little finger, *alone*, that for the moment continues the act of "Resting." Again, when we use the thumb twice in succession in such double-notes passages, since we cannot continue the Resting by means of the thumb during its repetition, it follows that the Resting must here be carried from key to key by the *other* fingers, so as to enable the thumb to rise and take its second key. These things should be carefully attended to by learner and teacher; for the formation of habits is easy, whereas the eradication of them is difficult.

[1] Such ample lateral movements of the hand and wrist, enable us to avoid any unnecessary, excessive "turning under" of the thumb, and the consequent helplessness of that member.

U

ON POSITION.

The curve of the thumb.

§ 13. The thumb, looking down upon it from above, should moreover always be more or less curved convexly, unless used *under* the hand, or upon two adjacent keys.[1] That is, *its nail-phalanx must always remain in a straight line with the key it is employed upon*, as shown in the accompanying Fig. 19; and not twisted, as for instance in Fig. 16, on page 283. The exceptions are: when the thumb is required to sound two adjacent white or black keys. The last-mentioned rule is then reversed, and the thumb is then extended almost straight from the hand, or it may even be concavely curved—curved outwards. The thumb must also be held straight, or even concavely, when it has to reach under the other fingers.

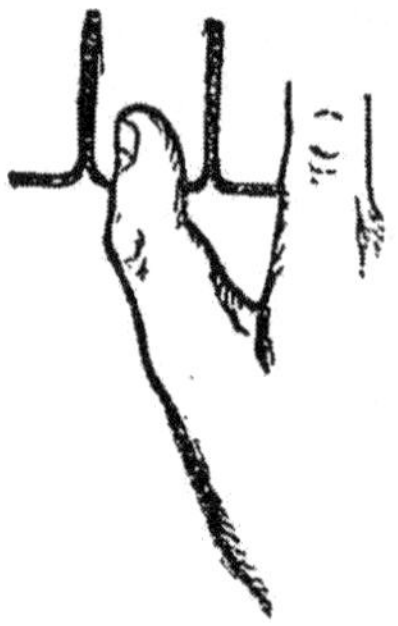

FIG. 19.—Correct position of the thumb.

§ 14. Finally, it need hardly be pointed out, that each finger should reach the very centre of its key. Unless we constantly endeavour to make the finger do this, we risk sounding two keys in place of the one intended, thus "splitting" our notes, or smudging them.

On note-finding.

§ 15. The fingers should find their keys *before* any attempt is made to depress either finger or key. It is quite wrong to reduce into a *single* action, the act of finding the keys, and the act of depressing them. The two actions may form a *continuous* movement, but they must be separate, mentally. The position of each key, should, moreover whenever possible, *be derived from the note or notes last played*. Close attention to this rule, forms an infallible cure for "wrong note playing."[2]

---

[1] One should especially be careful to train the thumb to prepare its note in turning-under while the preceding fingers are still engaged in sounding their notes. (*Vide to* § *24.*)

[2] Whenever practicable, we should not quit the key last used *until the next key is found;* and we can still retain our hold of the previously used key, although we may have allowed it to *rise*.

THE DETAILS OF POSITION. 291

Both these last rules become automatically fulfilled, if we insist on the *Act of Resting*, as set forth in Part III.

On sound-finding. § 16. Position INSIDE the keys, however, is an even more important matter, than the finding of the right notes.—Our ears must for this purpose be constantly on the alert, so that we may accurately observe *where* in its descent the key's speed must culminate, and our tone-making efforts cease. All accuracy in Expression depends on this.[1]

Position of the Hand and Knuckles. § 17. It is important that the Hand should be held *level*. That is: the knuckle of the fifth finger should be at least as well raised off the keys as the knuckle of the index-finger. It is better even to err on the side of giving the fifth finger the advantage in this respect. There is no difficulty in encompassing this, if we adopt the outwardly-turned Wrist as the normal position.[2]

§ 18. We now come to the much debated question as to the *height* of the knuckles off the keys. After study of Parts II. and III. of this work, there can be no difficulty about this question, for it is obvious that the height of the hand at its knuckle-end should arise solely as the direct result of correct action on the part of the fingers that support it there. If the finger activity is the correct one, and of requisite degree, then the correct position of the knuckle must of necessity ensue; and it is well to remember that it is of no use insisting on correct position here, unless it is provoked by the correct *condition* of balance between Finger-force and the other two components of Touch-structure.

---

[1] If we "play too late"—in key-descent, as so often already insisted upon, not only does this constitute loss of Energy, and loss of accuracy in Expression, but we are also then liable to overdrive the mechanism of the instrument, creating real hardness of tone, and even risking damage to the hammers and strings.

[2] Not only is the fifth finger placed at a great disadvantage, mechanically, unless we keep that side of the hand well up, but the *reach* of the thumb is also materially impaired. Also, if we allow the hand to slope towards the fifth finger, we shall find that the fingers will have to be used against the keys *at an angle*, instead of vertically as they should be; and the thumb will also be unable to reach its key with the *side* of its tip—close to the nail, as it should.

ON POSITION.

Relatively *to the wrist* the Knuckle may either be level or somewhat higher. (*Vide Figs. 6 and 7, page 151, also Figs. 8 and 9, page 166.*)

The actual height off the keys, and height *relatively to the fingers*, varies (a) with the form of touch employed, (b) with the size and conformation of each individual hand, and (c) with the height of seat habitual to the player. It is therefore quite a mistake to imagine that uniformity of position should here be a law. On the contrary, it is likely to lead to uniformity and restriction of touch "method"—to one-sidedness and want of colour in performance.

Thrusting-touch is nevertheless *usually* found more easy of attainment with the knuckle kept somewhat higher relatively to the finger than it is in Clinging touch,—but the reverse may even here be found more convenient with some hands. As the keys are an "unchangeable quantity," a large hand also usually finds a higher knuckle more suitable in all touches than does a small hand, this being particularly noticeable in thrusting-touch.[1] There is however one point that can be definitely laid down as a law, and this is: that the knuckle must never be *lower* than any part of the finger WHEN THE LATTER HAS DEPRESSED ITS KEY. The knuckle should therefore be kept well raised off the key-board *by the fingers*. It should be kept so well raised as to allow absolutely free passage and movement to the thumb, when turning under. Although the knuckle may thus under certain circumstances be level with the knuckle-phalanx, yet, as a rule, it is found best that it should form (more or less slightly) the *highest* point of the finger, when this is depressed. *Figs. 6 and 7, and Figs. 8 and 9 should here again be referred to.*[2]

[1] The knuckle-phalanx (from knuckle to first joint) will in these cases slightly slope *downwards*—when the finger is depressed on a *white* key.
When the same finger is on the contrary depressed with a *black* key, there may be hardly any such sloping noticeable. And with certain hands this knuckle-phalanx is normally thus held *level;* although the slightly higher knuckle does undoubtedly form the stronger position for thrusting-touch.

[2] The doctrine, that the knuckle should be "held in"—that the hand should be crushed down on the fingers and keys, cannot be too strongly condemned. It has done so much harm that it must again be referred to. Natural Law is no respecter of persons, however halo-crowned (and deservedly so) they may

THE DETAILS OF POSITION.

As already pointed out, the actual height off the keys varies with the form of touch employed.

The only exception, perhaps, to the rule of the well kept-up knuckles, is in the case of clinging-touch of the most sympathetic order, such as in that ultra-elastic touch-form so often required for the CHOPIN *melos*. In this case the fingers are left so "flabby," that the weight of the arm may then perhaps cause the knuckle slightly to fall in.

§ 19. All beginners, though they be young children, should at once be shown the necessity of thus keeping the knuckle (especially that of the fifth finger) well raised off the keyboard surface, and of keeping it either at least as high as any part of the depressed finger, or even as the highest point, slightly, of the hand itself. There is no difficulty in this, if we at once point out how the knuckle can easily be *kept up*

have been as artists. And as this "depressed-knuckle" fallacy has been so widely promulgated and adhered to, this renders emphatic contradiction all the more necessary. As a direct preventive of all ease in playing, nothing more effectual could possibly have been devised. To endeavour to play with the knuckle "in"—close to the keys, is quite as ridiculously uncomfortable, un-natural, and above all things, as mechanically *wrong*, as it would be to try to walk or run, while "sitting upon one's haunches!" Those who endeavour to play under such false conditions, may rest assured that they succeed to the extent they do, *in spite* of being grossly handicapped.

As already pointed out, Note 2 to § 18, and elsewhere, this misconception must have arisen through noticing that the knuckle *is lower* than the middle joint of the finger, when this is greatly raised as a preliminary to the act of tone-production. And as a well-raised finger is likely to lead to *free use of it*, one would be liable falsely to ascribe the good effect caused by such freedom to the position of the knuckle; and looking down upon the latter from above, one would also be liable to overlook the fact that the knuckle was not really any lower than usual *respectively to the keys*, but that the highly raised fingers created the delusion.

While on this point, a similar fallacy with regard to the WRIST-JOINT may also here be alluded to: This also arises from a similarly superficial observation of the real facts of "Wrist-touch" or Hand-touch:—In this case, if we raise the hand well as a preliminary to the act of touch, we shall find, that the knuckles are for the moment *higher* than the wrist-level. It follows, if we notice this, looking down from above, that we may fall into the error of imagining that "all octave-playing requires a lowered wrist"—a doctrine often promulgated by the adherents of "Methods" opposite to the one of the "Knuckle-in" dogma! Here again, obviously it is the preliminarily highly-raised knuckle that has created the delusion. As a matter of fact, as already noticed, most players find a wrist raised slightly *higher* than usual, the position most comfortable for rapid octave passages—especially if these are played in *thrusting* attitude, as they mostly should be.

from beneath—owing to the re-action of the finger-tip against the key, provided we insist on a proper balance being maintained respectively between the finger-exertion used and the hand-exertion and arm-weight behind it, and provided moreover that we do not employ mere brute down-arm-force instead.[1]

Hand-movement, vertical. § 20. HAND-touch (Wrist-touch) demands an actual vertical movement of the hand itself; the movement dating from the wrist-joint, and being visible as a movement of the knuckles, bodily.

This movement need be no greater than the actual depth of the key,—about ⅜-inch. The movement should indeed not exceed this actual necessity, when fullest speeds are required in Hand-touch. The hand should in this case rise only sufficiently with the key to permit of the finger-tips being *slid* on to the next keys, preparatory to their depression.

At slower tempi, it not only becomes possible, but even convenient and advantageous, to allow the hand to rise considerably—say an inch or so, provided such recoil of the hand is *in response* to the key's recoil. The knuckle may in this instance rise considerably beyond the level of the Wrist-joint in preparing for the act of touch. Excessive raising of the hand in hand-touch, however, is strongly to be deprecated. It is as futile and mischievous as an excessive raising of the

---

[1] Great care should especially be taken with children in this respect, since they are particularly liable to contract this vicious habit—that of forcing the knuckle in, by means of force derived from the down-exertion of the arm and body itself. To apply the full force of our bodies downwards, is the most natural error to fall into, when we first have the key-board presented to us, for it is the most natural way of applying force in ordinary life, when we *wish to force something away from us*. Children are especially liable to this fault, because their fingers are necessarily comparatively weak—although not so weak for Pianoforte purposes as generally supposed. We must therefore constantly (a) warn them against using arm or body-force, (b) remind them of the see-saw nature of the Key-lever, and the impossibility of producing any tone-effect once the hammer has rebounded off the strings, and (c) that the act of the finger in "bent" touch is *upwards* against the knuckle—" like sharply getting up from a chair by one's legs;" and (d) that Clinging-touch is an act of weighing the keys into sound. These things are quite easily understood, and gladly carried out by the little ones—who care for Music, and it is far more easy to teach them correct habits than their seniors, who, instead of "the clean slate," have theirs scribbled over with bad writing!

finger.[1] The hand should never be lifted to its fullest limit, any more than should be the finger, if perfect ease and certainty are desired. We must never forget, that all movements required at the instrument must be provided solely for the sake of *ease* in *using the key*, and certainly not for the sake of making our attitudes "look like Piano-playing."[2] (*Vide the strictures on this subject under Note 2 to § 18, and elsewhere.*)

Position of the Wrist vertically.
§ 21. The position of the wrist-joint relatively to the knuckle and relatively to the forearm and elbow varies with the size and general conformation of the player's hand and arm, and with the habitual height of chair. The actual height of the wrist does not materially influence either tone or ease. Inexorable rules are therefore undesirable here, and they would be even more out of place than in the case of the related position of the knuckle, discussed in § 18. It is well, however, to bear the following suggestions in mind:—

a) **Relatively to the Key-board**: the height of the wrist should arise naturally as the consequence of a proper balance between the three components of touch—the balance between finger-and-hand exertion and arm weight. The wrist should be

[1] It is difficult to find a phrase sufficiently condemnatory of the puerile idea, that "Wrist-action" consists in "throwing the hand *up* from the keys."

[2] As just stated, the Hand, preparatory to the act of touch, may be considerably raised off the keys—provided the passage is not too fast. In the early stages of learning, it assists the acquisition of Freedom thus to allow the hand to rise sufficiently. We can thus more easily learn to realise that it is essential to commence the act of Hand-touch by a complete release and consequent *fall* of the hand; and we can also (with such preliminary-raising) more easily perceive whether the hand-movement is unrestrained or not. But once we have arrived beyond the Instruction-book stage, we should learn to obtain this freedom *without much preliminary raising*. For the closer we keep to the key-surfaces in rapid octaves, etc., the greater will become our facility—rapidity and reliability. If we take care accurately to *cease* the employed exertions (and weight if used) the very instant each tone is completed, we shall find, that the recoil of the keys easily raises the loose-left-lying hand to the surface; and no greater "raising" than that is imperative.

To attempt to play rapid octaves—or slow octaves for that matter—with a flail-like purpose-*empty* flapping of the hand, forms one of those senseless Pianoforte-superstitions bred in the last century, but happily now exploded:—for we find that the greatest artists do not at all flap the Piano, but on the contrary, allow their rapid octaves to approximate very closely to a *glissando*,—a glissando executed *at the surface of the key-board*, with just sufficient Added-impetus for each octave given "in the nick of time."

high enough to give free play to the thumb. In rapid passages, especially, it is therefore desirable to keep it supported sufficiently high, to enable the thumb to reach its key with a slight downward slope. In slower passages, this does not so much matter.

b) **Relatively to the knuckle and fore-arm**: the height is greatly determined by the height of chair used. Sitting very low, causes the Wrist to be much higher than the fore-arm; while sitting excessively high, will cause it to be depressed below the arm and hand levels. Manifestly it is better to sit too low than too high.

On the whole, the wrist and knuckle are best placed about *on a level;* but one can play quite well with the wrist somewhat higher or somewhat lower than this, provided neither position be too exaggerated. With a large hand it is however usually found more convenient to allow the wrist to drop slightly below the level of the knuckles, for the long fingers of a large hand are else apt to set the thumb too far back near the edge of the keys.

c) In hand-touch—"wrist-touch": The movement of a limb is easiest when it is moved about the middle of its compass. Hence we should infer that the wrist would be in the most suitable position for octave playing and all other hand-touch passages, when placed about level with fore-arm and knuckle; and this, indeed, we find not only holds good in theory, but in practice also.[1] The argument is thus re-enforced, that the normal position of the wrist should be about level with the knuckle. Nevertheless, the precise position must be determined in the case of Hand-movement (as in Finger-touch) by the size of the hand, height of chair, and kind of touch used.

[1] We must be careful not to place the wrist too high, as this is likely to lead to the hand and digits being "jabbed" down on the keys by arm-force, in place of the proper down-activity of the hand during the moment of key-depression,—an activity, which by reaction bears *upwards* against the wrist.

Also, at other times, we must not allow the wrist to drop too low, since in this case we shall not be able to pass the thumb under, without changing the level of the wrist every time such passage is required.

THE DETAILS OF POSITION.

While the actual height of the wrist is thus quite a variable quantity, yet it is one of the points around which argument has most fiercely raged, and dogma has been most emphatic! (*Vide Note XX., Appendix to this Part:* "*The high wrist and low wrist dogmas.*")

Moreover, as in all cases of already fixed habit, if one is used to an exaggerated position either way, it will certainly be found awkward at first to attempt to play under the opposite position, or even a position midway between the two; so much so, that one is likely to allow sensation rather than reason to be the guide, and one will thus be tempted to pronounce emphatically in favour of——the already acquired habit!

Wrist-adjustment, with thumb on alternate black and white keys. § 22. The height of the wrist relatively to the fore-arm and knuckle, must slightly vary during rapid octave and chord passages in which *white* keys alternate in close succession with *black* keys. The same necessity arises when rapid *finger-passages* require the thumb on black and white keys in close alternation, as sometimes occurs.

In all such passages, the wrist-level should be *slightly higher for the white keys* than for the black keys. This slight kinking as it were, of the wrist upwards and downwards, permits us to reach white keys and black keys with equal facility. Thus we obviate any backward and forward movement of the Elbow (and upper-arm), which clumsy movement would otherwise have to be employed, to bring our fingers over their respective keys.[1]

Hand and Wrist movement, horizontal. § 23. The lateral movements of the hand and wrist, which enable us to place the fingers in position, respectively for five-finger, scale, arpeggio and double-note purposes, have already been

[1] Such change of wrist-level from note to note, should however be exceedingly slight; it should in fact be no greater than the difference in height between black and white keys. Moreover, during octave passages lying on alternate black and white keys, we should be careful to keep both thumb and little-finger (when on the white keys) close to the front ends (or edges) of the black keys; thus reducing the necessity for fore-and-aft movements as much as possible.

discussed in § 12. We there learnt that: (a) for five-finger positions, the wrist has to be so adjusted as to allow the middle-finger to be in a straight line with its key, no matter on what part of the key-board; (b) for the single-note scale, the wrist is slightly turned outwards—to ease the passage-under of the thumb;[1] (c) for the single-note arpeggio the same normal position applies, but the passage and extension of the thumb must be helped by slight lateral movements of the wrist; while (d) for double-notes passages, the wrist must normally be turned inwards when the passage is travelling in the direction of the fifth finger—to enable the longer fingers to be passed over the fifth finger and ring-finger.

In addition to these facts, we should now note, that for passages of short compass, we must allow the FORE-ARM to move with the hand, as we change from one fingering-position to another during the course of such passage; and that the WHOLE ARM must move in similar manner, when the passage is more extended,—is extended beyond the compass of two octaves or so. In this connection the following are good working rules:—

> a): For short velocity-passages which rapidly return upon themselves, within the compass of the octave, the Hand alone need move laterally—horizontally.
> b): For somewhat more extended passages of the same nature, the Wrist (and with it, the fore-arm) should move in addition.
> c): For similar passages, beyond the compass of two octaves, the Elbow itself (and with it the Upper-arm)

[1] It may seem incredible, but the suggestion has actually been made, that Scale and Arpeggio playing should be reduced to a sort of "Hop and skip" process, to avoid "the difficulty" of turning the thumb under, and the fingers over! This sounds more like one of MR. BERNHARD SHAW'S jokes than a serious suggestion, and is manifestly so absurdly puerile as to need no discussion. Such fallacy can only arise from an astounding ignorance of the requirements of the Pianoforte Repertory. There is no "difficulty" whatever in the turning under and over processes, if we but recognise the elementary necessity of horizontal Wrist-freedom. True, there are a few modern passages which depend on cleverly disguised skips, executed by Fore-arm movement; but such devices are subterfuges, and by their exception only prove the rule.

THE DETAILS OF POSITION. 299

must move in addition to the lateral Fore-arm-movement.

d): Finally, for slow passages, or such as move up the key-board or down, while not at once returning upon themselves, *both* Elbow and Fore-arm (the whole arm) must assist the transition from one fingering-position to the next.

§ 24. Thus, for instance, in learning or teaching the SCALE, we should insist on great care being bestowed on the character of the lateral movement that assists in connecting the successive fingering-positions. For example :—travelling up the scale of C, with the right hand, the thumb should be moving towards its note (F) while the index and middle fingers respectively play D and E. We must however not fall into the error of moving *the hand outwards* when the thumb reaches its F; on the contrary, the whole arm should already have been travelling slightly in the direction of the scale (with wrist turned slightly outwards), and while the thumb is engaged with its F, the arm should be allowed to travel still further in the same direction, sufficiently so to allow the index-finger to be brought ready over the G previously to its depression,—the thumb meanwhile assuming an extended (and inwardly curved) position,[1] owing to its being as it were "left behind" on the key-board. Similar procedure obtains during the next fingering-position and turning of the thumb under the ring-finger, and subsequent preparation of the index-finger over the octave d. The index-finger being thus always placed in position, *not* by a turning of the hand, but by the wrist itself being bodily carried up the key-board. In this way, we are enabled to adhere to the "outwardly-turned" wrist, as the normal position for the scale.

The ARPEGGIO is treated in like manner to the scale; slight movements of the hand and wrist, however, must here assist us :—

Taking the arpeggio of C for example: we start with the normally outwardly-held wrist, and the whole arm here follows the

[1] The inwardly turned thumb is shown in Fig. 19, page 290.

fingers, while the arpeggio begins to travel up the key-board in the right hand. But the wrist must be slightly turned still more outwards when the middle finger engages G, to enable the thumb easily to reach its c; and then, while the thumb is thus engaged on c (and is "left behind," as in the scale) the *Hand itself* must move slightly *outwards*, to enable the index-finger to reach its e;—this outward movement of the hand being only just sufficient to bring the wrist-position *back to the normal*. The arpeggio, in ascending, is thus accompanied by a gradual movement of the whole arm in the same direction, while wrist and hand ALTERNATELY also move *in the same direction*, relatively to the fore-arm and wrist respectively. The reverse movements of course accompany the return arpeggio.

Wrist-rotation.
§ 25. A rocking movement is sometimes required of the Hand and Wrist. This is really a rotary one of the Fore-arm with the Elbow as its apparent axis, and constitutes the "touch by side-stroke" of the Germans. Such "Rotation-touch" is suitable for passages in which we have to alternate notes lying under the opposite sides of the hand. Like Hand-touch, it is only available up to a certain speed, beyond which it must be supplanted by finger-movement. During an act of key-depression accompanied by this tilting or rocking movement of the hand, wrist and fore-arm, the fingers should remain unmoved relatively to the hand, as in the case of octave-playing;—the fingers should assume their depressed condition previously to such tilting.[1]

[1] We must recall, that such alternations of rotary activity and inactivity of the fore-arm, are also more or less required in *all* other touches, although the movement is that of the arm, hand, or finger, and although the adjustments are then invisible—not then taking the form of rotary movement. Without such constant readjustments rotarily, evenness must remain unattainable.

These matters have been fully dealt with in Chapter XVII., which should be referred to. The following additional positional hint is however noteworthy:

The Elbow, itself, should be placed a little more OUTWARDS than usual, when we require Rotation-touch at the more extreme ends of the key-board in the form of a free rotary movement TOWARDS THE THUMB. The same hint applies, when no actual tilting is required towards the thumb, but merely FREEDOM towards that side of the hand, when engaged near the key-board extremities.

THE DETAILS OF POSITION.

Position of the Fore-arm.
§ 26. The fore-arm position depends on the height of the wrist. As we have learnt that the wrist-height is determined by the height of the chair, and that of the knuckle, etc., it follows that also here we cannot lay down any definite and invariable rules, unless it be to warn against exaggeration and mannerism. With the wrist high, the fore-arm will slope somewhat downwards towards the elbow, while it may even slope *upwards* if the wrist is very low. The most natural position seems, as usual, to be midway between these extremes; and the fore-arm (from elbow to wrist) will then assume about a level position, or one, perhaps, that is somewhat higher than the key-level at the wrist, while somewhat lower than the key-level at the Elbow.

Position of the Upper-arm and Elbow.
§ 27. Coming now to the position of the Upper-arm and Elbow, we find that this is really a vital matter in playing. We must therefore recognise as the most important law of Position, that the SHOULDER SHOULD BE SUFFICIENTLY DISTANT FROM THE KEY-BOARD, to allow the Upper-arm to subtend an *obtuse* angle with the fore-arm—or nearly that. (*Vide Fig. 20.*) It is even desirable to err rather on the side of opening the arm out too much—to make it too straight, than to risk its approximating to a right angle, as in Fig. 21.

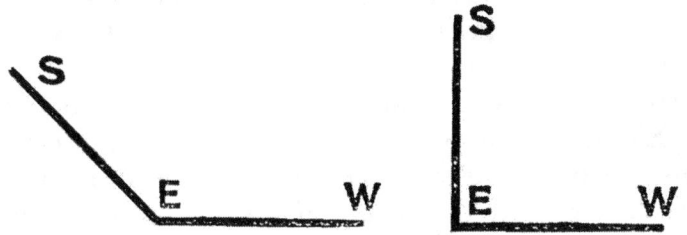

FIG. 20.—Approximately correct position of Arm. FIG. 21.—Incorrect position of Arm.
S represents the shoulder ; E the elbow ; and W the wrist-joint.

Unless the arm is thus sufficiently *open*—with the upper-arm sloping forwards, there can be no free movement of it in front of the body, *nor can the Weight of the upper-arm become properly available.* On the other hand, we must not really put the arm into a straight line (from shoulder to key); such unnatural position might lead to stiffness, and we should lose the very thing desired—the option of free Arm-weight.

§ 28. The distance of the Elbow from the Body, SIDEWAYS, varies with the part of the key-board the hands are engaged upon at the moment. Viewing the elbow from behind the performer's person, the Elbow should hang down in a straight line from the shoulder (or nearly so) when the hands are required upon keys exactly in front of the shoulder;—the Elbow meanwhile fulfilling the previous rule as to position *forwards*, when viewed in profile.

This normal position of the elbow (sideways) will however only allow us to reach about one octave of notes from the centre note of the position, by a movement of the fore-arm alone—with quiet elbow. To reach more distant parts of the key-board, we are therefore compelled to make use of a horizontal displacement of the Elbow—the whole arm in this case moving a little, sideways. Such lateral movements of the whole arm, should however be avoided, if a lateral movement of the fore-arm alone (with quiet elbow) will suffice to bring the fingers over their keys.[1]

Arm-touch. § 29. The vertical movements of the arm which form arm-touch, are of two kinds: (a) the fore-arm may move alone, in which case the elbow remains quiescent; or (b) the *whole* arm may move, in which case the elbow itself also moves vertically. As pointed out in Chapter XVII. such descent of the arm should arise solely from the greater or lesser relaxation of the arm-supporting muscles; the arm thus falling of its own weight, and *not owing to down-exertion.* Only rarely does one require the help of such down-exertion of the arm in addition to the fullest relaxation of the "up"-muscles; and then only in the slightest degree. And we must remember that the addition of such

[1] We should remember, that Fore-arm skips, to be executed with safety, demand that the Elbow be placed about *midway* between the two points to be reached, or even slightly nearer the *outer* note.

THE DETAILS OF POSITION. 303

down-exertion at once tends to colour the tone towards harshness.[1]

All important phrasings are executed by arm-movement. Since the key-board should be quitted with the last note of every important phrase by means of an Arm-movement, it also follows, that the arm must descend for the beginning of the next phrase; although it may do this quite gently.

In thus raising the arm, it constitutes good practice, to allow the finger-end of the hand to "remain behind" as it were; the tips of the fingers remaining on the key-*surfaces* a little while *after* the arm has begun to raise the wrist. This tends to ensure that supreme necessity of good Technique—a loose-lying hand.[2]

Position of the Body. § 30. The position of the Body, itself, is mainly determined by the necessity for sufficient space between Shoulder and Key—space to enable the arm to be sufficiently unbent, as explained in § 27.

To obtain this requisite space between shoulder and key (with its consequent downward and forward slant of the upper-arm) there are two opposite positions of the body available, including the modifications between these extremes:—

---

[1] *Vide* § 2 *of Chapter XII., and* § 2, *etc., of Chapter XVII.*

[2] It is well here to remind the student how imperatively needful it is, to pay attention to the law, that the Hand must never be supported by its own muscles during the act of tone-production; *i.e.* that it must never be *held* in the least. Whether the arm is fully supporting the hand at its wrist-end, or whether the arm itself is being supported by the fingers and hand, and however greatly we may therefore, have to *exert* the hand downwards momentarily, yet the opposite exertion of the hand, the up-holding one, must always be as carefully as possible eliminated during the act of touch. It follows, that the hand will remain lying on the keys, although the wrist is being raised by the arm,—unless we also at that moment choose to raise the hand on its own account.

Appreciation of the loose-lying hand, obviously led that excellent teacher LUDWIG DEPPE, to speak of the wrist as being "curved when the arm is raised;" a fact, however, of which he does not appear to have grasped the full *muscular* significance,—for his disciples only speak of its Position, not of its Condition. This wrist-"curvature," we are told, he insisted must only gradually be lowered into the normal "carried" *position* of the hand and wrist, the normal position not being fully regained, indeed, until the consummation of the tone-production of "the third note from the beginning of the phrase," he very properly premising, that the first note of every phrase should be played by arm-descent. *Vide* CALAND, *pp. 24 and 25,* "*Die Deppische Lehre des Clavierspiels.*" Also see: *Appendix to this Part; Note—XVII.* "*On Position-worship.*"

a) : We may sit *well away* from the instrument, and reach the key-board by *leaning slightly forwards*, from the hips;[1] or

b) : We may sit *somewhat nearer* the instrument, and can then reach the keys whilst remaining almost fully erect or *upright*.[2]

Each performer must discover for himself which of these two tendencies is best in keeping with his particular bodily conformation. But the Upright position (or one closely approximating towards it) is obviously the more graceful, and also the least fatiguing, when feasible.

This choice must be determined by the relative proportions of body-height and arm-length.[3]

As illustrating the forward-leaning type of position, a silhouette of ANTON RUBINSTEIN, is given as Fig. 22 on opposite page.

Position of Chair. § 31. One should be seated sufficiently distant from the instrument to enable one to open the arm to the necessary extent, as described in § 27. The chair or stool should also be in the centre of the instrument; the *E* on the first line of the treble staff may be taken to represent this centre. The height should be such, that the fore-arm is about level with the keys.[4]

---

[1] Such leaning-forward from the hips must not be understood to signify that STOOPING is to be countenanced.
In leaning forward, the back may, and should, remain perfectly straight; whereas in stooping, the spine itself would be bent. Stooping is objectionable from every point of view.

[2] We require to be *seated* rather *higher* for the forward-leaning position, than we do for the upright position of body.

[3] The relative height of the body from the hips, and the length of the upper-arm and fore-arm vary considerably—while the height of the keys is invariable; Body-position must hence vary almost for every individual.
As a rule one finds, that when the arm is long, relatively to the body, that the tendency is to sit higher and further away from the instrument while leaning forward ; and that a shorter upper-arm may prompt one to adopt a more upright position of the body, with a lower chair placed nearer the instrument.

[4] Piano-stools are as a rule made too high. In such a predicament, an easy remedy is, to sit further back than usual, and to lean forward, slightly, as described in § 30.

THE DETAILS OF POSITION. 305

Position of the feet.

§ 32. The position of the feet should be such, that the weight of the leg can rest upon the ground through the heel, when the toe or ball of the foot is engaged upon the pedal. The right foot

FIG. 22.—The outlined figure of the Master is probably from a Daguerrcotype. The stool and key-board have been drawn in.

should always be thus in contact with its pedal; the left foot, when not required for the *una corda* pedal, is best placed further back, with the sole of the foot only touching the ground, and with its toe almost as far back as the heel of the right foot —when the latter is engaged upon its pedal. This helps somewhat, when we occasionally have to employ those slight side-to-side movements of the whole body, which enable us to reach either extreme of the key-board with the *opposite* hand,

x

—movements especially required if our arms happen to be short.

Unnecessary movements. § 33. When we succeed in playing with perfectly unrestrained muscles, there remains nothing to *prevent* very free movements of hand, wrist, arm, and even of the body itself; movements, that are quite distinct from those demanded by the process of key-depression itself. Such movements are however often of great help to the player, indirectly, and several of these are indeed indispensable as "Tests," owing to their facilitating non-restraint, freedom, and accuracy of Tonal-aim. In the pupilage stages, these movements are therefore also practically unavoidable. On the other hand, there is this objection to one's giving way unreservedly to the temptation such movements offer, and that is, that the slightest movements of a performer become glaringly noticeable on the Concert-platform; and however comfortable, and even necessary they may be to the player, they prove undoubtedly disturbing and distasteful to the audience.

Hence, it behoves us to eschew all unnecessary movement so far as possible, once we have formed the habits of Freedom, and of careful Key-aiming, and to learn to reduce the *necessary* Test-movements to the smallest limits compatible with a due fulfilment of their purpose;—always provided that such self-abnegation does not lead to restraint and stiffness. The more quiet the artist's demeanour is on the platform, compatibly with good technique, the more is the hearer free to give undivided attention aurally, and the greater his enjoyment.[1]

SUMMARY: § 34. In conclusion, it must be reiterated, that most of these details of Position *should* demand but little attention, since they are likely to fulfil themselves

---

[1] If one is inclined to play at all stiffly—with a "held" arm for instance, then one really *dare* not move even a quarter of an inch without courting disaster! A rough estimate may indeed be formed of a performer's technical powers,—whether they are *probably* bad or *possibly* good, by observing whether all mobility of the body and arm is either completely absent, or in some measure present. A very *slight* swaying of the body and arms being really necessary, is therefore also not found objectionable by the listener. On the contrary, it may enhance the gracefulness of a performance visually,—owing to its unconsciously suggesting ease and comfort.

THE DETAILS OF POSITION.

automatically, provided we insist upon the correct muscular conditions. On many of these points, moreover, we find that it is obviously unwise to attempt to bind every individual down to the same conventions. On the other hand, it must also be reiterated, that there are several points where attention cannot be too carefully given. These are:—

a): Sufficient distance between shoulder and key, so that the upper-arm may lie sufficiently forwards; our chair being for this purpose also sufficiently removed from the instrument, but in the centre of the key-board.

b): The difference in the actual movement of the finger itself, exhibited most markedly when the finger is well raised previously to the act of touch; and which demands that we start with it far more fully bent for Thrusting-touch than for Clinging-touch.

c): Adjustment of the position of the wrist or hand laterally to the needs of the passage;—the hand being straight with the keys in five-finger positions; turned slightly inwards for scales and arpeggi; and turned in the direction the passage is travelling, in the case of double-notes passages.

d): Ample distance between Knuckle and Key-board, with avoidance of the inwardly-held knuckle.

e): Above all things, care in preparing every finger over every key, before *using* it; and care to aim Key-use to the place in Key-descent where tone emission commences.

RECAPITULATORY

OF CHAPTER XXIII., AND OF

PART IV

Finger, vertically considered.

1): Two quite distinct positions of the finger are available. The difference between the two is more noticeable when the finger is raised than when it is depressed with its key:—

2): The *Thrusting*-finger is more bent the higher the preparatory raising, and it tends to unbend as it descends towards, and with, the key.

The nail-phalanx consequently remains almost vertical (perpendicular) both in the raised and in the depressed position of the finger. This verticality of the nail-joint must carefully be insisted upon with the raised finger, otherwise we shall neither attain a true thrusting-touch, nor real brilliancy.

3): The *Clinging*-finger becomes more open, the higher its preliminary raising, and it tends to close upon the keys in descending; or it may even be applied to the key without any change from the preliminary flatter position, for the more extremely sympathetic tone-qualities.

4): The tip of the finger, close to the nail, reaches the key in Thrusting-touch; whereas the fleshy part, opposite to the nail, does so in Clinging-touch. In Clinging-touch the flesh is consequently pressed against the nail, and it even tends to creep round the latter.

5): In Bent-attitude, the fingers should all be nearly equally rounded. But if the little-finger is abnormally short, we may be compelled to use it slightly straighter, in spite of the consequent disadvantage for thrusting-touch.

6): Ample preliminary raising of the finger is healthy, when there is time for it, and provided we do so solely for the sake of using our fingers *freely*. We must, however, not allow such finger-raising to become our Object, in place of key-*use*. We must also carefully avoid hitting the key, in consequence of such ample raising. Raising the finger off the key should be avoided, when the same finger has to reiterate its note rapidly.

7) : It is upon the proper *condition* of the Upper-arm, that depends the proper *action* of the fingers in both attitudes, as explained in Part III.

The Thumb. 8) : The difference in movement between Bent and Flat attitudes is less exhibited by the Thumb than it is by the fingers. There is nevertheless a slight *tendency* for the thumb slightly to open-out towards (and with) the key in Thrusting-touch; and for it slightly to close upon the key in Clinging-touch.

9) : The movement of the thumb arises near the wrist-end of the hand. This may cause difficulties unless noted, owing to the fact that the movements of the other fingers arise at the knuckle.

The Fingers, in Hand-Touch. 10) : In Hand-touch (Wrist-touch), the required fingers should assume their depressed condition relatively to the Hand, *before* the latter descends. In rapid passages the required fingers "remain behind," as the hand rises from its preceding notes.

Finger-Staccato. 11): The return (or rising) movement of the finger differs in Staccato, in strict correspondence to the respective difference between the Thrusting and Clinging *conditions* of the finger and arm during the act of key-descent.

In Thrusting-touch, the front two phalanges of the finger rise from the key into exactly the same bent position they started from, before descent. In Clinging-touch, on the contrary, these two front phalanges *continue* their folding-in movement *slightly beyond the moment* of Tone-commencement; the necessary rebound of the key being assured by allowing the *knuckle-phalanx* to rebound at that moment,—just as happens in the bent-finger form of Staccato.

ON POSITION.

Fingers, Horizontally Considered.

12): Seen from above, the fingers should reach the centre of their keys. In the case of white-key passages the middle-finger should reach its white key *close to the front-edge* of the black keys, the remaining fingers reaching their keys slightly behind this position—slightly nearer the outside edge of the key-board, each finger according to its *relative* shortness.[1]

13): When the fingering-position requires the thumb on a black key, we must consider the edge of the black keys to form the limit of the key-board for the time, and the other fingers must, if required on the white keys, reach these *between* the black keys; and if necessary the hand must be slightly turned to permit of this, either to the left or to the right.[2]

Thumb Position.

14): The Thumb should have its nail-phalanx always in a straight line with its key; unless we require it to sound two adjacent keys simultaneously.

Key-Position.

15): The position of each key should, whenever possible, be directly derived from the position of keys previously played.

This is a vital matter, which however will accomplish itself automatically, provided we duly insist upon the Act of Resting, in one of its two forms, as previously explained.

16): The act of *finding* the position of a key, and the act of *depressing* it, should always be regarded as two distinct acts, although there need be no break in continuity between the two.

17): Position INSIDE the key is however the most vital point of all—the *place* in key-descent where the hammer is heard to reach the string, the place to which all tone-making effort must be carefully aimed to culminate and *cease*.

Hand, Wrist, and Finger, Horizontally.

18): FIVE-FINGER fingering positions (whether complete or not) lying on adjacent keys, diatonic or chromatic, should have the middle-finger in a *straight line* with its key—looking upon it from above.

[1] It is a total fallacy to suppose that the fingers must reach their keys all in the same line.

[2] *Vide* §§ *18-22.*

19): THE SCALE, owing to the required passage of the thumb sideways, demands a slightly *outwardly*-turned Wrist—or *inwardly*-pointing hand and fingers, as the normal position.

20): THE ARPEGGIO, in addition to this normally outwardly-turned position of the Wrist, as in the scale, requires slight lateral movements of the hand and wrist to enhance the lateral stretch of the thumb and fingers.

21): DOUBLE-NOTES SCALES, owing to the required passage of the longer fingers over the shorter ones, require an *inwardly*-turned Wrist (or outwardly-pointing hand and fingers) when the scale moves towards the end of the key-board natural to each hand; a position which is reversed on the return journey. In short: the hand and fingers must here be turned *in the direction the scale is travelling*.

22): OTHER DOUBLE-NOTES PASSAGES—arpeggi and the like, require in addition to the last, slight lateral movements of the hand and wrist.

23): In double-notes passages, we cannot transfer the Resting-weight in both of the parts forming the double progression at those points where the turning under or over of the fingers occurs. At such point the Resting-weight must be momentarily supported by a single finger which thus acts as a pivot, while the next two keys are prepared for depression.

The Hand.   24): The hand, at the Knuckles, should be kept sufficiently well raised off the keys by the fingers, to give the fingers ample space for free action. The knuckles should never be allowed to be *lower* than any portion of the finger, when the latter is (with its key) in a depressed condition. The knuckle may, on the contrary, form the highest point of hand and finger, especially in the case of large hands, and in the case of Thrusting-touch.

25): There is no difficulty in acquiring this habit, provided we remember that the knuckles should be kept up by the reaction of the fingers against the keys; and provided we do not viciously force the arm down upon the fingers.

26): The hand should be about level;—the little finger should keep its side of the hand as well raised as the index-finger side of the hand; or if anything, the little-finger side should be favoured. The only apparent exception is in the case of Rotation-touch, when the hand itself tilts a little from side to side.

27): Hand-touch (Wrist-touch), implies a movement of the hand during the act of key-depression. This movement arises at the wrist-joint, and is visible as a movement of the hand at the knuckle-end.

It is not necessary that this movement should exceed the distance from key-surface to key-bottom; but the hand may, like the finger, play "from a distance" when there is ample time for such preliminary movement. Any such preparatory raising of the hand, must however be followed by its *falling* upon the keys, thus remaking contact without any real hitting of the ivories.

28): The fingers do not move relatively to the hand in Hand-touch. (*Vide* § 10.)

The Wrist. 29): The height of the Wrist is determined by the position of the fingers. Its normal position is usually about level with the knuckles, or slightly lower, if these are well-raised. The wrist-level may, however, vary considerably without causing any discomfort, provided we do not confine ourselves either to an exaggeratedly high or low position of it.

Rapid octave passages are moreover usually found easier with the wrist-level slightly higher than the normal.

30): The wrist must alternately rise and fall, slightly, when a passage requires the thumb on alternate black and white keys. In this case the wrist is lower for the black key than for the white key. But the movement should not be greater than will just suffice to enable the Elbow to remain quiet.

Wrist and Arm. 31): Lateral movements are required of the wrist, fore-arm and upper-arm, to enable us to bring the finger-tips over their keys. The larger the distance to be reached, the larger is the portion of the limb chosen, by means of which to execute the movement.

32): These lateral movements of the fore-arm and upper-arm and their relationship to those of the thumb and wrist,[1] require very careful attention, when first learning the scale and arpeggio.

33) : A rotary movement of the hand and fore-arm may accompany the act of touch, when the extreme fingers of the hand are required to sound notes. This movement is then substituted for the more usual descending movements of the finger, hand or arm. In such "rotation-touch" the required fingers should be placed in their depressed position, preliminarily to the act of touch.[2]

34) : The actual height of the Fore-arm depends on the position of the Wrist. The most natural position is about level; or with the under-surface of the fore-arm slightly higher than the keys at the wrist, and slightly lower than these at the elbow.

The Upper-Arm or Elbow. 35) : Correct position of the upper-arm or elbow is most important. This is an absolutely vital matter; for it is impossible to obtain either freedom of reach, or the free *weight* of the Upper-arm, unless the latter *slopes sufficiently forward*, from the shoulder. The whole arm, from shoulder to wrist, must hence be *opened-out* almost into an obtuse angle.[3]

36) : The elbow, viewed from behind, should while thus lying forward, be neither pressed to the side, nor should it be unduly protruded sideways. The elbow must nevertheless freely change its position sideways, when a passage travels to the more extreme portions of the key-board.

Arm-Touch. 37) : Vertical movements of the arm are of two kinds, either of the whole arm from the shoulder, or of the fore-arm alone, from the elbow.

The beginning and the end of each phrase is usually accompanied by arm-movement.

Body-Position. 38) : The position of the body itself is mainly determined by the necessity for having the arm suf-

[1] *Vide* §§ *18-22.*
[2] We should recall, that rotary-adjustments must accompany almost every act of touch, although mostly unaccompanied by rotary-*movement*, and therefore invisible.
[3] *Vide Fig. 20, page 301.*

ficiently opened-out, as described in § 35. Sufficient distance is therefore required *between the shoulder and the key-board;* and to enable us to give this, we must sit sufficiently distant from the instrument.

This requisite distance from the key-board can be obtained in two ways: either (a) while sitting perfectly upright (or nearly so), or (b) while leaning forward from the hips—without stooping. This choice depends upon the length of the arm relatively to the height of the body from the hips.

Height of Seat. 39): The chair should be placed in the centre of the instrument. Its height is determined by the height and position of the body from the hips. When the chair is too high, we are compelled to move uncomfortably far away from the instrument, to ensure the requisite distance between shoulder and key, as described in §§ 35 and 38. Music-stools are often found insufficiently depressable.

The Feet. 40): The feet, when employed upon the pedals, should reach the latter with the ball of the foot, while the edge of the heel is placed upon the ground, and takes the weight of the leg.

The left foot, when not required upon the *una corda* pedal, should be placed further back than the right one (on its pedal) and with the sole alone reaching the ground.

Unnecessary Movements. 41): All unnecessary movements should be strictly eschewed. Even those secondary movements, required to enable us to *test* ourselves for freedom, and which must be greatly exaggerated in the learning-stage, should nevertheless subsequently be gradually reduced to the smallest limits compatible with a due fulfilment of their purpose.

Main Points of Position-Summary. 42): The main points requiring attention in Position, are as follows:—

RECAPITULATORY OF CHAPTER XXIII., AND PART IV.

a): **Sufficient distance between shoulder and key, with the seat sufficiently removed from the instrument to admit of this.**

b): **The distinction between the two kinds of finger-movement, with the finger sufficiently bent before its descent, in thrusting touch.**

c): **Avoidance of the depressed knuckle.**

d): **Lateral adjustment of the hand and wrist to each particular passage; the hand being turned inwards for single-notes scales and arpeggi, and turned in the direction travelled, during double-notes passages.**

e): **Above all things, one should insist (a) that each finger is in position, and *feels* each key, *before* the act of key-depression proper is commenced; and (b), that the position in key-descent is aimed for, where key-depression culminates in sound-beginning;——so that each key-propulsion is aimed, to culminate at the very moment that the hammer reaches the string.**

Subsidiary Points of importance are :—

f): **Not to allow the hand to slope towards the fifth finger——unless apparently so during the movement of Rotation-touch.**

g): **To keep the thumb well away from the hand,——with the nail-phalanx in line with its key.**

h): **Not as a rule to allow the fingers to reach the keys near the outside edge of the key-board.**

j): **The slight re-adjustments of wrist-height, in passages with the thumb alternately on black and white keys.**

k): **In Hand-touch, and Arm-touch, the assumption of the depressed position of the fingers relatively to the hands, *before* the down-movement of the hand or arm.**

l): **Attention to the two alternative return-movements of the finger in *thrusting* or *clinging* Finger-staccato, respectively.**

CHAPTER XXIV.

CONCLUSION.

Glossary and Summary of the main teachings of this work.

Part I, Introductory—the act of playing:

§ 1. THE Act of Playing demands perception and facility in two distinct directions: (a) Musical-perception, and (b) Technical-facility.

§ 2. Musical-perception implies that of Feeling and that of Shape.

§ 3. Technique implies (a) knowledge of the requirements of Taste, and (b) knowledge of, and facility in Key-treatment.

§ 4. Key-treatment, again, has two aspects: (a) Knowledge, or perception of the instrument's requirements, and (b) knowledge of, and facility in muscularly fulfilling these.

Part II, Instrumental aspect of Key-treatment:

§ 5. Tone-production can solely be wrought by causing the key to move.

§ 6. Loudness depends purely on the degree of speed attained by the key during its descent.

§ 7. Beauty of tone depends on our inducing this key-speed as gradually as possible. Tone control depends upon the same element.

§ 8. Opportunity for causing or influencing tone, absolutely ceases the moment the hammer reaches the string and rebounds therefrom.

§ 9. This moment, the beginning of the note (the moment of transition from Silence to Sound) must be listened for, so that our propulsion of the key can be accurately aimed to it.

§ 10. The key, in the shape of weight and friction, offers resistance to movement.

§ 11. The energy required to overcome this resistance,

SUMMARY AND CONCLUSION.

varies with different keys, and with the speed at which we try to impel them.

Part III, the Muscular aspect of Key-treatment.

§ 12. We can only gauge key-resistance, by physically feeling it through the muscular-sense, before and during Key-depression.

§ 13. The act of *Attention* during performance is dual, since it implies attention musically and attention instrumentally. We must listen inwardly and outwardly, so that we hear what should be, and so that we also hear the actual result; and we must meanwhile constantly *feel* the giving-way point of the keys, so that we can gauge the necessary efforts.

§ 14. Since the key must be reached so carefully, the contact should never be in the form of an actual blow, unless accuracy as to notes and expression do not matter.

§ 15. The act of Touch is consequently a Duplex process—excepting in the case of *ppp*-Tenuto or Legato:—

It consists of the two acts (a) of Resting, and (b) of Adding Energy to the key to move it.

§ 16. The act of Resting (which is continuous during each phrase) may either occur (a) at surface-level of key-board, or (b) at bottom-level of key-board.

This slight difference in Resting-weight constitutes the difference in Basis between Staccato and Tenuto, or Legato.

§ 17. The first (or lighter) form of Resting does not assist key-depression. The second (or heavier) form does;—being slightly heavier, it suffices to overbalance the key into deflection.

Both forms of Resting serve to tell us where the keys are, and their resistance.

§ 18. The absolute *pp* is obtained by employing this second form of the Resting, unassisted by any Added-impetus.

§ 19. The Added-impetus (Energy momentarily applied to the key during descent) is meanwhile required in all touches (except in *ppp*-Ten. or Leg.) to induce the requisite tone-amount and quality.

§ 20. This Added-impetus must absolutely cease to exist at the moment that sound-emission begins,—in Legato as well as in Staccato.

§ 21. The Added-impetus can be muscularly provided in the following three forms of Touch-construction or formation:—

1st Species: Finger-exertion alone, with passive hand and self-supported arm.

2d Species: Hand-exertion behind the finger, with self-supported arm.

3d Species: Momentary lapse in arm-support, behind the hand and finger exertions.

§ 22. The Muscular-components which provide the Act of Touch are therefore: (a) Finger-exertion, (b) Hand-exertion, and (c) Arm-weight.

§ 23. The sensations of correct touch are hence always UPWARDS—upwards by reaction from the key, against knuckle and wrist.

This, because we can only positively *feel* the actions of the finger and hand, and not the operation of arm-weight, since the latter is derived from *lapse* in muscular-exertion.

§ 24. Movement during key-descent, depends on which of these three components is slightly in excess of the other two at the moment. The resulting distinctions of movement are termed: Finger-touch, Hand-touch and Arm-touch.

§ 25. The third Species is available in either of two Sub-genera: either as "Weight-touch" or as "Muscular-touch." This, because the combination of the three touch-components may, in this Species, be *started* either (a) by Weight-release—that of the arm, or (b) by Exertion—that of the finger and hand.

The first makes for roundness of tone; the second for brilliance and even hardness.

§ 26. Hardness or harshness is bound to ensue if we apply arm down-force to any appreciable extent, and when we apply our efforts *too far down in key-descent*.

§ 27. We should therefore be careful always to play "only to the sound."

SUMMARY AND CONCLUSION. 319

§ 28. Quality of tone is moreover influenced by the two diverse Attitudes of the finger and upper-arm, respectively termed, the "Clinging" and the "Thrusting."

The first helps towards sympathetic (and carrying) tone, the second towards brilliant (and short) tone.

§ 29. It is the condition of the upper-arm (or elbow) that determines in which of these two ways the finger shall act.

§ 30. Most of the finger's work must be done by the Knuckle-phalanx; this applies equally in clinging and in thrusting attitude.

§ 31. To obtain the most sympathetic effect, we must provide key-descent through the co-operation of the clinging attitude with the third species, in the latter's weight-initiated form.

§ 32. Arm-weight, when employed in the Added impetus, must automatically cease its operation—in response to the accurately-timed cessation of the up-bearing stress at the wrist-joint.

§ 33. The transfer of the Resting weight should likewise be an automatic process, occasioned by the accurately-timed cessation of the supporting duty of the finger last used.

§ 34. Perfect freedom is imperative in all the movements and muscular actions employed in playing,—freedom from contrary-exertion.

§ 35. Rotary-freedom of the fore-arm must be insisted upon, as well as horizontal and vertical freedom of the wrist-joint. Rotary actions are required for every note.

Lack of rotary-freedom, especially, is one of the most common faults, since the here continually required adjustments mostly remain invisible.

Part IV, on Position: § 36. The shoulder must be at such a distance from the instrument, as will enable the arm to be opened-out almost into an obtuse angle, thus enabling us to employ its Weight when required.

We must be seated sufficiently distant from the instrument to admit of this.

§ 37. We must distinguish between the "flat" and "bent" positions and movements of the finger, that respectively accompany the Clinging and Thrusting attitudes, and their correlated upper-arm conditions.

§ 38. The wrist and hand must constantly adjust their position laterally, so that we can easily connect fingering-positions by means of lateral movements of the thumb, etc.
The wrist must meanwhile be neither too high nor too low; and it must change its height, slightly, when the thumb alternates between black and white keys.

§ 39. The hand must be level, since the little-finger would otherwise be placed at a disadvantage. More important still, the knuckles must never be permitted to fall in, as a normal position.

§ 40. The fingers should not move during key-descent, except in Finger-touch.

§ 41. The thumb, in its normal position, should be well away from the hand, and its nail-phalanx should always be in the same line as its key, unless it is required upon two keys simultaneously.

§ 42. Above all things, we must always insist on being properly in position over—and even on—each key, before using it, so that Energy can be applied to it, vertically.

§ 43. Each of the keys forming a passage must not be conceived as a separate unit;—each key's position must be conceived and must be found *as a particular distance from each preceding key*, or set of keys.

§ 44. In conclusion :

The student and teacher must once again be warned not to forget the *purpose* of Technique whilst studying its necessary details. The reminder is essential, for in studying these details, the mind is apt to dwell on *one* aspect of the problem, to the almost complete exclusion of the others. Thus, in endeavouring to secure the visible effects of correct Position and Movement, we are apt to forget that these are quite subsidiary to those of correct Condition—the muscular actions and inactions required of us by the key, at the moment.

Again, although we may not lose sight of this more important matter, we may so concentrate our mind on the required Muscular-conditions, as to cause us to forget to apply these, accurately-timed, to the key! And even if we do not forget this, we shall nevertheless fail, unless we do meanwhile use the key only in response to the promptings of our Musical-sense;—for "Execution" itself should always be prompted by the performer's wish to give expression to his Musical-sight.

Hence, we must study the details of Position only for the sake of obtaining the Muscular-act at its easiest, and we must apply the latter only in answer to the resistance the keys are constantly offering us in varying measure. And while thus muscularly judging the key, we must do so solely for the sake of the Musical-effect perceived to be necessary by our musical intelligence and feeling.

In short we must apply Energy to the key, only in strict response to what we feel is there needed to fulfil the Sound we musically wish at that moment.

A final Summary follows.

FINAL SUMMARY

OF SOME, OF THE MAIN TECHNICAL POINTS TO BE INSISTED UPON IN TEACHING OURSELVES AND OTHERS.[1]

I. We must remember: how sound can only be made through key-movement; and how beauty of tone can only be obtained by insisting upon the gradual depression (gradual propulsion) of each key; and how we must listen for the beginning of each sound, if we would accurately "aim" the efforts by which we intend to produce it.

II. We must remember: how Touch consists of the two elements, the Resting and the Added-impetus; how the one is continuous and the other not only dis-continuous, but always as short-lived as in Staccatissimo.   How the act of touch is muscularly mainly built up of the three components, Finger and Hand exertion, *versus* Arm-weight, etc., and why we must therefore always *feel* the act of touch as one of leverage upwards.
How these components can be combined into three main species of Touch-formation, of which the *third* offers us the two great distinctions between Weight and Muscularly-initiated touch, with the consequent divergences in Quality of tone; and how Quality is further influenced by the opposite Arm-and-finger conditions respectively termed Clinging and Thrusting.   How Weight must be ceased automatically, and how this also applies to the act of transferring weight in Legato.   Also the great importance of insisting upon the Rotary-adjustments of the forearm; and how the doctrine of *Ease* implies perfect freedom from contrary-exertion in all the movements and actions required, including those horizontal ones of the Hand and Wrist.

[1] These last Summaries are useless, unless the preceding portions of this work have been studied.

III. How Position, whilst mainly a result, and not a cause, includes nevertheless some points of importance: such as the sufficiently-opened arm; the difference between the raised bent and flat finger; the lateral adjustments of the hand; and the teaching, that every key must be felt before being played, and must be found as a lateral distance from its preceding fellow.

IV. Above all things, we must always remember that the ultimate purpose of our study is not to obtain correct Movements, nor correct Muscular-habits, but that our purpose is to obtain Command over Musical-expression. With this purpose in view, we must, in playing, constantly *feel* key-resistance, so that we may thus be muscularly prompted to fulfil the requirements both of Key and Music.

Good tone-production can in fact be thus defined:—we must allow Key-resistance and Musical-sense to prompt us easily to move each key at requisite speed and increase of speed, to a definite Place in Time and Key-descent.

FINAL SUMMARY

OF SOME OF THE MAIN TECHNICAL POINTS TO BE INSISTED UPON IN TEACHING OURSELVES AND OTHERS.[1]

I. We must remember: how sound can only be made through key-movement; and how beauty of tone can only be obtained by insisting upon the gradual depression (gradual propulsion) of each key; and how we must listen for the beginning of each sound, if we would accurately "aim" the efforts by which we intend to produce it.

II. We must remember: how Touch consists of the two elements, the Resting and the Added-impetus; how the one is continuous and the other not only dis-continuous, but always as short-lived as in Staccatissimo.   How the act of touch is muscularly mainly built up of the three components, Finger and Hand exertion, *versus* Arm-weight, etc., and why we must therefore always *feel* the act of touch as one of leverage upwards.
How these components can be combined into three main species of Touch-formation, of which the *third* offers us the two great distinctions between Weight and Muscularly-initiated touch, with the consequent divergences in Quality of tone; and how Quality is further influenced by the opposite Arm-and-finger conditions respectively termed Clinging and Thrusting.   How Weight must be ceased automatically, and how this also applies to the act of transferring weight in Legato.   Also the great importance of insisting upon the Rotary-adjustments of the forearm; and how the doctrine of *Ease* implies perfect freedom from contrary-exertion in all the movements and actions required, including those horizontal ones of the Hand and Wrist.

---
[1] These last Summaries are useless, unless the preceding portions of this work have been studied.

FINAL SUMMARY.

III. How Position, whilst mainly a result, and not a cause, includes nevertheless some points of importance: such as the sufficiently-opened arm; the difference between the raised bent and flat finger; the lateral adjustments of the hand; and the teaching, that every key must be felt before being played, and must be found as a lateral distance from its preceding fellow.

IV. Above all things, we must always remember that the ultimate purpose of our study is not to obtain correct Movements, nor correct Muscular-habits, but that our purpose is to obtain Command over Musical-expression. With this purpose in view, we must, in playing, constantly *feel* key-resistance, so that we may thus be muscularly prompted to fulfil the requirements both of Key and Music.

Good tone-production can in fact be thus defined:—we must allow Key-resistance and Musical-sense to prompt us easily to move each key at requisite speed and increase of speed, to a definite **Place in Time and Key-descent.**

APPENDIX TO PART IV.

THE FALLACY OF "POSITION" WORSHIP

Note XVIII.—To § 1, Chapter XXII., page 273: Most of the "teaching" of Technique, hitherto, seems to have consisted in insisting upon the adoption of such *visible* attitudes during rest and movement, as have been exhibited by successful players during performance. It was fallaciously assumed, that if one could only succeed in making Position and Movement correspond to those thus exhibited, that the result as to tone and agility would also correspond!

Now the previous chapters have demonstrated the fact, that it is almost entirely upon the paruticlar CONDITIONS of Action and Inaction of the arm, hand and finger that each particular kind and degree of tone and of agility must of necessity depend;—so that however closely one might succeed in observing and in reproducing the precise positions and movements employed by a successful player under all the varying requirements of Technique, yet this would not form the slightest guarantee that we should succeed in applying our forces against the key in the same manner as he, nor that our tonal results would prove similar. Indeed, owing to the fact that Position and Movement give so unreliable an indication of those ever-changing conditions of muscular-action and release which alone form the true *cause* of all tonal-effect, it is obvious that the most painstaking copying of "the look of the thing" will prove of no avail, unless we also happen to hit upon the required (but hidden) muscular-changes required. On the other hand, it is also abundantly clear, that provided we do adopt the correct Condition of the limb during key-descent, and apply such muscular-condition to the key in proper measure and proper time, that correct Position and Movement must almost of necessity arise as a *result* from such fulfilment of the laws of Key-treatment.

One may well marvel at the display of mechanical ignorance, want of power of analysis and observation exhibited by teachers and artists, who have spent their whole lives in endeavouring to help others to do the right things technically, while they have nevertheless totally failed to observe those most obvious rudimentary facts of muscular-action and key-action that form the direct cause respectively of technical failure and success, both in themselves and in their pupils and fellow-artists!

That the case is so black would be incredible, did we not every day have proof of it, and did we not remember how irksome most artistic natures find analysis and logical-reasoning. The consequence has been, that even the most celebrated teachers of this last century have wofully failed to discern the true causes of (or permits to) good Technique—the A, B, C of the Piano, as found in correct Key-treatment, instrumental and muscular.

For instance, in a work published last year, purporting to teach Technique, and which is avowedly the "only authorised publication of the teachings" of

LESCHETIZKY—the justly-renowned Artist-teacher,[1] we fail to find any description of the true causes and explanations of correct Technique. Instead, the little advice given relatively to tone-production, relies almost exclusively on Position and on Movement, and on the practice of carefully-planned methods of Note-practice,—on exercises, the practice of which does not, however, in the least ensure that the learner will happen to discover for himself HOW he should use the key or his own muscles, *i.e.*—what key-treatment and muscular-habit should be, in any of its manifold aspects! Thus, on referring to this work, Chapter XIV., "On Touch-varieties," after pertinently quoting "*C'est le ton qui fait la musique*," we find the following:—" If the Cantilene " is to be in the shape of a large strong tone, legato, then will Finger-force, " alone, not serve. One must here help by means of *Wrist-pressure* in the " following manner. One should reach the key lightly, and one should, " without discontinuing the contact with the key, press the latter down " deeply by means of a rapid upward movement of the Wrist-joint ;[2] wrist " and finger joints being fixed at this moment."

" The same effect can also be attained by a quick, downward movement of " the Wrist. The wrist must return to its normal position immediately after " the note is sounded, while the finger continues lightly to hold the key " down." . . . " In Staccato the keys are not to be pressed down, instead " they are to be sounded" (*i.e.*, hit down) "from above." . . . " The dif- " ference between Finger-staccato and Wrist-joint staccato depends on " whether it is the Knuckle-joint or the Wrist-joint *that provides the motive- " force.* Finger-staccato is, playing by means of *thrown* fingers. In wrist- " staccato, the bent finger is *thrown down* upon the key by means of the wrist- " joint. After a short sounding of the note (Nach kurzem Anschlag), the finger " is to be immediately sprung back by means of the wrist-joint." A few paragraphs further on we read, that the noise occasioned by the fingers tapping or hitting the keys " cannot be avoided in staccato " ! It is even suggested that this noise can help the musical effect " in burlesque moments " !

No further advice is tendered as to the Act of Touch—as to key-treatment and the implicated muscular-conditions. And while we find no distinctions drawn between the factors that cause Tone, and the factors that cause Duration (Leg., and Stacc.), we also find that Position and Movement are almost exclusively pointed to as the *cause* of all the effects—instead of recognising these as merely accompanying results, for the most part ! That is, instead of any attempt to analyse the muscular factors that are the immediate cause of all tonal effects, we find movements described and recommended, which it is assumed must lead to the desired effects,—movements moreover, in this case, which, as a matter of fact do *not* at all necessarily accompany the act of Singing-touch, although they *may* be allowed to *follow* such act of touch —when it is completed.[3] To the apparent non-recognition of the function of Arm-*weight*, may also probably be attributed a certain hardness in *forte* passages often observed in Leschetizky pupils.

All this does not detract from the splendid work done by this great Master-

---

[1] " Die Grundlage der Methode Leschetizky," Malwine Brée.

[2] " Man berührt die Taste leicht und zwingt—ohne den Contac tmit derselben aufzugeben— durch eine rasche Handgelencksbewegung nach aufwärts den Finger, die Taste tief niederzu- drücken."

[3] Obviously, the " rising " or " falling " wrist here alluded to, is an unconscious discovery (so often made by artists) of what I have described as the " Aiming-test " (*Vide Chapter XIX.*, *page 207*);—movements which certainly prove of use *provided they are employed* (as they should be) as a test to ensure the cessation (a) of all Action and (b) of all Weight, immediately that sound is reached, the wrist *rising*, when it is the Weight-element that *first* ceases its operation; and the wrist *falling*, when it is the Finger-and-hand exertion that first ceases its operation upon the key.

teacher; for although his results have apparently been achieved almost entirely by empiric methods, or by force of good example, yet he has proved himself to be one of the giants of the nineteenth century.

We find the same fallacy—of relying mostly on the phenomena of Position and Movement—exhibited by those who profess to teach the methods of another of the last century's really great teachers—LUDWIG DEPPE, who indeed was probably the most advanced of all the well known nineteenth-century teachers. He, for instance, clearly recognised the necessity for the free wrist, and its source, the "carried" arm; also he instructed in touch by weight-release, although he perhaps hardly recognised that the released weight of the arm was the cause. (*Vide* "*Die Deppeschs Lehre des Klavierspiels*," E. CALAND.) On reading this little work one clearly perceives that Deppe himself must have been able to obtain the true "sympathetic" touch-quality, and that he stimulated his pupils to do likewise. His idea of the "arm-carried hand" lapsing "upon the key," being indeed within reach of that full realisation of the real facts of the case, which, after all, seems to have eluded him. And this, in spite of what was truly a monumental striving after Truth in the matter; especially when we take into consideration the state of absolute ignorance of first principles—and disbelief in there being any—in which he found the musical world. (*Vide Note to* § *29, Chapter XXIII.*)

"*THE STRAIGHT FIFTH FINGER*"

NOTE XIX.—To Note of § 6, Chapter XXIII., page 281 :—The doctrine that the little finger should be held straight, or nearly so, even in "bent-finger" touch, is another of those fallacies, which, having first arisen through inaccurate reasoning, have then become a tradition. That the little finger owes its frequently supposed weakness to its being short, was the beginning of the fallacy.

The very fact of using it "flat" while the other fingers are employed in the rounded form necessary for brilliance, would place it in a comparatively disadvantageous position. To begin with, it would be more elastic than the others. This would also most likely lead to its attempted re-enforcement, by surreptitious thrusts from the arm, or else by a rotary poking action from the hand; for it is difficult to give the requisite thrusting action of the finger, if we start with it straight. We must remember that "thrusting touch" implies a slight tendency of the finger to *open-out* towards the key; true, this uncurling must indeed be slight, but it must be sufficient to permit the finger to be applied *vertically* to the key—and this we cannot do, if it is straight in the first instance, for it will then be compelled to pull inwards upon the key, as in clinging touch. Moreover, the little finger is by no means so "weak" as it is popularly supposed to be, as we find, when we ask even a child to grip us with it. As already indicated, its apparent weakness at the instrument results in most cases from failure to adjust the Fore-arm Rotation-element to its needs.

As the finger is a lever of the third order, it requires no very high grade of elementary mechanical knowledge to prove how great is the delusion that the finger gains in power by being straightened! On the contrary, since its muscular force is applied *between* the fulcrum (the knuckle) and the resistance (the key), it follows that the straighter we hold the finger, the further off is its work placed, and the *less* is its power.

The same argument, also, in another form, *viz.*: that the fingers must be placed in as straight a line as possible on the keys—that their tips should be in as straight a row as possible—is the climax of foolish reasoning.

The nearer the finger is applied to the edge of the key, the *greater* is the leverage (or power) exercised over the key, hence, again, we give the little finger less power when we straighten it, for it then approaches nearer the fulcrum of the key !

Moreover, the fingers form separate units, as a matter of fact; each one is provided with its own individual muscles. Evenness of result is hence attained by the individual training received by each finger to fit it amongst its fellows— the muscles of the weaker ones are taught to exert themselves slightly more than those of the stronger fingers. They are thus taught to create the same relative effect upon the keys, each finger at its own particular point of contact relatively to the others.

Meanwhile, do not let us lose sight of the fact, that evenness of finger is induced, not so much by training the fingers into equal strength (or weakness), as by obedience to the law, that the tone-making stresses should all be given in strict response to what the keys themselves suggest—by their resistance. That is, if we constantly watch Key-resistance, as we should, then each finger will more or less unconsciously adapt itself to the needs of the moment, and evenness *thus ensues automatically.* And it could then be obtained even if we used the fingers with the hand turned upside down !

"THE HIGH WRIST AND LOW WRIST DOGMAS"

NOTE XX.—To § 21, Chapter XXIII.:—While the height of the wrist is perhaps the one point in Position which least demands hard and fast rules, since it may (and must) vary considerably owing to so many considerations, yet it seems to be the point around which debate has flourished most hotly and dogmatically, probably owing to this very fact—that the precise actual height may vary with impunity according to personal idiosyncrasy ! For we find players, with excellent technique, who strictly adhere to "low wrist," because they have been brought up on that fad; while we find others, equally excellent, who employ the "high wrist" whenever they possibly can. Obviously, neither position is harmful, provided it is not exaggerated. Personally I find that one position suits certain passages, while the opposite one suits others. It is the unflinching adherence to one position that proves objectionable. As a rule quick passages are found really easiest with a *higher* wrist, especially in the case of double-notes passages.

The point of real importance (as insisted upon in Part III.) is, that the wrist-joint *must be free.* And it is this necessity, imperfectly recognised, that has no doubt led to these two opposite dogmas on the subject. Thus we found, that all Agility-technique demands that the arm be self-supported, with the hand lying loose. If we unconsciously obey this rule—and imperfectly recognise its real significance, it follows that our instinctive feeling may cause us slightly to *raise the wrist,* since this will be more suggestive of the "dangling" sensation of the loose-lying hand. Conversely, if we desire a singing touch, and have more or less unconsciously recognised that it requires the loose-left arm to weigh the keys (and hand) down, such elastic and almost flabby state of the wrist and knuckle (here required at the moment of key-descent) may naturally suggest a dropping-in of the wrist—and even of the knuckle.

So little, however, does the actual position of the wrist relatively to the hand influence tonal-result, that the wrist-joint may at times be allowed to rise quite high up, without in the least disturbing one's Technique. I have seen LISZT himself assume an absurdly exaggerated position of this nature (obviously the result of his unconscious *sense* of the correct muscular-conditions) although he, of course, did not affect it normally. I have also seen others imitating a similar position, or the opposite exaggeration, obviously hoping to induce thereby the much coveted "sympathetic touch"; but as they had *not* realised the requisite muscular conditions—of really "weighing the key" into sound—their movements were reduced to mere meaningless contortions and mannerisms.

It seems almost superfluous to add, that such great alterations of position are not only *not* required, but that they are also in themselves not in the least suggestive of the desired tonal results! Nevertheless it is obviously in this way that the various wrist "methods" have arisen—through imperfect reasoning. For instance, superficially it must have seemed to be an unimpeachable syllogism to say:

a) "The wrist-joint must be free."
b) "If I let the wrist drop, then the wrist-joint is free."
c) "Hence a dropped wrist (*i.e.*, a low wrist!) means a free wrist."

Of course this would form admirable logic, were it not that its conclusion depends on a mere word-quibble!—For a dropping (or falling) wrist may certainly be assumed to be free at the moment, provided it be really falling. But a wrist that *is placed* in a "dropped" or low position, is no more necessarily in an unrestrained condition, than if it were placed high, or midway between either extremes. The wrist-joint we must remember, is only free when none of the opposing muscles are permitted to act,—provided none of those muscles are allowed to act, that are *opposite* in function to those required of the finger, hand, and arm. And the wrist is not truly free, unless it is so not only vertically, but also horizontally, and rotarily, as discussed in Chapter XVII. (*Vide page 193, and preceding pages.*)

EDUCATIONAL WORKS FOR PIANOFORTE BY TOBIAS MATTHAY

With 22 Illustrations. 8vo, pp. xlii + 328. 10s. 6d.

THE ACT OF TOUCH
IN ALL ITS DIVERSITY.

Musical Times says:

"When Mr. Tobias Matthay first published his work, 'The Act of Touch, in 1903, it was received with very mixed feelings by the musical profession. Many scoffed at the mere fact that an acknowledged expert required some 300 pages of closely printed matter to explain how to play the pianoforte; others regarded the book as **a 'one man's fad,'** which would have its day and be gone; others indignantly denied that anything could be wrong with existing methods, which had produced a Liszt, a Rubinstein, a Madame Schumann. But the wise, even if unable to grasp a tithe of the new gospel at first, recognised the fact that here was something giving food for thought and experiment.

"And now? The 'one-man's fad' has within ten short years **altered radically the whole system of modern pianoforte teaching.** The Matthay Principles, Matthay Doctrines, Matthay Methods, call them what one may, are known the world over, and **probably never before in art has an almost world-wide revolution been accomplished in so short a space of time.** Truly of art did Schumann say, 'Es ist des Lernens kein Ende.'"

Crown 8vo. 4s. 6d.

THE FIRST PRINCIPLES OF PIANOFORTE PLAYING

Being an extract from the Author's "The Act of Touch." Designed for School use, and *with two additional Chapters*—"Directions for Learners and Advice to Teachers."

Crown 8vo. 2s. 6d.

COMMENTARIES
ON THE TEACHING OF PIANOFORTE TECHNIQUE.

A Supplement to "The Act of Touch" and "First Principles."

LONGMANS, GREEN & CO., 39 Paternoster Row, London, E.C. 4

Quarto. 7s. 6d.

RELAXATION STUDIES

In the Muscular Discriminations required for Touch, Agility and Expression in Pianoforte Playing. Cloth bound (150 pages, 4to), with numerous Illustrations and Musical Examples; with a Portrait of the Author.

BOSWORTH & CO., Heddon Street, Regent Street, W.

Quarto. 1s. 6d.

THE PRINCIPLES OF FINGERING, LAWS OF PEDALLING, etc.

An Extract from above.

BOSWORTH & CO.

Quarto, with Illustrations.   2s. 6d. net, cash.
THE FOREARM ROTATION PRINCIPLE
ITS APPLICATION AND MASTERY.
Sole Agents for Great Britain and Colonies:
JOSEPH WILLIAMS, 32 Great Portland Street, London, W.

Sole Agents for U.S.A:
THE BOSTON MUSIC CO. (SCHIRMER), 26 West St., Boston, Mass.

Quarto, with Illustrations.   3s. net cash.
THE CHILD'S FIRST STEPS IN PIANO PLAYING
Written for Children, but also for Adults as an Introduction to their teaching.

Sole Agents for Great Britain and Colonies:
JOSEPH WILLIAMS, 32 Great Portland Street, London, W.

Sole Agents for U.S.A.:
THE BOSTON MUSIC CO. (SCHIRMER), 26 West St., Boston, Mass.

In Three Books.   Books I and II, 3s. net, Book III, 2s. 6d. net.
THE PIANIST'S FIRST MUSIC MAKING
The Music Material to accompany above, by FELIX SWINSTEAD and TOBIAS MATTHAY.

THE ANGLO-FRENCH MUSIC CO., 109 Baker Street, London, W.

Practice Card No. 1.   1s. 6d. net, cash.
DOUBLE-THIRD SCALES
THEIR FINGERING AND PRACTICE.
Sole Agents for Great Britain and Colonies:
JOSEPH WILLIAMS, 32 Great Portland Street, London, W.

Sole Agents for U.S.A.:
ARTHUR P. SCHMIDT, 120 Boylston Street, Boston, Mass.

Crown 8vo, with Illustrations, pp. xiv + 163.   Paper covers, 7s. 6d. net; Cloth, 10s. net.
MUSICAL INTERPRETATION
Its Laws and Principles, and their application in Teaching and Performing.

Sole Agents for Great Britain and Colonies:
JOSEPH WILLIAMS, 32 Great Portland Street, London, W.

Sole Agents for U.S.A.:
THE BOSTON MUSIC CO. (SCHIRMER), 26-28 West St., Boston Mass.

7s. 6d. net ; Card, 1s. 6d.
THE T.M.P.S. PRACTICE TRIANGLE AND CARD
Exercises for Rotational Freedom, Finger Extension and Freeing.
Sole Agents:
JOSEPH WILLIAMS and THE BOSTON MUSIC CO., as above.

THE PROBLEMS OF AGILITY.   1s. 3d. net.
THE ANGLO-FRENCH MUSIC CO.

ON METHOD IN TEACHING: A Lecture.   3s.
THE ANGLO-FRENCH MUSIC CO., 109 Baker Street, W.

CPSIA information can be obtained
at www.ICGtesting.com
Printed in the USA
LVHW081215160323
741694LV00037B/880